IN THE BEST INTERESTS OF THE CHILD

In the Best Interests of the Child

Loss and Suffering in Adoption Proceedings

Mili Mass
Translated by Jonathan Orr-Stav

berghahn
NEW YORK • OXFORD
www.berghahnbooks.com

Published in 2018 by
Berghahn Books
www.berghahnbooks.com

Originally published by Resling as
Beshem tovat hayeled – ovdan vesevel behalichei haimutz in 2010

Library of Congress Cataloging-in-Publication Data

Names: Mass, Mili, author.
Title: In the best interests of the child : loss and suffering in adoption proceedings / Mili Mass ; translated by Jonathan Orr-Stav.
Other titles: Beshem tovat hayeled. English
Description: First Edition. | New York : Berghahn Books, [2018] | Includes bibliographical references and index.
Identifiers: LCCN 2017052482 (print) | LCCN 2018000705 (ebook) | ISBN 9781785338038 (ebook) | ISBN 9781785338021 (hardback : alk. paper)
Subjects: LCSH: Adoption--Israel. | Adoption--Law and legislation--Israel. | Adoption--Moral and ethical aspects--Israel. | Adopted children--Family relationships--Israel. | Parental deprivation--Psychological aspects. | Children--Legal status, laws, etc--Israel. | Parent and child (Law)--Israel. | Loss (Psychology) in children.
Classification: LCC HV875.58.I75 (ebook) | LCC HV875.58.I75 M3713 2018 (print) | DDC 362.734095694--dc23
LC record available at https://lccn.loc.gov/2017052482

British Library Cataloguing in Publication Data

A catalogue record for this book is available from the British Library

ISBN 978-1-78533-802-1 hardback
ISBN 978-1-78533-803-8 ebook

In Memory of 'Dalit':
who fought over her children
but was denied the chance to raise them –
in the hope that one day they will read her story
and, unlike her, know who their mother was
and how important they were to her

Contents

Acknowledgements

This book is a testimony to the loss that children experience when forcibly separated from their parents. It is based on my work as an expert witness, but came into being only after I had found a witness to my own story, and had experienced the power of testimony.

Since 1987, I have occasionally served as an expert witness in legal proceedings over the state's petitions to declare children eligible for adoption without their parents' consent, on the grounds that the parents were incapable of raising them. In the course of fulfilling my duties – which were primarily to assess the ability of parents to raise their children – I repeatedly witnessed the state's punitive attitude towards the parents, its denial of the loss inherent in adoption, and of the harm caused by the secrecy surrounding adoption in relation to all three parties of the adoption triangle: children, parents and prospective adoptive parents. Whenever I shared what I had seen with colleagues and friends, I almost always encountered disbelief and scepticism – to the point where I ceased confiding in people and limited myself to giving expert testimony in court.

After I was exposed to Professor Adi Ophir's ideas about the term 'political', I shared with him my views on Israeli adoption law and policy and the distress I was feeling at that time as I monitored the painful adoption case of 'Dalit' and 'Tal' (as described in Chapter 3 of this book). He advised me to write the book, and stood beside me throughout the long and frustrating process of its publication in Hebrew.

'Elinor' and her parents, whose story is also told here, gave me permission to document our relationship, which continues to this day, years after my official role in this affair ended. The profound significance of their presence in my life has accompanied me throughout the writing of this book.

In the course of my work, I needed help on more than one occasion, and many came forward with assistance. My colleague Mira Barkai, as always, has been my compass, steering me in the direction of common sense, which often becomes buried under the thick layer of prejudices and moralistic contortions surrounding the issue of adoption. Dr Ruth

Zafran, Judge Moshe Drori, Judge Yaffa Hecht (retired), Attorney Miby Moser, Attorney Moshe Brown, Attorney Yossie Mendelson and my friend Yossie Godard all offered me much-needed help and advice at various stages of the work on the Hebrew edition. I am also grateful to the Radzyner School of Law, Interdisciplinary Center Herzliya, to the Minerva Center for Human Rights at the Faculty of Law, Tel Aviv University, and to the Department of Social Work at Ben-Gurion University for their generosity in holding conferences in honour of the book when it came out in Hebrew.

Dina Hurvitz, who edited the original Hebrew edition of this book, introduced me to a very high standard of editing, and the translation of the book into English by Jonathan Orr-Stav certainly maintained these high standards. I am particularly grateful for his understanding of the nuances of the expressions I was sometimes looking for. Debby Diamond edited the English translation with much of the same attunement.

The publication of the Hebrew edition of the book (Resling, Tel Aviv, 2010) was supported by grants from the Minerva Center for Human Rights at the Faculty of Law, Tel Aviv University, and the Council of Deans of University Schools of Social Work.

Resling, the publishing house of the Hebrew edition of the book, welcomed the book graciously and gave its blessing for the publication in English. I am grateful to Dr Ruth Zafran, Professor Alon Harel, Professor Adi Ophir and Professor Vered Slonim-Nevo for their support of the publication of the book by Berghahn, and to the publishing house itself, of course.

Mili Mass
Tel Aviv, 2017

Note on Translation

Since this book was destined for a British publisher, British spellings and idioms were used in the translation. However, for the benefit of readers in North America and elsewhere, very UK-specific terms, such as 'Reception', 'flat', 'lift', 'lavatory' and 'Year 5', were replaced with more universal or American equivalents ('kindergarten', 'apartment', 'elevator', 'bathroom', 'Grade 5').

While laws in English-speaking countries are typically referred to as Acts, the accepted translation of Israeli laws refers to them simply as Laws – hence, for example, the Adoption of Children Law.

Introduction

Moses and Oedipus

The desire to save children from a bitter fate confers upon adoption an aspect of benevolence. Adoptive parents are the object of esteem rarely accorded to birth parents. That is the bright side of adoption. The dark side is the very fate from which the child is being saved – a fate thought to be an existential danger, the product of indifference and callousness or even spite and malicious intent. The roots of this equation – which lauds adoption while condemning the circumstances that result in children being placed for adoption – may be found in mythology, in tales such as those of Moses and Oedipus, who owed their lives to adoption. In both stories, the hero's genealogical ties play a prominent part, but in other respects they are fundamentally different: one concerns the wish to give a child the chance of a better life – or indeed, life itself – while the other is about the desire to control destiny and rewrite one's personal history.

The Moses legend is about a child whose mother tries to save him from death, as decreed by Pharaoh upon all sons of the Israelites. However, the Bible stresses that Moses, the father of the nation, was not entirely cut off from his roots. Pharaoh's daughter, who retrieved him from the river, recognised him as 'one of the Hebrew's children', and put him in the care of a Hebrew nursemaid (who was, in fact, his mother), and he remained with his own people until he was weaned. Only then was he taken into the house of Pharaoh, and on reaching adulthood, 'went out unto his brethren' (Exodus 2:2–11). The text is unclear as to whether Moses knew that the nursemaid was his mother, if he was still aware of his birth identity and whether, on reaching adulthood, he knew that the Hebrews were his people. However, what is undeniable is the significance attached to the preservation of the genealogical ties in Moses' life. Today, this significance is acknowledged in what is known as 'open adoption', in which contact between the adopted child and his birth parents is not severed, and the child is not torn away from his genealogical kin.

The adoption of Oedipus was also intended to save him from death, but in this instance it is the father, the King of Thebes, who was out to have him killed, in an attempt to foil the prophecy of the Oracle that his future son would kill his father and sleep with his mother. Oedipus is therefore hidden from his parents, adopted by a royal family in another country and utterly cut off from his birth identity. His story represents the desire to control fate,[1] and although it ultimately leads to horrendous tragedy, its enormous potency appears to be at the heart of the doctrine that sees secrecy as an essential component of adoption. Accordingly, 'confidential adoption' – also known as 'closed' adoption – severs the ties between the adopted child and his birth parents, in a bid to provide a 'clean slate', as if the life of the adopted child begins with his adoption.

Adoption policy in Israel follows the Oedipal model. The Adoption of Children Law states that adoption must completely sever all ties between the child and his birth parents. His adopted identity and location must remain hidden from them, and as soon as adoption procedures are completed, he too must know nothing about them.[2] From the moment the court has decreed a child eligible for adoption, not only is his contact with his birth parents terminated, but his birth identity is as well. As in the case of Oedipus, hidden from his father's murderous intent, the child is completely cut off from his genealogical relations, to protect him from the threat and dangers allegedly posed by his birth parents.

The condemnation of the birth parents is even more explicit in cases where a child is put up for adoption without his parents' consent.[3] This occurs in instances which, in the words of one court judgement, 'like a necklace of misshapen and defective stones strung together – are the abandonment and neglect of a child, and total failure in the fulfilment of parental duties – for no reasonable cause or justification'.[4]

To this list of grounds for adoption, another was added, namely the parents' inability to raise their child[5] – an argument originally designed to ensure that a home is provided for children who have spent many years in children's homes or other institutions, due to their families' inability to raise them at home, or because the parents refused to put them up for adoption.[6] Today, however, this argument is also being cited to justify the removal of children from their birth parents' custody without the parents' consent, once it is shown that they are incapable of raising them. While this charge is ostensibly different from the 'misshapen stones' situations described above, inasmuch as it involves no 'element of culpability',[7] the parents' 'acquittal' from such a charge is not unequivocal.[8] While on the one hand, in the view of the same presiding judge, 'the pernicious effect of these phenomena has extended to the interpretation of section 13(7) of the Adoption of Children Law – giving rise to the incapability argument',[9] he also pointed out that 'the root of this unfortunate state of affairs is precisely in the meaning of section 13(7), in that the particular grounds cited in section 13 of the Adoption of Children Law are nothing but instances of [it]'.[10]

To protect children who, in the view of adoption officials,[11] are in jeopardy as long as they are in the custody of their birth parents, the law sanctions the use of emergency orders. In these instances, the child is removed from the parents' home, his birth identity is changed and a temporary one given to him by the adoption officials, his location is made secret, and access to him is limited exclusively to the adoption officials, who are also entitled to hand him over to the intended adoptive family even before the court has approved his removal from his birth parents' custody. To obtain such approval, the adoption authorities must appeal to the courts no later than fourteen days after the child's removal from his parents' custody.[12] The adoption authority in Israel – known in Hebrew as Hasherut Lema'an Hayeled (literally, 'The Service for [the Sake of] the Child', henceforth SSC)[13] – represents the state, and is the body that petitions the courts for the child to be declared eligible for adoption. The courts are authorised to give such approval *ex parte*, that is, without the parents being present.

The law therefore empowers adoption officials to enforce the Adoption of Children Law, and the SSC is the only point of contact for all parties in the adoption triangle. The adoption officials – all SSC employees – act as the child's guardians from the moment he is removed from his parents' custody until the court's decision, at the state's bidding, to declare the child eligible for adoption. During this time, the child is kept behind a wall of secrecy, and access to him is permitted only through adoption officials and under their supervision.[14] At this stage, the child's birth identity has already been removed, in favour of a new, temporary and confidential identity. All contact between him and his birth parents is conducted exclusively through the adoption officials, even though the latter are a party in the legal proceedings, with an interest in putting the child up for adoption. Thus, the same procedures used by adoption officials to put children up for adoption also entitle them to portray the parents as posing a danger – not only to the court but to the child as well. The child is thus left struggling to understand why he was taken away from his parents and why his contact with them is limited to certain prescheduled times and strictly under close supervision. At this point, in effect, any reasonable doubt over the charge that the parents cannot raise their child has already been removed. They are presented as people from whom the child must be hidden, much as Oedipus had to be hidden from his father.

Although, by legal precedent, the law courts are 'the father of orphans'[15] and the sole authority in the decision to put a child up for adoption and to order his adoption,[16] the law delays court intervention until *after* the child has been removed from his birth parents' custody and handed over to the intended adoptive family. In practice, therefore, authority resides in the hands of the SSC, which operates in secret, rather than in the justice system, which is expected to operate transparently to protect the rights of all parties involved – children, birth parents and adoptive parents. Entrusting all contact between the child and his birth parents to adoption officials – who, by definition, have a vested interest in severing this contact – allows them to present matters in a manner that is calculated to sway the court's decision. They are able to sabotage the relationship between the child and his parents, for example by controlling and policing their encounters, and by keeping secret the child's testimony about the nature of his relationship with his parents. The restrictions imposed on the child's contact with his parents are carried out on grounds of 'the best interests of the child', but in a way designed to make it a self-fulfilling prophecy.[17] Indeed, so zealous is the pursuit of 'the best interests of the child' – a principle conceived to counter the view that a child is his parents' property[18] – that it appears merely to replace the parents' ownership of the child with that of the state (in the guise of the adoption officials).[19] However, by denying the child his right to express his views, the state defeats the ultimate purpose of 'the best interests of the child' principle – namely, recognising the child as 'a person with an independent personality'.[20] The Adoption of Children Law in Israel[21] does not mandate that the child himself must be represented in court as a party to the proceedings.[22] Instead, he is usually represented by the adoption officials who, at the same time, are petitioning for him to be declared available for adoption.

Adoption proceedings portray the child not as an independent person, but as an atomistic entity detached from all genealogical ties and devoid of any identity.[23] Adoption policy in Israel is founded on a pointed disregard of any risk that removing the genealogical ties from the adopted child's life may result in an irreplaceable loss.[24] Although there is some acknowledgement that denying the child the chance to grow up with his birth parents may have some adverse effect on him, adoption is portrayed as a fitting substitute and as compensation for that damage. This view centres on the original causes of the damage[25] – namely the parents' conduct and failures – and therefore does not require the child's own testimony. Thus, the state's assessment of the parents' conduct is presented as a reflection of the child's assessment of his relationship with his parents.

As previously noted, when the child is adopted, he is given a new identity, in an attempt to erase any trace of the ties he once had with his birth parents,[26] and the parents' very disappearance, in turn, is presented as justifying the necessity of the Gordian knot forged between the adoption procedure and eradication of the child's genealogical ties.

This book examines the proceedings of four cases that I encountered as an expert witness called upon to assess the parents' ability to raise their child, during court hearings held to approve the emergency orders and the state's petition to have the child declared eligible for adoption on these grounds (against the parents' wishes).[27] In all four cases, I witnessed the accounts presented by the adoption services, under the veil of secrecy imposed allegedly to protect the privacy of the children and their parents: accounts of denials that adoption entails loss; of refusing to allow the testimonies of the children involved as to the special meaning of their relationship with their parents; and of the questionable premise underpinning it all, namely that adoption is a fitting substitute for lost genealogical ties. My goal in this book is to describe the injustice inherent in the systematic and routine denial of the loss experienced by the child, and the wrong done by the muzzling of its expression in any form.[28]

As part of the detailed description of the chain of events in each of the cases documented in the book, I also attempt to decipher the children's relationships with their respective parents, and to examine the SSC's intervention and the legal proceedings. Each case focuses on one or more of the catchphrases typically used in the adoption establishment's linguistic style of controlled expression: 'parental capability'; 'belonging' and 'continuity'; 'the wilderness generation' and 'the best interests of the child'; and 'a sacred calling'.

The term 'parental capability' is used when assessing a parent's ability to raise their child. It is a vague term, given to many interpretations,[29] the most common being one in which the parent's ability is presented as a fixed feature of their personal makeup. According to this interpretation, the relationship between parent and child is unidirectional: the parent determines the child's development and the nature of their relationship. The child, in this scenario, is perceived merely as the passive object of the parent's care – and thus the significance to him of his removal from his parents may be ignored. This construct is, in Chapter 1, set against an alternative view that defines the parent's ability in terms of the solution that he finds for the conflict between the need to preserve his resources and the need to provide for his child's needs, which draws upon those same resources. This presents the child as someone who actively forms an attachment with his parent, and since this attributes equal weight to the child's attachment to the parent as to the parent's attachment to the child, it requires consideration of what removing a child from his parents means to him.

The terms 'belonging' and 'continuity' highlight the inherent paradox of closed adoption, which purports to provide continuity in the child's life while severing his ties to his birth family. The contradiction at the heart of this paradox is deliberately obscured by denying the significance of the child's bond with his birth parents, and presenting the underlying false premise that adoption is compensation for the damage allegedly inflicted upon the child by his birth parents through their parental shortcomings.[30] Only when the child is given an opportunity to testify openly to the loss he experiences with the disappearance of his parents from his life – for example, when he is returned to them after being removed under the terms of an emergency order, as recounted in Chapter 2 – is the singular significance of that irreplaceable relationship revealed.

The phrases 'the wilderness generation' and 'the interests of the child' have been used in relation to child welfare policy in Israel at various points in its modern history, and feature in the case described in Chapter 3. In the pre-state period and in the first years following independence, the phrase 'the wilderness generation' was a central plank in the country's approach to the role of parents in their children's life, echoing the ethos that the new society should be built not by those who had wandered about in the proverbial wilderness (as in the biblical story of Exodus), but by those who, unlike their parents, were born free – that is, liberated from the shackles of exile. In the 1970s, this term was phased out in favour of the phrase 'the best interests of the child', but the underlying ideology behind the two expressions is the same: protecting the child means protecting his interests, rather than his relationship with his parents. Both terms are evident in the closed adoption approach.

Preceding the inclusion of Chapter 3 in the book were legal proceedings that made me realise the need for a distinction between 'secrecy', which entrenches the state's ownership of the child, and 'privacy', in the sense of protecting the relevant parties involved from public exposure. To this end, I present Chapter 4 as an interlude discussing secrecy as a construct; the relationship between it and the need for open government in a democratic society; and how all these issues are reflected in adoption policy and in the legal proceedings concerning whether the adoption case described in Chapter 3 could be made public. The general method used in the book – of devoting each chapter to a detailed description of a single chain of events – is discussed here in terms of the potential conflict between this method and the protection of privacy.

The term 'sacred calling' is usually cited in response to any criticism levelled at the SSC staff, to suggest that such criticism is heretical. In reality, however, the term is a faithful reflection of the SSC's current mindset and procedures, which are designed to safeguard its authority. Chapter 5 describes a case that reflects the adherence of adoption officials to the belief that birth parents and adoptive parents must be strictly segregated – even when the adoption is said to be open – and the zealousness with which this directive is observed, as though it were a religious ritual aimed at consecrating traditional customs, even at the price of silencing the child's voice.

The book concludes with an epilogue that juxtaposes two moral viewpoints, one drawn from a moral judgement on the issue of parent culpability, and the other about concern for others, aimed at preventing unnecessary suffering and loss – first and foremost of the child, but also of the parents. It is the latter which this book aims to advance in an attempt, as Adi Ophir put it, 'to disrupt the order of production and distribution of these evils'.[31]

Notes

1. Mili Mass, 'Adoption in the Bondage of the Oedipal Myth', *Journal of Psychiatry and Law* 22 (1994), 263–67.
2. Civil Appeal (CA) 2169/98, *Anon v A-G*, Verdict #53 (1) 241, 264 (1999):

   'The general rule is the "full" or "closed" adoption.' [However, the possibility of an open adoption was present already in the first Adoption of Children Law in Israel, 5720/1960 henceforth, Adoption of Children Law, 1960), and is preserved in the current version, as amended in

1981. It is known as 'Restricting the results of the adoption' – Adoption of Children Law, 5741/1981 (henceforth, ACL), 16a].

3. ACL 13(1–6), 8.
4. Supplementary Civil Proceedings (SCP) 7015/94, *A-G v Anon*, Verdict #50 (1) Repeat Trial (RT), 113 (1995).
5. This was added to the ACL 13(7); Nili Maimon, *Child Adoption Legislation* (Tel Aviv: Israel Bar Association, 1984), 321–22 [Hebrew].
6. Report of the Adoption of Children Law Inspection Committee, Jerusalem (Justice Ministry, 1979).
7. CA 418/88, *Anon v A-G*, Verdict #44 (3) 1, 9 (1990).
8. When speaking about an unidentified parent, I have chosen to use the masculine form, although the role is usually associated with the mother. Since the mother is generally cast as the one bearing responsibility and blame, the masculine form helps to underline that the father, too, is part of the parental equation.
9. SCP 7015/94, *A-G v Anon*, 114.
10. Ibid.
11. The term 'adoption officials' is henceforth used in this book as shorthand for welfare officials operating under the ACL. Since all adoption officials in Israel are women, I refer to them throughout the book using feminine pronouns.
12. Provision for removal orders of this sort is made both in the Youth (Care and Supervision) Law, 5720/1960 (henceforth, Youth Law) 11a, and in ACL 12c. The licence given by law, as an emergency procedure, for adoption officials to transfer a child to an intended adoptive family even before the issue has come before the courts is designed to spare children unnecessary upheavals should they be declared eligible for adoption; Maimon, *Child Adoption Legislation*, 191.
13. Not to be confused with 'Child Services', which is a separate and distinct entity. The Service for the Sake of the Child is the Israeli Adoption Authority in all but name.
14. Maimon, *Child Adoption Legislation*, 196–97.
15. CA 488/77, *Anon v A-G*, Verdict 32 (3), 421, 437 (1978):

    The father of orphans – in terms of the authority to make a final determination of their future – is the court of law and the court of law alone: this must not be given to anyone else, however good their intentions, lest they establish facts on the ground that force our hand.

16. ACL 16.
17. 'Because the raison d'etre of the state's involvement is to "ensure the best interests of the citizen", the benevolent state feels morally justified in governing the private lives of its citizens.' Signe Howell, *The Kinning of Foreigners: Transnational Adoption in a Global Perspective* (New York: Berghahn Books, 2006), 10.
18. Pinhas Shifman, *Family Law in Israel*, Vol. 2 (Jerusalem: The Sacher Institute for Legislative Research and Comparative Law, Hebrew University Faculty of Law, 1989), 218 [Hebrew].

19. 'Experience has shown that when the parents' rights are expropriated, they are transferred not to the child but to the state'. Betty Reid Mandell, *Where Are the Children? A Class Analysis of Foster Care and Adoption* (Lexington, MA: Lexington Books, 1977), 64.
20. Shifman, *Family Law in Israel*, 218.
21. ACL 2.
22. On the child's participation in legal proceedings that deliberate the relationship with his parents, see Mili Mass, 'When Family Relationships Stumble into the Finality of Legal Proceedings', *IDC Law Review* 18 (2014), 323–62 [Hebrew].
23. It is interesting to note that this practice is attributed to transnational adoption: 'The child is denuded of all kinship; denuded of meaningful relatedness whether its destiny is known or not. As such, the child is the example *par excellence* of the autonomous individual – so central in contemporary Western thinking. But this also, paradoxically, renders him or her a non-person; in a sense, non-human'. Howell, *The Kinning of Foreigners*, 4.
24. On the meaning of the term 'loss', see Adi Ophir, *The Order of Evils: Toward an Ontology of Morals, trans.* Rela Mazali and Havi Carel (New York: Zone Books, 2005), 89. On the presence of loss in the lives of adoptees, see David M. Brodzinsky, 'Stress and the Coping Model of Adoption Adjustment', in David M. Brodzinsky and Marshall D. Shechter (eds), *The Psychology of Adoption* (New York: Oxford University Press, 1990), 3–24; Harold D. Grotevant, 'Coming to Terms with Adoption: The Construction of Identity from Adolescence to Adulthood', *Adoption Quarterly* 1 (1997), 3–27.
25. Ophir, *The Order of Evils*, 129; Mili Mass, 'Baby at a Crossroads: The Dispute over the Meaning of Adoption', *Tel Aviv University Law Review* 31 (2008), 219–40 [Hebrew].
26. In Israel, adopted children are issued new birth certificates attesting to their birth to their adoptive parents (according to correspondence with the director of the Population and Passport Registry of the Ministry of the Interior, 21 December 2008). In a written reply from the director of the Child Services Agency on 27 January 2009, it was further clarified that:

    1) A new birth certificate is indeed issued to the adoptee, as set out in section 20 of the Population Registry Law of 1965.

    2) The original birth certificate is considered null and void. The Ministry of the Interior's position is that it will not provide any document that is considered invalid.

    3) It should be noted that, under the ACL 30b: 'A welfare official may allow an adoptee aged eighteen and above to examine their details in the Registry…'. The adoption file includes identifying details of the biological parent.

27. The names of those involved have been changed and identifying details obscured, including details of prior verdicts on these cases, without affecting the substance or significance of the testimonies.
28. Ophir, *The Order of Evils*, 165.
29. According to the courts, the wording of the argument set out in ACL 13(7) (which allows a child to be declared eligible for adoption even without the parents' consent, on grounds of their parental incapability) is insufficiently clear. CA 418/88, *Anon v A-G*, 5, and Chapter 1.
30. On the issue of damage and compensation, see Ophir, *The Order of Evils*, 128.
31. Ibid., 14.

1

'Parental Capability'

The Story of the Ziv Family Children

Children in Danger

'There's nothing here for me to salvage', I thought to myself grimly as I read through the documents presented by the state in support of its request to declare the children of the Ziv family – Yitzhak (age six), Galit (five) and Orr (three and a half) – eligible for adoption. Every time I am asked to give an expert opinion, I read the reports and testimonies submitted by the SSC to the court, and am plagued by a sense that it is impossible to preserve the contact between the parents and their children. And on almost every occasion, when I listen to the parents' and the children's accounts, a very different picture emerges, even in the cases where I agree that declaring the children eligible for adoption is unavoidable.

Understanding the parents' point of view is, in my opinion, essential to assessing their ability to raise their child. Unlike the parents' legal counsel, whose job is to defend the parents' position and rights, the expert is required to understand the parents' point of view and distinguish it from her own.

With the appointment of an expert witness, the court provides the parent one more opportunity before ruling on the future of their relationship with their child, and the child's fate. Therefore, when making a preliminary assessment as to whether to serve in this capacity, I take particular care to first examine the documents provided by the court. In the case of the Ziv family, when the mother's legal counsel asked me to serve as an expert witness on her behalf, I was fairly dismayed by what I read in the documents.

In support of its petition to declare the Ziv children eligible for adoption, the SSC had presented a report whose main points were as follows. The Ziv couple were well known to their local welfare services almost from the start of their life together. The mother and father were not married. The mother had immigrated to Israel at the age of fourteen with her mother and three brothers. They settled in a town in southern Israel, where she met her partner, a man about twelve years her senior, from a very troubled background, who had not served the three-year military service customarily required of all Israeli men on reaching the age of eighteen due to his criminal record. Since her family objected to their relationship, the couple eloped to the north of the country to live with the young woman's grandmother. During their time together, they produced three children. The father frequently became physically abusive towards the mother, and on several occasions she responded by filing official complaints with the police. In addition, he did not provide for the family financially, and would abandon them for long periods. When he did return, he would fall back into the pattern of physical abuse towards the mother and ignoring the children's physical and emotional needs. The mother and children often found themselves without food, and had to rely on donations to buy basic food items. The home had no furniture or equipment, apart from a baby crib, a playpen and a blanket on the floor. The couple received monetary assistance to buy basic house furnishings (beds, refrigerator, wardrobe), but the father sold most of them. He moved from one workplace to another and found it difficult to provide for his family. According to the mother, much of his income was squandered on card games.

In the view of the local welfare officials,[1] the children were at physical and mental risk.[2] Despite the support given to the family, they suffered from neglect. Yitzhak (the eldest) had also been beaten by his father for no apparent reason, and suffered bruises on one eye and one leg. Galit exhibited signs of disciplinary problems. Both were developmentally delayed, physically as well as mentally. Orr, too, in his infancy, was malnourished and restless. When the children were aged three, two and six months, respectively, an interim order[3] was issued for them to be removed and placed with foster families. This was subsequently extended several times, for periods of up to eight months at a time, whereupon they were returned to their parents under a supervisory care order for a probationary period. The parents were each placed in rehabilitation care programmes, and their relationship improved. After seven months, however, it worsened again, the police once again received complaints of physical abuse, and even the mother began to be absent from the home, leaving the children alone at night. After two months, in view of the deterioration in their condition, the children were removed from the mother's custody with the help of the police, and placed in a children's home[4] in another town, where they had been staying ever since. Six months later, the father was sentenced to six months in prison for robbery. The mother, Sophie, returned to live with her mother in southern Israel, where she took on only a part-time job due, she says, to her ill health. She visited the children once a month, at prescribed intervals, but other than that, from one visit to the next, was said to have had no interest in them. Given the children's poor condition and the parents' incapability of raising them properly, the SSC asked the court to declare them eligible for adoption.

The report went on to detail the children's severe condition while they had lived with their parents: their attendance at their respective daycare centres or preschools had been erratic; they were often absent or late, and when they did attend they were clearly neglected and dressed in dirty clothes. Yitzhak and Galit had lice in their hair; Yitzhak was sad and withdrawn and spoke about violence at home, and Galit exhibited developmental problems. Orr, as the youngest of the three, appeared to be in the best condition. Once they arrived at the children's home, the staff reported that Yitzhak and Galit were totally out of control. They would snatch the food that was served to them, and had no personal hygiene habits. Yitzhak would constantly engage in reckless behaviour, and Galit hoarded objects and toys. In addition, she exhibited sexually flirtatious behaviour towards one member of staff. During Sophie's visits to the home, staff observed that there appeared to be no bond between her and her children. Sometimes she would visit the children in the company of her own mother, and on more than one occasion she and her mother were verbally and physically abusive towards members of staff.

The caregivers at the children's home were quoted as saying that the children's poor condition might be too much of a burden on any single family seeking to adopt the two older children. With regard to Orr, the youngest child, there seemed to be no need to justify his separate adoption, because the staff thought there was no significant bond between him and the two older children. The authorities were therefore recommending that the siblings be separated from one another.

The disturbing description of the children's condition and the parents' failure to care for them illustrates the circumstances that provide justification for adoption without parental consent, for what is known as 'parental incapability'.[5] However, according to the courts, the wording of the rationale for non-consensual adoption on the grounds of parental incapability is insufficiently clear: 'The words that the legislature has used are vague and highly unclear. Expressions such as "incapable", "care properly" etc. are highly intangible and lacking in any directive'.[6] Indeed, this rationale can be subject to various interpretations, two of which are demonstrated in the legal proceedings surrounding the case of the Ziv children.

One view sees the parents' capability of raising their child as a manifestation of a natural mechanism that is instinctively activated at the child's birth, and innate to the parent's personality. This mechanism is what is examined in the psychological tests used to assess the parents' ability to raise the child, while the effect of the parent-child relationship upon the parent, and the circumstances in which the parent cares for the child, are hardly taken into account, if at all.

Another interpretation sees the manner in which the parent raises their child as an expression of how they resolve the inherent conflict in parenting between providing for the child's needs – which depletes their resources – and their need to preserve their resources. The parent's resolution of this conflict is what lies at the heart of the assessment of the parent's ability, according to this approach.[7]

The SSC report on the Ziv case was founded on the former approach, as it focused on the parents' personalities. The father was described as a violent man who took no responsibility for his wife or children, while the mother was portrayed as a helpless woman who did not protect her children from their father, and even now, after they had been removed from her custody, was seemingly indifferent towards them and continued to neglect them. The report therefore concluded that she suffered from a character disorder, an assessment in keeping with the notion of 'lack of parental capability', which was made after important details in the chain of events had been omitted from the SSC report and that of the children's home to the court. Thus, for example, in the state's petition there was no mention of the fact that the decision to remove the children from the mother's custody was taken while the father was in detention after the mother had filed a complaint against him in an attempt to protect herself and her children from him; that the mother had fought against the children's removal from her custody and was even arrested for refusing to reveal their whereabouts; that the police department, which had helped the welfare officials track down the children, had to forcibly remove the children from their mother's custody; that for several months the mother was not told where her children were being kept, and that when she finally discovered where they were, she was allowed to visit them only once a month for one hour at a time, despite her repeated requests to extend the visit duration; that the distance of the children's home from the mother's home meant that she had to spend many hours travelling by public transport to visit, and when she was unable to arrive at the stipulated time, she was prevented from arranging an alternative date and time and had to wait until the next scheduled monthly visit in accordance with the inflexible timetable that had been presented to her. Had all this information been included in the case report, it would have focused the evaluation of Sophie's parental capability on the particular solution that she had found in her struggle to save her motherhood.

The dialectic between these two approaches to assessing the mother's capability to raise her children lay at the heart of the legal proceedings in the case of the Ziv family children.

The Parental Mechanism

The justification for adoption without parental consent on grounds of the parent's incapability to raise their child appears to contradict the conventional view that a parent's ability to protect and nurture their child is 'innate'. In fact, the very idea behind the notion of 'parental capability', namely that it is a personality-based mechanism that is triggered at the child's birth, suggests that it is 'natural' and 'normal', and its absence – the so-called 'parental incapability' – is therefore a 'pathology'. Thus, instead of parental failure serving as a reason to question the notion that parental capability is innate, the term 'parental incapability' reinforces it.

The benchmark used for distinguishing between 'normal' and 'pathological' when assessing a parent's 'capability' is evident in the tests used, which are often referred to as 'parental capability tests', but are really personality tests. These assessments were attached to the state's petition to declare the Ziv children eligible for adoption, and their summaries were included in the SSC's report. In them, the father was reported to be:

> extremely childish … of a poor and limited personality, [with] a low frustration threshold, and insufficient control over his impulses … He is rash, reckless, with signs of psychopathic tendencies, and no indication

> of any feelings of guilt over what he has caused his wife and children ... No real ability to empathise (towards his wife and children) ... a young man of normal intelligence, but of disturbed character ....

As for the mother, she was found to be:

> truly infantile, incoherent, of uncertain identity, even if she now tries to put on a façade of someone who knows what she wants ... She lacks judgement, has only tenuous contact with reality (due to excessive infantility), does not plan her actions ... She is a young woman with a character disorder (over dependency), who has become a parent prematurely ... She cannot defend herself or her children.

The assessment clearly demonstrates the view that the parent's ability to raise a child is indicative of a particular personality makeup. The use of the word 'capability' reflects a belief that every individual has an innate aptitude that lies dormant within the innermost recesses of their personality, to be activated the moment their child is born. However, that term ignores not only the effect of the parents' living conditions, but also – and especially – the effect of the child on the parent themselves. It also suggests that the parent needs the child as much as the child needs them, and therefore the parent's bond with the child must be a reflection of the child's bond with the parent.[8] Parenting – be it an expression of normality or of pathology – is perceived as the predominant factor in the child's development, and the parent as one who determines the quality of their relationship with the child. The term 'parental capability' presents the parent as the possessor of a mechanism innate to their personality, and the child as merely the object of that mechanism. Consequently, the child's bond with the parent is evident in the parent's behaviour, and the child's point of view is ignored. Parental 'capability' is equated with the child's bond to the parent. If the parent 'fails' in their care for the child, it means that the parent–child bond must be lacking, and therefore the child must be taken away from the parent for the child's sake. For this reason, in the state's petition to declare the Ziv children eligible for adoption there is no mention of the nature of the children's interaction with their parents, although there were plenty of opportunities to observe it, for example when the children were placed with foster families, then returned to their parents, and ultimately sent to the children's home.

As I shall explain later, I do not share the belief that a parent's capability to raise their child is a natural mechanism that reflects the bond between them. Nonetheless, when I read the account of the Ziv children's dire condition, I thought that it was indeed necessary to remove them from their parents' custody, for their own protection. I could not, I thought, recommend in good conscience that the children be returned to their mother's custody, as her legal counsel expected of me. The rhetorical power of descriptions of the danger that children allegedly are in, and the desire to put an end to it, without delay, is often overwhelming and clouds one's comprehension of the true situation. For this reason, when I first read the SSC staff report, I did not 'hear' the silence of the children and Sophie.

The doubts I harboured about the benefit of appointing me as expert witness on the mother's behalf, and the belief that I would not be able to form a different assessment from that which I read in the documents provided by the SSC, grew stronger after reading the conclusions of a psychologist appointed by the SSC to observe two meetings between the mother and the children. These conclusions, which were presented in court as part of the testimony in support of the state's petition to declare the children eligible for adoption, were among the documents provided to me by the mother's legal counsel.

The psychologist, like other experts, appeared to recognise the limitations of using personality tests of the parents to assess their ability to raise their children, and therefore thought it necessary to observe the interaction between the mother and her children. To her credit, she qualified her conclusions:

> An opinion based exclusively on observations during two time-constrained meetings with no intimacy, and in circumstances that were stressful and threatening for both the mother and the children, is necessarily of limited validity and can only serve as one factor in a range of considerations for the 'child's best interests' that are based on prior acquaintance of the family, psychological diagnoses and reports about each of the children from the children's home.

Nonetheless, her observations as to the mother's ability to regain custody over the children were summed up as follows:

> In the two meetings at which I was present, what stood out was what was missing in the relationship between the mother and the children. In both meetings there was no evidence of any joy, or even excitement at seeing each other again; there was no apparent moment of intimacy or familiarity that arises from living together, in a bid to relive shared positive experiences of the past. In the children's case, none of them appeared to show a glimmer of memory or fondness for their mother, either physically or emotionally. Clearly, at this point, when the children have been for a comparatively long time at the children's home, the memory of being close to their mother diminishes with time (I do not know how close they were when they were still living together) – especially when it is apparent that all three are, to one extent or another,

attached to the children's home staff, teachers and psychologist. In this respect, there was a deterioration from one meeting to the next. If in the first meeting Yitzhak and Galit associated their mother with 'home' and once even used the word 'Mum' and tried, off and on (and rarely, at that) to ask her or tell her something or attract her attention, and gave up, by the second meeting they arrived without expectations, and did not attempt or even avoided making contact or cooperating with the mother. Orr, too, who at the first meeting responded passively to the mother's approaches, was more distant in the second meeting, when the mother kissed him and lifted him onto her lap. Yitzhak and Galit's avoidance of her at the second meeting and their refusal to cooperate were much more pronounced than on the previous occasion, and nuances in their behaviour hinted at residual bad memories of their relationship with the mother. The children's needs for gentleness and affection were all addressed to the children's home staff, and, over time, to uncles as well. As previously noted, based on the evidence of these encounters, we can see that the three children, notwithstanding their differences of age, temperament and gender, do not see their mother (or grandmother) as a source of warmth, protection, or even as an adult who is attentive to them, can answer questions or be appealed to for help in mundane matters such as 'to go potty', to adjust a piece of clothing that had become uncomfortable, or to dispose of a sweet that they no longer wanted – instead, they appealed to the home staff. ('Test forays' during the first meeting were the exception that proved the rule.) All attempts at verbal communication with the mother during the meetings were disappointing as far as the older children were concerned, and Orr never once approached the mother of his own accord.

On the mother's part, the monthly meeting was an opportunity to bring the children sweets, and little gifts that were not necessarily suited to their respective needs – most of it involving new clothes. The clothes, however, were chosen with care, attention, and with due thought for the needs of each child. They were high quality, smart and of the correct sizes, and carefully chosen to distinguish the clothes for the boys from those for Galit. During these visits the mother appeared to be all alone before what seemed to her like a panel of judges (occasionally she brought other relatives with her). Although, in practice, the staff members tried to facilitate the communication and contact between the mother and the children and intervened as little as possible, the mother was undoubtedly perennially conscious of the fact that her children are in a children's home and of the unspoken threat of adoption as an accusative finger aimed at her. She could not use the hour that she had to foster a sense of intimacy with the children and to create an atmosphere of spending time together – be it by playing a game, through conversation, displays of affection or physical play. Playful interactions, physical bonding and emotional closeness [for the children] all occurred with the home staff, rather than with the mother or grandmother. Apart from holding Orr on her lap, the mother did not

> approach him, or take him to her. She did not initiate physical contact, questions about how they were, small talk or joint play. Once she gave them the toys or sweets, she showed no further interest in the children's reactions. What was particularly striking was that she appeared to treat the children as if according to a premeditated plan, which she insisted on executing with an almost childish determination, irrespective of the needs of each child, without any attempt to listen to them or to try to adapt her plan to their needs, or instigating any verbal communication with them, be it through questions or replies. Indeed, she tried to sidestep the few initiatives that they made, appearing not to hear their questions or statements, and when obliged to respond, giving a banal, irrelevant reply – be it about their father, or a complaint about hurting them while dressing them, or getting them ready for a photograph together. She neither listened nor paid any due attention …

The estrangement between Sophie and her children, as described in the psychologist's assessment, is attributed mainly to her conduct towards her children. The psychologist did not consider the possibility that the children's diffidence itself affected Sophie's responses. This unidirectionality in assessing the interaction between them is influenced, as previously noted, by the view that the parent's ability is the outcome of their inborn personality mechanism that governs their ability to respond to their child's needs. Although the children's responses to Sophie were also noted in the psychologist's assessment, according to her they did not serve to explain the mother's behaviour.

The psychologist's observations did not relieve the bleak picture portrayed in the SSC officials' report. The description of the children's attitude towards their mother did not prompt me to think that it was essential to preserve their relationship with her, nor did the description of her behaviour during the encounters with her children improve the impression that I had received from the report. I expressed these doubts with Sophie's legal counsel, and suggested that she reconsider her request to appoint me an expert witness, but she decided nonetheless, perhaps for want of any alternative, to call on my services after all. I tried, therefore, to hold on to the only glimmer of hope that I could find in the gloomy picture: Sophie's tenacious struggle to regain custody of her children, which stood in marked contrast to her alleged passivity and indifference portrayed in the documents I had been given.

The struggle waged by parents for custody over their children is often attributed to ulterior motives, as evident in the words of a district judge at a meeting of the Israeli parliamentary Labour and Welfare Committee:

> I can cite examples that I have witnessed in court about mothers who fought like tigers against petitions to have their children declared eligible for adoption. The reason is social: social stigma, self-respect, personality disorders, hurt egos. It has nothing to do with love for the child. I want to tell you – without wishing to make generalisations – when I began to hear adoption cases and encountered this kind of people, it was new to me. I had dealt with cases of family law, I know people in all kinds of situations, but the weirdest and least acceptable things I saw in cases of adoption involving parents who have their children taken away. I would like to assume that everyone who is present here today is a normal person who likes children and knows how to raise them – but not everyone is like that. We must not view these kinds of people as being all alike. The same applies to mothers who change their minds about adoption – it's not always because of love for the child.[9]

Despite professing that he wished to avoid generalisations, the judge in question viewed birth parents whose children are taken away for adoption as the 'kind of people' who are not 'normal', and therefore, in his view, their motives for fighting for the right to raise their children should be treated as suspect. In the above statement, he ignored what 'that kind' of parents did have in common: the struggle against the death sentence that the court was liable to pronounce on their parenthood. A desperate struggle of this sort is liable to bring about 'unacceptable' behaviours. Parents who are perceived to have 'failed' will always find themselves in a double bind. If they are compliant, and meekly accept the rules that have been imposed on them without enquiring after their child between one visit and the next, they are supposedly demonstrating that their bond with their child is unimportant to them and therefore justifying the removal of their child from their custody, but if they fight for the right to maintain custody of their children, their motives are declared suspect. According to this approach, any deficiency in the parental mechanism is presented as a deviation from the norm, and blurs the distinction between two axes for assessing the parent's ability: normality/pathology, normativity/deviance.[10]

Since I do not share the views expressed by this judge, and do not entertain preconceived doubts of the sincerity of the parents' struggle for custody of their children, even if they are perceived as having failed in raising them, I searched the documents that were given to me for an explanation for the discrepancy between Sophie's tenacious struggle now and her alleged indifference towards her children as described in the SSC's report. While I was doing so, I received a transcript of a discussion that had taken place in court several weeks earlier, before the case had been brought to my attention, in which the children's home staff psychologist (not the one whose observations are cited earlier) testified that, during the previous visit, there had been a change in Sophie's conduct towards her children. This time she sat and drew with them, helped them put a jigsaw puzzle together, and was generally more active during the meeting. According to this psychologist, the two older children cooperated with her. At the court hearing, the director of the children's home also testified that during her most recent visit, Sophie had started playing with her children on her own initiative, but added:

> We were very surprised. In late May, she did this of her own accord, and surprised us and the children – because it was different from her behaviour that we had seen in the previous two years … My feeling was that it was an act, put on because the court hearings were about to begin. The contrast between her attitude towards the children over two years and that meeting was very marked.

(I should point out that the director's account was inaccurate. At that time, the children had been at the home for twenty-one months, during the first seven of which Sophie did not know their whereabouts, so naturally could not visit them. When she did find out where they were, she was initially prevented from visiting them on a regular basis, and the frequency of visits had increased – under court orders – only in the previous month or so.)

The director's testimony about the time and context in which the change in the mother's behaviour was observed – namely, the start of the court hearings in her case – was no doubt intended to present her as manipulative and seeking to deceive the court. The fact that the meeting in question took place only after there had been regular meetings between the mother and her children and after they had become more frequent was not raised as a possible explanation for her change of behaviour. That said, I would not entirely rule out the possibility that the change in the mother's behaviour was related to the prospect of imminent court hearings in her case – however, not necessarily because she was attempting to influence the court, but because by this time a lawyer had been appointed by the court to represent her, and supported her in her stand against the state. The importance of a lawyer representing the parent can hardly be overstated, not only because, given the nature of the legal system in Israel, this is the only means by which the parent can present their position to the court, but also because of the helplessness of the parent, who more often than not comes from the margins of society and is obliged to face a seasoned and powerful system, and defend themselves against accusations that they have 'failed' in their 'natural' role of parenthood. For such parents, their legal counsel is often the only support they have.

The children's home psychologist, who had been present at the time of the supposedly exceptional meeting between Sophie and her children, did not attribute much significance to the changes that he observed in Sophie's behaviour, since, as he put it:

> The test should not be based on all kinds of things that one sees externally – because a month earlier, the meeting had been a disaster. The real question … is whether the mother is able and capable, in terms of her personality, to assume responsibility and care for these three children, and not everything that one sees on the surface.

The psychologist's downplaying of the significance of the change in the mother's behaviour during her meeting with the children was explicitly due to his view that a parent's ability to raise their children is a fixed and immutable mechanism. Here lies the advantage, as it were, of the term 'parental capability' as it is currently defined. The law demands that the assessment of a parent's capability also consider the possibility that it might improve, with the help commonly provided by welfare services,[11] but if parental capability is defined as fixed and immutable, the requisite forecast is predetermined – that is, it will not change – thereby relieving the assessor of the need for any further examinations. A parent who is found to have a deficient parental mechanism will forever be 'lacking parental capability'. Moreover, equating that mechanism with the parent's personality, which according to the theory behind this notion is determined in one's infancy, presents it as something impervious to any subsequent environmental influences. Thus, not only are the parent's living conditions ignored when evaluating their ability to raise their children, but so too is the context in which the observations are made of their interactions with their children. Consequently, for example, parental visits are conducted at a frequency determined by the SSC, and in most cases, since the location of the children's home is secret, at the offices of the SSC which, like any other governmental offices, are highly impersonal and alienating, under close supervision of SSC staff, who are present in the room throughout the visit. (In the case of the Ziv children, at least two such staff members were present in the room at all times during Sophie's visits.)

In the subsequent hearings in the Ziv family case, it transpired, following an investigation by Sophie's legal counsel, that the psychologist (whose report was quoted above in detail) had held her observations several months before the court hearings. In response to the lawyer's question, 'Do you know for how long the children had not seen their mother prior to the first visit that you observed?' the psychologist replied, 'As far as I remember, I was told that the visits were held once a month'. However, as Sophie's lawyer pointed out:

> According to what Sophie said, this visit in fact took place *three* months after she had not seen the children. Might this explain why the children turned to the staff members when they asked if they could go to the bathroom, or when they wanted certain toys?

The psychologist replied:

> Yes, that can certainly explain why, at that time, they were more attached to the staff members, and had grown distant from the mother.

Perhaps the psychologist's memory had failed her, but the fact is that she had not noted how long had passed since the mother's previous visits as part of the information pertaining to her observations – perhaps because of the little significance that she attributed to this detail.

The omission of the context of the parent's life circumstances from the assessment of their bond with their children is most glaringly apparent – to the point of absurdity – in the attitude of the adoption officials towards the idea of meetings between the father and the children, as summed up in the verdict:

> The aforesaid decision [that the father can visit the minors whenever he is on parole from prison] was made while the adoption official … was not present in court. When she arrived and was told of it, she objected, saying 'I shall consult with the facility where the children are being held … There is a very big problem with regard to the father. He has not seen them for two years. I think that to foist him on them at this point is problematic…' She omitted to point out that the father had appealed several times, through the prison social worker, to see the minors, and had been turned down. In her own testimony to the court, the senior adoption official repeated the claim that visits by the father had not been held due to his lack of interest. Later, in response to the question by the father's counsel, she replied, 'He said that he had requested, but it wasn't something with a follow-up, end and beginning…' This statement contradicts what was stated in the SSC report – which [the senior welfare official] had signed off on … and the testimony of the [local] adoption official ('[The father] reports putting in repeated requests to visit the children, which in his words were always denied'), and other documents to the effect that the father repeatedly asked to see his children, but was turned down.

Presenting the fact that no meetings had been held between the father and his children as evidence of his alleged lack of interest deliberately ignored the fact that he was in prison during that time, therefore the option of visiting his children was entirely at the discretion of the authorities.[12] Here too, then, the parent's ability to raise their children is presented as an innate mechanism supposedly isolated from environmental influences, and in defence of the premise that 'lack of parental capability' is a pathology and a deviation, the parents' motives are always thought to be suspect and they themselves are vilified, in a bid to justify their removal from the children's lives.

Demonisation of the Parents

If the 'lack of parental capability' diagnosis served its purpose – to highlight the parent's inability to raise their children – defining it as a pathology beyond the person's control would relieve them of responsibility for their actions. It is true that the ruling pointed out that the claim of 'lack of parental capability' does not require a blame element, unlike other transgressions that justify adoption without the parents' consent;[13] however, the definition of the parent's child-raising ability as 'natural', or 'normal', does suggest a normative benchmark. This is evident in the words of the judge cited earlier, in which he doubted the sincerity of the parents' struggle to have the children returned to their custody after they had failed to take proper care of them; it is as if deficient care were indicative of deliberate, or perhaps even malicious, behaviour towards the children. Indeed, the state's coercive intervention has a punitive connotation, which is apparent not only in the judge's remarks, but also in the court's official rulings,[14] despite declarations to the contrary.[15]

The legal proceedings in the matter of the Ziv family revealed the attempt to create an inevitable association between the incriminatory meaning of the phrase 'lack of parental capability' and the removal of the children from their parents. The children's home psychologist testified:

> There was one incident at the birthday of one of the children where there was a lot of shouting and swearing. It was one of the most horrendous visits I have ever witnessed at the home. For an entire family to come to a birthday party with a big cake, and then do nothing but shout and threaten people – but not one of them was able to pull themselves together and actually celebrate anything. And the one who actually sang 'Happy Birthday' to [the boy] was only me.

On another occasion, the psychologist continued, Sophie swore at him, and threatened him: 'You're a dead man! We'll find you! I have friends where you live!' In response to Sophie's legal counsel's question about whether the psychologist knew that before the second violent visit the adoption official had spoken with the mother and grandmother and told them that the children would be placed for adoption, the psychologist denied that the two incidents in fact occurred so close to one another. However, even if Sophie and the grandmother had been told of this on some other occasion, there is no disputing the fact that it did take place directly before one of Sophie's visits – a timing that, at the very least, indicates a callous insensitivity to the mother's psychological condition before meeting with the children. With regard to another visit reported by the psychologist, the grandmother recounted in an affidavit to the court that her eleven-year-old son – Sophie's younger brother – who had accompanied her on one of the visits, asked Yitzhak if he wanted to return home, but the psychologist

> shut him up and said 'No one's talking about home', so I turned to [him] and said, 'Why are you saying that he doesn't want to go home?', and then the [psychologist] grabbed the children, held them tightly, and wouldn't let us talk with the children, and then the children began to cry, and I got the impression that the children wanted to come home and [the psychologist] wouldn't let them…

The court learned about two further incidents involving violence by the family. One took place at the welfare offices near Sophie's home. The mother arrived for an interview in which she was supposed to hear about the SSC's future plans for her children, but since the officials did not have a clear answer, Sophie began shouting, whereupon the officials called the police and filed a complaint against her. Another incident took place after a meeting at which she was informed of the impending petition to have her children declared eligible for adoption. Shortly after that meeting, the adoption official in question received a telephone call at her home, in which she was threatened 'with a bullet to the head'. The adoption official filed a complaint with the police, but, as the court notes, 'N.B.: There is no word as to who made the threats, in what context, how it has to do with any of the respondents, or the results of the police investigation [into the matter]'.

Based on these incidents, the adoption officials argued that the two parents were violent, and in order to protect the witnesses summoned on the state's behalf, asked that the court

> instruct that the testimonies of welfare officials and expert witnesses be heard not in the presence of the respondents [the parents]; that the respondents not be told the dates when the authors of said documents will testify; that the documents and transcripts of their testimonies not be disclosed to the respondents; and that the respondents' counsel be prohibited from disclosing any details whatsoever that may identify the authors of said documents…

Since the father was in prison at the time, and only the mother appeared at the hearings, this request was clearly aimed mainly at her. On this point, the court's ruling was:

> Without detracting in any way from the seriousness that should be attributable to any sort of violence, if we take into account the manner in which the minors were taken from their parents' custody; the fact that they were held for such a long period at a secret location far from their parents' home, without the possibility of reasonably frequent visitations and without any information given to them as to what to expect down the road, it is not surprising that the feelings of helplessness, frustration, uncertainty and anxiety were eventually manifested, including in the form of bursts of rage. The problem is, instead of reflecting on what had happened, the adoption officials chose to draw up an exaggerated and tendentious report and to file an exceptional request – perhaps in order to stir up the court into joining it in the perverse course that it chose to conduct matters from the outset.

This was not the only case in which I witnessed the adoption officials' attempt to cast the parents as bullies. In another case, the father's violence towards the adoption official was presented to the court as justification for banning him from visiting his daughter.[16] The daughter, Revital, had been taken from her mother at birth; her father learned of her existence only during the hearing on the state's petition to declare her eligible for adoption, since the mother was unable to raise her. Revital stayed with an undisclosed foster family with whom she had been placed by the SSC, and her father visited her regularly at the offices of the SSC. When Revital was seven months old, I saw her for the purposes of assessing her father's ability to raise her at his home. In the assessment that I subsequently submitted to the court, I wrote that the baby's condition indicated that she had been left for hours at a time on her back without movement – the back of her head was bald – and the delay in her development was clearly evident. She was utterly passive; she looked at a face put in front of her, but did not follow it with her eyes; when a toy fell from her hands she did not follow it; and when it was handed to her, she did not reach out to take it.[17]

Several months later, the SSC petitioned the court, pursuant to the Legal Fitness and Guardianship Law, 1962, to approve an operation for a skin transplant operation on Revital's knee. Boiling water had been spilt on her at the foster family, causing her severe burns. The incident was referred to as an 'accident'. Revital remained in the care of that foster family, and no inquiry was launched into the matter by any external authority. To add insult to injury, the adoption officials tried to make the father appear to be the villain. For several weeks after the incident, he was not allowed to see his daughter's bandaged knee during his visits, and when the bandage was finally removed and he saw her scarred knee for the first time, he was aghast and shouted, 'This is what you call the "best interests of the child"!?' (the argument that had been cited to deny him custody of the child). The adoption official left the room, and when she returned and tried to pick up the baby, the father pushed her hand away. During the following visit, he says, he was observed from behind a one-way screen, and a minder was stationed by the door to supervise him. On the day of his next visit, he found he was unable to be there, but when he rang to notify them of this and to reschedule, he was asked how he thought he could raise his daughter if he was incapable of maintaining his visits to her. At this point the father threatened the adoption official and said that he would kill her. He was then barred entirely from seeing his daughter. In an attempt to salvage matters, he wrote to the court, describing the chain of events, and apologised to the adoption official in question, attributing his aggressive behaviour to the humiliation and sense of persecution he had felt at the hands of adoption officials, and his profound pain at seeing the injury his daughter had incurred, and assured the court that at no point did he have any intention of carrying out his threat.

This is a story of a father who, when confronted by his infant daughter's disfigured knee, was screaming from the intensity of the pain he felt. None of the SSC staff thought of offering him any words of comfort or sympathy, lest perhaps that might be taken as an admission of the adoption service's responsibility for the child's injury. The father was simply presented as a violent and dangerous man whose complaints must be rejected. When this attitude enraged him and prompted him to threaten the adoption official, the tactic paid off: he did indeed act in a violent and threatening manner, and the court cancelled his visitation rights altogether.

The case of the Ziv children was different. The court rejected the request to hold the hearing without the parents present, on the following grounds:

> Needless to say, the court regards any assault on public servants a matter of grave concern, and upholds the right of public servants to testify freely without fear or anxiety – a right that the court must protect with all means at its disposal. On the other hand, the right of the respondents – whom the authorities are seeking to deny that which is dearest to them and to permanently revoke their parenthood over their children – to be present at the hearing and for their case to be presented before the court in the optimal manner … the right of a litigant to be present at hearings concerning them is a basic constitutional right … which the

> court has a public responsibility to protect. Accordingly, when it was claimed that this right clashes with the right of witnesses to protect themselves, special provisions were made in the court decision with regard to hearing testimony.

The court agreed for the witnesses to appear behind a screen, but this was removed in the course of the hearings. The court ruling explained why:

> The mother sat huddled in a corner of the hall, and it was enough to see from the manner in which she sat and the helplessness that she displayed to understand that it was not fear of her presence that had led to the [witnesses'] exceptional request. Even the witnesses who appeared at the witness stand one after the other testified that she is a passive woman, quiet and restrained, whom they neither feared nor claimed to be afraid of at any stage … With hindsight, it is difficult to avoid the impression that the request in question was meant mainly for dramatisation purposes and to de-legitimise the respondents, in a bid to undermine their position from the outset.

Indeed, a certain degree of dramatisation was needed to persuade the court of the SSC's contention that the children would be in danger if they were returned to their mother. State Counsel argued that the petition to declare the children eligible for adoption had been submitted with the approval of all welfare services involved in the adoption case. His attempt to present a unified position was key to how he represented the state's position. Thus, for example, the director of Sophie's local welfare service office, who had been invited to testify on its behalf, explained that their plan was to ensure that the children be returned to the mother's custody, but with the addition of a safety net. In response, State Counsel asked the court to declare her a hostile witness. When the judge expressed frank surprise at this, State Counsel explained, '… I could not anticipate what the witness would say today. Given her testimony today, she should be declared a hostile witness pending a more extensive investigation'. The witness also revealed that the committee in charge of settling the dispute between the local welfare department and the SSC over the Ziv family children had held a stormy meeting, with raised voices: 'I heard someone remark that if there were programmes like this in the community, there would be fewer children available for adoption, which would adversely affect families seeking to adopt'.

'As if that weren't enough', the court ruling noted later, when the court ordered all material relating to the Ziv family in the files of their local welfare services to be made available to the parents' legal counsel, it transpired that:

> Counsel for the petitioner [the SSC] had taken matters into his own hands. He had submitted a copy of the welfare file [from the mother's local welfare office] without transcripts of two discussions about the minors ... When these were finally received ... they turned out to be not 'internal records', nor 'correspondence between legal counsel and client', but transcripts of discussions at the SSC with social workers [at the mother's local welfare office], with staff at the children's home, and with State Counsel .... State Counsel had attached out of date transcripts to the petition to have the children declared eligible for adoption, on the assumption – so it seems – that the transcripts of those later discussions would never be found – [and which] put an entirely different complexion on the matter.

The two transcripts in question cited the objections of officials at the mother's local welfare offices to the SSC's petition to declare her children eligible for adoption. The conduct of the State Counsel[18] in this case prompted the judge to issue an unusual warning against the lack of protection for children inherent in improper representation by the state:

> It saddens me that this is the State Counsel's position. In at least two respects, adoption cases differ from run-of-the-mill civil cases being considered by the court. Here the petitioner is the Attorney General, and the law permits the petitioner to produce documents that would not be admissible in a regular civil court – such as – among the attachments to the petition to declare a minor eligible for adoption – reports containing hearsay testimonies; impressions and documents whose authorship is unclear; the circumstances in which they were written and the motivation for their writing often uncertain; and whether their motivations were pertinent or governed by ulterior motives. All this in proceedings whose outcome is the most difficult kind that the court is required to rule upon. The assumption behind this licence is that when a petition is made by the Attorney General rather than by an interested party of some kind, its intentions are honourable. Moreover, its purpose is to enable the courts to be open-minded by bringing before it all the material, including the deliberations, the arguments on both sides, so that the court may rule on the difficult disputes placed before it based on the entire picture of the situation. I do not believe that the role of the Attorney General should be limited to presenting the SSC's position exclusively, and if there is a dispute on such a fateful question, it is difficult to expect the respondents – who are the biological parents – to act with their hands tied, while the other party holds information that could lead the court to rule in their favour, and that this information should be concealed from the court to cater to the narrow interests of the opposing party...

Having the legal department of the Ministry of Welfare – which works in close association with adoption officials – represent the state in this matter, rather than the Attorney General itself, as is customary with other government ministries,[19] creates a united front that can be threatening to the parent in legal proceedings, presenting him or her as someone who is not part of the 'normal' population.

The Place of the Children in the Parental Mechanism Model

Giving 'lack of parental capability' an incriminatory meaning presents all parents that the state defines as the 'carriers' of this deficiency as people who endanger their child through mere contact. Accordingly, their children are removed under emergency orders to a secret location, and all contact with them is conducted exclusively through the adoption officials. Adoption officials are given enormous power. At the same time that they serve as 'gatekeepers' of the contact between the children and their parents, they also act as a party in the legal proceedings over whether to declare the children eligible for adoption. They are able to manage the contact between parent and child in a manner that confirms their portrayal of such contact as dangerous for the children, and supports their petition to declare the children eligible for adoption. The court's ruling in the matter of the Ziv children reveals how the adoption officials acted in this case:

> At the first hearing, as previously noted, the petitioner's counsel [the SSC] argued that the visits must be stopped immediately, on the grounds that '... in view of the evidence attached to the petition, a picture has emerged of harm caused to the minors as a result of previous visits...'. The court's decision not to terminate the visits (which in any event, as later transpired, did not take place prior to the petition – even at the rate of once a month, as previously agreed), remained effectively a dead letter ... Once proceedings got under way, a picture began to emerge from the evidence presented to the court of a pattern of obstructions to visits and making it difficult for the mother to visit, from the moment that the children were taken from their home ... and despite this – notwithstanding this Procrustean bed of a single visit a month, for one hour only, for three children, which was often cancelled on one pretext or another – the mother was not given sufficient opportunity to communicate with her children. From the descriptions we have heard, it is clear that every effort was made to undermine and weaken the children's bond with their family.

While considerable distance between the mother's residence and the children's home may not have been the result of a deliberate attempt to make it difficult for her to maintain contact with her children, it was certainly a major factor in her difficulty in keeping up her visits at the appointed times set by the authorities. Her legal counsel relayed her complaint that the continuity of previous visits was repeatedly disrupted. For example, she arrived late to one of the visits because the taxi she had taken had been involved in a road accident, but the children's home officials told her that they could not arrange the visit to be held later that day, and that the next visit could only take place a month later, that is, two months after the previous visit. Another visit was postponed – once again, by a full month – because on the date in question the mother had to undergo emergency dental treatment, resulting once again in two months between visits. The children were given no explanation that the mother's visits had been postponed because of the home's strict rules, because, as the home's psychologist put it, 'the children don't need technical explanations'. Nonetheless, the children do need the mother's visits to be regular and continuous. As it is, the frequency of one visit a month was probably not enough to give them confidence in their mother's bond with them, and when in addition to that a promised visit was abruptly cancelled, they likely felt abandoned. To protect them from feeling this way, the authorities could have offered the mother an alternative date within days of the originally scheduled visit, instead of simply cancelling the visit altogether. However, the manner in which the children perceive their relationship with their parent through such regimented visits is cited as yet another justification for the decisions of the SSC staff, rather than as a means of evaluating their decisions since, as we have said, the parenting evaluation is not about the children's relationship with the parents, and accordingly, the impact of the SSC intervention on this relationship is of no consequence.

Once the contact between the parent and the child is policed in this fashion, the parent is perceived by the child as being helpless. As the alienation begins to permeate the relationship between the parents and their children, and given the presence of the caregivers during their visits, the parents are no longer perceived by the child as the people to turn to with their problems – be they real or imaginary. Meanwhile, for the psychologist who observed the interaction between the Ziv children and their mother, the fact that they did not appeal to her for help was a sign that there was no bond between them. Even if we were to ignore reports of mistreatment in children's homes run by the SSC, children will always have difficulties adjusting to different settings. However, here the parent is presented to them, not as someone who can support them and defend them from their surroundings (as many parents do, for example in relation to the child's school), but as a source of danger. The children are conveyed a message that their relationship with their parents is harmful; otherwise, why aren't they seeing their parents at home rather than in forbidding and impersonal offices, and why are the visits conducted under supervision?

The story of the Ziv family children indicates the risk inherent in the very separation of children from their mother. As the court said in its ruling:

> The director of the children's home described the children's condition thus: 'The children have now been at the children's home for a year and three months. Time has acted partly in their favour, but in the past six months there has been a deterioration in the condition of the two older children, particularly the elder one ... five-and-a-half years old, an intelligent, clever child ... emotionally in a state of total despair, signs of depression and violent outbursts towards other children and to himself. Situations in which he goes absolutely berserk ... the danger is both to himself and to [other] children. When he isn't throwing a tantrum he goes into withdrawal, a vacant stare and sadness in his eyes ... Also, the fantasy that he began to harbour [about returning home] as a result of the mother's visits becoming increasingly regular may have undermined his confidence...'. Even the minors' deteriorating state was not enough to alert the adoption officials, and when the [mother's local] social worker notes that 'one hour for three children is not enough time to share one's attention' and repeats the mother's request to see the children every two weeks, the response of the chief adoption official is: '[I] suggest that the visits not be changed given the children's difficult responses...' (and no one suggested to her that perhaps the children's difficult condition was deteriorating because of the harsh separation from their family).

Declaring parents to be lacking in parental capability and excluding them from their children's lives is done 'in the best interests of the child', yet the children themselves have no say in the matter. The children's condition serves as apparent 'proof' of the state's position, and yet they are denied the chance to bear witness. Even if they do manage to break through the wall of secrecy and express the wish to return to their family, the officials in charge of their welfare and protection immediately dismiss the importance of what they are saying. Referring to Yitzhak's wish to return home as a 'fantasy' silences his testimony and denies the profound significance of his bond with his mother and his fear that it will disappear – an anxiety that repeatedly arose during the assessment that I conducted not only with him, but with Galit as well, as I shall describe later. The deterioration in their condition should have indicated the gulf that arose between the reality in which they found themselves and their ability to express their wish to reinstate their relationship with their mother.[20] Dismissing

Yitzhak's wish as a 'fantasy' speaks volumes about how, in the eyes of the caregivers, the severing of his contact with his mother was a *fait accompli*, even though the court – which is the sole arbiter in this matter – had not yet declared him eligible for adoption. At that time, the children's wish to return home was by no means a fantasy, but defining it as such denied the loss they felt as a result of their dwindling contact with their mother due to the strict regime of visitations. On this point the court said, *inter alia*:

> The request to stop the visits was also justified on grounds of 'the best interests of the children' – even though at no point was it explained to the court why their best interests required them to be cut off from their family and mother, nor was there any assertion that the mother was abusive to the minors or had hurt them in any way ... 'The best interests of the child' argument is not a mantra, nor can it serve as a 'fig leaf' for any request or as justification for any act or failure.

As far as the SSC was concerned, the decision had already been made to remove the children from their home, so it was in no hurry to submit the petition to declare the children eligible for adoption until they had spent a full twenty-one months in a facility that, in everyone's view, should have been only temporary. Giving permission for parent visitations appears to have been done to create the impression that the state respects the court's authority in the matter of the children, but these visitations seem to have been conducted in such a manner as to ensure that by the time the court reached a decision, the children's relationship with their parents would be irreparably harmed.

With regard to the point that the law as it stands places the fate of the parent–child relationship in the hands of a body which, by definition, is an interested party in the legal proceedings, the court said:

> The impression from this case (as in other cases involving a petition to declare a minor eligible for adoption) is that the minor is 'prepared' for adoption from the moment they are removed from their parents' home, such that, when the issue comes before the court to decide, the court's hands are often tied, since it does not have the means to turn back the wheels of time ... The parent's visits then became a tool that the SSC used to achieve this objective. If the parent does not arrive [for a visit], they are accused of neglecting the minor and not expressing any interest in him; if they are late they are told that the children's home cannot possibly reschedule the visit for another time, and they are turned away; and when a visit is possible, it is conducted with a stranger's eyes scrutinising every movement and utterance.

Often it seems that the removal of the child from their parents' custody is aimed not at protecting the child's well-being, but at preserving the idealised image of parenthood as a natural phenomenon. Parents who fail to live up to that image are criminalised and presented as lacking parental capability, because their conduct belies that image.

Parenting as an Expression of the Parent's Solution to the Struggle for Survival

The perception of the parent's ability as a 'natural' or 'normal' mechanism makes it possible to ignore the context in which the parent is obliged to operate, their life circumstances and the effect that the child has on them, and to present parental capability as something that is fixed and immutable. An alternative approach might be to see parenting as a solution that the parent finds to the inherent conflict between the demands posed by the child (which deplete the parent's resources) and the need to maintain these resources to create suitable conditions in which to raise the child and provide for the family, and to manage their life to the best of their abilities.[21] Changes in the conditions of parenting – including the child growing up and developing – may result in changes to the solutions that the parent develops for this purpose. The parent's struggle for survival is an intrinsic part of parenthood and comes to the fore when, for example, the parent lacks the proper conditions in which to raise their child, or when the child has special needs.

The notion that the child is a drain on the parent's resources runs counter to the prevailing (and idyllic) view of a child as a tender creature totally dependent on the parent's care, but is consistent with studies that find that the child makes unconditional demands for care from the moment of birth.[22] Defining parenting as a struggle for survival also dispels the somewhat idealised notion that it is a natural ability that is activated automatically at the child's birth. Conceptualising parenthood as a conflict between responding to a child's needs and the parent's need to preserve their resources focuses attention on the parent's considerations when trying to reconcile this conflict,[23] and on both the parent and the child as individuals. To do this requires knowledge and understanding of parents' living conditions, the personal resources they have available and the demands placed on them by their child. Children vary in the nature and intensity of their requirements and their ability to express them, and parents vary in terms of their ability to understand these requirements and respond to them. The reciprocal relationship created between the parent and the child reflects the effect of the child's needs on the parent and the effect of the parent's solution on the child and his or her demands.

Perceiving the parent's parental capability as a solution to their struggle for survival therefore requires one to also be attentive to the voice of the child – acknowledging the child's position as subject as much as that of the parent. Understanding the parent's ability as a solution to conflicting needs applies to protective and nurturing parenting as well as harmful parenting that may endanger the child – without defining the latter as a pathology. At the same time, it is important to note that focusing on the solution that the parent arrives at makes it difficult to forecast future changes in the parent's ability to raise their child, as legally stipulated.[24] Changes in the parent's future circumstances, the demands made by the children as they grow up, and their impact on the parent – all these are unpredictable. This difficulty requires great caution before arriving at a conclusive assessment.

The court's ruling with regard to the Ziv children acknowledged the effect of life circumstances on parenting. After reviewing the history of the couple and their life together as described in the adoption officials' report, it focused in particular on its impact upon the mother:

> Respondent A [the mother] – a mere adolescent – found herself in an impossible situation, often without food or basic supplies, far removed and cut off from her family of origin, withdrew within herself, and the combined effect of her [very young] age and poor circumstances appear to have affected the children's condition, as well. She found it difficult to care for her children, and in particular, to protect them from the rage and violent outbursts of Respondent B [the father]. From the appendices to the petition, it appears that the minors were repeatedly moved from one location to another prior to the petition to declare them eligible for adoption, and kept away from the respondents' home for long periods at a time .... Meanwhile [six months later, after the children had been returned to their home] respondent B was arrested – an opportune time, one would think, to invest in and provide support for the mother. However, for reasons which have not been made clear to me, it was precisely at this moment, when the chief culprit of the [mother's and children's] suffering and distress had disappeared, that it was decided to remove the minors from their mother's care. The mother, in her desperation, sent the two older children [to her parents' home], and claimed that the little boy was the son of another man, with whom she arrived, in the hope of countermanding the order that way. However, it was all to no avail. The children were seized and removed from her custody under police escort ... and placed in a children's home.

It should be noted that the orders declaring the children as wards of the court and the orders revoking the parents' custody were issued by different judges in courts at different locations, and were extended without in-depth discussion (or with no discussion at all), based solely on the

> testimony of the welfare officials – which, it would appear, was not always balanced or accurate (as in the case, for example, of the surprising declaration by the [respondents' local] welfare officer that 'the extended family had no objection to having the children removed from their mother's custody', even though it later transpired that the extended family were in fact hiding the children and the mother was even arrested for not revealing their whereabouts – to avoid having them removed). From the time that the minors were transferred to the children's home [in the Central region] until the state's filing of a petition to declare them eligible for adoption, all requests made by the welfare officials were approved without substantive discussion – presumably due to the court's great faith placed in the welfare officials. The issue of visitation and maintaining contact with the parents during this long period was left by the courts to the discretion of welfare officials, and every time the emergency order was extended, the ruling stated that 'the place and times of the visits will be determined by the adoption officer'.

The description of events in the court's ruling and the one provided in the adoption officials' report differ not only in the different emphases given to the facts, but also in the explanation given for the mother's failure. In the judge's statement, the mother was not portrayed as someone driven by some 'parental mechanism' but in terms of her living conditions and subjective experiences – as a young woman virtually paralysed by her hardships following her hasty decision to link her fate to that of her partner, causing her to fail to protect her children and care for their needs.

The court attributed the children's behavioural difficulties not only to the father's violence and the mother's helplessness, but also to the instability in their lives after their removal by social services and placement with foster families. It also portrayed the children's removal from the mother's custody and placement with the SSC as dramatic events, in stark contrast to their matter-of-fact presentation in the adoption officials' report, as if they were just another unremarkable incident in the chain of events. It described the arrest of the violent father as a moment when there was a real prospect of improving Sophie's ability to provide for her children's needs; instead, it became the precise moment when social services chose to remove the children from her care. The repeated resort to removing children from the home, even at the moment that might have been a turning point, when the mother shook off the passivity that had gripped her until then and fought like a tigress to hold on to her children, became an aim that justified the step whose alarming and threatening nature in the eyes of children cannot be overstated: Sophie was arrested by the police and the children forcibly removed from where they had been hidden precisely to prevent such an occurrence. In the court's ruling, the execution of the emergency order was presented not as a means of protecting the children, but as the starting point of a deliberate attempt to remove the mother from their lives. The psychologist from the children's home told me that he objected to the children being returned to their mother because 'the children have no confidence in their mother's ability to protect them', and yet he saw no connection between this alleged 'lack of confidence' and the manner in which the children had been removed from their mother. How could they trust her and her ability to protect them when she was unable to prevent the authorities from taking them away from her?

The manner in which the children were forcibly taken from their mother, and the harsh regime imposed on that relationship, was governed by the authorities' denial of the significance of the children's relationship with their mother. Therefore, when I was asked to assess Sophie's parental ability, I had to try and break through that wall of denial. The court's decision to mandate regular visits by the mother to her children – issued before I was asked to serve as an expert witness – made this possible.

The Transactional Nature of the Relationship between Mother and Children

A few days before I observed Sophie's meeting with her children, I spoke with her alone. I did this for three reasons. First, to minimise the negative impact of my presence on her interaction with her children, since the very act of observation during such a meeting is an invasion of the privacy of the relationship. Although this privacy was already routinely violated by the children's home staff who were present during any meeting between Sophie and the children, my presence, as an unfamiliar observer, was liable to add yet a further sense of alienation. The second reason was to try to forge a relationship of trust with her that would distinguish our relationship from the one she had with the SSC staff. The third reason was to try to better understand the significance of the children in her life.

My meeting with Sophie was held at the offices of her legal counsel. She was no more than twenty-two years old at the time, petite, pleasant and soft-spoken, but very withdrawn, and it was a great effort to get her to talk. She hardly said anything of her own accord, and her responses were laconic. She explained that she found it difficult to express herself, partly because Hebrew was not the language she normally spoke. She did tell me that she kept a journal of all her experiences since she met her partner, written in her native tongue. Despite our efforts, we could not secure a budget to translate the journal. During the conversation, she spoke about how, for many months after the children had been taken from her, she did not know where they were or to whom she could turn in order to see them. She was unable to name the organisation that eventually helped her locate the children, but even when she discovered that they were being held by the SSC, she was not allowed to visit them, and when she was finally permitted to do so, as previously noted, any difficulty she encountered while trying to get there on time led to the visit being cancelled and postponed for another month.

The conversation was strained. Sophie's tone was monotonous and without affect. I wondered how much she had really been engaged in raising her children. I asked her to describe to me what was characteristic of each child and his or her relationship to her, which she did without hesitation. When she spoke about her children, her face suddenly lit up, and her tone of voice became vigorous and lively. The individual attention she gave each child was clearly evident. She said that she had loved to play with children ever since she was a young girl, and her family used to leave children in her care. She was therefore astonished when her children were taken from her based on the claim that she could not raise them.

The meeting was brief, and when it was over I did not know if I had won Sophie's trust. It was difficult to tell whether her remote and indifferent tone was due to language difficulties, her sense of alienation, her shyness or depression. The only convincing element was her strong attachment to her children, although that in itself was not enough evidence of her ability to raise them. Nevertheless, it was a first crack in her alleged obliviousness as described in the documents I had read before the meeting.

To reduce the sense of alienation during the upcoming observation, I also visited the children's home to get an idea of Yitzhak, Galit and Orr's daily routine, and to establish a benchmark when assessing their behaviour during their meeting with their mother. The staff in the children's home had opted not to tell the children that I was about to be introduced to them, lest this raise their hopes that a permanent solution for them was about to found, since the court had not yet reached any decision. Children who are brought to the children's home know that their stay there is temporary, therefore the question as to whether a family has been found 'for me' is always on their minds. The Ziv children had spent twenty-one months in a setting that was supposed to have been temporary – a very long time, even by SSC standards. During this time, they had seen many other children come and go, assigned to adoptive families or returned to their families after a brief stay at the home. Nonetheless, the fact that the staff had sought to protect the children from possible disappointment by hiding the true purpose of my visit – although they knew that the children would sense I was coming to see them, if only because they had not been sent off to preschool that day – is indicative of the authorities' mindset in this and in other cases of adoption, and can serve as a clear example of their refusal to recognise the children's position as subject. Children's expressions of disappointment, anger or protest – especially in response to situations brought about by the SSC – are regularly blocked in various ways. Although the child's best interests are said to govern his/her life, it is the authorities who define them. Children are not involved in the discussion of what constitutes their best interests. I resented the staff's decision not to introduce me to the children, because by complying with it I effectively became a partner in the treatment of the children as objects of observation. However, I had no alternative but to accept the rules laid down by those in charge of the children on a daily basis.

The meeting was held in the morning. Only the Ziv children were present at the home. Orr, the little one, was being carried about in the arms of the home's director and looked as if he enjoyed it very much. He was the only one who asked who I was, and in response was told that I was a friend of the director's. Yitzhak and Galit looked neatly dressed, but their lovely faces were expressionless, apathetic and impassive. Neither of them gave any direct acknowledgement of my presence. They wandered aimlessly into the yard, watched what one of the maintenance workers was doing, and occasionally threw a glance in my direction. It was clear that they understood very well that I was observing them. I decided to cut my visit short to end the unease and secrecy that hung in the air, but despite the barrier that I had encountered between me and the children, the visit helped me 'read' their behaviour with their mother during the next session, and gave me clues as to how I should conduct myself during the meeting.

A week later, I arrived at the SSC offices to observe the meeting between Sophie and her children. This was the third in a series of monthly visits that had been held consecutively, following the court's intervention. I met Sophie at the elevator. Knowing that the children were already on their way to the meeting, she had gone out to buy them some drinks and three large bags of candy. When we entered the designated room, I wondered if her reticence and uncommunicativeness were covering up her tension, and in fact these disappeared after a few minutes, when we heard running footsteps and Sophie said, excitedly, 'Here they are!' and went to the door. Yitzhak appeared first and kissed her warmly. Then came Galit, but I did not witness the moment of their meeting. The children's home house mother also entered the room. Galit asked to go to the bathroom, and Yitzhak joined her. Sophie went with them and I followed her out into the hall, where I saw Orr sitting on a raised platform, holding the hand of the children's home director and looking at her. I said hello to him and the director told me proudly that Orr remembered my name from my previous visit the week before. She then picked him up and carried him lovingly in her arms. Seeing the close contact between them, I wondered if and how Sophie would be able to make any connection with the toddler.

When we returned to the room, Yitzhak and his mother had formed an immediate bond. Yitzhak had taken a Lego game, sat down next to his mother and they were building things together with the blocks. Sophie watched him as he played, while trying to get Galit to join them, but Galit held back. Orr, who was sitting on the director's lap, shrugged his shoulders as if to say 'No', when Sophie reached out to pull him in closer. The director, by way of encouragement, suggested that she 'let him warm up a bit'. Sophie then went up to Orr and tried to touch one of his eyebrows, above an eye that had reddened, but he shrank back and she relented. Yitzhak was quiet and engrossed in what he was doing. Suddenly he raised his head and asked where the candy was. Sophie gave him some, and offered some to Galit and to Orr, but it was clear that the candy was less important to them, and Sophie did not use it to try to create a rapport with them. Yitzhak, still absorbed, went on building things with the Lego. Sophie went up to Orr again, sitting him on her lap this time and tickling him. He laughed and the ice between them was broken. Once again, she tried to examine his eyebrow, while offering him a toy from the closet. He chose a jigsaw puzzle, and Sophie knelt down to play with him and asked what gift he wanted for his birthday. He asked for shoes, but she said she would bring him sandals because the weather was already warm. Then he asked for jeans – 'but overalls', he stressed – and she said she would bring them to him on her next visit, when they would celebrate his birthday.

All this time Galit walked aimlessly around the room, without focusing her attention on any particular person. She busied herself with the candy, offered some to the house mother and hung about near where I sat with the home director, rather than where her mother sat with Yitzhak and Orr, but here, too, her gaze wandered. She drank noisily from a drink that her mother had given her, and looked at me in a friendlier manner than during my visit to the home. When I remarked that one can drink faster without a straw, and in larger gulps, I earned a real smile. Meanwhile, Sophie had managed to get Yitzhak to join her and Orr in putting together the jigsaw puzzle that Orr had chosen, and it was clear that she was trying to get them all engaged in the game – no easy task, considering that the children ignored each other, and each of them related to her differently. They were also affected by the presence of three other adults in the room (the home director, the house mother and I). Galit asked her mother to hand her a large teddy bear from the top of the cupboard, but even then did not fully acknowledge her. When she got the bear, she asked me to hold the candy while she held the teddy bear and told me defiantly that she was holding it 'by the bum'.

Sophie became absorbed in the jigsaw puzzle. Orr tried to draw her attention to the location of certain pieces, and in doing so tripped and fell, but she did not seem to notice it. This took a few seconds, and she returned immediately to focus on the children. Perhaps she needed to relax and rest a little from the effort involved in dealing with the children and adjusting her own rhythm to that of each of them, all while being mindful of the home director. When she recovered, she went back to focusing on the children, and suggested a game of cards. Orr took some cards out of the closet and asked if he could hand them out, but Galit, who had finally joined the game, brusquely grabbed many of them for herself. Orr protested and asked Galit to give him some cards, but the girl refused, and Sophie patted her affectionately on the leg, asking her gently to give up some of the cards. Galit refused, and Sophie did not press the matter any further. Now the two older children wanted to go to the bathroom, and Sophie got up to go with them. Orr asked if he could join them too, and when the director offered to accompany him, said emphatically, 'No! I want to go with Mum'. The children ran down the hall, with Sophie behind them. When they returned, the card game was abandoned, and Sophie suggested they go back to the Lego game, asking Galit and Orr to join Yitzhak. They refused, and Yitzhak began to build a house by himself. Galit sat down next to Sophie who was observing Yitzhak and asked if she had a baby at home. Sophie said no, adding that Orr was her smallest child.

In addition to her effort to adapt herself to each child, Sophie appeared to me to be engaged in a struggle with the home director over who would play the role of 'parent', the adult responsible for the children's well-being. At the start of the visit, Sophie asked if they had celebrated Orr's birthday, and was told they had not. She wondered why this was, and the director explained that a party had been held at the nursery – and, by way of evidence, asked Orr to tell his mother that the shirt he was wearing was a birthday shirt – but that 'at the home' they don't always manage to celebrate the party on the precise date. This was a curious explanation, given that there are no more than twelve children at the home, a number that does not justify the postponement of a birthday party. Although a toddler of Orr's age does not know precisely when his birth date occurs and how it related to the date on the calendar, coordinating the three events – the celebration at the children's home, at the nursery and with Sophie – could help provide a measure of coherence to the life of a child who has been cut off from home. The child's body, name and birth date are, after all, all that they have left from their past life. Such a coordination might also help to bridge the gulf that opens up between the child and their parents after being removed from their custody.

At this point, Sophie also noted that Galit's hair had been cut. The home director said that this was necessary to keep it clean, but added that it would grow again. As if in retaliation for the implicit criticism in Sophie's remark, the director then commented that Galit had told her that her mother dyed her hair a different colour each time. Sophie, somewhat defensively, replied that her hair colour was the same as it was on the previous occasion. The director countered that last time she had been a redhead, not a blonde, but Sophie insisted this was not so. To defuse the growing tension, I told Galit that even if her mother changes the colour of her hair, she is still the same Mum. To change the subject, and to regain her place in the children's lives, Sophie then asked Yitzhak if he would be going to school next year, and he replied that he would still be going to kindergarten, but 'kindergarten for big kids' (apparently it had been decided, without consulting the mother, to keep him in kindergarten for another year). The director, once again playing the role of the children's spokeswoman towards Sophie, told her that Galit had asked if the guard at the entrance was their father. She suggested that they ask their mother where their father was, but Sophie did not answer. Instead, she reddened and tears welled up in her eyes. I asked if the subject was a difficult one for her, and she replied quietly that she didn't know where the children's father was, to which the director responded that she could say that, too. Feeling defensive again, Sophie pointed out that Galit had asked her the same question while they had been in the bathroom and that she had replied to her there. Hurrying to change the subject – and implicitly criticising the home – Sophie then asked the children why they were not wearing the shoes that she had brought them. The children replied that the shoes were lost, and Galit added that the same thing had happened to a particular dress that her mother had given her. The house mother then interjected that nothing was lost, and everything was still available. It should be noted at this juncture that children often complain that items they have received from their parents go missing at the children's home, and while the staff's denials are probably technically true, they ignore the possibility that the children are trying to tell them something. Children possibly sense that there is a conflict between the parents and the children's home staff, and by complaining they are externalising their feelings, in the hope perhaps that the adults will settle their differences. When parents and the children's home staff are focused on the conflict itself, arguing over whether or not certain items are lost, they are actually making the situation worse. It is also possible that, for the children, the objects symbolise the bond and sense of belonging they feel towards their parents. If so, by complaining about the disappearance of these items they are, in fact, talking about the disappearance of their parents under a legitimate guise, and perhaps also protesting against their relationship with their parents being presented as something dangerous and forbidden.

By now, Yitzhak and his mother had forged a great physical intimacy. Towards the end of the session, as they were building the house out of Lego, Yitzhak looked intently at his mother and told her that her earring was open. She explained that that's how the earring was designed, and he gently touched a necklace that she was wearing. There was a sense that he was looking for a way to preserve the closeness that had developed between them in the room. His face was sorrowful, quite unlike his blank expression when I had visited the home.

The allotted hour came to an end, and Sophie suggested to the children that they have their picture taken together. Yitzhak asked for the Lego house that he had built to remain as it was until the next time. Galit, still defiant, refused to part with the teddy bear. The director tried to forcibly take it from her, but Galit physically resisted. Sophie suggested that she pick Galit up and together they put the bear back in its place high at the top of the cupboard. Galit relented, and the dispute was settled amicably. Orr continued to be cheerful. Sophie suggested once again that they go out and be photographed together, but the children, perhaps in a bid to prolong the visit as much as possible, insisted on going to the bathroom again with her. Finally, they had their picture taken near the elevator. Each of the children also wanted to take a picture themselves, and Sophie helped each of them to do so. Yitzhak protested, 'I know by myself', so she let him take the picture alone. The home director thought it better that they parted before getting into the elevator. I suggested that perhaps we go down together as far as the taxi, but the director whispered to me that saying goodbye next to the taxi would be a 'melodrama', refusing to believe, it seemed, that the children truly found it difficult to part from their mother. In the event, the parting went quietly, albeit very sadly. Sophie and I stayed inside the building, beside the door, as Yitzhak gazed at his mother through the glass door while holding the house mother's hand, and Orr waved goodbye to her repeatedly. Galit, at first, did not look back, but joined in with Yitzhak as he shouted goodbye. Yitzhak continued to gaze at her as he got into the taxi.

Sophie's behaviour during this visit was similar to that described by the home director as 'unusual'. The new regularity of the visits appeared to have an effect, and perhaps my presence gave Sophie a sense of protection. (That, at least, was my intention when I made the comments that I did on seeing the defensive look on her face whenever the home director made a remark implying that the children needed protection from her.) In my assessment of Sophie's meeting with her children, I noted how she had coped well with the challenge of relating to each of them in a particular manner and addressing their different appeals within the space of one hour. In the face of such difficult conditions, she showed courage and sensitivity. I was favourably impressed by the patience she showed while waiting for the children to make their choices, and particularly how she dealt with the girl's truculence, both in the matter of the cards and in resolving the girl's refusal to part with the teddy bear (far more successfully than the home director, who tried to do so by force). The manner in which she drew Orr closer to her, despite his apparent attachment to the home director, was also remarkable, but the greatest bond was undoubtedly the one that she had formed with Yitzhak. Their interaction was the most prolonged, compelling and touching – especially on Yitzhak's part. This confirmed what she had said about the children at our first meeting: Yitzhak helped her, and it was clear that she trusted him to allow her to divert her attention occasionally to his siblings; Galit was obdurate; and Orr turned all his captivating charm on Sophie when she finally managed to capture his interest.

That said, I wondered if the frequency with which she switched from one game to another indicated a certain limitation in her relationship with the children. Although the explanation for this may have been simply that this was her response to the children's own choices, it may also have been an attempt on her part to offer a new stimulus on each occasion, in the hope of engaging all three children in the short time available.

In the brief conversation that she and I held afterwards, she said she had been very nervous on the way to the meeting. She told me that her local social worker had asked her why she doesn't talk with the children during the visits, and she admitted that it is hard for her, both because the children are very attached to the director and to the psychologist – when they are present the children prefer to remain close to them – and because she knew that she was under scrutiny at the meetings. She complained about the long intervals between one visit and the next, and that the home director always asked about the father's whereabouts, even though Sophie explicitly asked them not to reveal to the children that he was in prison. She also talked about Orr's reluctance to come to her, explaining that she tickled him to make it easier for him to reconnect with her. She said she did not want to celebrate his birthday this time before knowing what present he wanted from her. She also revealed that while they were in the bathroom, the children had asked her where she lived, whether she had a new home and whether she no longer lived with Grandma. Galit also told her that she constantly changed the colour of her hair, and she replied that even when she does so she still stays the same mother (possibly repeating what I had said to Galit a short time earlier), and then added that 'Galit is like that…'. When I asked her what she meant by that, she explained that 'whatever game she's interested in is more important to her than being with the caregiver'. Possibly she was referring to 'caregivers' others than herself, because the children had been under the care of so many until then.

She spoke about how, on previous occasions when they parted, the children would fling themselves on the floor, next to the elevators, weeping bitterly, and she would tell them to stop, that there was no need to cry like that. Emotional restraint appeared to be very important to her. She also expressed her annoyance at the fact that the children kept asking to go to the bathroom, since each visit lasted only an hour, and this meant time was being wasted. The children had, indeed, gone to the bathroom three or four times. According to the home director, such frequent visits to the bathroom were typical of the children's meetings with their mothers, but not of their daily lives at the home. I thought of several possible explanations for this. The meeting made the children excited, and running down the hall is a way to relieve the tension of such emotionally charged meetings in a crowded room, under the watchful eye of outside observers. It was possibly also a way of gaining some physical contact with Sophie, but when Sophie told me about the conversations she had had with the children in the bathroom, I wondered if the real reason was that this was a chance for them to gain a measure of privacy and perhaps even intimacy with their mother, away from the children's home staff and various observers.

The interaction between the mother and her children revealed how important their relationship with her was to them. This was particularly apparent in Yitzhak's attitude to his mother, but it was significant that Galit, too, her defiance notwithstanding, needed her mother's assurance that she does not have a 'new' baby at home. They both turned to her, rather than to the staff, when asking to go to the bathroom, and Orr even rejected the home director's offer to take him there. Clearly, the interaction between Sophie and her children was very different from that which had been observed and reported by the psychologist. My observation provided a completely different impression from the one I had received on reading the case file and from my initial conversation with Sophie. Instead of wretchedness and helplessness, I saw sensitivity, animation and resourcefulness. I also saw how the home director's intervention intimidated Sophie, and – as I later learned from the conversation I had with her after the meeting – almost paralysed her.

Although I was favourably impressed by Sophie's ability to relate to her children with sensitivity and individually, I still wondered whether she was able to provide a safe and stable home environment. I thought that I might learn this through another conversation, so I made an appointment with her. This time she arrived straight from a visit with the children. The diffidence that had characterised her facial expression during previous meetings had disappeared. She was impassioned, her eyes were large and open and her speech flowed freely. When I asked her how the visit had gone, she told me that it had been very good, and with a beaming smile added that Orr had told her that she was 'the most beautiful mother'. I remarked that this time she was noticeably more open towards me, and she explained that she was 'too happy' after what had happened at the meeting with the children, and added that since this was our third meeting, she felt more relaxed in talking with me. Her happiness with the successful meeting with the children was also evident in the fact that she spontaneously recalled things that the children had said or done that indicated that they were still strongly attached to her. Orr wanted to hold her hand (which, she said, 'I never thought would happen'), followed by Galit, and when Yitzhak joined them as well, she had no free hand available, so she invited him to hold on to her blouse. I asked her how Galit had behaved this time, and she replied that Galit had come up to her and was more attentive than in the previous session. The children had asked her to buy 'something' and take it home, so that they could see it when they returned home, and at the end of the meeting they were surprised and excited to see pictures of themselves in her purse. She was more determined than ever not to give up the children.

Her excitement was contagious. I now realised that she needed the children's affirmation that their relationship with her was important to them. She attributed the big change in their attitude towards her in the past two months, and in her own behaviour, to the home staff's response to her demand that they stop making remarks or intervening in her conversations with the children, because these were *her* meetings with *her* children. 'They get to see the children all the time', she said, and asked that during the visits they 'let me have my time with them'. Since then, they have indeed not intervened (judging by the meeting that I had attended, I could only imagine how much they must have intervened on previous occasions). This time, when celebrating Orr's birthday party, she arranged the table herself and rejected the staff's offer to help.

The constant competition with the home staff members for the children's attention made things very difficult for her, and she believed that they occupied the place that was rightfully hers in the children's hearts. She attributed the change in the children's attitudes not to the regularity of the meetings – which was now maintained under court order – but to the staff members 'conceding' the place that they had held with the children. This explanation indicated just how much Sophie's self-image as a mother had been devastated by the forcible removal of the children to an environment that regimented her contact with them and severely compromised her ability to maintain a close bond with them.

The behaviour observed in these later meetings between Sophie and her children lends support to the view of parenting as solutions found in the struggle for survival. Sophie had rehabilitated herself, was now renting an apartment and earning a living as a housekeeper. In addition, she was now allowed to meet with her children on a regular basis. The newfound confidence that she had acquired was reflected in her relationship with the children, and they, in turn, reacted joyfully and showed her just how much she meant to them. Their responses moved her and told her that she had not been obliterated from their lives. The touching expressions of their relationship that appeared only after the visits were put on a regular footing – such as Galit's question about whether her mother had a new baby at home, and Yitzhak's request to have the house that he had built in Lego be kept for him until the next meeting – indicate that they had experienced the separation from the mother and the earlier irregular pattern of visits as a kind of abandonment. Previously, their behaviour indicated that they had given up, as it were, on their relationship with the mother, and she, in turn, reacted with indifference and what appeared to be mechanical responses. This is an example of a vicious cycle of a damaged relationship in which the children's feeling of being abandoned feeds back to the parent, who feels that they are no longer important to the children, which reinforces the children's feeling, and so on. The children's surprise when they saw their photograph in their mother's purse, and Sophie's surprise when Orr wanted to hold her hand, reveal the extent of the damage that had been wrought on the relationship. The children had found it difficult to believe that, despite the physical separation between them, they still held a central place in their mother's life, and she in turn found it hard to believe that she was still important to them.[25]

It is not only children who need expressions of warmth and love from their parents; parents need such responses from their children, too, to replenish their resources. With the positive change of direction in their interaction in these later meetings, the damaging effect of the forced separation between mother and children over many months became apparent. But the scale of that damage emerged only after the court's intervention removed the restrictions that had been imposed on the visits in an effort to pave the way for the children to be declared eligible for adoption.

In the expert opinion that I submitted to the court, I was able to state wholeheartedly that Sophie's success in reversing the vicious cycle and re-establishing warm and meaningful interactions with her children indicated the depth of her attachment to her children, the strengths that she could call upon to retain her place in her children's lives, and the children's yearning for a close relationship with her. Her achievement was all the greater considering the obstacles that had been put in her path, the deliberate sabotaging of her relationship with her children by the disruption of the regularity of her meetings with them and denying her any role in their lives. That said, I found it difficult to determine how capable she would be to assume responsibility for the children, since they had been removed from her care for over two years. During that time, her life had undergone many changes, the impact of which I could not evaluate since the children were not in her custody. However, thanks to the dogged efforts of her legal counsel, who brought representatives of Sophie's local social services to testify in court, it transpired that her local welfare services department recognised the adverse effects of her living circumstances on her ability to raise her children and the help that it could provide in mitigating those effects. As the director of the local welfare department testified in court:

> In the evaluations of [Sophie's] parental capability, it was repeatedly noted that she is needy and childish. If I close my eyes for a moment and see before me the many women who have been through my office [in my capacity as] a social worker and director ... I think that you don't need to be a genius to understand that if a fourteen-year-old girl marries someone far away from home, in a town whose social norms she would have difficulty adjusting to just by virtue of her being a new immigrant ... She had the misfortune to be married to an abusive husband, and I think this entire picture shows that she was powerless ... Ever since she's returned to [the town] I have witnessed her gradually acquire an increasing understanding of her surroundings and an ability to deal with it ... I think we are witnessing a process of change and growth and development...

Although I did not agree with the assessment that Sophie was 'lacking in parental capability', I did recognise a possible difficulty in her mothering – namely, a vulnerability that, under certain conditions, might derail her care of the children and possibly harm them. With the support of the local social services, however, I thought that the impact of this vulnerability might be minimised. However, due to a surprising development, I was never cross-examined in court.

Happy Ending? Time Will Tell

The court rejected the state's contention that the mother should be kept apart from her children, and granted Sophie's request to have the children home over the New Year holiday. In response, SSC officials claimed that the children's home where they had been kept was not set up to take children back after spending time at the parents' home, unless the arrangement included a plan for further visits. No justification was provided for this argument, but it too was likely presented to quash any hopes that the children might have about returning to their mother before the court had reached a decision about the petition to declare them eligible for adoption. The court was therefore asked by the SSC workers not to instruct that the children be returned to the children's home after staying with the mother over the holiday, and instead to recommend that they be 'prepared' [*sic*] to be returned to the mother's custody within ten days. In response, the court said:

> Hanging in the air is the question, how is it that the Service for the Sake of the Child – whose very name suggests that it should be responsible for the welfare of minors – is willing, just like that, to release minors to their mother's care, when it had unequivocally and adamantly insisted throughout the proceedings (and, indeed, ever since their removal from their home) that their well-being demanded that the mother's visits cease altogether and that all contact with her be severed. At what point, then, were the children's best interests being considered: when they had asked for a complete cut-off – or now, when they are recommending for the children to be simply returned to the mother's custody? … After all, nothing has changed, by the looks of it, apart from the testimonies of the welfare officers … and discovery of the transcripts of discussions about the minors and decisions that were not implemented.

These documents, as we recall, were presented to the court only at the demand of Sophie's legal counsel, but had been known to SSC staff from the outset, even before legal proceedings in the children's case had begun.

The ruling went on to say:

> Under these circumstances, I have ordered the minors be handed over to their mother's care for a trial period of six months, and that until then they shall be suitably prepared by the staff of the children's home, and that from the moment they are returned to the respondent's custody, the family shall be under the care of the [mother's local] social services department, and that the director of that department submit monthly reports to the court about the minors and notify the court immediately in the event of anything untoward. However, as any reasonable person might expect, ever since the authorities' looming presence has been withdrawn and the mother's contact with her family has been renewed, the children's condition has improved immeasurably.

Yitzhak, Galit and Orr returned to their mother's custody. At first, they behaved in a very tentative manner, apparently for fear of being taken away again, but over time this self-imposed exemplary restraint gradually gave way, and difficulties and behavioural problems began to emerge. Local social services praised the mother's ability to create a family environment, while noting the needs and difficulties of each child. In their report, they said:

> The children appeared calm, very attached to their mother, a great deal of eye contact and physical contact between mother and children ... the interaction between mother and children featured parental authority and an emotionally very expressive relationship, both verbally and physically.

This confirmed my own earlier observations that Sophie demonstrated an impressive ability to accommodate the children's wishes by understanding their respective personalities and wishes, and acting accordingly.

Several months later, a taxi in which Sophie was travelling was in a road accident, and she suffered severe stomach injuries. In their reports to the court, the local social services praised how she arranged matters:

> There is a huge improvement ... The respondent tried to assimilate everything she had learned from social workers and other community resources ... Today, while she is hospitalised, the entire family and community have pulled together [!] to help. She is making tremendous efforts to recover more quickly and has chosen to put aside rest and pampering and to remain with residual symptoms of injury for the sake of getting back on her feet and functioning on her own...

Six months after the children's return to their mother's custody, the court decided to dismiss the case and reject the state's petition to declare them eligible for adoption.

I learned about the aftermath of this story from an article that appeared in the newspaper after the ruling's publication, about a year and a half after the children had been returned to their mother.[26] Excerpts of the court ruling included two additional comments: one was that the SSC had strongly disagreed with the court's ruling, the other was that the three children had been sent by the mother to a residential centre. Objections to court rulings usually result in an appeal, but in this case none materialised. The manner in which information had been leaked that the children had been placed in the residential centre suggests that the SSC thought the judge was wrong to return the children to their mother. The fact that Sophie had been seriously injured in a car accident, which had made her unable to function for a long period, was conveniently omitted from the article. Instead, it stated that the Minister of Labour and Social Affairs had launched an independent commission to look into the case and recommend any remedial actions that may be needed. In fact, to my knowledge, no such commission was established. Following the article's publication, I contacted Sophie's local social services department, and was told that they had supervised the family for a year and that the mother had taken good care of the children, but because of the injuries she had sustained in the accident, she had sent her children to a child care residential centre. Every two weeks, the children come home for the weekend, and Sophie makes sure that all three come home on the same weekends, to preserve the family structure and the relationship between the siblings.

The placement of the children in a residential centre was presented in the newspaper article as evidence that the state had been right to ask for the children to be declared eligible for adoption. This portrayal of events was consistent with the conventional view that adoption is the best solution as it provides children with a legally created family framework, as opposed, for example, to fostering, which according to the conventional view condemns them to instability, or placement in a residential centre, which supposedly condemns them to an impersonal and alienated environment. This is a common belief, although the success rates of adoption in Israel have never been subjected to any methodical study.[27] While there is no dispute that the legal (and often personal) commitment of adoptive parents is greater than that of the foster parents or of staff at children's residential centres, that is not the only factor at play in adoption.[28] The other factor is the complete severance of the child from their past and the denial of their identity, as required under the terms of closed adoptions.[29] The case of the Ziv family illustrates how assessing the mother's 'parental capability' as if it were a personality trait made it possible to ignore the significance of the severance of the child's contact with the parent and the denial of their identity.[30] Presenting the placement of the children at a residential centre as something unacceptable ignores the significance of maintaining a continuous relationship between a mother and her children. Moreover, the solution put forward by the state – adoption – would have meant that the siblings would have been separated from one another, and even that was not thought of as detracting from the advisability of adoption.[31] That the mother made sure that the siblings were always together during their home visits was also ignored in the article, which implied that the mother placing the children in a residential centre was evidence that the judge in this case had erred in her decision.

Six years later, I contacted Sophie. Her injuries and numerous surgeries had left her partially physically disabled, and her vulnerability, which I had recognised when evaluating her ability to function as a mother, prevented her from overcoming the difficulties caused by her physical handicap. She could not raise the children at home. This is how vulnerability becomes actual limitation. No one could have foreseen the accident, of course, nor does this necessarily attest to any change in her relationship with her children. The three children were now at the same boarding school, and still coming home together on holidays. Sophie was full of praise for how they helped around the house when at home, and was very proud of Galit's success at school. All contact with the father had been lost, however.

What lessons might we learn from the handling of the Ziv children case? There is no question that at the time when they were removed from their mother's care, they had suffered serious harm. They had been living in an environment where violence was a daily occurrence, and they were developmentally delayed. It is by no means certain that merely removing the father from the family would have put an end to that harm, but it is doubtful that removing the children from their mother's custody protected them from further harm – due both to the violent manner in which this was done, and because they were held for nearly two years at a facility that, by the SSC staff's own admission, was meant only for short stays, and because of the SSC's flagrant and persistent undermining of their relationship with their mother. It is not inconceivable that the positive change that the mother underwent in forging an independent life for herself was made possible by the fact that she had been relieved of the burden of caring for her children on a daily basis. However, even if such relief were necessary to allow her to make her own way after an abusive and immature marriage, this could have been done in a more supportive manner, for example through a consensual arrangement, involving securing a safe environment for the children near their home, allowing her frequent and regular meetings with them, and helping her to find a source of income.[32] But to do this would have meant recognising her struggle for survival and the importance of her relationship with her children as key factors in her ability to raise them. The thinking that 'parental capability' is the product of some innate parenting mechanism does not foster such an approach (to put it mildly), and leads to erring on the side of over-intervention rather than under-intervention. It is this mindset that a court's ruling was referring to when it stated:

> in the proper measure, the means used will, on the one hand, provide an appropriate response to the special needs of the ward of court and the risks that they face, while not exceeding the limits necessary to avoid inappropriate violation of individual rights and family autonomy.[33]

The mother's local welfare authorities had acted in accordance with this thinking. Placing the children in residential centres was meant to provide the children with a safe and nurturing environment, while allowing their relationship with their mother to be maintained.

The story of the Ziv children – just another chapter in the annals of adoption policy in Israel – is about the denial of the unique bond that forms between parents and children. The implicit censure in the court's ruling of the way in which Sophie had been demonised, and the harm inflicted upon her relationship with her children, is no compensation for the suffering and loss that the children experienced in the two years that they were cut off from her. It is unclear what scars will remain with them from this period. The thinking behind the concept of 'lack of parental capability' makes it possible for the state to abruptly remove the mother from her children's lives, and then return her as if she were merely a lost plaything, whose restoration undoes all the harm done.[34] Only the children can tell whether the mother's return to their lives indeed mended the rupture in the fabric of their existence created by their forcible removal from her care and the subsequent strict regimentation of their contact with her, and only they can say if they have regained a sense of belonging or whether they still live under the shadow of loss from that period of their lives.

The next chapter examines the central role played by the sense of belonging, and its inherent denial in the adoption process.

Notes

1. In Israel, the term 'welfare officials' refers to social workers authorised to operate under the terms of the Youth Law ('Youth Law welfare officials'). These are employed by local welfare authorities and are distinct from adoption officials, who, as noted in the Introduction, are authorised to implement the ACL, and are employed directly by the Ministry of Welfare. Hearings pursuant to the Youth Law are conducted in youth law courts, while hearings under the Adoption of Children Law are held in family courts.
2. The use of the term 'risk' with regard to the Ziv family children is in keeping with the conventional terminology used by welfare services with regard to their client population. See, for example, *Report of the Public Committee into the Condition of Children and Youth at Risk and in Distress*, chairperson Hillel Schmid (Jerusalem: Prime Minister's Office and Ministry of Welfare, March 2006), 33 [Hebrew]. The broad and indiscriminate use of this term does not distinguish between the condition of *at risk* (a high probability of harm), *in danger* (actual harm) and *vulnerable* (a susceptibility that might develop into actual harm). However, such a distinction is necessary for the intervention to be focused and differentiated. Judging by the description of the condition of the Ziv family children, they were well beyond 'at risk' and were now 'in danger', i.e. of being physically harmed and delayed in their development. To protect them, it was important to tackle the source

of the danger, as indeed was pointed out in the court's ruling (as excerpted later in this chapter). For further discussion of this distinction, see Mili Mass, 'Risk, Danger and Vulnerability in the Parent–Infant Relationship: A Method for Assessment and Intervention', *Society and Welfare* 12 (1992), 391–405 [Hebrew].

3. The interim order was issued under the Youth Law, whereby a minor is declared a *ward of court* as stipulated in the law. In this case, it seems the children were declared wards of court under section 2 of the law: 'A minor is a ward of court when one of the follow conditions applies ... (6) their physical or mental well-being has been harmed or is liable to be harmed for any reason'.
4. Children are placed in this children's home after an emergency order is issued pursuant to the ACL 12c. Its location is secret, and children are kept there pending the court's decision on the state's petition to declare them eligible for adoption. During this time, all meetings between the children and their parents are held at the offices of the SSC, and on dates and times of its officials' choosing.
5. ACL 13(7).
6. CA 418/88, *Anon v A-G*, 5.
7. Mili Mass, '"Parental Capability": "Parental Instinct" or "Survival Instinct" – On Expert Opinion', in David Yagil et al. (eds), *Psychology, Law and Ethics in Israel: Psychological Evaluations, Psychotherapy and Judicial Decisions* (Tel Aviv: Probook, 2008), 217–35 [Hebrew].
8. This approach originated in certain leading schools of thought in psychoanalytic theory, which perceive the mother's need for contact with the baby as a mirror of the baby's need for contact with her. If the baby's relationship to its mother is defined as symbiotic, so too is her relationship with the baby. Helena Deutsch, 'Motherhood and Sexuality', *Psychoanalytic Quarterly* 2 (1933), 476–88; Deutsch, *Neurosis and Character Types* (New York: International Universities Press, 1965), 190; Christine Olden, 'On Adult Empathy with Children', *The Psychoanalytic Study of the Child* 8 (1953), 111–26. Today, the baby's relationship with the mother is defined as interpersonal, and so too is the mother's need for contact with the baby. See Jessica Benjamin, *Bonds of Love* (New York: Pantheon Books, 1988), 1. According to this approach, the degree to which the mother needs her baby, and the significance she attributes to that bond, determines the quality of her relationship with her child.
9. Protocol Knesset Labour, Welfare and Health Committee, Transcript 189, 14 June 2006 [Hebrew].
10. Vered Ben-David, 'Judicial Bias in Adjudicating the Adoption of Minors in Israel', *Children and Youth Services* 33(1) (2011), 196–203.
11. ACL 13(7).
12. The father's position is not stated here, since the question of returning the children to his custody was not under consideration at the time, although he did have legal representation.
13. See CA 418/88, *Anon v A-G*, 9:

Options (4)–(7) of s 13 are mutually complementary, and all involve situations in which a parent avoids fulfilling their duties towards their child. Option (4) deals with a parent who has abandoned their child, or avoided maintaining contact with them; Option (5) deals with a parent who has avoided fulfilling their duties towards their child; and Option (6) talks about a parent who has refused to receive their child into their home. What the three causes have in common is that the parent, as we said, acted in a manner without reasonable cause or justification. In other words, a 'blame' element of some kind is needed (to distinguish between the words 'without reasonable cause' [as stated in (4) and (5)] and the words 'without justification') in relation to (6(, see CA 316/86, Miscellaneous Appeals (MA) 415/86 [6], p. 551). A parent who is terminally ill, or imprisoned for a long period, will not, therefore, be included in these options. Accordingly, and complementarily, the additional option in s (7) has been added, in relation to a parent who is unable to care for their child properly, due to their behaviour or situation, whatever the reason may be, whereby no reasonable financial or care assistance, as customary in welfare authorities, could bring about a change in the situation.

For more on the question of the relationship between the definition of parents' harm to their children and pathology and responsibility, see Nigel Parton, 'The Natural History of Child Abuse: A Study of Social Problem Definition', *British Journal of Social Work* 9 (1979), 431–51.

14. Mira Barkai and Mili Mass, *The Meanings of 'Parental Capability' and 'The Best Interests of the Child' in Supreme Court Decisions Regarding the Adoption of Minors* (Jerusalem: Sacher Institute for Legislative Research and Comparative Law, Faculty of Law, The Hebrew University, 1998), 144 [Hebrew]. Judith Modell states that 'Termination does not let anyone forget the punitive side of adoption customs in the US. The parent whose rights are terminated takes the role of the "evil" mother who never totally disappears from the culture of child placement'. Judith Modell, *A Sealed and Secret Kinship* (New York: Berghahn Books, 2001), 105.
15. Barkai and Mass, *The Meanings of 'Parental Capability' and 'The Best Interests of the Child'*, 177–79; CA 166/81, *Anon v A-G*, 327.
16. Adoption File (AF) 34/97, *A-G v Anon et al.*, Family Law Precedent (FLP) 99(2) 121 (1999).
17. Selma Fraiberg, 'Intervention in Infancy: A Program for Blind Infants', *Journal of the American Academy of Child Psychiatry* 10 (1971), 381-405; Sally Provence and Rose C. Lipton, *Infants in Institutions* (New York: International Universities Press, 1962).
18. Complaints about lack of integrity and misinformation have been made by all three parties to the adoption triangle. Anne L. Bable, *Ethics in American Adoption* (London: Bergin and Garvey, 1999), 119–21.
19. Decision of Judge Drori, District Appeal (DA) 707/05, *A-G v. Unknown Father*, para 6 (unpublished), in Nevo Archive (14 April 2005):

This is not the place to expand on this matter at length, but I cannot conclude my opinion without expressing a position – however preliminary – about the manner in which the appellant's position was represented in this case. The appellant's title – the Attorney General – suggests that it should be representing the interests of the public as a whole, but in this appeal it has been quite apparent that it showed a clear preference for the prospective adoptive parents – complete with forecasts of the scope of adoptions in general – which guided the argument brought forward by appellant's counsel, instead of considering the basic rights of the parents – and, in this case, of a father(s) who is (are) unknown, but traceable. May these brief words serve as a kind of 'warning postscript', that may in future be worth developing into practical rules governing the agency representing the public's interest in cases such as this, in which the SSC has an 'agenda' of its own, which in my view, on more than one occasion, eclipsed the broader view of the Attorney General, which was represented by members of the Ministry of Welfare's legal department, who are in constant contact with the SSC, and see themselves as lawyers acting on the latter's behalf.

20. As Ophir puts it: 'A deliberate widening of the gulf between the sense of loss and the ability to express it is a kind of abuse'. *The Order of Evils*, 93.
21. Ann Ferraris Oliviero, 'Infanticide in Western Culture: A Historical Overview', in Stefano Parmigiani and Frederick S. vom Saal (eds), *Infanticide and Parental Care* (Chur, Switzerland: Harwood Academic Publishers, 1994), 105–20; Sarah Blaffer Hrdy, 'Fitness Tradeoffs in the History and Evolution of Delegated Mothering with Special Reference to Wet-Nursing, Abandonment and Infanticide', in Parmigiani and vom Saal, *Infanticide and Parental Care,* 30–42; Margo Wilson and Martin Daly, 'The Psychology of Parenting in Evolutionary Perspective and the Case of Human Filicide', in Parmigiani and vom Saal, *Infanticide and Parental Care,* 73–104.
22. For example, T. Berry Brazelton, Barbara Koslowsky and Mary Main, 'The Origins of Reciprocity: The Early Mother–Infant Interaction', in Michael Lewis and Leonard A. Rosenblum (eds), *The Effects of the Infant on Its Caregiver* (New York: Wiley, 1974), 49–76; T. Berry Brazelton, 'Evidence of Communication during Neonatal Behavioral Assessment', in Margaret Bullowa (ed.), *Before Speech* (New York: Cambridge University Press, 1979), 79–88.
23. Mili Mass, 'The Determinants of Parenthood: Power and Responsibility', *Human Relations* 50 (1997), 241–60.
24. ACL 13(7).
25. Theresa Benedek, 'Parenthood as a Developmental Phase', *Journal of the American Psychoanalytic Association* 7 (1959), 389–417.
26. Ruth Sinai and Moshe Reinfeld, 'The Judge Did Not Understand Why the Children Had Been Separated from Their Mother', *Ha'aretz*, 21 September 2000 [Hebrew].

27. For more on the issue of assessment of the results of adoption, see Chapter 3 and Chapter 4: Interlude.
28. According to Modell, the same is true for the US. 'The Act [US 1997 Adoption and Safe Families Act] then restricts the notion of permanency to legal relationship between parent and child. Emotional attachments, loyalties, obligations, and exchanges between adults – none is considered a guarantee of the child's safety and security over time'. *Sealed and Secret Kinship*, 108.
29. Lee Gronrot-Kaplan, 'Forgive Me for Not Raising You', *Ynet* (column), 7 November 2008, http://ynet.co.il [Hebrew].
30. Modell states that 'the US 1997 Adoption and Safe Families Act simplifies the concept of "parenthood" as the most expedient strategy for policy makers, thereby obstructing the goals of the policy, i.e. to serve "the best interests of the child"'. *Sealed and Secret Kinship*, 127.
31. As described by Peter Marsh and June Thoburn: 'The tendency to encourage the use of the adoption solution should be considered in the light of the principles set out in the UN Convention of the Child's Rights – i.e. "the rights to family life" and "the principle of proportionality"'. 'Adoption and Permanence Debate in England and Wales', *Child and Family Social Work* 7 (2002), 131–32.
32. Expressed by Martin Downs: 'A child's circumstances may "require" statutory intervention, perhaps even their indefinite or long-term removal from the family and his or her placement with strangers, but that is not to say that the same circumstances will necessarily "require" that the child be adopted'. 'When Adoption without Parental Consent Breaches Human Rights', *UK Human Rights Blog*, 25 November 2014, http://ukhumanrightsblog.com/2013/10/01/when-adoption-without-consent-breaches-human-rights/.
33. Family Law Court (FLC) 6041/02, *Anon v Anon and Welfare Officer under the Youth Law (Care and Supervision), 1960*, 58(6), 246, 274 (2004).
34. Ophir, *The Order of Evils*, 84.

2

'BELONGING' AND 'CONTINUITY'

Elinor's Story

Disappearance

'Just a minute, Your Honour.' The mother jumped to her feet when the judge was about to declare as final her earlier temporary decision, to return Elinor to the mother's custody. The mother approached the witness stand and said, 'I want to thank you for returning Elinor to me – I know that not everyone…'. She choked up with tears and turned her face to the window to recover. 'I don't know what would have happened if Elinor had not come back to me. And I also want to thank you for your attitude towards me', she added. It was the end of the hearing at which, by mutual consent of the two parties, the state's petition to declare Elinor eligible for adoption was denied.

More than seven years later, when I told her about Elinor's *bat mitzvah* (twelfth birthday) celebration, the same judge asked me what Elinor would say today if she were asked about the decision to return her to her mother after spending many months with her designated adoptive family, to whom she had become very attached. I replied that Elinor would be unable to answer: her conscious memories of that period were vague, and according to her mother, she wanted to shut out the pain of that chapter of her life. The blurred remnants of her loss made it impossible to determine if the pain was associated with the memory of her forced separation from her mother at that time, or with the disappearance of the foster family from her life.

The question of the disappearance of a significant person, and the risk of it inflicting a loss that overshadows an adoptee's life, were at the heart of the legal proceedings concerning the state's petition to declare Elinor eligible for adoption. Elinor had been placed with a foster family, who were designated to adopt her once she was declared eligible for adoption. Returning her to her mother's custody meant that the foster family would disappear, and she would not see them again, thereby creating yet another upheaval in her world. Conversely, keeping her with that family under the terms of a closed adoption (which the family insisted on if the adoption were to go ahead) would have meant cutting her off from her genealogical ties, the loss of which might have haunted her throughout her life. Her story is representative of the conflict between belonging and continuity created by the adoption procedures practised in Israel.

Removing the Mother

The mother had given birth to Elinor at the age of thirty-two, while in the throes of a severe drug addiction that had afflicted her since the age of sixteen. She had married in her teens, and gave birth to her eldest child when she was nineteen, but the marriage ended two years later when her husband was jailed for robbery and manslaughter. That child grew up in institutions, and the father, rather than the mother, raised him after his release from prison. A few years later, the mother gave birth to a girl, who was immediately placed for adoption without objections on the mother's part. Elinor's father was a repeat offender who was also involved in illegal drugs at the time of her birth. He did not marry her mother, but acknowledged his paternity of Elinor, who was his second daughter. (His first daughter had been born to him in a marriage that ended in divorce, and he lost touch with her for many years.)

Elinor's birth was premature – a common occurrence among drug-addicted pregnant women. After birth, the baby was kept in the hospital for observation and to determine the effects of the circumstances of her birth. To enable continued monitoring of her condition, she was then placed with a foster family,[1] where the mother visited her regularly. When the baby was a year old, she was returned to the mother after the latter had moved in with her own mother, who agreed to assume responsibility for the care of her granddaughter.

At that time, the father was in prison for various drug offences and thefts. Despite her repeated promises not to, the mother persisted in her drug habit, but the grandmother kept her word. Elinor was treated well by her grandmother, developed nicely and regularly attended a nursery, but at the age of three was reported to suffer from nightmares and to form attachments with everyone, indiscriminately. This type of attachment is deemed to be 'undesirable', as a child is already expected to show signs of discriminate attachment – preferring certain individuals over others – in the first year of their life.[2] This was later cited as evidence that the mother was unable to raise Elinor.

Ascribing the pattern of Elinor's indiscriminate attachment to improper care by her mother is indicative of the prevailing view that attributes any difficulties that the child may have to faulty care by their parent, while ignoring all other factors that may have affected the child's development, some of which may not even be known. In Elinor's case, her particular pattern of attachment may have been due at least in part to reasons that had nothing to do with the mother's lifestyle at the time, in particular the circumstances of her birth and the fact that she was raised by a foster family during her first year, then returned to her mother's custody at the age of one. However, for the authorities, the conspicuousness of her mother's lifestyle – drug addiction and fraternising with criminals – justified presenting her as the source of Elinor's developmental difficulties and nightmares. One day, when the mother lost consciousness after a drug overdose and was taken to hospital in a state of clinical death, the SSC issued an emergency order under the Adoption of Children Law.[3] While the mother was literally being brought back to life, Elinor, who was a little over three years old at the time, was seized by the SSC directly from her nursery preschool, without even being given the chance to say goodbye to her mother or grandmother. Later, the mother admitted that she did not object to Elinor being taken from her in this way, as she felt guilty for not keeping her promise to stay away from drugs.

Elinor's removal to protect her from her mother's lifestyle did not take into account the harm involved in abruptly severing her ties with her mother without the chance to say goodbye. The mother was deemed a harmful agent, and as such – in line with the medical approach that the cause of a disease must be removed for the patient to be cured – she was summarily removed from her daughter's life. Moreover, since the emergency order was issued based on the view that a child's development is exclusively determined by how they are treated by the parent (particularly the mother),[4] the fact that Elinor was also removed from the care of her grandmother, who, according to the local welfare services, cared for her with unstinting devotion, was clearly not taken into account in the decision to remove her from her mother's custody. The principal consideration behind this decision was to protect Elinor from her mother, rather than to ensure any measure of continuity in her life. While it is true that the mother's lifestyle might well have been harmful to Elinor – if only because it left her at the mercy of criminals – her grandmother's dedicated care was certainly a protective factor, and the harmful impact of abruptly removing her from her grandmother's care should have been considered as well. This factor would have assumed greater weight if the significance of the bond with the birth family in maintaining continuity in the child's existence had been recognised, and if the intervention that was meant to protect her was aimed at avoiding a pattern of repeated separations from attachment figures.[5]

Elinor was placed in a children's home, and once the emergency order had been issued, State Counsel petitioned the court to declare her eligible for adoption on grounds of the mother's 'lack of parental capability'. Meanwhile, the mother and grandmother visited Elinor regularly at the offices of the SSC, and were alarmed at her poor condition, which included a perennial cold and a look of profound dejection. It was at this point that the mother realised how serious the situation had become, and that if she did not pull herself together, she was liable to lose Elinor forever. Two months after Elinor's placement in the children's home, the mother voluntarily checked into a rehabilitation centre that offers comprehensive treatment and assumes complete control over its clients' lives, including restricted visits to her daughter. After extensive consideration of this potential turnaround in the mother's life – notwithstanding the assessments of two experts that she was 'lacking in parental capability' to raise her daughter – the presiding judge in the proceedings decided to give her a chance to continue her rehabilitation before ruling on the state's petition to declare Elinor eligible for adoption.

Just when the mother had shown commitment to undergoing treatment for her addiction, and despite the fact that the court had granted her another chance, the SSC decided to place Elinor with the foster family whom they had designated to adopt her should she be declared eligible for adoption. (The law permits adoption officials to do so even before the court decides that the child is eligible for adoption.)[6] The family's location and identity were kept secret, and access to the child was exclusively controlled by the adoption officials.[7] The pretext for the timing of this handover, they said, was that the children's home where Elinor had been staying was not intended for an extended period. Thus, far from deferring the adoption procedure, as the court had decided, the turnaround in the mother's life served to hasten her removal from her daughter's life. Elinor's placement with the foster family was accompanied by a declaration to the court that the mother's visits to the girl would continue to be held regularly, as before, subject to her leaves from the rehabilitation centre where she was staying at the time.

When Elinor was placed with the foster family, she had not seen her mother for several weeks, and repeatedly asked them, 'Maybe my mummy doesn't know where I am – because I went away suddenly? Maybe she's worried about me?' When, about a month later, she saw her mother again for the first time since arriving at the foster family, she flew into a rage after returning from the meeting, shouting, 'My mummy's better now! She can take care of me – *I don't want to be here!'*

According to the foster parents, she could not be placated for three days, and State Counsel asked the court to terminate the child's meetings with her mother to prevent any further mental turmoil and anguish. The court acceded to this request, after two experts testified that it was necessary, but since the judge still harboured some doubts, she also invited me to provide an additional expert opinion on whether such an injunction was indeed called for.

This decision by the judge was an early indication of how she chose to manage the proceedings. Rather than limit herself to deciding which of the information provided by the two sides is more credible, as is usually the case in the adversarial approach that is practised by the Israeli judicial system, she proactively sought out the information she needed.[8] 'If I had been separated from my mother', she said, 'I, too, would have reacted as the girl did – I do not understand what is so troubling about her furious angry response', adding that if the mother persevered in her rehabilitation treatment, it was worth reassessing her ability to raise her daughter. In marked contrast to the adoption officials and the experts, who dismissed the significance of the mother's announcement of the turnaround in her life (based, it seems, on their belief that no one is truly conscious of their motives, and therefore a person's declarations are not a reliable indicator of their intentions, let alone their actions),[9] the judge was insisting that she wanted to hear what the daughter and mother had to say.

The experts' presentation of Elinor's furious reaction after seeing her mother for the first time in weeks as an expression of the 'difficulty' caused by the meeting itself, rather than of the pain of being kept forcibly apart, was rooted in a professional approach that is at least half a century out of date with regard to understanding the reactions of children who are separated from their parents. In the past, for example, parents were forbidden from visiting their hospitalised children because the children's crying at the end of the visit was seen as a sign of the suffering caused by the visit itself, and a disruption in the work of the medical staff. However, this practice changed after a milestone study by Joyce Robertson and James Robertson in the 1950s,[10] which introduced the explanation that the children's crying was in protest at the parents leaving them at the end of the visit, not because of the 'suffering' caused by the visit itself. This insight currently guides the attitude of caregivers when children are forced to part from the significant adults in their lives. Children's departments in hospitals, for example, now typically allow parents to remain by their children's bedside throughout the day and night; indeed, absence of the parents is assumed to cause depression and apathy in children, which may impede their recovery. Thus, by arguing that Elinor must be spared the emotional turmoil allegedly caused by her mother's visits, these experts were ignoring well-established current knowledge, and denying Elinor's protests that clearly showed that her relationship with her foster parents had not expunged the loss of her mother. Only by having her mother returned to her life, Elinor was saying with her crying, would she regain what she had lost.[11]

Both the judge's questions and the expert opinions highlighted the issues of continuity in Elinor's life, and the turnaround in her mother's life. However, while the judge was asking the experts if there had been a change in the mother's ability to raise her daughter, the experts were saying that, since the mother's personality makeup – like that of any person – is immutable, no improvement could be expected, and therefore there was no prospect of a turnaround. The judge thought that Elinor's protest was a sign of her need for continued contact with her mother, while the experts were recommending keeping them apart so that the girl's relationship with her foster parents would eventually supplant the one she had with her mother. Elinor's sense of belonging implicit in the judge's words was entirely absent in the experts' assessment, and the significance of her unique bond with her mother was disregarded in their recommendation to cut her off entirely from her mother. This question of belonging and continuity lies at the very heart of the adoption issue, and I took it upon myself to respond to the judge's questions, and to try to determine whether the girl's ties with her mother should be severed entirely. But first I had to verify if the mother had indeed turned her life around.

At this point in the proceedings, the court learned that the mother had decided – on her own volition, without first securing her caregivers' consent – to check out of the rehabilitation centre, in favour of outpatient treatment. It was strongly emphasised, however, that this did not mean she was relapsing into drug abuse, as is often the case in such instances.

Evaluating the Turnaround in the Parents' Lives

Since I base my opinion on the parent's and the child's viewpoints and on an understanding of the relationship between them, I must have open and, to the extent possible, frank conversations with the parent. Naturally, my own viewpoint comes into play in such conversations, which always makes me concerned that it might colour my understanding of the case and bias my dialogue with the parent and child. In the case of Elinor's mother, I had even more reason to be concerned, since my image of her had not entirely shaken off the 'drug addict' label – an image of someone who had given up all control over their life for the sake of immediate gratification. Moreover, the parent also complicates the evaluation process by bringing their own anxieties, suspicion and often antagonism to our meeting. To coax the parent into expressing themselves freely, I must first win their trust, despite them knowing that the opinion that I ultimately submit to the court may result in the removal of their child from their custody.

In one case, in which I was asked to meet again with a mother after I had recommended her daughter to be declared eligible for adoption because I believed she was unable to raise her, the mother pointed to the room where we had sat during the evaluation and said to her own mother, 'You see? That's where I sat and opened up to her – and she stabbed me in the back'. On more than one occasion, I have yearned for some sort of distance between myself and the parent, similar to the distance between examiner and examinee in psychological tests. On the other hand, I have learned that it is precisely the freeform evaluation, free of any standardised template, that makes it possible to uncover unexpected details, which other, standardised approaches would likely miss in their uniform and structured evaluation.

In the case of Rachel, Elinor's mother, I was surprised by the very first thing she said to me when we met: 'I don't care what you say about me – I know I can be a good mother to my daughter'. I marvelled at her boldness in telling me this right off the bat. Although she knew that my opinion would carry much weight in the court's decision, she had no hesitation in telling me that she did not care what my opinion was, one way or the other, even after two experts had already declared her unfit to raise her daughter.[12] The forthright manner with which she said this reinforced the crisp impression of her neat and clean appearance and her lively facial expression, which largely dispelled the unease that I had initially felt at the sight of her orange-dyed hair and tight-fitting blouse (which was also orange). Uncertain as to what her behaviour might mean, I soon learned that her boldness was not due to lack of understanding of the serious implications of having her rights as a mother revoked, nor was it characteristic of her, since she had generally been quite cooperative, especially at the outpatient clinic that she had checked into of her own accord. Rather, it was a sign of her determination to fight for her right to raise her daughter, of her profound conviction in her ability to do so, and of her self-confidence, after successfully completing the first and most difficult stage of kicking the drug habit. While this optimism had not extinguished her sense of failure after years of addiction to illegal drugs, or her sense of guilt over the suffering that she had caused her daughter and her son from her previous marriage, she also asserted her moral right to start a new chapter in her life and to raise her younger daughter.

The roots of her boldness became clearer when she revealed to me how she had become a drug addict in the first place. In her childhood, she said, her father continually engaged in extramarital affairs with other women, and would leave home from time to time. She never understood why her mother tolerated this, or why she forgave him for being unfaithful, but when he left home for good when she was sixteen, she felt particularly hurt. She was considered the most beautiful girl in the family, and his favourite daughter, but after he left her mother, he never returned, not even to see her. The shock of the sudden transition from being his favourite daughter to feeling abandoned may be what pushed her into drugs. However, the fact that she had been considered special in the first place may also be what gave her the strength she needed when she sought to start a new life as an independent person at the age of thirty-six. Recognising her own strength held the promise that she would be able to successfully tackle the difficult challenges that lay ahead, namely low-skilled employment (due to her lack of education), low income and having to raise a child and provide for a family on her own, without a partner. The knowledge that she had once been loved and considered special was evident in her highly personable manner, which won her many well-wishers and much goodwill, including among the staff at the outpatient clinic.[13] The assessment by the outpatient centre director that Rachel's unilateral switch from hospitalisation to outpatient care was justified (despite being unauthorised) was also in her favour. It confirmed my impression that she was capable of independent judgement and of standing up for her rights when she thought it appropriate.

Given all this, the turnaround that Rachel was making in her lifestyle was promising. Her proven success in rehabilitation – albeit still in its early stages – and the tenacity that she projected in her determination told me that she was capable of maintaining this positive transformation. The modesty with which she said that she was able to lead a 'normative' life, as she put it, also struck me as a positive sign. My opinion also took into account the positive reports by her probation officer, especially in view of the fact that she had been considered one of the most severe cases of addiction that they had encountered. This fulfilled an important condition laid down by the Adoption of Children Law, namely the ability of a failing parent to change in the foreseeable future, given the customary care provided by welfare services.[14] Indeed, from a normative perspective, there was a substantial change for the better in Rachel's condition, and the grounds for continuing to deny her custody of her daughter – in this respect, at least – were now questionable.

However, the normative benchmark is not the only (or indeed the primary) benchmark for evaluating a parent's ability to raise their child. Parents must be attentive to the child's wants and provide them with a safe environment that is responsive to their developmental needs. To evaluate this dimension of child-rearing ability, one must observe how the parent and child interact with each other. Since Elinor had not been in her mother's custody for seven months, all I could do at this point was to examine how Rachel perceived her role as a mother, and the extent of her understanding of her child's condition and needs. In that respect, the manner in which she conducted the conversation raised some concerns in me, since just her account of her own rehabilitation nearly filled the entire hour of our meeting. I wondered whether this was a sign of self-absorption, or merely that she was proud of her success. The answer, however, came when I asked her what she could tell me about her bond with Elinor. She immediately shifted her attention to that topic, easily and naturally. She told me that when she became pregnant with Elinor, she decided that she wanted to raise her, and not to repeat the mistakes of the past, as she had done with her son, who had grown up in institutions. She had not challenged the decision to remove her other daughter, who was born while she was heavily addicted to drugs, from her care, because she knew that she was in no condition to raise her at that time. With Elinor, however, she felt it was different. She wanted to raise her, and was convinced that she could do so.

During her pregnancy with Elinor, Rachel was not allowed to enter rehab. The policy practised in Israel in this regard is something of a Catch-22. On the one hand, rehab treatments are forbidden during pregnancy, due to the risk of miscarriage; on the other hand, there is a tendency to deny the woman the right to be a mother, because drug abuse during pregnancy is considered a form of child abuse. Rachel pointed out that although she was still addicted to drugs at the time, she did care for Elinor until the age of three. In the first weeks after birth, she visited her at the neonatal ward every day, and saw her regularly during the first year of her life, when she was with a foster family, and subsequently at the children's home. When Elinor lived with her grandmother, Rachel made sure that her health needs were being met and arranged for suitable daycare, and when she was in a good mood – that is, when she was under the influence of drugs – she spent time with her.

That said, she noted that one of the experts who had examined her during the legal proceedings was wrong when he said she was capable of functioning as a mother only while under the influence of drugs. While it is true that she used to play with Elinor in that condition, the psychologist had focused purely on the physical aspect of the drugs' effect, she thought, and failed to recognise that the emotional aspect is the most important one – and that aspect is deadened by the drugs. As she put it, one cannot measure child-raising merely by the ability to play with the child; one must also have the ability to feel for the child. Now that she was 'clean' and her emotions had reawakened, she understood that she could be a good mother only when she is clear-headed. She had been devastated when Elinor was taken from her, and alarmed at her poor condition at the children's home. By way of evidence, she showed me a picture album of Elinor, and indeed the difference in her facial expression while living with her grandmother versus when she was at the children's home was readily apparent. At her grandmother's she looked happy and was laughing, with an open expression, while at the children's home she was downcast, pale and sad.

With regard to Elinor's father, Rachel told me that he too had entered rehab after his release from prison, but that she was not interested in re-establishing contact with him. Their relationship, she said, was one of her past mistakes, and had only come about because of the drugs: he was a dealer, and she needed them. She also had a dim view of his conduct as a father. He had no contact whatsoever with his eldest daughter, and on his release from prison he was in no hurry to see Elinor either. It was clear that she had no feelings for him, though she had no objection to him having some kind of contact with Elinor.

The issues that Rachel chose to focus on during our interview indicated that she fully understood the level of responsibility that was expected of her. This was not at all self-evident in her case, given her past record as a failed mother, and although she had shown herself capable of staying off drugs, she had not been off them for very long. Her responsibility towards her daughter had yet to be tested in her actions. Although she said that the big turning point in her understanding of her responsibility towards Elinor – the decision to kick the drug habit – occurred when she understood that she might lose her daughter, it was precisely that declaration that made me concerned that perhaps she was more motivated by the threat than by a genuine desire to provide for Elinor's needs, and that once Elinor was returned to her, she might relapse into addiction. However, I weighed that concern against my understanding that perhaps the prospect of having Elinor taken from her was even more alarming to her than having to deal with the enormous difficulty of weaning herself off her addiction, and it was that that motivated her to enter recovery. It was possible, therefore, to read Rachel's declaration at face value, namely as a sign of the supreme importance that she attributed to raising her daughter and to her understanding that she could not gain that privilege as long as she remained an addict.

Rachel's determination to raise Elinor persuaded me she was sincere. After her eldest son had grown up in institutions and she witnessed the suffering that he went through, and after she had agreed to place one daughter for adoption, I believed that her decision to raise Elinor was taken after sober reflection and of her own volition, rather than because of a conventional notion that a mother should raise her child, or for fear of the social consequences of breaking that taboo. Still, it was difficult to draw any conclusions as to her ability to raise her child. I needed some proof of her ability to live up to her determination and to translate the turnaround in her lifestyle into protective measures tailored to the child's needs, since that, after all, is the true sign of a parent's understanding of their responsibility. I hoped that observing Rachel's interaction with Elinor might provide that kind of evidence.

The perception of responsibility is a sign of a parent's ability to assume the role of a protective adult towards a child, while an evaluation of the relationship between a parent and a child reveals the parent's ability to identify with the child, to see the world through the child's eyes.[15] Parenting requires this kind of duality, which is why I divide a parent evaluation into two: assessing their understanding of their responsibility, and evaluating the quality of the emerging relationship between them and the child. The latter requires winning the child's cooperation, understanding and appreciating their point of view.[16] In the event, evidence of Rachel's ability to identify with Elinor came to me by chance, after an incident that caused great pain to them both.

Rachel arrived at our second meeting with red and expressionless eyes. She had spoken with Elinor a few moments earlier. It was a call that she had looked forward to for a long time, but it was abruptly terminated after Elinor told her about costumes for Purim (a kind of Jewish Halloween), and mentioned the name of Haggai, one of the children in her foster family. Rachel heard someone at the other end say, 'That's enough! Say goodbye', and the receiver was slammed down, but not before Rachel heard Elinor crying and shrieking. Rachel wept as she told me about the moment the conversation was abruptly cut short, saying, 'How could they do that to her? Why did they forcibly stop the conversation like that?' A few minutes later, they rang again and Rachel assumed that they were allowing Elinor to say goodbye properly in order to placate her.

At this point in our conversation, Rachel protested against the court's decision to terminate their meetings, her words almost echoing those of the judge cited earlier: 'I don't understand – is it unnatural for Elinor to cry after she saw me?' She was very anxious about Elinor and the effect that the abrupt termination of the phone call would have on her. I no longer had any doubt about her ability to identify with her daughter. Inwardly, I wondered if mentioning Haggai's name was not a deliberate attempt on Elinor's part to introduce some continuity into her existence by forging some form of connection between her mother and the family with whom she was living. Children usually understand very well which topics are off limits in conversation, and perhaps Elinor's 'slip of the tongue' was meant to challenge that prohibition. Rachel herself was highly preoccupied with the question of continuity in Elinor's life, and told me how the foster family had changed her name. At their first meeting after Elinor's placement with the foster family, the girl told her that her name was now 'Linor'. Rachel did not want to use that name, and told her that she doesn't know her as 'Linor', only as 'Elinor', and that for her she was 'Elinor' and always had been. Rachel was intelligent enough to link the significance of this moment with Elinor's first question to her foster parents, 'Does my mummy know where I am?' By telling Elinor that she would always know her as 'Elinor', she was, in effect, signalling to her that she was preserving the continuity in Elinor's life and the bond between them. Now, in her conversation with me, she added that Elinor had probably undergone some kind of brainwashing by her foster family, since otherwise, 'Why was that the first thing she said to me after two months apart?' It is possible, of course, that Elinor began their conversation at that meeting by announcing her new name not because of brainwashing, as Rachel surmised, but to get Rachel's approval for the relationship that had formed between her and the foster family. Deciding between these two interpretations reflects the question at the heart of the evaluation of Rachel's capability: did the mother's emphasis on continuity of the bond stem from the fact that she understood Elinor's situation and was concerned that severing that continuity would hurt her, or was it an expression of her own need for continued contact that she projected onto Elinor? The latter possibility could not serve as a basis for a recommendation that Elinor be returned to the mother's custody. The living conditions that Rachel was likely to face in years to come would mean that raising Elinor on her own, with meagre financial means, would often require her to sacrifice her own needs in favour of Elinor's, something she could do only if she could accept the child's viewpoint even when it differed from her own. I could not answer that question in my meetings with Rachel without Elinor being present. To do so, I would need to observe the interaction between them.

The possibility that Elinor's behaviour was an attempt to receive her mother's blessing for being part of the foster family and for the severing of ties with her raises another question: is it right to expect the mother to give such a blessing? Would it not mean that Rachel was effectively giving up on Elinor? If Rachel did give her blessing, Elinor might interpret it as a kind of abandonment – a feeling that often haunts adopted children.[17] I could not help but resent the loyalty test that Elinor was being put to at such an early stage, when no decision had yet been made to declare her eligible for adoption. The wall of secrecy that surrounds the child from the moment they are removed from their parents under an emergency order obscures these questions, and leaves the child to deal with these dilemmas on their own, while their SSC chaperones effectively urge them to detach themselves from their parents, in their conviction that the child must be given up for adoption. In Elinor's case, as I was to find out later, the reality was even worse.

To assess Rachel's ability to raise Elinor, I asked to meet Elinor's father, Meir, as well. While it was generally accepted that he could not assume responsibility for raising Elinor, and an assessment of his ability to raise his daughter played no part in the legal proceedings, I surmised that if Elinor were to be returned to Rachel's custody, there would be some degree of contact with the father at some point, and therefore he too would have some impact on her life.

I met Meir at the hostel where he lived during his rehab programme. Like Rachel, he was good-looking and highly personable. When I arrived, the radio in his room was blaring Middle Eastern pop songs, and he turned down the volume, saying, 'Those songs will probably not help you'. Having thus established himself as the host, he got quickly to the point of what he wanted to say: the discrimination against the Mizrahi community (Jews originating from North Africa and the Middle East) was what led him to neglect his studies and, indirectly, to descend into a life of crime. I understood that he saw me as a member of the discriminatory establishment. He decided to leave the life of crime because, he said (in a loose quotation of a biblical phrase), 'Shall we live forever by the sword?' But, he added, with a wink, 'There's a younger crowd that's taking our place, now'. While trying to win me over with such banter, he clearly wanted to avoid taking responsibility for his past criminal behaviour, but he was very proud and even surprised by his rehabilitation and by his proven success at work. When the subject of Elinor came up, he became very serious. He understood that he was in no position to assume the burden of raising her, and yet – he said with evident embarrassment – he did not want his daughter to be placed for adoption. During his time in prison, he had encountered men who had been adopted in their childhood, and – visibly blushing – he urged me not to recommend such a fate for Elinor. Although he was not interested in maintaining a relationship with Rachel, he was hugely impressed by the transformation she had undergone. While he could not say how much support, financial or otherwise, he would be able to provide Rachel in raising Elinor, he certainly appeared to be anxious not to undermine the bond between mother and daughter.

In the wake of my meetings with Rachel and Meir, the evaluation that I submitted to the court stated that the two parents had truly turned their lives around. State Counsel tried to invalidate this assessment on the grounds that it was not based on personality tests, as was customary (including projective tests, which are designed to reveal the anxieties that the subject is dealing with), but merely on conversations that I had held with the parents. These, State Counsel said, were not enough to reveal the innermost recesses of the parents' dynamics and anxieties, and reflected only how they wanted to present themselves, and were therefore not objective.

While it is true that personality tests are good for providing a uniform benchmark for classification after standardisation, and are ostensibly little affected by the circumstances in which they are conducted, a closer inspection of their validity reveals that only a few of their constituent items truly examine what they are purported to, and the added value provided by such projective tests in relation to the insight that is acquired during an interview is, in reality, marginal and negligible.[18] Moreover, the process of classification itself creates a difficulty, in that it is endlessly iterative, with each classification yielding a sub-classification, which leads to another, and so on,[19] in a potentially infinite cycle that in essence serves to generate hypotheses to be tested during treatment, and is inherently at odds with the finite nature of legal proceedings.[20] Nonetheless, the 'objective' and 'scientific' use of personality tests supposedly justifies the application of classifications generated from various hypotheses to irreversible decisions such as abrogating parental rights or removing children from their parents. In its bid for accuracy or supposed validity of its findings, this process often results in a multiplicity of labels, as in the case of Rachel, who was found to have 'an antisocial personality disorder with elements of borderline personality and needy obsessive-compulsive personality ... with a borderline intellectual constitution' – a quadruple classification that suggests a severe pathology, with a predictable effect on the decision of a court called upon to pronounce judgement upon her capability.

The court overruled State Counsel's objections to my opinion, and I, for my part, noted that my evaluation was not yet complete. In assessing the turnaround that Elinor's parents had effected in their lives, I had addressed the question of whether they were capable of maintaining a lifestyle that did not endanger Elinor, but I had yet to establish whether the mother was capable of conducting herself in a manner that took into account her child's needs, or what Elinor's relationship with her mother meant to her. To that end, I asked the court for Rachel's visits to be resumed, if only so that I could observe their interaction and complete my evaluation. The court agreed, and ordered that the meetings resume, at least until my opinion had been submitted.

In the Bosom of the Foster Family

Before observing a meeting between Rachel and Elinor, I asked to visit Elinor at the home of the foster family, to get an idea of her present life environment and the effect of her being cut off from her mother, and to provide a baseline when evaluating their interaction during the observation. In response, State Counsel demanded that an adoption official be present during the visit. I thought this would interfere with my work, for the simple reason that, to cultivate an atmosphere of openness, it would be better to have as few participants as possible, and because I saw no need for any additional professionals to take part. This was especially true since the adoption officials had objected to my appointment in the first place, and I was concerned that they would communicate this attitude to the family, intentionally or otherwise. The judge agreed with me and overruled State Counsel's request, but as I later discovered, the adoption officials found another way to intervene in the process of forming a connection with the foster family.

At the outset, I experienced a little of the difficulty that Elinor might have been experiencing, when I telephoned the foster family to set the date for my visit, and wondered how to refer to her in my conversation with them. To minimise any unwanted friction before our first meeting, I decided to use the name they had given her – Linor.[21]

I arrived at their house a little late, and the foster parents were waiting for me impatiently. They lived in a handsome house in a well-tended suburb. Dorit and Zvi were both in their thirties, native Israelis, simple, pleasant and hospitable, and as I later came to realise, straightforward and sincere. They had two other children – Mia, who is two years older than Linor, and Haggai, who is five years older.

Linor was pacing up and down the living room in a state of considerable agitation. She was (and still is) a very pretty girl – tall, open faced with a high forehead and long, straight, glossy hair, physically very like her father. Dorit placed her on her lap and asked her what they had said about me, but she did not answer. Dorit then said that before I arrived she had explained to Linor that I was coming to hear how she felt in her new home, and Linor replied that she didn't want to return to the children's home. Dorit said that Linor was very excited and suggested that she bring her photo album. Linor showed me the pictures and, with Dorit's help, explained what they were about. All the pictures had been taken since her arrival in the foster family, and in all of them she looked happy. She laughed out loud at the memory of some events, and made a point of stating the name of each child and adult whose merest foot or hand appeared in the picture. Dorit said that it was important for Linor to remember them all, because she had so many people to meet at once. She spoke about the good memory that Linor was blessed with, and that, contrary to what the adoption official had said, she did in fact remember her past. A few days earlier, she said, Linor had been talking about her grandmother, but couldn't remember her name. When I now asked Linor about her, she tried to remember her grandmother's name, but failed, and only said that she was very pretty. She then got up and imitated the walk of a woman walking heavily and erect.

Elinor's efforts to remember the name of every member of the foster family, followed by an attempt to remember her grandmother's name, confirmed my suspicion that traces of the disappearance of the mother and grandmother still lingered in her relationship with the foster family. Her effort to remember every detail was possibly a sign that she was afraid that the memory of her mother and grandmother might disappear entirely, and that she needed to cherish the presence of their loss, lest they vanish from her life entirely. As Ophir puts it, 'To lose means to remember; the continuous presence of the loss depends on a constant effort of remembering'.[22] This interpretation was fundamentally different from the explanation put forward by Dorit, who was not interested in Linor's past being a chapter in her life, and wanted her entry into the life of the foster family to mark the beginning of her history, with all previous traces of her past expunged. This desire, which characterises the closed adoption approach and the conventional adoption practice in Israel, was encouraged by the adoption officials' promise to Dorit that the child would not remember anything of her past.

As I was about to leave, Linor asked if I could stay. Dorit said that she found partings difficult, although things had improved somewhat. In the early days, whenever guests were about to leave, Linor would cling to them. Linor asked if I could draw something before I went, and I suggested that we exchange drawings. As she went to bring the coloured pencils, she knocked her leg against something and cried bitterly, and when Zvi tried to treat the pain she hurt herself again, this time in her neck, and her crying became even louder. I wondered if her crying was only because of the physical pain. The fear of separation was a recurring theme in her attitude towards me during that visit. Perhaps she was afraid, as she had told Dorit, that my visit heralded yet another separation. These difficulties in saying goodbye were indicative of how central the experience of separation was in her short life, not only with regard to her present separation from her mother, but the series of separations she had already experienced in her past: in her transition from her foster family to her grandmother's home at age one; from her mother and grandmother to the children's home at the age of three and a half; and three months later to a new foster family.

After she had quieted down, Linor sat down to draw, but this time hurt her finger. I remarked that on some days it seems 'one is constantly getting hurt all the time', and she laughed. She sat down in front of the large box of coloured pencils, and was momentarily embarrassed as she tried to divide up the work between us. As she took out a pencil from the box, she whispered 'Mummy Rachel' (at that time she still referred to her mother by that name, as distinct from her foster mother, whom she referred to as 'Mummy Dorit'). I wasn't sure that I had heard her correctly, and asked her what she had said. She replied that she had said that it was she herself who had chosen that colour. Dorit explained: 'Linor said that these are the pencils she received from Mummy Rachel in a package with a lot of surprises in it'. Linor turned her attention back to the drawing, blushed and said nothing, as if a forbidden subject had come up. The fleeting reference to the pencils she had been given by her birth mother indicated the importance that she attributed to them, but the almost surreptitious way in which she said it was a sign that she sensed that contact with her mother, or even mention of her name, was somewhat illicit and had to be concealed. Even the foster mother's matter-of-fact mention of Rachel's name did not remove the taboo associated with Elinor's bond with her.

Besides her attempt to come to terms with her separation from her birth mother (the nature of which became clear to me in my conversation with Dorit) and to preserve her memories of her past, it was clear that Linor was trying hard to fit in with the family that had been offered her, including uncles, aunts and so on. She was told that next year she would go to the nursery school which 'her sister' Mia had attended, which made her happy because she was already familiar with it. The pictures that she showed me in her album indicated that she was happy in her new surroundings and proud of being so well informed about them. During the conversation, she also pulled out several pictures showing the family home during construction, and said that she would show me how to build a house. Perhaps she was trying to say that she was building her home in the bosom of her new family, but perhaps she was also asking about what a home is, since this was already the fourth home that she had lived in during her four-year lifespan.

My visits to the foster family cracked open the wall of secrecy surrounding the work of the adoption officials, and revealed their *modus operandi*. The moment Linor was out of the room, Dorit told me:

> When we received her, we were told that she had already been declared 'free for adoption'; that she was to meet with her mother another two or three times to say goodbye, and that the remaining administrative steps needed to complete the adoption procedure would be completed within six months. Now we're told that 'things are a little more complicated'.

> No one's telling us what's going on. We didn't want to harm anyone; all we wanted was to adopt a child.

While the law does indeed state that 'the court shall not issue an adoption order unless and until the adoptee has been with the adoptive family for at least six months before the order is issued',[23] this requires the child to have been declared eligible for adoption already, a precondition that had not yet been met in this case.

It later transpired that it was not only the foster parents who had been misinformed, but the child as well. Dorit spoke about how Linor had 'thrown a hissy fit' on returning from her first meeting with her mother, bursting into bitter tears and pushing Dorit away from her, after she had already been with them for a while. This went on for three full days, during which time Dorit and Zvi were at a loss over what to do. 'Instead of moving forward, we're falling back', they thought, despairing at the situation. The adoption official referred them to a psychologist, who advised them, over the telephone, to tell the child that the judge had already decided she would grow up with them until she was eighteen, and that she could see her mother then.[24] This advice, it should be noted, was given not only before the girl had been declared eligible for adoption, but even before the court had granted the request made by the adoption officials and experts to end the meetings with her mother. The psychologist was therefore advising the foster parents to lie to the child, although they themselves did not actually know that what he was suggesting was untrue. The denial of the loss inherent in adoption creates a slippery slope in which it is easy to disregard the protest implicit in the child's stormy response, and from there it is but a short distance to outright fraudulent misrepresentation.

I came away from the foster parents' home with an acute sense of unease on discovering that, in direct violation of the court's orders and without its knowledge, Elinor had been told that she was to grow up with the foster family. I realised that she was making a sincere effort to adjust to the family and to come to terms with her separation from her mother. In these circumstances, my request to observe a meeting between her and Rachel was liable to undermine Elinor's apparent acceptance of the situation, without my being able to offer any guarantee that such contact could continue if, after my opinion had been submitted, she was declared eligible for adoption after all. However, without observing the interaction between Elinor and her mother, which was essential to my evaluation if I was to gauge the significance to them both of their relationship, I could not conclude my opinion. If I did not submit an opinion, Elinor would be declared eligible for adoption purely based on the actions taken by the state's representatives, as indeed had happened with other cases in the past. I shall expand on this point before continuing Elinor's story.

The Slide into Deceit

Now that I understood the false pretences under which Elinor had been placed with the foster family, the significance of the condition set by the SSC – that my visit be held only in the presence of an adoption official – was clear. The adoption officials were anxious that the deceitful manner in which Elinor had been placed with the foster family not be revealed to the court or to the foster parents. When I raised the matter in court, the adoption official claimed that I was distorting what the foster parents had said, and that they did not, in fact, tell me that they had been assured that Elinor had been declared free for adoption. Later, the adoption official went even further and claimed, in court, that another conversation I had held with the foster parents had been recorded without my knowledge, and that it showed that my reports to the court were false. However, despite the court's demand for this to be submitted as evidence, it was never confirmed. When I subsequently confronted the foster parents and asked why they had surreptitiously recorded my conversation with them, they explained that they did so because the adoption official had told them that I was lying in court, and they wanted to ensure that their memory was not misleading them. The recording in fact proved to them that I had quoted them accurately.

This was not the first time that I had encountered the deceit involved in the placement of children with designated adoptive families under emergency orders, before they had been declared eligible for adoption. The secrecy and monopolistic nature of the adoption process in Israel make such deceptive practices possible. To ensure the secrecy of the procedure, adoption officials serve as the only point of contact for both the prospective adoptive families and those parents whose children are removed from their custody.[25] Indeed, the Adoption of Children Law allows adoption officials to execute an emergency order that allows a child to be placed with a designated adoptive family even before the court has approved his removal from his birth parents' custody.[26] The reasoning for this practice is purportedly to protect the child from unnecessary upheavals once they are declared eligible for adoption, but in practice, because of the false representation of facts by adoption officials, the court often finds itself facing a *fait accompli*, and must decide whether or not to remove the child from a family in which the child has been told they will grow up. In this way, adoption officials secure control over the adoption proceedings, even at the price of violating the basic rights of the children, the birth parents and the prospective adoptive parents.[27] On more than one occasion, the court has been sharply critical of the fact that it had been forced, in effect, to rubber-stamp a situation that had been engineered by adoption officials,[28] and yet the unchallenged status given to the adoption authorities under the law, and the secretive structure of the SSC, remain unchanged. The foster family that had been designated to adopt Elinor was the third such family that I had encountered in my capacity as an expert witness. In all three families, the children were placed under the terms of an emergency order; all three were told that the child had been declared eligible for adoption and that only a few administrative formalities remained before the adoption order was approved to complete the process; and in all three cases, the question as to whether the child should be declared eligible for adoption had not yet been decided in court.

In the case of another child – Natalie/Vered – the duplicity surrounding her placement with a foster family that had been designated to adopt her affected how her meetings with her mother were conducted, and consequently the court's decision in her case.[29] Natalie had been removed from her mother's custody at the age of one. The mother was promised that the court would discuss her case, and that in the meantime, Natalie would be cared for by an undisclosed foster family. The mother met with her daughter every two weeks at the offices of the SSC, and was not told that the state had petitioned the court to declare Natalie eligible for adoption. Meanwhile, the foster parents who had received Natalie under the emergency order were told that she had already been declared free for adoption, so they changed her name to 'Vered'. Only during my visit to their home, in preparation for my expert opinion, did they learn that the child had not yet been declared eligible for adoption. The birth mother discovered the real purpose of the SSC procedure only several months after Natalie had been removed from her custody. When the child began to speak, she referred to herself as 'Vered', and addressed her birth mother by her first name. The mother, taken aback and very angry, repeatedly demanded from her daughter that she call herself 'Natalie', and to call her 'Mummy'.

While the mother's insensitivity in this case may not have been exclusively due to the SSC's manipulations, the test that she was put to during these meetings clearly tripped her up, and posed a threat to her daughter. As an expert witness on behalf of the court, I judged her to be incapable of raising her daughter, based largely on the total lack of understanding that she displayed of the repercussions of the child's return to her life. However, my recommendation to sever all ties between the mother and her daughter through closed adoption was based on my observations of the meetings between them, in which the mother became a threatening figure, not least due to the manipulation of the situation by the SSC's actions.[30]

In another case, the SSC in effect determined the court's decision. When Doron was five years old, he was taken from his mother's custody on the grounds that her lack of judgement placed him in clear jeopardy. The mother, who had been raising him on her own, loved him dearly, but could not refuse him anything nor did she forbid him from engaging in dangerous behaviour. Her lifestyle raised questions about her mental state and its implications for her ability to raise Doron, but a psychiatric examination was inconclusive and the case was handed over to the SSC for evaluation. Under an emergency order, Doron was placed with a family who intended to adopt him; the state petitioned to declare him eligible for adoption, and the foster parents were told that the legal proceedings had been completed and that the petition to declare him eligible for adoption had already been approved. In this case, I was invited by the court to serve as an expert witness on the mother's behalf, and in that capacity I observed a meeting between the mother and son, and witnessed the strong bond between them. Doron played happily with his mother, his cheeks dimpled with pleasure throughout the entire session, something that I had not seen in him while with the foster family. Nevertheless, when he asked about their dog and the mother replied that the dog had disappeared because she had left their front door open, he said with a tense laugh, 'At night, as well' – alluding, perhaps, to a sense of insecurity that he had felt while living with her. He told her very animatedly of his doings with the foster family, and it was clear that he felt well and protected there. When they parted, and he was taken by the adoption official back to his foster parents, he turned around to have one last look at his mother until he could see her no more.

While there was no doubt that the mother in that case was incapable of using appropriate judgement or being responsible for Doron's well-being, it was equally clear that Doron was attached to her with every fibre of his being. In my estimation, Doron's well-being meant that his foster parents should be given full parental rights and duties, while maintaining some contact with his birth mother in 'open' adoption, which is quite common today in Western countries but still regarded as an exception in Israel.[31] This option had not been included in the terms under which the SSC placed Doron with his foster parents, so the court authorised me to present it to them. Although the standard procedure was that all contact with the designated adoptive family should be made exclusively through the adoption authorities, the court nevertheless decided to make an exception in this case, probably in the belief that it would be better if the open adoption option be presented by someone who was not opposed to it, rather than by the SSC, which clearly was. However, in direct contravention of the court's decision, the adoption official phoned the foster parents to alert them as to the purpose of my visit. When I arrived, they were resolutely against the proposal, and even if their response was not attributable to how the proposal had been presented to them by the adoption official, the fact that they arrived at our meeting with a digital recorder to record our conversation, and the father's parting remark – 'You've made a very good impression on us' – were most definitely due to the adoption official's advance warning.

The foster parents had asked to adopt a child 'to have a fresh start', despite the fact that Doron was already five years old and had been living until that time with his loving mother. As far as they were concerned, his history began on the day he arrived on their doorstep. In my conversation with them, I repeatedly said, with all due respect, that although it was easy for me to sit in an office and propose an open adoption to them, while they would have to live their lives by it, severing all ties between Doron and his mother, to whom he was so attached, would likely drastically reduce his world and impair his sense of continuity. To this they both replied that they too had left behind childhood memories in their countries of origin, and did not think that continuity was all that important. Their position confirmed my long-held belief that the fact that closed adoption is the default option in Israel – despite its contravention of traditional Jewish law which explicitly forbids an 'orphan' from being adopted[32] – may have something to do with the fact that Israeli society was built by immigrants. The legislative preference for the closed adoption arrangement, which encourages a denial of the loss of genealogical ties, may be a reflection of how Israeli society as a whole is attempting to start a new chapter in Jewish history, which, in part, involves a deliberate disregard of the yearning that its immigrant residents may have for their countries of origin, while emphasising Israel's *raison d'être* as the motherland.

In the case of Doron, it was difficult for me to decide what would be more harmful to him: severing his ties with his mother, or transferring him from his present foster family to another that would agree to an open adoption. I wanted to meet with him alone, but the adoption official objected. Unsurprisingly, perhaps, so too did the foster parents. I thought that it would not be right for me to meet with Doron alone in defiance of the adults who were caring for him and to whom he had already grown attached. As I parted with them, the foster mother escorted me to the door, saying somewhat plaintively, 'I don't want him to think that we took his mother away from him'. I refused to help her have her cake and eat it too by offering her any reassurance. Instead, I summed up the dismay and bitterness that I felt at the SSC's deliberate misrepresentation with nothing more than a shrug.

With a heavy heart, I recommended to the court that Doron be left in the custody of his foster parents, and that his ties with his mother be severed. I feared that transferring him from that family, after he had been promised that he would grow up there, would make it difficult for him to adjust to another adoptive family that might agree to open adoption. In view of that, Doron needed someone to serve as 'a bridge' between his two families. His mother, because of her shaky mental condition, could not be that bridge, and the SSC workers objected to this solution. It was the lesser of two evils. Under the present circumstances, the harm incurred by being transferred to another family would likely have been worse than the harm caused by being cut off from his mother.

In response to my recommendation, the judge did something unprecedented.[33] She observed a meeting between the mother and her son from behind a one-way mirror, then brought the two parties together and told them she could not understand how one could separate the child from his mother to whom he was so clearly attached. On receiving no reply at the meeting, she then followed this up with a visit to the foster family (who lived a fair distance from the court) for one final attempt to persuade them to agree to the child preserving some contact with his mother, but they remained adamantly opposed.[34] In her subsequent ruling, the judge wrote:

> There is no denying that the environment in which the minor is today is a safe and desirable one for him. The foster/adoptive family is clearly very motivated and able to deal with the challenges involved, and to provide for the minor's every need. It has given him, for the first time ever, good and safe parenting, and treats him as if he were their own child. There is also no question that the minor is attached to his [birth] family – his mother, grandfather and aunt – but, as previously made clear, this relationship was fraught with upheavals and inconsistency. His relationship with his mother was destructive, unhealthy, and put

> him in danger. Despite his young age, the minor is gradually coming to terms with the foster/adoptive family, and it appears as though he belongs to it. That said, he also needs the meetings with his birth family and contact with it. However, in the absence of suitable preparation and mutual consent, such contact cannot be maintained without undermining what has been invested to date by the foster/adoptive family.

Elinor's case, then, was the third one in which my encounter with the foster family exposed the duplicitous manner in which the SSC had conducted itself vis-à-vis the court, the child, the birth parents and designated adoptive parents. In many cases in the past, as in the other two I have cited here, the court, despite its sharp criticism of being confronted with a *fait accompli*, ultimately ruled in favour of the adoption officials' recommendations.[35] In Elinor's case, however, the court decided to return the child to her mother. Moreover, in the wake of this case, procedural changes were made whereby when a child is placed with a family under an emergency order, the foster parents must be informed of the child's legal status, and confirm this notification in writing on a specially designated form. Although I have never been told explicitly that this change was introduced because of Elinor's case, I do believe it was prompted by the court's refusal to accept the situation that the SSC had tried to engineer, and the heavy emotional price that, in this case, the designated adoptive family was obliged to pay for the licence that the adoption officials had taken.

Protecting the interests of the families designated to adopt children who have been taken from the custody of their birth parents is vital to the function of the SSC, whose sole purpose is adoption, but in all three cases cited above, the children were also harmed as a result. Natalie/Vered felt threatened during her meetings with her mother, who reacted furiously to the discovery that the adoption officials had deceived her and used the girl to fight back. The child, of course, had no understanding of why her mother was behaving this way and saw her as an unfamiliar and frightening woman. Doron was abruptly cut off from his mother, with whom he had a very strong and warm bond; and Elinor encountered various difficulties, both at the legal proceedings stage and subsequently, as I shall detail presently.

Although the new procedure restricts the power of the SSC to place children with designated adoptive families and to declare them free for adoption, adoption officials can still exploit the cover of secrecy and exclusive access to act behind the court's back towards both birth parents and prospective adoptive parents. In a family court ruling delivered approximately five years after the introduction of the procedure requiring a foster family to declare that it is aware of the child's legal status, one judge wrote (in relation to the adoption of another female minor):

> I do not think it right to give approval for the minor to be left with the 'host' family, given that the placement was made improperly and illegally, and the petition submitted in a manipulative manner, by means of deception and fraudulent representations to the court … The disingenuous presentation of the family as the 'foster family', when in reality it was a family that intended to adopt the minor, is a serious act of deception and fraud towards the court … One expects public officials to operate honestly and to help the court to administer justice. It is not acceptable for a minor be placed with a family in an underhanded fashion for the purpose of securing an illegal and improper adoption. While the principle of the best interests of the child is paramount, the end does not justify the means; just as national security does not justify presenting false data to the court and/or failing to present the whole truth and concealing facts, neither does the child's best interests.[36]

In another case, the judge wrote:

> Regrettably, we find in the case before us that the [adoption] officials decreed that the respondent's minor children must have one and only one fate, namely to be given up for adoption, and once they did so they did not shy away from contributing to the evidence brought before the court – to the extent of nearly tying the court's hands and placing before it a *fait accompli*, and more's the pity. There is nothing wrong with an [adoption] official's professional assessment that a minor is better off being declared eligible for adoption, but a very clear distinction should be drawn between that and … actually contributing to the circumstances in which the petition is made. It is both wrong and indefensible to approve what has happened in this case, whereby the [adoption] official determined the procedure's outcome in advance and accordingly chose what information to bring to the court's attention, what to emphasise and what to omit entirely, instead of presenting the full picture to the court and letting it decide. There is nothing wrong with an [adoption] official making a professional assessment that meetings between a parent and a minor are not in the best interests of the minor. However, it is wrong to translate that assessment into action by preventing meetings between the parent and the minor before the court has ruled on the matter – particularly when this contravenes the court's decision. It was both improper and unjustifiable to make a false representation to the respondent, when he sought to meet with his children, by telling him that legal proceedings had been started against him, when in fact no such action had yet been taken.[37]

The slippery slope, in which the denial of the loss inherent in adoption slides into deception, is intrinsic to the closed adoption model and part of the history of adoption in the Western world ever since children who were born out of wedlock were given up for adoption and denied knowledge of the circumstances of their birth, on the pretext of shielding them from the image of being the product of 'bad seed'.[38] Such adoption explicitly involves deception. The practice of revealing to adopted children that they are adopted began in the first half of the twentieth century, in the light of experience showing that the chances of successfully hiding such information indefinitely are extremely low, and because of the risk that when adoptees learn this by chance, they feel betrayed by their adoptive parents. Today it is generally agreed that it is better to tell an adopted child that he is adopted once he is capable of understanding.[39] Nonetheless, the very act of adoption – that is, removing a child from his birth family and planting him into an adoptive one[40] – is an attempt to create a fictional reality[41] when the adoptee is provided with a new birth certificate and the original one is hidden,[42] a practice that has become synonymous with the adoption procedure.

Indeed, so entrenched and essential has deception become in closed adoption that it has been robbed of its meaning, and is now seen as a legitimate part of social consciousness. Thus, the Supreme Court rejected the petition of birth parents to receive information about their child during the course of an adoption, in part on the grounds that it would be wrong to involve the child in this, and on the other hand stating that if he were not told that the adoptive parents were communicating with his birth parents, the matter would lead to keeping of secrets from him and undermining the trust in his relationship with his adoptive parents, with 'repercussions on his emotional development for the rest of his life'. However, as the custom today is to tell adoptees that they are adopted, their life is still shrouded in secret and false identity.[43] In this regard, it has been noted that:

> the adoptee is presented with an opposing, irreconcilable dilemma: on the one hand, she is told early in her life that she comes from a different family of origin. She comes to learn, but not to understand that the mother of whom she was once a part has been inexplicably lost. When she questions who her original parents were, where they are now, and why she was relinquished, the adoptive parents tell her they have little or no knowledge about them.[44]

Denying the deception that lies at the heart of the adoptee's life, which is profoundly embedded in the conventional notion that the adoptee has to be presented as if born to their adoptive parents, serves the ruling of the court in cases when deliberating the option of exchanging information between birth parents and adoptive parents. Such was the case in which a child was declared eligible for adoption without his father's knowledge because of 'improper conduct of the welfare authorities'[45] and the absence of any hearings in the family court, hearings that 'should have been held'.[46] In that case, not only did the court reject the father's appeal to reverse the declaration of his son as eligible for adoption, even though not all statutory requirements for such a decision had been met, on the pretext that the child had already been living with the adoptive family for over three years; the court also prohibited any information from being conveyed to the father, to prevent 'the creation of a web of lies within the family'.[47]

The process of evaluating Rachel's ability to raise Elinor was therefore overshadowed by the distortions created by the adoption officials. Re-establishing the meetings between her and Elinor, which was necessary to complete the evaluation procedure, contradicted what the foster parents had told Elinor at the behest of the psychologist acting on behalf of the SSC: that she would not see her mother again until she was eighteen. In addition, there was a risk that after resuming the meetings, all contact between Elinor and her mother would be cut off again if the court decided to declare Elinor eligible for adoption. Nevertheless, I believed that Rachel's impressive progress in recovering from drug addiction, and her strong sense of commitment to Elinor's well-being as evidenced in my meetings with her, justified the risk involved. Even if the court decided in favour of adoption, and decided that it would be necessary to sever all ties and for Rachel to disappear from Elinor's life, at least Elinor would have been given a chance to part with her mother properly, something she had not been able to do on previous occasions. I therefore asked the court to order the resumption of regular meetings between Elinor and her mother. My request was granted, and before the first meeting, I spoke once more with Dorit and Zvi, the foster parents. During this conversation, which was not held in Elinor's presence, they responded sharply to the court's decision to resume the meetings between Elinor and her mother, even if the purpose of such meetings was only to decide about the future of their contact together. They had formed a very negative view of the mother from the information they had received from the adoption officials. They viewed her not only as a drug addict who led a very dubious lifestyle, but also as a mother who had failed to raise her eldest son, or maintain any contact with him, and who had already given up one child for adoption in the past. By law, details of this sort are not supposed to be given to a foster family. Secrecy in adoption is supposed to work both ways, not only to keep the birth parents unaware of details about the adoptive family, but to prevent information being given to the adoptive parents as well. This violation of secrecy by adoption officials had of course been deliberate and calculating, since by the same token they could have also told them that Rachel was intelligent and charming, and that her success in the first stage of rehabilitation from drug addiction was a sign of great courage.

During our conversation, Dorit and Zvi repeatedly stated that their primary concern was Elinor's best interests, but Zvi added that they had to take into account their extended family as well, who would likely be affected by the appearance of another figure in the family. The wording and presentation of their arguments are common in cases of this sort. After initially claiming that the only consideration is 'the best interests of the child', the actual reasoning at play is revealed, namely how the child's interests fit in with other interests.[48] Such considerations are only natural, of course, but the use of the term 'the best interests of the child' is often cited as a pretext for measures that have little to do with the child. When I raised the prospect of continued contact between Elinor and her mother, Dorit and Zvi were indignant. What would happen, for example, if after they had raised Elinor she chose to return to her mother, and the mother would reap the benefits of their care and efforts? The mother, they had been told, had never taken care of the child. As they saw it, it suited her very well that the child was being fed and cared for by others, and she only had to visit from time to time and bring gifts, free of the need to deal with the drudgery of the daily routine.

Rarely have I encountered references to raising a child in such explicit and blunt terms of expected rewards for investing in the child's upbringing, or compensation for efforts, as when these foster parents frankly described their predicament. I was taken aback to hear such an argument from people seeking to adopt a four-year-old child, particularly after hearing how devoted they had been to raising her and their sincere efforts to adjust to her needs and to make it easier for her to fit in with the family. As the conversation went on, the real issue became clearer: they wanted to be a 'normal' family, with three children, and allowing continual contact between Elinor and her mother would compromise that sought-after 'normality'. Their desire to adopt a child so as to be a 'family like all families' was not unique to them, and indeed is an explicit factor in the Adoption of Children Law. The law states that 'adoption can only be undertaken by a man and his wife together', in an effort to create 'standard' families. To that end, the law permits the removal of children from the custody of 'deficient' parents, such as those suffering from that irreversible functional disorder known as 'lack of parental capability', termination of their parenthood and redrawing the demographic map of society, all in the name of preserving the vaunted 'standard' family, that is, erecting clear boundaries around the nuclear family.[49] Severing the child's bond with his birth parents is integral to this approach as the child's bond with his adult caregivers is supposed to be exclusive. For the same reason, the foster parents saw no problem in abruptly ending Elinor's phone call with her mother when she mentioned her foster brother by name; according to them, it was a conference call, and it was the adoption official who disconnected it, to prevent the girl from giving any further information to her mother. Preserving the secrecy appeared to them to be essential to protecting the exclusivity of their bond with Linor, in line with the mindset behind the closed adoption model. Continuity with Elinor's past had been imposed upon them, and they were now seeking to limit and qualify it. After hearing from the adoption official that I had my misgivings about Elinor's name being changed, Dorit explained that when she first met Elinor and heard her name, she was taken aback. 'We're a strictly secular family, so we have no *Els* [the contraction of the word God, in Hebrew] in the family', she explained, which is why they changed her name to 'Linor'. While the caregivers at the children's home objected to the name change, the adoption official, who fervently argued in court that Elinor's adoption was essential, agreed. At the nursery school, Elinor was registered under the name given to her by the foster family, despite the girl's own objections (to appease her, she was told that 'Linor' was merely a nickname). Just as the foster parents attributed little importance to the continuity of Elinor's identity, they were also dismissive of the notion that cutting her off from her mother would be a loss. Dorit even offered to provide Linor with psychological treatment to erase the traces of her birth mother's disappearance from her life. Throughout the entire conversation, there were numerous such glimpses into how the foster parents associated the erasure of all traces of Elinor's identity and her loss with their need to entrench the exclusivity of their bond with her, as a sign of the family's 'normality'.

I saw their efforts to expunge Elinor's identity as a denial of her being a person in her own right, for what is it that turns a child from a mere body into a person, after she has been cut off from her familiar surroundings and the significant figures in her life, if not the identity that she received at birth? An echo of such a denial is evident in an interview with Rafi Gonen, an African who had been adopted as a child by an Israeli citizen: 'My dad wanted to take a plaything with him from Bophuthatswana and it struck him that a little black baby would do nicely'.[50] That 'little black baby' grew up and became an

Israeli youth who had a loving and very close relationship with his adoptive father, but the image of himself as a 'plaything' still dogged him in his late twenties.

Dorit and Zvi's position was also evident in their reaction to another suggestion that I put forward, namely that Elinor remain in their care until her mother was fully rehabilitated, should the court decide to return her to her mother. As they saw it, that idea was a complete non-starter. When I asked them if this was because they saw it as a form of exploitation, Dorit agreed, since that indeed was how they felt, but also because they thought that returning the mother to Elinor's life would not be to Elinor's advantage. Quietly, but firmly, they said that had they known that the adoption issue had not yet been settled, they would not have agreed to take the child. My previous visit had been their first intimation that the process was not proceeding as promised by the SSC representatives, and that the promised adoption order would not be issued at the end of the six-month period. But even before that visit, Dorit pointed out, she had repeatedly told her husband, 'Look, we keep asking them, and they [the SSC staff] keep avoiding giving us a straight answer'. They also said that they were considering appealing the court's decision if it did not approve their adoption of Linor.

They were clearly very distressed. They had both become attached to Linor, and had sincerely tried to make her feel part of the family, and meeting with me now put all of their efforts in question. I thought it necessary for the judge to meet with them, even though they were not a legal party to the proceedings and had taken no part in it, so that they might reconsider their position despite the misinformation they had been given about the legal status of Linor. I also thought that it was only fair to let them know that they would be unable to appeal the court's decision because prospective adoptive parents hold no legal standing before the child is declared adoptable. The judge agreed with my request and, once again going beyond the call of duty as the arbitrator in the dispute between the birth parent and the state and the person in charge of the child's well-being in the complex situation that had arisen, invited them to her office. After that meeting, she wrote:

> I learned to my astonishment that, according to [the foster parents], when the minor was placed in their custody, they were not told that she had not yet been declared eligible for adoption, and indeed that they were told that there would only be two or three more meetings with the mother until they were finally parted.[51]

However, even after the conversation with the judge, the foster parents remained adamant that they would immediately relinquish custody of Elinor and sever all contact with her if the court ruled in favour of resumption of meetings between her and her mother, and most certainly if it ruled that she was to be returned to her mother. Their unwavering opposition ruled out the possibility that Elinor might go on living with them while her mother found a place to live and started to lead an independent life. However, much to my relief, the issue of the mother's accommodation was resolved when she took up the suggestion of an official at the Prisoner Rehabilitation Service to apply for a place at a special hostel established to help former women prisoners and their children to make the transition to independent living, find employment and restore the relationship with their children. This was a sign of the seriousness of Rachel's intentions, of her good judgement and her preparation for the heavy responsibility that would be placed on her inexperienced shoulders in the event that Elinor was returned to her care. Meanwhile, her meetings with Elinor, who was still at her foster parents' home, resumed, and I began preparing my written opinion.

Resumption of Meetings between the Mother and Elinor

To assess Rachel's ability to raise Elinor, during my observations of them together I tried to find answers to three questions: (1) Was Rachel's understanding of her responsibility also evident in her behaviour with Elinor? (2) Was Rachel able to relate to Elinor's needs when they were incompatible with her own? (3) What was the nature of the bond between Elinor and her mother?

As previously noted, the circumstances that had arisen very much restricted the possibility of receiving answers to these questions. The mother's responsibility could only barely be tested in a meeting of such brief duration, in an unfamiliar environment while being observed by others, and the forced separation that had been imposed on them was liable to impinge upon her ability to relate to her daughter's needs and to her daughter's responses to her. I was, however, able to answer these questions, perhaps because Rachel did in fact exhibit great responsibility and understanding of Elinor even in the restrictive conditions under which their meeting was held.

The first meeting between the two, after a seven-month break, took place at the offices of the SSC. Apart from myself, observers included the chief adoption official, the adoption official who had been in contact with the foster family, and a representative of State Counsel. Rachel arrived with her lawyer, and in a possible attempt to calm her nerves, spoke animatedly about the party that had been held in her honour at the rehab centre on her successful completion of treatment there. Elinor arrived, escorted by the adoption official, took one look at the entourage that waited outside, and entered the room with her mother with a blank look on her face. A one-way mirror allowed us to observe the meeting. From time to time, Elinor left the meeting room and came into the observation room where we sat. She was curious to see us and the adoption officials, whom she knew, no doubt seeking in this way to defuse the intensity of the meeting that was taking place after the painful separation and after being told that she would not see her mother again until she reached eighteen.

I could see that Rachel had prepared in a mature and responsible manner for the challenging situation that Elinor was in, having to contend with this re-established encounter with her mother and with the memories of her birth family amidst the sense of belonging to the foster family. Rachel had brought along an album of pictures of the family and letters from Elinor's aunts, which were sealed with lip prints as a sign of kisses. She immediately said yes to a softly spoken request from Elinor, possibly the first sentence that the child uttered spontaneously: 'Mum, next time could you possibly bring Grandma with you?' When Elinor referred to Dorit as 'Mum' as well, Rachel did not object or correct her.

As far as the bond between Elinor and Rachel was concerned, however, the picture was less encouraging. Initially, Elinor tried to keep a physical distance from her mother, did not respond to her hugs, and wiped her face with her hand after Rachel kissed her. Although she tried to remain next to her mother, she avoided eye contact, something that children do after a painful parting from an important figure in their lives, either to protect the connection from their anger, or in an effort to maintain control of themselves despite the emotional turmoil invoked by the renewed meeting.[52] In response, the mother tried to impose her closeness on Elinor. Both, it seemed, appeared to be agitated, Elinor because of the mother's imposed proximity, and Rachel because of Elinor's diffidence. Rachel's behaviour may have been the result of her great joy and excitement at the renewed contact, of her desire to succeed in the 'test' that she was being put to, but it might possibly also have been because – as occurred to me in my introductory conversations with her – she was too self-absorbed to see Elinor's evasions. However, when she saw that Elinor was not responding to her suggestions of things to do together, she gave up and went along with whatever activity her daughter chose. When Elinor began colouring in a drawing, Rachel joined her, and as they began to talk, an intimacy began to form between them. At first, Elinor seemed distant and indifferent, but in an apparent attempt to introduce some coherence into her life story, she suddenly asked her mother if she knew how old she was. Rachel, immediately understanding the real significance of the question, replied, 'Of course I do! I gave birth to you…'

The gulf that had opened up between them, however, was evident when Rachel tried to play on musical instruments in the room and to sing a well-known children's song with her, one that may have suited Elinor at the age that she was when she was taken from her, but which she had now outgrown, as evident from her reluctance to join in. When Elinor asked Rachel for an accordion, Rachel said that she would bring one next time. Towards the end of the meeting, when Elinor had become less inhibited about the physical intimacy, Rachel helped her gather up her belongings and pack the gifts that she had brought her, sat her down on her knees and – after the adoption official had agreed to another meeting – quietly explained to her that they would meet again in two weeks' time. In these final moments, there was a sense of great closeness between the two. The adoption official denied Elinor's request to take a picture of her mother, to which Rachel acquiesced without demur, but did allow her to take a picture of her grandmother with her.

This painful meeting vividly illustrated the impact of the forced separation between mother and daughter. For the mother, time had stopped, as it were, while Elinor had become more distant from her mother, had grown and developed. I was, however, unsure from the observation whether Rachel sensed the distance that Elinor put between them, that is to say, whether she was able to notice that Elinor's needs were distinct from her own. To receive an answer to that question, I asked to observe them again during their next meeting.

The second meeting was more relaxed. Elinor immediately became physically close to her mother, and readily responded to her hugs and kisses. Rachel's displays of affection were fewer than at the first meeting, but her attempts to initiate games were still very awkward. The incongruity of her reactions to Elinor in terms of Elinor's level of development was still very pronounced, only this time it was apparent in her *over*estimating Elinor's level of understanding, for example when she argued with her that she should say a 'male cat' and not a 'boy cat'. Adjusting her expectations to her daughter's true level of development is clearly a difficult test that parents are not normally required to face. However, these momentary altercations themselves appeared to have the positive effect of opening up the communication between them. I also observed the readiness with which Rachel joined in whatever Elinor initiated. She apologised to Elinor that she had not been able to find an accordion, and agreed to Elinor's suggestion that she visit more shops. Later, Elinor asked to see her brother (the mother's eldest son, whose picture Elinor had identified during the previous visit – 'that's my brother' – although she couldn't remember his name), and once again asked for her grandmother to visit, and the mother was obliged to say that she would, when she could. Once again, Elinor sought some measure of continuity of her life, this time by asking how she used to drink milk when she was a baby, and when Rachel told her, Elinor demonstrated by finding a bottle and sucking on it. She then sat on a tricycle, and while she pedalled, said something in a cheery voice. The mother burst into a loud, but uneasy, laugh – the reason for which I learned only later, during my conversation with her. At the end of the meeting, Rachel promised Elinor – again, with the permission of the adoption official – that from then on, they would meet every two weeks.

After the meeting, I asked Rachel to stay on and chat with me about the two meetings. She told me that this meeting had gone much better than the previous one because on the previous occasion Elinor did not want to come close to her. This reassured me that she was able to distinguish between her needs and Elinor's, allowing me to attribute greater weight to her expressions of understanding and sensitivity than to her previous attempts at imposing her physical proximity on Elinor. She told me that she had cried after the previous meeting, because Elinor had been so preoccupied with the question of who she was, which, she thought, was abnormal. This also indicated a good understanding on her part of Elinor's situation. As she put it, part of her difficulty during the previous meeting was because she was so excited. She had, she said, never felt like that before, pressing a hand on her chest to illustrate where her love for Elinor emanated from. She did not know how to fully express her love. She felt, she said, 'like a rose opening up from inside'.

Without any prompting on my part, she then went on to explain that when Elinor was pedalling on the tricycle, she had playfully said out loud the surname, town and street name of the foster family. Rachel had responded by laughing nervously, not really hearing what Elinor said, both out of embarrassment since she knew that Elinor had been forbidden from talking about such matters, and because she feared that it would result in another intervention like the one when Elinor had let slip the name of her foster brother over the telephone and the call was abruptly disconnected. With this single gesture, Rachel demonstrated the duality that is expected of a parent – taking a responsible position while identifying with the child – and struck the golden mean between not violating the secrecy that had been imposed upon Elinor, and not insulting the child, who had given the information to signal her closeness with the mother. However, it also expressed the situation of tension that Rachel was in, for fear that her contact with Elinor might be severed once again. I wondered if one could draw any conclusions from that as to Elinor's feelings, since this was not the first time she had tried to transmit information to her mother about her whereabouts. Perhaps she wanted to break through the wall of secrecy that stood between her life with the foster family and her mother. In the meetings that were to follow, Elinor was to express her wishes even more clearly.

Rachel also told me that she had suggested that Elinor's father come with her to the meeting, but he had refused, for fear of being rejected by the child. Her attempt to create a connection between the father, with whom she herself did not want a relationship, and Elinor revealed the importance that she attributed to continuity in Elinor's identity, and was further evidence of her ability to distinguish between Elinor's needs and her own. She added that she had also wanted to bring along one of her sisters and her own mother, but in a telephone conversation prior to the meeting, the adoption official had told her that anyone else joining her would be turned away, so 'they might as well save themselves the trouble'. This blunt refusal by the adoption officials might be regarded as mere callous insensitivity, particularly with regard to the grandmother, since they too had heard Elinor's moving appeal, but in fact it was fully consistent with their determination to erase all traces of Elinor's previous life. Moreover, it undermined Rachel's position, as she had promised in good faith to bring Elinor's grandmother with her on her next visit, so it made her appear unreliable in Elinor's eyes. When I asked the court to allow the grandmother to take part in future visits, the judge was dumbfounded at the reason given by the adoption officials for their refusal: 'The court's ruling [only] said that the mother should visit'. 'Nowhere was it said that the grandmother or aunts should be prohibited from seeing [visiting]. Anyone may visit, unless the court has explicitly forbidden them', said the judge in response. Ultimately, however, the grandmother's visit did not take place, because Rachel's own subsequent visits, which the adoption officials had explicitly agreed to, were later denied by the same officials. The next scheduled meeting was cancelled at their request on the grounds that Zvi, the foster father, was abroad. This blatant violation of the mother's promise did not prevent the same adoption officials from subsequently castigating her in court for breaking her promise to bring Elinor an accordion. Rachel, in response, was so mortified she did not even mention that she had apologised to Elinor about this during their second meeting. As far as the adoption officials were concerned, the mother was on trial, while their own actions were beyond reproach, even when they caused disappointment to the child.

It became abundantly clear at this point that the tension between Rachel's bid for continued contact with Elinor and the adoption officials' desire to put an end to it and complete the adoption proceedings was growing, as it became increasingly likely that Rachel would not be declared 'lacking in parental capability'.

Continuity (with Whom) and Separation (from Whom)

In the wake of my two observations, I felt there was little reason to deny the mother's right to custody of Elinor. The two meetings demonstrated Rachel's ability to treat her daughter astutely and appropriately to her daughter's situation. I was also impressed by the responsibility she showed in not subjecting Elinor to a 'loyalty test' between herself and the foster parents. Last but not least, her decision to accept a place at the hostel run by the Prisoner Rehabilitation Service (PRS) meant that Elinor's immediate return to her custody was possible at a practical level as well.

On Zvi's return from abroad, he and Dorit demanded an immediate end to the meetings between Elinor and her mother. There had been a marked deterioration in Elinor's behaviour; she had begun to be insolent towards them and aggressive. They therefore asked State Counsel to declare that if they were forced to bring Elinor for another meeting with Rachel, they would send her along with all her belongings with no chance of returning to their home. Accordingly, State Counsel asked that the next meeting between Rachel and Elinor be postponed, to allow Elinor to bid a proper goodbye to her foster family and not feel as though she were simply being kicked out.

The mother's counsel responded by insisting on her client's right to continue meeting with Elinor, as arranged, adding that if the foster parents did indeed make good on their threat, the mother should be allowed immediately to take custody of her daughter at the PRS hostel. Fearing that Elinor would once again be taken from her adult caregivers to whom she had become attached, without the chance of parting with them properly, as she had been from her mother and grandmother, I sided with State Counsel on this point. I thought that Elinor should be given a chance to part with her foster parents properly, and estimated that their decency and the attachment they had formed with Elinor would overcome their feelings of hurt and pain, and lead them, despite their anger, to allow Elinor to part with them in a considerate and compassionate manner. The court agreed, and State Counsel promised that this did not mean they would seek to derail the apparent emerging outcome of Elinor's return to her mother's custody, even if it meant severing her ties with the foster family.

However, the adoption officials had a different opinion, and contrary to State Counsel's promise, tried one last time to rewind the dispute back to square one. Once again, my opinion on the mother's ability to take custody of her daughter was called into question, on the grounds that the foster parents could provide Elinor with better care than her mother. This was a clearly irrelevant argument since, by law, the only criterion for declaring a child eligible for adoption without parental consent is if the parent is shown to be incapable of raising the child.[53] The adoption official then claimed that Elinor told her privately that she 'would die' if she were returned to her mother. Such a declaration was in such marked contrast to Elinor's furious outburst a few months earlier (after her first meeting with the mother while with the foster parents) that it could only attest to the impact of the enforced separation from her mother, of the supervision of their meetings, and of the sanctions imposed on her when she tried to break through the wall of secrecy, making her believe that her mother was a dangerous person. Next, the adoption officials demanded that Elinor be first examined by an expert, to establish the harm that would be caused to her if she were to be separated from the foster parents. This, too, was patently unreasonable, since any such harm to Elinor would result not only from her separation from her foster parents but also from the nature of the future evolving relationship with her mother after returning to her mother's custody, which could not possibly be known at that time. Moreover, any such expert examination would delay proceedings by several more months, deferring the parting from the foster family and providing yet another pretext for not returning Elinor to her mother, given her ever-deepening attachment to her foster family.

The judge, rejecting the state's petition out of hand, ruled for Elinor to be returned to her mother, but in a controlled, gradual fashion, and charged me with implementing the decision.

The process of returning Elinor to her mother was difficult and painful for all concerned: for Elinor, who was torn between the adults who wanted to raise her; for the mother, who was afraid she might not be up to the task of taking care of Elinor once she returned to her care; and for the foster parents, who promised to help Elinor as much as they could during their parting from her, despite their fervent opposition to the court's decision. Elinor asked – indeed, begged! – not to be cut off from either the foster parents or from her mother. She suggested that her mother come and live with the foster parents – which would have been an ideal solution, except that Elinor's world was far from ideal.

Elinor's anxiety at being returned to her mother, and the estrangement that had crept into their relationship and had not yet abated, were clearly evident in her first visit to the hostel that her mother had moved into. It was preceded by resistance on Elinor's part to the very visit, coupled with a great curiosity about her mother's present life, now that she was 'well again'. When we arrived at the hostel, she protested, 'This is not where Mummy lives!', but significantly, upon ringing the intercom bell at the entrance, she emphatically announced herself as 'Elinor!', not 'Linor'. Her mother had prepared an accordion for her, as she had promised, which Elinor responded to with feigned pleasure. The contrast between the foster family's spacious, well-lit and pleasant home and the bleak and modest hostel dwelling was stark, and made me profoundly despondent, as it seemed to encapsulate the economic repercussions of Elinor's transition from her foster parents to her mother's care. I withdrew into a corner of the room, partly to avoid casting a pall over the occasion, but also to allow Rachel and Elinor to renew their relationship one on one, without interference by any third party. During the visit, Rachel cleverly turned the unfamiliarity into a voyage of discovery, until it was time for supper, when Elinor's definite dislike of the food, which was very different from what she had become accustomed to at her foster parents' home, highlighted how far they had grown apart since their separation. Rachel and her friends, who were present at the meal (life at the hostel does not provide for much privacy), smiled at the names that Elinor gave the food, but Rachel respected the girl's taste and tried to direct Elinor to the dishes that she might agree to eat.

During the visit, I repeatedly found myself wondering whether the decision to cut Elinor off from her foster parents had been the right one, even though it was mandatory under the law once her mother was deemed capable of raising her. The answer to this troubling question was provided by Elinor at the end of the visit, when Rachel accompanied us to the car and Elinor clung to her for dear life. For nearly an hour, Rachel and I tried to relax her grip on her mother and to get her to say goodbye, with endless promises that she would visit again in a few days' time. The terror that seized her as she parted from her mother expressed all that she had suppressed over the long time they had been forcibly kept apart. It revealed the difference between the terror that one feels on suffering a sudden, inexplicable traumatic event,[54] such as when Elinor was forcibly removed from her mother and grandmother, and the pain one experiences in anticipation of a blow from an identified and known source, such as her impending parting from her foster parents. Elinor was in an unbearable predicament, and none of us adults could remain immune to her cries of distress. She made each of us feel the sheer magnitude of the pain and fury she was experiencing, and tried to enlist each of us to help her avoid the horrible choice she was forced to make.

'You do realise, I hope, that you're carrying out a Judgement of Solomon on this poor girl!', Dorit scolded me when I brought Elinor back very late, due to her reluctance to part with her mother. Elinor was clearly in pain, and in shock. Even if it had been a mistake to place her with them, Dorit added, one cannot correct a mistake by making another one, and taking the child back to her mother was, in her view, another mistake. In effect, she was comparing Elinor's removal from them with her removal from Rachel – an understandable comparison, but for the fact that the former was a bond between a birth mother and child. Dorit was all too ready to quote the girl when she complained that 'Nobody's listening' to her when she asked not to leave her foster parents, but when it came to Elinor's plea for her mother to come live with them – that is, for the contact with the mother to be not only preserved but made permanent, and continuous – Dorit and her husband argued that they had to be considered too. If indeed this is a Judgement of Solomon, I thought to myself, it is because of the deceitful manner in which the adoption officials had placed Elinor with the foster family in the first place.

Over the next two weeks, I took Elinor to visit her mother every other day. On these occasions, I picked her up either from the foster parents' home or from kindergarten, and brought her back the next morning. During these visits, Elinor made sure to show her ambivalence towards me too, oscillating between refusing to enter my car, pouncing angrily on any mistake or clumsiness on my part, refusing to go at all or fearing abandonment when I pointedly ignored her attempts at evasion when I came to pick her up, to unexpected, poignant pleas for love, such as 'Do *you* want to be my mum?' To their credit, Dorit and Zvi had thought of everything. They asked the kindergarten teacher that on Elinor's last Friday at the kindergarten, she would be made 'Sabbath Queen'; on one of the visits, before she had parted with them for the last time, they sent her along with her toys, as a way of communicating to her the true meaning of the parting, and made her help in packing. They also explained to her repeatedly that she was going back to the mother whose tummy she came out of, just as their children were staying at their home, with the mother whose tummy they had come out of.

Given how strongly they had objected to the court's ruling, the decency with which Dorit and Zvi handled the parting with Elinor was remarkable. They did everything possible to make the experience as painless as possible, so that she might preserve her memories of the time she had stayed with them. The ever-precocious Elinor, however, was not fooled. When they gave her an album with pictures of her from the time she lived with them (without their own pictures, of course, because of the secrecy that was in effect), and told her that when she misses them she could look at the pictures, she replied, 'What good will it do? You're not going to be there'.

Dorit and Zvi's decision to sever all ties with Elinor hurt Rachel very much too. 'What am I, a witch?' she asked. However, it is also possible that she was not only offended, but also feared that she might not be up to the task of caring for Elinor on her own, and had been hoping to be able to call on the support of the foster parents, whose successful care of Elinor was all too evident. From my perspective, however, these very anxieties on Rachel's part, after initial confident declarations that she was able to raise Elinor, made me all the more confident in her ability to deal with her daughter's return to her care. It meant that she understood the magnitude of the step she had taken, and Elinor's pain, and the difficulties she would face in her relationship with her daughter. She wrote the foster parents an emotional letter in which she told them she had no intention of intervening in what happened between them and the authorities, but wanted to thank them for the devoted care they had taken of her daughter, and hoped that they could stay in touch. Dorit replied in a warm letter of her own, in which she explained that repeated meetings and partings might make matters more difficult for Elinor, and wished her success in caring for her wonderful child.

Elinor's final parting from the foster parents was heartbreaking. Mischievously and charmingly, when Haggai refused to let her kiss him, she kissed him on his back. In a bid to delay the final departure from the foster home, she ran back into the house time and again, for another kiss, and another, and another request for ice cream. With her tears, stubbornness and protests, Elinor was demanding that her pain be noticed. She rejected Dorit's attempts to placate her with a bar of chocolate, and when Zvi said that they would meet again when she was grown up, she wept and said, 'I won't grow up with my mother'. Finally, in a heart-rending gesture, when we were already sitting in the car, the foster father ran back into the house and fetched her the doll with which Mia, the older daughter in the family, used to fall asleep. As I drove off, Elinor was screaming on the back seat as if being scalded.

In the short drive from the foster parents' house to the hostel, Elinor fell asleep, as she usually did, but this time I had a hard time waking her up when we arrived. Perhaps she was worn out with crying, or perhaps she did not want to awaken to the new, painful reality.

We found Rachel at her wits' end with impatience and worry. As our parting from the foster family had taken longer than expected, she had feared that Elinor's return to her had been cancelled at the last minute. In my wish to keep a promise that Zvi had made to Elinor before we left, I suggested that the three of us go and eat ice cream together. That was a mistake. Elinor was too agitated to enjoy the occasion, and it would have been better if I had let her spend time alone with her mother, at a pace that suited them both. Moreover, Rachel had not secured permission to leave the hostel with Elinor, and when they returned she was severely reprimanded by a member of staff, who ignored the special circumstances. Rachel, in response, lashed out at her, giving vent to the anxiety and tension that had been pent up as she waited for Elinor to arrive. This vocal altercation was a dismal welcome for Elinor, but she bravely continued in her attempts to adjust to her new situation.

A few days later, Rachel took Elinor to kindergarten, and Elinor reacted with an acute anxiety attack. Rachel guessed that it was because it was from a kindergarten (albeit a different one) that Elinor had been seized by the SSC a year earlier, when she had originally been taken from her mother.

Two weeks later, Rachel was given leave by the PRS to attend a *bar mitzvah* celebration held by relatives of hers. In the run-up to the event, the family bought Rachel and Elinor some nice new clothes. Shortly before the event, Rachel (inadvertently) violated one of the hostel rules and was ordered to cancel the trip, but she refused, saying that it was important to her to keep her promise to Elinor. On her return, she was punished by being banned from leaving the hostel for a month, apart from going to work and picking up Elinor from the kindergarten. Punishing the mother meant imprisoning Elinor too, within a few short weeks of her difficult parting from the foster family.

This incident illustrated contrasting interpretations of the notion of responsibility. The hostel staff saw responsibility in terms of obeying authority, while Rachel saw her responsibility in keeping her promise to her daughter, even though she knew that refusing to obey the hostel rules would result in her being punished.[55] In my opinion, a parent's responsibility is measured in their response to their child's needs, even if it runs counter to the norms imposed on the parent; in the eyes of the hostel staff, however, the hostel is a micro-cosmos of the outside world, and abiding by its rules is indicative of a resident's ability to readjust to society. The strict demands to comply with all rules of the house left little room for expressions of pain, anxiety and rage. The mother and Elinor clung to each other, and Elinor reacted to the most trivial of frustrations with outbursts of tears and anger. Nonetheless, despite all the difficulties that it entailed, living at the hostel undoubtedly provided the mother and daughter a safe environment at a time when they needed it most.

The hostel provided special therapeutic activities for the children, which Elinor happily took part in. The court had prescribed psychotherapy for Elinor and Rachel, which greatly helped both of them in the early, difficult stages of their lives together. Elinor loved the therapy sessions, but these were stopped after ten months, as the state had capped the budgets allocated for the purpose. This was tantamount to the state denying responsibility for the enormous suffering that had been inflicted on Elinor by the actions of its own authorities and by the deceitful manner in which they had been conducted, since if the foster family had been told the truth about Elinor's legal status in the first place, she might very well have been returned to her mother without losing contact with the foster family, thereby avoiding a loss that compounded, and possibly re-enacted, the losses she had suffered in the past. The authority given to the adoption officials to suspend the law in the name of the law, puts them in a position whereby they are able, however inadvertently, to harm the child with impunity.[56] They can carry out an emergency order which allows them to place a child with a designated adoptive family and create a situation whereby an attachment is formed between the child and the designated adoptive parents, even before the court has confirmed that the child is eligible for adoption. A decision that the child is not eligible for adoption and is to return to his birth parents inflicts on the child unnecessary loss as he has to part from the designated adoptive parents to whom he was already attached.[57] When Elinor was returned to her mother's custody, Rachel was still under probation, and both mother and daughter were living together in the hostel that was run according to strict rules. Although Rachel had excellent social skills and knew how to 'work the system' to suit her needs, she was still in the early stages of rehabilitation from drug addiction, and found herself being endlessly tested, in part because of Elinor's behavioural difficulties. Since I believed that Rachel needed continuous support, I asked, and received, her permission to continue to visit them, even after my official, court-appointed role as Elinor's chaperone during her return to her mother's custody had ended.

While they lived at the hostel, I served mainly as a lightning rod for the tension, anxiety and frustration that arose in the relationship between the two as they tried to adjust to the hostel's rigid framework of rules. Elinor interpreted their confinement to the hostel as a punishment imposed on her by the judge (who, as she saw it, had also decreed that she should be cut off from her foster parents). Yet, a year later, when it was time for them to leave the hostel, she became anxious again. In part, this was possibly a reflection of the anxiety that Rachel was feeling, but in time I realised that every transition triggered enormous anxiety in Elinor, presumably because of the repeated transitions that had been imposed upon her in the past.

The two moved to a nearby apartment, which allowed Rachel to go on seeing her social worker at the hostel, and Elinor to stay in touch with the place and particularly to continue taking part in the psychodrama sessions of which she had grown very fond. Rachel overcame her anxieties about the transition to independent life by throwing herself into creating new social contacts. In short order, she created a pleasant family environment for herself and her daughter, where the atmosphere was often very cheerful. Elinor's response to this was immediate and positive. About a year after she had been returned to her mother, we went to mark the impending New Year at the same place where we had eaten ice cream on the day Elinor had left her foster family. Elinor remembered this, of course, and I remarked that this time we were more cheerful. It is difficult to describe the relief that I felt that evening, compared to the serious dread that had haunted me a year earlier. When we returned home, Elinor exclaimed, 'I had fun today!' This was an extraordinary declaration. At that time, Elinor usually complained about wanting things, perhaps because of the many disappearances that she had experienced. I understood this to be a positive summary of events that began over a year earlier with such difficulty and pain.

Life with Mum

Rachel's departure from the hostel at the age of thirty-seven marked the beginning of her life as an adult. It was the first time that she had to make a living for herself and manage a home as a mother. Her exceptional social skills, charm and sensitive understanding of nuances in relationships helped her a great deal in creating social contacts in her new surroundings, but these were somewhat constrained by the fact that the area in which they lived – which she had chosen for its proximity to the hostel – was well-to-do. Her feeling that she would not be accepted into this environment and be able to provide for Elinor's needs, certainly not in the same way as the other families living in the area, threatened to dash her hopes of fitting in with the 'normative world'. These difficulties grew when Elinor started going to school; her struggles to meet the demands of study and to obey the rules of the classroom environment failed to be noticed by the school, and she was neglected. Rachel had no chance of receiving public housing in this town, because, as a single mother with one girl, she was only eligible for public housing in a development town, where her chances of finding work would be small. She decided, therefore, to return to the town where she had grown up, where her mother and brother, with whom she was on good terms, still lived. While technically it was a development town, it was growing quickly and was close to a large city. I was against the idea, because I feared the consequences of her returning to the place where she was known as a drug addict, but she argued that the housing issue was more important, and that returning to her previous environment would not bring about a relapse in her situation; she was convinced that people who knew her would respect her for turning her life around. This decisive reply was indicative not so much of her confidence in her successful return to her former home town, as of her difficulty in dealing with complex situations and her desire to banish uncertainty by taking decisive action. This became apparent as I accompanied her during her tour of the various schools there before deciding on a school for Elinor. Encounters with past acquaintances did result in a few awkward moments, for example when they would peer at her and ask, 'So, are you OK now?' Nonetheless, the move back to the town proved to be the right decision.

After a period of forced unemployment (and a somewhat uncontrolled spate of spending), Rachel began building a life of settled routine. Her knack of enlisting the help of those around her proved very useful, and she managed to get the apartment that she wanted from public housing, turning it into a tidy and pleasant home. After failing to find any work locally, she found a job as a residential counsellor at an institution. She maintains a close relationship with family members, and has the occasional romantic fling with a man. To date, she has not found a partner with whom she can build a life, but the relationships she has formed are sincere and serious, and she is very loyal to her friends and family. Elinor has done well at school thanks to her high intelligence, the personal attention that the school provides to each student, and the constant cooperation between mother and school staff.

Rachel's devotion to Elinor is absolute, although as Elinor has grown older, their relationship has often been stormy. These clashes have somewhat eroded the softness and warmth in their relationship, and the moments of intimacy that they used to enjoy so much have become less frequent. Elinor is capable of putting off and alienating people with behaviour that is unpleasant and even hurtful. In the early years, she did not meet much with friends, preferring instead to spend long hours alone, playing computer games, or with her mother. This was a heavy burden on Rachel, particularly since she had little time or energy for games or recreation. Towards the end of Fifth Grade at school, Elinor began attending an after-school programme that ran from lunchtime to seven PM. This suited her and fitted in well with Rachel's late return from work. It also resulted in a marked improvement in Elinor's performance at school and a calmer environment at home. Once the summer holidays began, however, the programme closed, and the relationship between the two reached crisis point again. Elinor dominated every move that her mother made, and for the first time in many years the mother lashed back at her very aggressively. Raising a pre-teen girl in a tiny apartment leaves precious little privacy for a parent, particularly a single one. A few months earlier, Rachel had ended a relationship with a man after a series of rows that went on for a month. Perhaps Elinor's outbursts were in belated response to those rows, or perhaps they were due to an early onset of hormonal changes that accompany early puberty. Towards the end of the summer, Rachel learned that the after-school programme would close down, but a space had become available at a home-like institution accommodating twelve children run by a young couple living on the premises with their own children, and she decided to send Elinor there. The institution is not far from Rachel's home, and Elinor was able to continue attending the same school as before. She received a key to their apartment, and popped in on her way to school every morning. She spent the weekends with her mother, and often slept at home during the week as well. Her move to the institution initially sparked some anxieties and great sadness in both of them, and in her first weeks there Elinor cried every evening when her mother came to visit her, but in time she settled in well in the new environment. Her conduct there was impeccable, and she continued to make progress in her studies, and even began to make some close friends.

Shortly after returning to her mother, Elinor saw her grandmother again, whom she had missed so much, but was taken aback to find an old woman who spoke with a heavy foreign accent. Although she lives nearby and Elinor often tags along when Rachel visits her, after many months of enforced separation during her time with the foster parents, the special relationship that Elinor used to have with her grandmother has, sadly, gone. However, she often visits one of her aunts who lives in another town and has a daughter of the same age. Rachel also makes sure to take her to all extended family celebrations, of which there are many.

My contact with Elinor and her mother continues to this day. A few months after Elinor had been returned to her mother, I took them to an art workshop at a museum. The instructor asked Elinor if I was her grandmother, and Elinor, who was very preoccupied with the whole question of belonging at that time, somewhat fiercely replied, 'That is *not* my Grandma!' When another instructor asked the same question, Elinor (who was five at the time) lost her patience and said, slowly and emphatically, 'She's. No. Grandma!' Thereafter, for a few years, those three words, *'She's No Grandma!'* became a catchphrase for the three of us and a shorthand reference to me and my role in their lives. Nowadays, however, Elinor no longer needs to define my role in her life. After the first few years, when I visited them once a fortnight and kept in touch with them regularly by telephone, the frequency of my visits diminished, and today they are less lonely and leading a normal, routine lifestyle. However, I still ring them from time to time and talk with them over the phone and occasionally meet or go out with them. To this day, however, Elinor has not fully come to terms with the irregularity of my visits, although I always consult them before turning up, and occasionally plan joint activities with her, such as attending various shows. She always receives me with a frown on her face, a vestige, perhaps, of the many forced partings she had to endure in the past, and only relaxes and becomes friendly after a while.

My ongoing contact with Elinor and her mother has provided an opportunity to examine the validity of the expert opinions presented in Rachel's case during the legal proceedings over Elinor's custody, both mine and those of the two preceding expert witnesses. Rachel, as we recall, was assessed as having only 'borderline intellectual capacity', and her difficulties were thought to be indicative of an 'antisocial personality with elements of borderline personality disorder and a dependent obsessive-compulsive personality disorder'. This opinion was delivered in the early stages of her rehabilitation from drug addiction. Drug addiction is often seen as indicative of an antisocial personality, but once she had recovered from it, it was a stretch to see how that definition could still apply to her, and to view her undoubted manipulative abilities, for example, which are often essential when one is dependent on public services, as a form of antisocial behaviour. The underestimation of her intellectual capacity was perhaps affected by her limited knowledge, but failed to give credit for the considerable intelligence she displays when organising her life, particularly with regard to social relationships. Her social skills mask her cognitive difficulties, which might be mistaken for a borderline personality, and what was defined as an 'obsessive-compulsive disorder' might explain her occasional dogged determination to pursue the priorities that she sets herself, but also her abilities as a hard worker, a single breadwinner and mother seeking to provide a stable and predictable environment for her daughter. While she is inclined to seek an authoritative figure to depend on in times of crisis, a trait said to be a sign of a 'dependent personality' in the opinions of the other experts, she demonstrated considerable independence and courage when she established a home and family at a fairly late age. However, even if we apply the broadest possible interpretation to these assessments of Rachel's personality and the manner in which she raises her daughter, and even if we were to endorse the validity of the classifications applied to her, it is clear that we cannot draw unequivocal conclusions from them as to her ability to raise her daughter, as one must when such assessments serve the basis for an irreversible court ruling. It is not the accuracy of the classification that rules it out as a valid basis for evaluating a parent's ability to raise their child, but the fallacy of trying to deduce from a person's attributes how they might conduct themselves down the road. Rather, that conduct is largely determined by the person's life circumstances and their relationship with others, who are also affected by it in return.

In light of my acquaintance with Rachel, I was able to examine my own initial estimation of her ability to raise Elinor, based on the degree to which she understood her role as a mother and her relationship with her daughter. I now realised that Rachel displays great responsibility towards Elinor, even though the child's needs often mean that she must forgo satisfying her own. Nonetheless, Elinor can still be a very trying girl at times. Her frustration threshold is low, and she is inclined to furious outbursts, mainly towards her mother, and this can often easily turn into a form of tyranny. On one of these occasions, Rachel had to stop herself from phoning me to ask that I come and take Elinor. 'Don't do anything you might regret later', she told herself. This was likely not the only time that she felt this way. She constantly shifted between patience – confirming my assessment that she understood the meaning of the responsibility that she had taken upon herself – and grounding or punishing Elinor out of anger and offence, which reflects her tendency to be self-absorbed (which I had also noted during the observations). However, when she is not angry, Elinor's demands have also been helpful to her, as they serve as a guide as to how to act, thanks to her ability to identify with her daughter's needs. After Elinor's tenth birthday, Rachel told me that the days leading up to the celebration were very difficult. 'I forget that when she's excited, she tends to fly off the handle', she said.

Her innate generosity also leads her to give Elinor encouragement and help her overcome hurdles. For example, when Elinor refused to show me her first report card, which was not very good, Rachel astutely persuaded her by asking her, 'But we have to show Mili your report card – how else will she know that you've improved next term?' Elinor's occasionally harsh responses to her mother may, of course, spring, in part, from her resentment over the difficult experiences she went through in the first years of her life, due to Rachel's drug addiction (a fact that she learned about during their time at the hostel) or perhaps because of the disappearance of her foster parents from her life. Her low frustration threshold may also have a physiological component – the product of a premature birth and exposure to illegal drugs during Rachel's pregnancy.[58]

Rachel's perceptiveness towards Elinor and her ability to understand her difficulties, which struck me when I first assessed her, were also apparent on many occasions. Thus, some six months after they had left the hostel, when their apartment had been flooded during heavy rainfall, she decided of her own initiative to move out within twenty-four hours. Elinor got into the spirit of things and helped a great deal. In the evening, when all their belongings had been moved to the new apartment, Elinor took her dog onto her lap, hugged it and said, 'Now I just want to cry', and burst into tears. The mother, realising that this was her daughter's way of relieving the tension that had built up over the move, which naturally filled her with anxiety, let her cry until she had calmed down, but when she told me about it she was full of admiration for Elinor's ability to articulate her feelings. I, for my part, admired Rachel's perceptiveness. I also greatly admire her ability to provide Elinor with the support that she needs due to her harsh mood swings. In one of these moments, a few weeks after she had been returned to her mother, when Elinor cried in frustration and anger about something, Rachel suggested that she lie down and put her head on her lap, while she stroked it and said to her, 'You had a nice day today: you had a celebration at the kindergarten, and now we're going on a trip', and Elinor's bawling soon subsided, and she calmed down. On other occasions, Rachel proved that she was able both to empathise with Elinor and play the role of the responsible adult. On one notable occasion, two days after Elinor's sixth birthday, I came to fetch them for a Saturday drive to see some wild flowers. Elinor insisted on wearing one of the smart dresses that she had received for her birthday. Rachel advised her not to go out in that dress, but Elinor ignored her. As she climbed up a hill, Elinor was stung by a nettle and began to cry. The mother took her into her arms and said, 'I told you that you shouldn't wear a dress like that for such trip, didn't I?' She then asked if we could go back to the car so that Elinor could change into a tracksuit that she had brought along precisely for such an eventuality (without telling Elinor or me).

This ability to work out what to allow Elinor and how to compensate for the child's lack of judgement characterised Rachel's mothering in the first years after Elinor had returned to her care. However, as the years went by, the flare-ups between them became more frequent, with Elinor expressing her dependency by endlessly criticising her mother, and Rachel, feeling that she had no choice, giving in to Elinor's demands, even when it was against her better judgement, until finally she lost her patience and snapped. This scenario is not uncommon in mother–daughter relationships during puberty, but it was very hard on Elinor who, because of her low frustration threshold, needs predictable and stable responses. Their living conditions were also not conducive to reducing the tension, with Rachel struggling to make a living, while Elinor spent her time alone at home after school. It meant that Rachel often felt as though she could not provide Elinor with a supportive environment, and she feared that the continual quarrelling that had begun to take hold of their relationship might undermine Elinor's development. For this reason, Rachel thought it best to send Elinor to a residential centre, which, she believed, would provide her with a protective environment while allowing her to stay close by.

On Loss and Belonging

On the face of it, Rachel's placing of Elinor in a residential centre was confirmation of the prevailing belief within the SSC that 'all children who are not given to adoptive families and returned to their parents end up being sent away from home',[59] and that court decisions to return children to their birth parents' care are wrong. Setting aside the fact that many adopted children end up being sent to institutions as well,[60] in Elinor's case we can examine this claim in light of the circumstances in which her mother decided to put her there. Specifically, Rachel's decision is indicative of the huge impact that living circumstances have on a parent's ability to raise their child, and on their relationship. Rachel found it difficult to balance her own needs, as a single breadwinner who also wanted an intimate relationship with someone, with providing for Elinor's needs. While she would have preferred merely to send Elinor to a day centre, this had been closed down in the wake of budgetary cuts, and she was under pressure to accept the residential option because the social worker at the local welfare office told her that if she did not take advantage of the one place left at that establishment, the welfare office would not be able to help her should difficulties arise later in the year. After a year at the residential centre, Elinor had calmed down a great deal, and made very good progress at school. Rachel thought of bringing her back home as the next school year approached, but then discovered that at the junior high school that Elinor was about to enter, the school day ended early while Rachel was still working until the early evening every day. This meant that once again Elinor would have found herself at home alone for hours on end, precisely in a period of transition, which is always difficult for her. Once again, therefore, circumstances dictated that the residential centre option was the best practical solution.

Given the impact of the sociocultural context on Elinor's life, I am often reminded of what Dorit, Elinor's foster mother, had told me, somewhat reprovingly, in our final telephone conversation: 'That girl had a chance'. Her words reverberated in my thoughts for a long time afterwards, making me wonder on more than one occasion whether Elinor had in fact been done a disservice by being returned to her mother. I presume that Dorit was suggesting that Rachel might once again relapse into drug addiction, which did not happen. However, there is no denying that, had Elinor stayed with the foster parents, she would have had the chance for a more solid and broad-based education that would have allowed her to develop her intellectual abilities and artistic talents and enrich her life. It was with great sadness, therefore, that I watched Elinor's considerable curiosity that I had noted at the start of our acquaintance gradually grow dimmer to the point of extinction. Rachel is aware that she can provide her daughter with few educational opportunities, but does not attempt to change the situation, which is similar to her own childhood. She shows little interest in anything that does not have an immediate bearing on solving the problems in her daily life. As she admitted, Elinor occasionally mentioned with some wistfulness the range of extracurricular activities that she enjoyed taking part in when they lived in the big city. Elinor avidly attends dance classes, and occasionally expresses genuine wonder when confronted with something of artistic merit. While watching *The Sound of Music*, for example, she sat awestruck, saying softly at the end of the first song, 'That was beautiful!'

The paucity of opportunities offered by growing up with her mother was given less weight, in the court's ruling, than the decision to cherish the sense of Elinor's belonging to her birth family. This is in recognition of the possibility that, had she been given up to a closed adoption, the disappearance of her mother from her life would have left her with a permanent sense of loss.[61] This choice was put in the court ruling itself:

> The impression is that this is a girl with great potential, who, in order to fulfil herself, needs a fertile soil – i.e. parents who are also well educated and financially secure, who can give her the basis for good development. In this respect, Elinor's best interests lie in growing up in the foster home. On the other hand, progress and intellectual development are just one of many facets of a person's makeup. It is hard to believe that a child can grow up to become a happy and mentally adjusted human being when the only solid ground that they know is pulled out from under them, and they are cut off from their roots. Elinor has a mother whom she misses desperately, which she expresses by every possible means, and we cannot know for certain that, had [her mother] succumbed to the request to have Elinor declared eligible for adoption, she would not have grown into a permanently frustrated person, forever seeking the mother she loved and who never stopped caring for her.

The significance that her mother's disappearance from her life held for Elinor was evident in something she said shortly after being returned to her mother. On their way to kindergarten one day, she quietly sang a song to herself that she had learned at the children's home, '*My Mother is So, So Dear to Me*', and immediately burst into tears, saying, 'You were sick, and it was very sad'. On another occasion – with the encouragement of the psychologist who was treating them at the time – Elinor turned to her mother and said, 'I want you to tell me why you left me'. At the same time, Elinor was very aggrieved by the disappearance of her foster parents. 'I only want to visit them!', she begged. Perhaps to protect their memory from her anger, she clung fervently to the belief that it was the judge who prohibited her from visiting them, and toyed with the idea of running away to them after she and her mother had left the hostel. Her cravings for the food at the foster parents' home dogged her for years after she had returned to her mother, who in turn made an effort to make her the same kind of dishes, at Elinor's request. That said, a few months after returning to her mother, Elinor also recalled less favourable memories of her time with the foster family. During one of our joint days out together, she suddenly told us, while holding Rachel's hand and mine, that 'Mummy Dorit' allowed her to light Sabbath candles, and her long hair had caught fire for a moment. On another occasion, when I brought her a present on her fifth birthday, she burst into tears and said that when she was with the foster family they had celebrated her birthday together with Haggai's – 'and I wasn't his age, and he wasn't my age!', she wailed bitterly. Perhaps raising these memories precisely during moments of intimacy with her mother and me allowed her to conjure up experiences that she had had with her foster parents, which, as with any relationship, were fraught with difficulties, instead of the idealised image that had been magnified by her inability to visit them. Once she had developed an intimacy with her mother, she appears to have been gradually able to emotionally let go of the foster parents who had vanished from her life, instead of fixating on what she felt was a punitive ban on seeing them.

In the first two years after returning to her mother, Elinor would tell new acquaintances that she had been with another family, and pointed out that she had 'another mother', but as time went on, she stopped mentioning them. After five years, she suddenly asked to look at the album of pictures they had given her when she left them. At first, there appeared to be no specific trigger for her request, but it was on the New Year, and Rachel, with her great sensitivity, pointed out to her brother, 'Look: it was just at this time that she came back to me', which indeed was the case. She intuitively understood that Elinor's request was an 'anniversary reaction', a well-known human response on the anniversaries of significant events.[62]

Rachel tried to preserve the traces of the foster parents in Elinor's life. Several years after Elinor had returned to her care, she asked me to contact them, but I could not help her. My contact with them had continued only for a short time after Elinor's return to her mother. Thanks to their decency and honesty, I had formed a productive and useful relationship with them, even though they knew that it was my expert opinion that led to them having to part with Elinor. They used to phone me every week, and, with Rachel's permission, I would give them reports on how Elinor was doing. These conversations proved to be very useful, as they would provide tips on Elinor's daily habits. However, after a few weeks, Dorit rang me, very upset and hurt, after the adoption officials had forwarded to them the long and detailed report I had written about Elinor's return to her mother (this was a violation of confidentiality, since it had been addressed to the court and should not have been shown to them, as they were not a party to the proceedings). Although I had not presented them in a negative light – on the contrary, I greatly appreciated the sensitive way in which they tried to help Elinor part with them – they were not the intended recipients of the document, and I had not taken special care to avoid offending their sensibilities. Reading the report while still feeling the pain of separation from Elinor heightened their sense of injury, and after that they stopped phoning me, and contact with them was lost.

As Elinor's *bat mitzvah* (twelfth birthday) approached, her mother toyed with the idea of inviting the foster parents, as a way of celebrating Elinor's life while acknowledging the role they had played in her early years, but in the years since Elinor had asked to look again at the album of her time there, she no longer mentioned them, and when asked about them, said that she had no memories of that period. When I invited her to ask me questions about that time, a smile lit up her face, but she couldn't think of anything to ask me, neither then nor since. It is unclear whether the repeated difficulties that arose between Elinor and her mother were precipitated by traces of the period in which she experienced a double loss – first that of her mother, then of her foster parents. Both were superfluous losses that led to avoidable suffering.[63]

Elinor's preoccupation with the question of belonging to her family – which at first involved distinguishing her connection with her birth mother from that with her foster mother, as evident in statements such as 'I didn't know that you were my real mum', or 'I just thought that I had two mothers'[64] – was most apparent in the relationship she forged with her father, Meir. As previously noted, during the proceedings the father had stayed away and tried not to be involved, but connecting with him was important to establishing the genealogical connection in Elinor's life. Once Rachel regained custody of Elinor, she tried to get the father involved in raising her. To help Elinor maintain her connection with her father, Rachel made sure that she used her father's surname, rather than her own, as stated on Elinor's birth certificate. To this end, she enlisted the father's cooperation, and got him to agree to his name being registered in Elinor's documents.

Within a few weeks of leaving the hostel, while they were still living in the big city far from where the father lived, Elinor asked her mother if it was okay to invite her father to spend the Saturday with them. This embarrassed Rachel, as the invitation would have entailed him staying over on Friday night (public transport in Israel does not operate over the Sabbath), and she had no intention of renewing her relationship with him. She agreed nonetheless, seeing how important it was for Elinor. During his visit, Elinor played the perfect hostess. Seeing herself as the one responsible for providing him with hospitality, she gave him a tour of the various venues of her life – the kindergarten and the playground that she would often go to with her mother – while he and Rachel took care not to treat it as a joint date of their own. A few weeks later, Meir invited Elinor and her mother to spend the weekend at the rented apartment that he shared with two students as part of his own rehabilitation programme.

The relationship between Elinor and her father did not live up to these hopeful beginnings. Once she had established the connection with him, Elinor allowed herself to lash out at him over every frustration, and he, not having the same patience as her mother, responded by backing off. Rachel does not appreciate his responses. At times, she is angry at what she sees as limited financial help on his part in raising Elinor, nor does she refrain from telling Elinor what she thinks about him. Nonetheless, when the father invited Elinor to celebrate the Passover Seder with his family, Rachel sent her along with a change of clothes in case she chose to stay the night there, but reminded her that she could also return home at any time if she so chose. Elinor, too, oscillated between being offended and distancing herself from her father and renewing contact with him of her own accord. These repeated initiatives of hers eventually helped Meir to stay in touch, since before this he had never been in a relationship where he was the responsible adult in charge of a child, and it wasn't easy for him to play the role of father. When Rachel went into hospital for an operation, Elinor stayed with a next-door neighbour; Meir made no special effort, not even visiting or enquiring after her.

However, since Elinor's move to the residential centre close to the mother's house, there has been a considerable change in her relationship with her father. He is often invited over for lunch on Saturdays with Elinor and her mother, and invites Elinor to his family's events, or to spend time with him. When Elinor broke her leg at school, and Rachel, who works out of town, could not arrive immediately, he rushed to her aid and took her to a doctor. In the following days, when Elinor was confined to bed and Rachel had to go to work, the father looked after her in their home. When Elinor celebrated her *bat mitzvah*, Meir took full part in planning the event and paying for expenses. By this time, it was clear that the decision to return Elinor to her mother's custody had ultimately also brought her father into her life.

Elinor's father and mother, respectively, represent two types of parenting. The father represents an acquired ability that emerges from, and is bolstered by, the relationship with the child; the mother, on the other hand, was blessed with a natural ability to balance identifying with Elinor's needs and her own role, as an adult, responding to those needs. She serves as Elinor's 'safe base from which to explore',[65] for example when she supports her wish to spend time away from home, while reminding her that she can return home at any time. While Rachel's abilities sometimes fail her in the face of Elinor's outbursts, she recovers and makes herself available once more to help her daughter.

In my description of Elinor's return to her family, her two parents' rehabilitation may have come across as self-evident, but it is worthy of special emphasis. Rachel and Meir, who from a young age had lived outside the law and on the margins of society, are examples of successful rehabilitation. As Elinor grows up, I hope she will learn to appreciate the courage and determination that they needed to rebuild their lives. By now, her sense of belonging to her family often helps her to overcome her fits of frustration and anger, both her anger over her parents' past, and the typical upheavals of adolescence.

Family

The story of Elinor's return to her mother challenges the idea that the key criterion when assessing a child's best interests is whether or not a family is a 'standard' one.[66] The family of Elinor and her mother also includes Rachel's elder son, who grew up in children's homes. Over the years, Rachel's relationship with her elder son, who is financially well-to-do and works with his father in his father's business, has grown much closer. When his girlfriend became pregnant with his child, Rachel, unlike his father, supported his decision to marry her. 'Even if it turns out to be a mistake, I'll support you', she promised him. He now has two children, and Rachel and her daughter-in-law have a warm relationship. She visits her grandchildren, who live in another town, at least once a fortnight, and often has them over to her place. In the meantime, Rachel's other daughter, the one whom she gave up for adoption in the depths of her drug addiction, has also joined the family. The SSC delayed the daughter's request to meet with Rachel for over a year ('Think very carefully if you want to do this – then come back to us'),[67] but when she turned nineteen, it finally allowed her to contact her. Their first meeting, which took place, as usual, at the offices of the SSC, was emotional. The two have since formed a close bond, despite the SSC's attempts to undermine the relationship by giving the daughter false information (for example about her father's background), and warning her not to give her address or phone number to her mother. The daughter has been accepted into Rachel's family, is invited to family events, and keeps in touch with her elder brother. She, they learned, had been sent to a residential centre by her adoptive family. When she met Rachel, she was already married; since then she has divorced, and has had a son out of wedlock. She raises him by herself, but lives near her adoptive parents, with whom Rachel is on good terms. She avoids calling Rachel 'Mum' or even using her first name, a reluctance that Rachel understands and ignores. Meanwhile, Meir's eldest daughter has also joined the family since he re-established contact with her, and he occasionally spends time with her son, his grandson.

Elinor's *bat mitzvah* celebration was a unifying experience. The degree of cooperation between the parents was evident, in part, in the handsome invitation they sent out, in which they appear together under the father's surname (which, as previously noted, is also Elinor's). To fulfil Elinor's dream of having a celebration in an event hall with all the usual bells and whistles, Rachel worked overtime, cleaning schools as well as her usual work, to pay the deposit. At the reception, mother and father stood on either side of Elinor, three good-looking, smartly dressed people, to welcome the guests. All the family members arrived for the event, including the daughter who had been given up for adoption (who arrived with her baby daughter and adoptive mother), and Meir's eldest daughter. At the candle-lighting ceremony, Elinor gave the first candle-lighting honour to her maternal grandmother, who cared for her in her infancy, followed by her paternal grandmother, her elder half-brother and her elder half-sister, and, of course, her parents. For me, this ceremony was a consecration of the family framework that had formed following Elinor's return to her parents' lives.

This account is not intended as a challenge to the conventional view that children must not be sacrificed for the sake of their parents' lives, but to point out the lack of compassion inherent in the notion that 'the best interests of the child' and 'parental rights' are inherently contradictory,[68] which underpins the alacrity to prescribe adoption rather than other solutions whenever parents have difficulties raising their children. It is difficult to say to what extent Elinor's presence in her mother's life helped Rachel to reconnect with her eldest son or with the daughter she had given up for adoption and her adoptive parents, or whether Meir might have summoned up the courage to reconnect with his eldest daughter if he had not experienced fatherhood with Elinor. The contribution that children can bring to their parents' own development is precluded and denied when the state sees fit to intervene in situations where parents encounter difficulties, or are perceived to fail. In such situations, any protest against the severing of ties between parents and children, and its attendant consequences, is presented as an attempt to sacrifice the children for the sake of the parents, and ignoring 'the best interests of the child'. Elinor's story demonstrates how misguided such generalisations can be, and the destructive chain reaction they can generate, ultimately to the detriment of the child's life as well. If Elinor had not been returned to her mother's custody, we would never have known what the extent of the loss to Elinor and her family members would have been.

The story of Elinor's return to her family reveals what a family is really all about. The absence of a 'standard family' framework has not prevented Elinor from having family relationships that have successfully grappled with, and withstood, crises, failures, separation, disappointments and loss. The lesson of her life experience is that the sense of belonging to a family is an unconditional one, and rooted in mutual commitment. It is this belonging, rather than any measure of 'normality', that represents the true meaning of 'family'. The destructive effect of the alternative – not having such a belonging – is described in the next chapter.

Notes

1. Pursuant to the Law 3(b).
2. John Bowlby, *Attachment, Vol. 1* (London: Pimlico, 1997), 299–330.
3. ACL 12(c).
4. There is no empirical evidence for this premise. Although there is general agreement that the manner in which a parent cares for their child contributes to the child's development and affects it, there is no substantiation for the claim that it determines the child's development. See Arnold J. Sameroff and Michael J. Chandler, 'Reproductive Risk and the

Continuum of Caretaking Casualty', in Frances D. Horowitz (ed.), *Review of Child Development Research,* Vol. 4 (Chicago,IL: University of Chicago Press, 1975), 187–244.

5. *The Committee of the Rights of the Child,* UN Human Rights Office of the High Commissioner General, Comment no. 13 (2011), 'The Right of the Child to Freedom from All Forms of Violence: "respect must be given to the least intrusive intervention as warranted by the circumstances'". (CCRC\C\gc | 13, 2011, Article 19, para. 54)
6. ACL 12(c1).
7. Strictly speaking, the full official name of such a family is a 'foster family with prospect of adoption', which, as the name suggests, means that it is designated, in due course, to adopt the child in question. For the sake of simplicity, I will henceforth refer to them simply as the 'foster family', 'foster parents', 'foster father' and 'foster mother', as appropriate.
8. In the adversarial approach, the parties in dispute are responsible for presenting all the evidence to be taken into consideration, and the judge serves as an arbitrator and decides which of the two claims is more credible.
9. Rom Harré and Paul Secord, 'Why Not Ask Them?' in Harré and Secord, *The Explanation of Social Behavior* (Oxford: Blackwell, 1972), 101–25.
10. *A Two Year Old Goes to Hospital,* film, by Joyce Robertson and James Robertson (London, 1952); Joyce Robertson and James Robertson, 'Young Children in Brief Separation: A Fresh Look', *Psychoanalytic Study of the Child* 26 (1971), 264–315.
11. Ophir, *The Order of Evils,* 89.
12. It was only twelve years later that I learned that Rachel had been told that Elinor had already been declared eligible for adoption, and that the proceedings in her case were purely a formality. Because of her ignorance of legal matters, Rachel believed this, and it was only in a casual conversation with me twelve years later that she learned she had been lied to.
13. This might be seen as an example of continuity that is sustained throughout the lifetime when a favoured daughter's feeling is re-enacted in the relationships she creates. In a study of the elements in a person's development that serve to predict or forecast their future life, continuity was found only in the pattern of relationships that the person creates. Michael Rutter, 'Continuities and Discontinuities in Socioemotional Development: Empirical and Conceptual Perspectives', in Robert N. Emde and Robert J. Harmon (eds), *Continuities and Discontinuities in Development* (New York: Plenum Press, 1978), 41–65.
14. ACL 13(7).
15. Theresa Benedek, 'Psychobiological Aspects of Mothering', *American Journal of Orthopsychiatry* 26 (1956), 272–78; Benedek, 'Motherhood and Nurturing', in James E. Anthony and Theresa Benedek (eds), *Parenthood: Its Psychology and Psychopathology* (Boston, MA: Little Brown, 1970), 153–66.
16. Mili Mass, 'Legal Parenthood and the Continued Parent–Child Relationship: The Moral and Experiential Aspects of Parenting', *Adoption Quarterly* 2 (1999), 39–69.

17. Hila Ha'elyon, *Adopted: The Adoption Experience from the Standpoint of Adopted Women in Israel* (Haifa: Pardes, 2010) [Hebrew].
18. Scott O. Lilienfeld, James M. Wood and Howard N. Garb, 'The Scientific Status of Projective Techniques', *Psychological Science in the Public Interest* 1 (2000), 27–66; Stephen A. Newman, 'Assessing the Quality of Expert Testimony in Cases Involving Children', *The Journal of Psychiatry and Law* 22 (1994), 181–235.
19. See discussion of this issue in Plato, 'Sophist', in his *Complete Works*, ed. John. M. Cooper (Cambridge: Hackett, 1997), 235–93. The ever-continuous classification is evident in the constant renewal of the DSM-IV-TR, *Diagnostic and Statistical Manual of Mental Disorders* (Washington, DC: American Psychiatric Association).
20. Moshe Almagor, 'The Place of the Clinical Psychologist in Assessing Parental Capability', *Psychology* 8(1) (1999), 39–49 [Hebrew]; David Yagil, 'Considerations and Uncertainties in Diagnosing Parental Capability', in Yagil et al. (eds), *Psychology, Law and Ethics in Israel: Psychological Evaluations, Psychotherapy and Judicial Decisions* (Tel Aviv: Probook, 2008), 183–205 [Hebrew].
21. Henceforth, whenever describing her life with the foster parents, I shall refer to her by that name.
22. Ophir, *The Order of Evils*, 91.
23. ACL 6.
24. The psychologist presumably cited the age of eighteen because that is the age when the law allows the adoptee to apply to the SSC directly about making contact with his or her birth parents. ACL 30(b).
25. This procedure is implemented through the appointment of special welfare officers under the ACL. See also Maimon, *Child Adoption Legislation*, 85 [Hebrew].
26. ACL 12(c[1]).
27. Mili Mass and Adi Ophir, 'Care, Supervision, and Abandonment: On Non-Consensual and Confidential Adoption', *Tel Aviv University Law Review* 29 (2006), 257–310 [Hebrew].
28. As previously noted, the court had been very explicit in its opinion, see Introduction to this volume: 'the father of orphans ... and no one else is entitled, for whatever reason, to create facts that will force us to decide based on them'. (CA 488/77)
29. For a more extensive description of this case, see Mass, 'Legal Parenthood', 48–53.
30. AF (Jerusalem District Court) 51/86, *A-G v Anon* (unpublished [15 March 1988]).
31. This type of adoption is discussed in Chapter 5 of this book.
32. Shifman, *Family Law in Israel*, 50.
33. In this case, too, the judge acted in accordance with the continental approach, whereby judges do not limit themselves to the facts presented by the parties in dispute, but seek the additional information they require to reach a decision. This is in contrast to the adversarial system normally practised in Israel.

34. Mass, 'Legal Parenthood', 53–59.
35. See, for example, CA 166/81/88, *Anon v A-G*, 9, verdict 36 (4) 321 (1982); CA 320/84, *Anon v A-G*, 9, verdict 38 (3) 419 (1984); CA 138/85, *Anon v A-G*, 9, verdict 39 (3) 631 (1985); CA 3236/90, *Anon v A-G*, 9, verdict 45 (3) 460 (1991); CA 6953/94, *Anon v A-G*, verdict 53 (3) 418 (1999).
36. AF (Rishon Lezion) 67/02, *Minor v A-G* (AF), LP (Legal Precedent) 2003 (2) 27, [1], 19(g), 20 (2003).
37. AF (Beer Sheba) 32/05, *Minor v A-G* (AF), para 7 (b,c,d,e) (unpublished), Nevo Archive (21 June 2006).
38. 'Adoption Narratives', *The Adoption History Project*, www.uoregon.edu/~-adoption/ (accessed 11 July 2007).
39. See E. Wayne Carp, *Family Matters: Secrecy and Disclosure in the History of Adoption* (Cambridge, MA: Harvard University Press, 1998), 133; John Tristeliotis, *In Search of Origins: The Experience of Adopted Children* (London: Routledge and Kegan Paul, 1973), 19; Maria Berger et al., 'Some Thoughts on the Question of When to Tell the Child that He Is Adopted', *Journal of Child Psychotherapy* 8 (1982), 67–88.
40. See Family Appeal Petition (FAP)377/05, *Anon and Anon Designated Adoptive Parents of Minor v Biological Parents et al.*, verdict 60 (1) 124, 169 (2005).
41. Judith Modell, *Kinship with Strangers: Adoption and Interpretation of Kinship in American Culture* (Berkeley, CA: University of California Press, 1994), 225–30. A fictional depiction of the reality of the adoptive family can be found in Shai Golden, *The Good Son* (Or-Yehudah: Zmora Bitan Dvir, 2008) [Hebrew], in which he calls his adoptive family environment – whose surname he bears – 'Goldenland'.
42. See above, Introduction to this volume. This procedure is documented in Ronit Krown Kertsner's film, *The Aforementioned Minor* (Israel, 2006) [Hebrew], in which a California woman who was adopted in her childhood speaks about her 'amended' birth certificate: 'It bothers me that two thirds of my birth certificate are a lie'.
43. Lihi Kander, *A Flower Named Sigal* (Tel Aviv: Tcherikover Publishers, 2000), 50.
44. Marshall D. Shechter and Doris Bertocci, 'The Meaning of the Search', in David M. Brodzinsky and Marshall D. Shechter (eds), *The Psychology of Adoption* (New York: Oxford University Press, 1990), 79.
45. FAP 778/09, *A-G v Anon and Lawyer Yaron Hod Legal Guardian Ad Litem for Minor*, 2009 (4) 3142 (SC), decision of Justice Arbel, para 49 (2009).
46. Ibid., decision of Justice Arbel, para 48 (2009).
47. Ibid., para 65.
48. Shifman, *Family Law in Israel*, 221.
49. Mass and Ophir, 'Care, Supervision and Abandonment'.
50. Neri Livneh, 'An Abandoned Baby from Africa', *Ha'aretz*: *Dad, Mum, and Me* (special supplement), 16 April 2003 [Hebrew].
51. In that conversation, the foster parents confirmed the information that I had given in court, thereby refuting the adoption official's claim that I had given a false account of what they had said to me.

52. Mary Main, 'Avoidance in the Service of Attachment: A Working Paper', in Klaus Immelman et al. (eds), *Behavioral Development: The Bielfield Interdisciplinary Project* (Cambridge: Cambridge University Press, 1982), 651–93.
53. 'The fact that children's welfare would undoubtedly be improved by their adoption has, historically, never been sufficient justification for their admission to the process.' Kerry O'Halloran, *The Politics of Adoption: International Perspectives on Law, Policy and Practice* (New York: Springer, 2009), 34.
54. Lenore Terr, *Too Scared to Cry* (New York: Harper and Row, 1990).
55. Mili Mass, 'The "Subject", the "Citizen", and the Failed Understanding of Responsibility', paper presented at the conference *A Second Look at the Practice of Casework*, Paul Baerwald School of Social Work and Social Welfare, Hebrew University, Jerusalem, 13 November 2005.
56. Mass and Ophir, 'Care, Supervision and Abandonment', and see Chapter 3.
57. However, I finished writing Elinor's story when she turned twelve.
58. On the notion that the frustration threshold of some children inherently takes longer to mature, see Ross W. Greene, *The Explosive Child* (New York: Harper Collins Publishers, 1998). This book helped me understand Elinor's outbursts, and I read the author's suggestions on how to deal with the difficulties presented by such a child together with Rachel, who learned to try and reduce the number of situations in which her daughter's low frustration threshold is tested – contrary to common belief that, for a child like this, it is important to set clear limits.
59. Yaffa Glick, 'Double Agent', *Tsomet Hasharon*, 24 June 2004 [Hebrew].
60. The number of adopted children sent to residential centres has not been systematically documented, but one study found that 19 per cent of the children whose adoptive parents were interviewed were sent to institutions for various periods. See Dori Rivkin and Shoshana Baumgold, *Follow-Up of Older Children Who Have Been Adopted* (Jerusalem: Myers-JDC-Brookdale Institute, 2001) [Hebrew]; see also Chapter 4: Interlude.
61. Haim Walder, 'Please Do Not Uproot What is Planted: The Story of an Adopted Child Who Has Grown Up', in Walder, *People Speaking about Themselves: Life Stories* (Bnei Brak: Sifriati Publishing, 2002), 82–91 [Hebrew]. The 2002 Adoption of Children Act (UK) lists the considerations to which the court must have regard, including 'the likely (lifelong) effect on the child (throughout life) of having ceased to be a member of his original family and become an adopted person. This novel requirement imposes on the court the duty to take a long-term view of whether adoption will continue to meet the needs of the subject throughout his adult life…' (1(4[c]).
62. See Josephine R. Hilgard, 'Anniversary Reaction in Parent Precipitated by Children', *Psychiatry* 16 (1953), 73–86.
63. Ophir, *The Order of Evils*, 317.
64. This remark by Elinor reveals a situation that is described in the professional literature, in which adoptees live with two sets of parents: the real (the adoptive parents) and the imaginary (the birth parents). Paul M. Brinich,

'Some Potential Effects of Adoption on Self and Object Representation', *The Psychoanalytic Study of the Child* 35 (1980), 107–34; Steven L. Nickman, 'Losses in Adoption: The Need for Dialogue', *The Psychoanalytic Study of the Child* 40 (1985), 365–98; Murray Ryburn, 'Identity Formation', in Ryburn, *Open Adoption: Research, Theory and Practice* (Aldershot: Avebury, 1994), 21–32.

65. Mary D. Slater Ainsworth, *Infancy in Uganda: Infant Care and the Growth of Love* (Baltimore, MD: The Johns Hopkins University Press, 1967), 332.
66. Ayelet Blecher-Prigat, 'On Rights, Boundaries, and Family', *Tel Aviv University Law Review* 27(2) (2004), 539–86 [Hebrew].
67. The ACL authorises the Chief Adoption Officer to allow the adoptee, on reaching the age of eighteen, to inspect their adoption file (ACL 30[3(b)]). For more on how this part of the law is implemented, see Ruth Zafran, 'The Right of the Adoptee to Track Down the Identity of His Biological Parents: A Critical Observation from a Comparative Viewpoint', *Family in Law* 1 (2007), 225–55 [Hebrew].
68. Shifman, *Family Law in Israel*, 217.

3

From the 'Best Interests of the Child' to the 'Wilderness Generation'

The Story of Dalit and Her Daughter Tal

Child Protection

'Who are you anyway?' This is how Dalit interpreted the responses of her pre-verbal, two-and-a-half-year-old daughter Tal, who had been returned to her following a legal custody battle that had gone on for nearly two years. This interpretation was not accidental. Dalit herself had been adopted in her infancy, and with these words she expressed both the erasure of her own identity and genealogical ties,[1] and the grievous blow to her motherhood inflicted by the authorities' attempt to make her redundant and remove her from her daughter's life.

The story of Dalit's feeling of being redundant is representative of the 'wilderness generation' ethos that prevails in adoption practice in Israel, and which dominated educational thinking during the *yishuv* period (the pre-independence Zionist Jewish community in Palestine, 1882–1948) and in the early years of Israel's existence as an independent state. Of all the interpretations of the story of the Israelites wandering in the wilderness for forty years, Zionism chose to embrace the one that states that the Promised Land could be conquered only by the generation that had been born free, that is, after the Exodus from Egypt, and that those who had lived as slaves in Egypt had to die out in the wilderness.[2] This interpretation was consistent with the glorification of the *yishuv*, which was usually coupled with a commensurate depreciation of the Jewish diaspora tradition and which dominated educational thinking and immigration absorption policy at the time. To this end, the bonds between children and their parents had to be loosened.[3] And indeed, the redundancy of the parents, and cutting off of children from their cultural legacy, was a persistent theme in the assimilation of immigrants in the country.

Traces of the loss that these children experienced came to light publicly only many years later, after they had grown up.[4] Only then was the term 'the wilderness generation' discarded. Its replacement, the principle of 'the best interests of the child', which has governed child welfare policy in Israel since the late 1970s, represents a departure from the view that the parents' role must be rejected simply by dint of their generational affiliation; instead, social services limit their intervention to instances where the child's welfare is compromised (at least in the eyes of the authorities). However, the potency of the ideology that equates protection of the child with rejection of the parents remained unchanged, and is clearly evident in the Adoption of Children Law passed in 1960 and in its revised version of 1981. This reflects the hegemony of the secular Jewish (i.e. Zionist)[5] approach, which explicitly rejects the traditional Judaic dictum that 'although it is a *mitzvah* [good deed, commandment] to raise an orphan in one's home, adoption does not make the orphan the adopter's child'.[6] Moreover, the modern Adoption of Children Law that has been in place since 1960 prescribes as default the most extreme form of adoption: closed adoption. The application of the 'best interests of the child' principle within the Adoption of Children Law effectively continues the previous, pre-independence tradition in which the idea of state protection is focused on the child, rather than on his relationship with his parents.

The evolution of the policy of child protection from 'the wilderness generation' notion to 'the best interests of the child' is evident in Dalit's story, albeit in reverse order (hence the order of their appearance in the chapter title). As a child, she was adopted following the state's petition to the courts, on the grounds that it was in her 'best interests', but when she grew up and became a mother herself, she was designated a member of 'the wilderness generation', and the state petitioned for her removal from her daughter's life, once again on the grounds of 'the best interests of the child'.

Dalit's Childhood and Youth

I learned the story of Dalit's childhood in her own words after being appointed by the court as an expert witness on her behalf, and I recount it here in chronological order, as I reconstructed it, rather than in the order in which it was revealed to me in the course of the legal proceedings.

Dalit was adopted at the age of fifteen months. She knew nothing about the circumstances of her adoption other than the fact that her mother had been addicted to drugs. She did not even know where she lived prior to being adopted.[7] Whether her mother voluntarily gave her up for adoption, or was forced to do so, Dalit's adoption was clearly carried out on the principle of the best interests of the child, that is, to grant her a family. Her adoptive parents were already raising another adopted child, a boy, four years her senior.

When she was in Grade 1 at school, Dalit told her parents that her classmates were making fun of her for being adopted. Her parents suggested that she tell them that while they had only one family, she had two, and that, unlike them, she had been *chosen* by her parents. In years to come, this explanation led Dalit to feel guilty for having failed to meet her parents' expectations.

Dalit always felt that her grandmother, her adoptive father's mother, really loved her. The grandmother lived with them, and would visit the kindergarten during the day and watch Dalit play. When Dalit began attending school, which was situated opposite their house, the grandmother used to go out to the balcony and wave to her at recess. She felt that her father loved her too, and preferred her over her brother, while her mother preferred her brother. The father used to take her to the zoo, and on school holidays would let her come with him to his place of work. Nonetheless, her special bond was with her grandmother.

When Dalit was nine years old, as she recalled, she arrived at school one day bruised: her mother had hit her. Her father knew about this and tried to make it up to her. A year and a half later, Dalit underwent psychological tests and was found to have a learning disability. Although certain treatments were prescribed, including family therapy, it is difficult to determine from Dalit's account if these were indeed acted upon. In any event, throughout that period, the physical abuse by her mother never ceased, and to make matters worse, her adoptive brother began sexually abusing her as well. She told no one about this. On one occasion, she told her mother that her brother had been touching her inappropriately, but the mother refused to believe her, so she said no more about it. She was angry at her parents whenever they left her alone with her brother. Only one social worker suspected that her brother had been abusing her: when she drew her family members, she placed a large 'X' over his character. But when the social worker advised Dalit to file a complaint with the police, Dalit denied the matter and stopped seeing the social worker. Since the abuse occurred within the family, she was ashamed about it, and did not see it as a form of rape.

With hindsight, Dalit dates the final rift in her relationship with her parents to the death of her grandmother. When she was twelve years old, she returned home from school and saw obituary notices, which she was barely able to read. Finally, she guessed that her grandmother had died, and that she had already missed the funeral. Two weeks later, she celebrated her *bat mitzvah* with her friends, but after the party she felt that no one cared about her anymore, so she hid in the stairwell of their apartment building to see if anyone would come looking for her. Her father did look for her several times, but eventually gave up, she said, so she ran away to her friend's house and began wandering the streets. After a few weeks of living on the streets and engaging in various acts of delinquency, social services transferred her, at the behest of the juvenile court, to a youth home for delinquent girls. She spent the next three and a half years in institutions of this sort. In recounting her story to me later, she mentioned her adoptive parents very little in relation to this period, and it seems as though – from her point of view at least – they were largely absent from her life during this time.

Dalit was alarmed by what she saw at these institutions, including acts of violence and suicide attempts, and as she stayed there her behaviour began to deteriorate. As she put it, one must go along with delinquent norms of behaviour to survive in such places. If she refused, she was forced to serve the girls who had leadership status. As one of the girls deemed to be, in her words, 'a troublemaker', she was confined to the 'secure wing' throughout her stay at the institution, unlike other girls, who were kept there only for a few weeks or months, at most. However, as she saw it, life in the secure wing actually helped her adjust to the institution and to make some progress. In the institution's report about Dalit, this period is described as follows:

> It is possible to see, in the past few months, a process of calming down, moderation and stability in Dalit's behaviour and function. Her willingness and readiness to change are apparent at the group level – by giving up the prestigious status [of leader] with all its attendant benefits – and

> at the personal level, in her summoning up huge strength to file a complaint of rape [against her brother]. …
>
> Since the last discussion, Dalit has been following the rules, carrying out her duties, obeying authority, knows how to listen and to receive criticism … Dalit is liked and respected by the various staff … Dalit's status in the group is good and solid.

While at the institution, Dalit trained to become a hairdresser. At this time, there was still some contact between her and her adoptive parents. They used to visit her at the institution, although she did not visit them on holidays. She still felt a special bond with her father, while her mother continued to favour her brother, who by this time, she told me, was in prison for robbery and rape. During one of the visits, she told her parents about how he had sexually abused her. Her mother still refused to believe her, just as she had refused to accept it when he was tried and convicted for rape.

When Dalit turned sixteen, the court order expired and Dalit was released from the institution. She began wandering the streets of an area populated by ethnic minorities, mainly Arabs, who lived on the margins of society. She began spending most of her time with them, abusing drugs, and was eventually sent to a rehab centre. There she encountered people who were addicted to hard drugs, and, seeing the effects of withdrawal symptoms, fled the centre shortly afterwards, for fear that she too might end up that way. In one session with a social worker, she said that she missed her time at the youth home, so she was sent back there. This time she arrived of her own volition, so there were no restrictions placed on her actions; she broke all the rules, resulting in her being expelled and ending up back on the streets. In the wake of (unfounded) suspicions that she was involved in crime, the police turned up at her adoptive parents' door. Although she was subsequently acquitted of all charges, her father never forgave her for the 'disgrace' that she had brought upon the family, and Dalit, when recounting this period of her life later, justified his reaction: 'They did me a favour by adopting me, and I repaid them badly'. When I met her, about two years later, she still regretted hurting her father. She accepted her adoptive parents' refusal to have anything more to do with her with a mixture of justification and confirmation of the suspicion that had dogged her throughout her childhood, that she was never really important to them.

Dalit's perception of her adoption as a 'favour' done to her by her adoptive parents is perhaps the most telling testimony of its failure, as the whole purpose of a closed adoption, which entirely severs all contact between the adopted child and their birth parents, is to make the child feel that they are as much a part of the adoptive family as a child born to it.[8] Adopted children who do not feel that they truly belong to the adoptive family or who, for various reasons, like Dalit, do not grow up in it, are therefore wronged twice: once when they are cut off from their birth family and from their genealogical ties, and again when they are shunned by the adoptive family.

Realising the Principle of the 'Best Interests of the Child'

The attempt to protect Dalit through adoption had failed. It is difficult to prevent failures in adoption, since the selection of an adoptive family is carried out in a type of simulated environment, before it is known which child will be placed with the family. Although the law requires the adoption order to be issued no earlier than six months after the child has been placed with the new family, to ensure that the placement is suited to the child, in practice, only in particularly difficult cases is a child removed from his designated adoptive family after being there six months or more. Moreover, what Dalit described as physical abuse by her adoptive mother likely did not begin during the trial period; the dynamic nature of any parenting relationship, including that of adoptive parents, emerges as the relationship with the child evolves. Given all this, one might question the considerable investment that the state puts into selecting adoptive parents, and the stress and anxiety induced by these selection tests. Instead, it may be more appropriate to use much broader criteria for selection, such as whether the lifestyle of the designated family is indicative of good judgement and an ability to forge meaningful relationships.[9] Removing the presumption involved in the present lengthy and complex selection procedure would foster greater willingness to recognise failures, and to deal with their consequences. In Dalit's case, this did not happen. When she ran away from home, claiming that she had been physically abused by her adoptive mother, the authorities should have sought another way to protect her, but failed to do so. When Dalit herself became a mother a few years later, the family court, which accepted her account of abuse by her adoptive mother, said the following in its ruling:

> What is even worse, nothing was done, even after it was known that the adoption had failed, to provide her with an alternative adoptive family, or a foster family: [instead,] the social services were content to place her in institutions, where she was naturally exposed to girls with behavioural problems or from troubled backgrounds, and to a barrage of

> social workers, psychologists, welfare officials and probation officers. From the documents submitted to me it appears that – apart from the psychologists asked to provide evaluations from time to time – nine social workers were involved in her case [here the ruling cites the names of nine professionals]. Social services also did not seek to appoint a guardian other than her adoptive parents, nor to appoint a 'friend', as stipulated under section 3(2) of the Youth Law.

The state attaches supreme importance to providing an alternative family for children whose birth parents have been deemed by social services to have failed, to prevent them from being placed in institutions. That, after all, is the justification cited for severing the contact between the child and his birth parents, as occurs when a child is declared eligible for adoption. However, this principle clearly did not extend to the case of Dalit's failed adoption. Instead, after she had fled her adoptive family at the age of only twelve, the Youth Law was brought to bear, and she was placed in institutions so that she could be 'supervised'. The use of youth homes for such a purpose raises doubts as to whether social services were indeed guided by the principle of 'the best interests of the child' when dealing with Dalit, or whether it was an attempt to dodge responsibility for the failure of her adoption, implying that she herself were to blame for her situation.

For Dalit, being blamed for the failure of her adoption meant adding insult to injury, given the sexual abuse she experienced at the adoptive family home. Sexual abuse within the family is sometimes referred to as the 'unspoken crime'.[10] It rocks the very foundations of the child's trust and sense of security. The family, which is supposed to be a safe haven, becomes a lair where lawlessness prevails and the weaker members are exploited as prey. When Dalit felt this way about her adoptive family, which had been chosen by the state specifically to safeguard her welfare, the wrongdoing effectively extended further, tarnishing the very authorities that were supposed to protect her. However, instead of going out of their way to prove to Dalit that they were sincere in their efforts to protect her, the authorities treated her as a nuisance, a nagging reminder of a truth they wanted to suppress. Thus, they denied the responsibility that the state had assumed when it put her up for adoption. Nowhere was this more blatantly apparent than in the testimony given by the adoption official in court, when asked whether she understood why Dalit had no trust in social services:

> The harm caused to Dalit occurred in the first two years [of her life] … when she had to be given up for adoption because her mother couldn't take care of her. That is the age at which trust, the bonds of relationship

> with some kind of parental figure, be it more or less benevolent, are formed. That's when the rupture occurred.

Even at this point, years after the full details about the adoption failure had become known, the adoption official could not bring herself to recognise the injustice that had been done to Dalit. After many long and bitter months of legal wrangling over Dalit's right to raise her daughter, I asked two adoption officials, individually, 'Have you ever told Dalit that you know that the failure of her adoption had severely harmed her and that you were sorry about that?' Both replied, 'The adoption official who met with her to open her adoption file [in response to Dalit's request for details of her birth family] was very empathetic towards her'. But it is not compassion or competent care that is called for when recognising the serious damage that the state had caused Dalit, even if this damage was the result of the inherent flaw in the adoption system itself, but recognition of moral responsibility. This has never been forthcoming.

The moment the Youth Law was applied in her case, Dalit was handed over to the disciplinary system, which uses a combination of punishment and treatment[11] that focuses on the dialogue between the youth in its care and society's authoritative position, and defines their welfare according to its values. Nonetheless, Dalit's placement in the disciplinary system did have some benefit. While in the 'secure wing' of the youth home, she acquired a vocation that she was proud of, and she herself noted that at both institutions where she had stayed there were some individuals whom she felt positively about and indebted to. These apparently were the ones who helped her resist the pressures to adopt the delinquent norms that prevailed in those environments and the adverse effects of the conditions of despair, and probably prevented her further slide into delinquency. But her perennial feeling of being redundant, and her image of herself as a nuisance, did not change while under the auspices of the disciplinary system.

Dalit's lifestyle after her expulsion from the institution is further illustration of the state authorities' failure to protect her. Her roaming of the streets and associating with marginal groups was the consequence not only of being literally homeless, but also of her feeling rejected by society. Shortly after she turned seventeen, she became pregnant by a young Arab man. The moment she realised she was pregnant, she ceased using drugs. She had known someone who had been born to a drug-abusing mother, who was prone to acute fits of rage, and she was determined that this would not happen to her own child. She had been using cannabis and ecstasy, she said, not hard drugs, so it was easy for her to wean herself off them on her own, but she also broke off ties with the gang she had been hanging out with for two months, to avoid temptation, until she knew for sure that she had kicked the habit. Seeking a place to stay during her pregnancy, she entered a home for unmarried pregnant girls run by the SSC. There she was tested for drugs, and found indeed to be clean. She left that home a short time later, however, for fear that if she stayed there she would be forced to give up her child for adoption. She wanted to raise the child herself.

To decide the fate of her unborn child, a Resolution Committee,[12] a quasi-statutory body that meets at the local social services offices to formulate care programmes for children deemed to be 'at risk', was convened. This committee decided that an emergency order must be issued, pursuant to the Youth Law, to take away Dalit's baby at birth, followed by a petition to the courts to declare the baby eligible for adoption. In the conclusion to his presentation to the family court during the legal hearings that followed, Dalit's legal counsel described the discussion at the Resolution Committee as follows:

> The proceedings within the committee are clearly conducted like a legal proceeding, but the 'defendant', namely, the respondent in our case, was not informed that her case was being discussed; no legal representative was appointed to represent her position; nor was she given the elementary rights to present her case ... At that meeting it was decided that an emergency order should be issued the moment the baby was born. The transcript of this committee meeting reeks of something akin to a lynching. None of the welfare officials, including Ms [—] who knew the respondent better than anyone else, represented the respondent's interests. Indeed, Ms [—] spoke as though she was citing up-to-date information, when in fact the reports that she possessed were six months out of date. The welfare official Mr [—], who had no knowledge of the respondent whatsoever, stated, 'it is fairly clear from her history that this is a baby that needs to go up for adoption – this won't reach the hearings stage – she doesn't have the wherewithal'. Welfare official Mrs [—] further added: '[This is] a very serious case. In the worst cases, the decisions are the easiest'. It is clear from their discussion that the welfare officials sought to exploit the respondent's weakness when dealing with them as an established authority, and did not expect her to fight back and fend for herself. Indeed, such is their bias, that at the end of the transcript, they wish themselves good luck (with an exclamation mark!).

The committee's decision meant that Dalit was once again placed in the hands of social services, welfare officials and the SSC. This was another moment when these services could have acknowledged their responsibility for Dalit, having failed in their attempt to protect her through adoption, and sought a way to help her raise her daughter. Instead, they decided that, for the baby's protection, Dalit had to be removed from her life. This was based not on any examination of her ability to raise a child, but merely on the assumption that she constituted a threat to her own child. This is evident, for example, in the SSC's report submitted to the family court, which described Dalit's stay at the youth home as follows:

> characterised by many escapes and severe behavioural problems, failure to comply with the rules of the establishment, lack of willingness to rehabilitate, violent outbursts, smuggling drugs into the centre, inviting members of ethnic minorities into the centre, and threats against girls.

The state chose to cite the report from Dalit's most troubled period, shortly after checking into the youth institution of her own accord, rather than the positive reports about her progress when she had been placed there under the Youth Law. The deliberate preference for the more negative report confirms the claim by Dalit's legal counsel that social services sought to besmirch her character to justify their wish to take away her daughter. When Dalit testified in court, the tragic consequences of the authorities' attitude towards her were very apparent. She described her stay at the centre only as 'a messed up time', and when I remarked that she was undermining her own cause by omitting to mention how she had learned a trade at the centre, she said, 'Everybody knows what went on there, why do I have to go into detail?'

Dalit's lifestyle, disengagement and roaming of the streets did undoubtedly justify marking out her mothering as vulnerable, since her difficulties were likely to undermine her ability to keep her daughter safe and to care for her. However, it was precisely this vulnerability that signalled Dalit's need for help in matters such as securing suitable living accommodation (which might have partially made up for the state's liability for the failure of her adoption). Instead, the state chose to apply a normative benchmark, and her vulnerability was presented as grounds for disqualifying her as a mother. Although Dalit's lifestyle was clearly non-normative, the life experience she had gained had given her significant survival skills. She had secured the help of a non-profit organisation whose purpose was to 'rescue' Jewish girls who had become romantically involved with Arabs, and which had promised her and her baby a place to live. But the welfare authorities, who decided without Dalit's knowledge to take her baby away from her, knew nothing about that.

Member of the 'Wilderness Generation'

Dalit's initiation into the 'wilderness generation' was dramatic. After the Resolution Committee's decision to take away her baby at birth, all hospitals in town were notified to alert social services when she checked in to give birth. Accordingly, while Dalit was in labour, helped only by a member of her benefactor organisation (whose purpose, as we recall, was to keep her apart from the baby's father), a Youth Law welfare official entered the delivery room and flatly notified her of the committee's decision to take away her child as soon as it was born. Months later, in the court hearings about the case, this timing was justified on the grounds that the decision had been made only a few days earlier, and the committee did not have time to notify Dalit in advance. Dalit's own reaction to the notice, as she recounted two years later, was: 'I didn't want the baby to come out!'

In its subsequent ruling in the case, the district court said the following about this episode:

> While the respondent was lying in bed, about to give birth, she was told by the welfare official that the girl would be taken from her, and she would not be permitted to raise her. Respondent's counsel has described this scene as 'the cruelty of the welfare officials knows no bounds'. While this wording is extreme, one does nonetheless wonder how it is that the welfare authorities, who are mandated to care for their clients' welfare, chose this particular manner and time to notify the mother that she would not be permitted to raise her child, just when she was about to give birth.

Welcome to the 'wilderness generation'. Dalit, as a person, no longer existed. She mattered only as a means of ushering in the next generation, whose welfare the state would care for as it understood and saw fit. Dalit had already experienced at first hand how the state protected the next generation, and the story of the first months of her daughter's life confirmed her fears.

Dalit left the hospital alone. Under the terms of the emergency order she was forbidden from taking her daughter, Tal, home with her from the hospital. Tal remained in the hospital for various tests, and these confirmed what the SSC already knew: Dalit had not abused drugs during her pregnancy. They also found that Tal was free of HIV. A week later, under the terms of the Youth Law,[13] welfare officials applied to the juvenile court to grant retroactive approval for removing the baby from her mother's care.

It is easy to imagine the effect that this forced separation had on a mother whose sensitivity and vulnerability were all the greater after the birth of her first child – particularly given that she was all alone. Since the Youth Law does not mandate the defendant to have legal counsel, Dalit arrived at the juvenile court hearing by herself and, in her anxiety to retrieve her daughter, despite the concerns she had about the heavy responsibility that this would entail, asked to speak with the welfare official (who was there on the state's behalf) to formulate a joint plan for Tal's care. Led by her recognition that she did need help and support, Dalit suppressed her usual rebelliousness and provocative behaviour, but the welfare official dismissed her request out of hand, preferring instead to go ahead with the planned legal proceedings.

The judge, however, saw no justification for denying Dalit the right to raise her daughter, and ordered Tal to be returned to her. Meanwhile, Dalit undertook to live in the accommodation offered to her by the benefactor organisation that had taken her under its wing. In subsequent hearings held under the Adoption of Children Law at the family court over the issuance of the emergency order, Dalit testified that the following six months of her life, her first as a mother, were an endless game of cat-and-mouse, with the welfare authorities watching her every move while she tried to elude them:

> I couldn't [manage] by myself. Why? You can't take care of [the child] … I was living under threat, [thinking] how to make them not take away the girl – unlike every other mother, who thinks about things like how to go for a walk, and all that…

In the six months in which Tal was in her care, Dalit resided either at the home of Mrs N., a member of her benefactor organisation, or at a hostel run by the organisation in the same neighbourhood. As she explained to me, she took Tal for her routine medical check-ups at different family health centres, to avoid tracking by social services, and for that reason also refused to show welfare officials Tal's immunisation card, for fear that they wouldn't return it to her, as an additional pressure to take her baby from her. The reports provided by Mrs N., who had been appointed by the court to serve as Dalit's 'friend' (as stipulated in the Youth Law), varied according to their recipient. To the welfare officials, she complained that Dalit continued to fraternise with Arabs (which her organisation was at such pains to prevent), and would leave the baby for hours on end in her care. When it came to testifying in court, however, she refused to repeat these accusations. Dalit herself confessed that at first she hid the fact that she was seeing her Arab boyfriend (who she claimed was Tal's father) from Mrs N., but then decided she did not want to be dishonest and hide the connection. Despite this confession, the organisation decided that she could continue to reside at their hostel, and continued to help her. When Tal was two months old, she suffered stomach cramps in the middle of the night, and Dalit rushed her to hospital, despite Mrs N.'s attempts to dissuade her because of the late hour. The hospital staff agreed that Dalit had done the right thing, and she stayed by Tal's bedside for four days straight. During this time, unlike when Dalit had been daily ministering to her daughter's needs at her benefactors' facilities, there were public officials on hand who witnessed her dedication. Nonetheless, when her legal counsel presented this months later, when the case was brought before the family court, the adoption official responded:[14]

> Let's qualify that: I doubt very much that she *did not actually move* [from her daughter's bedside] – of course she moved. What is true is that she was … well, from Mrs N. I know that there were Arab men there…

The judge turned to the official at this point and asked her sharply, 'And what significance, pray, am I to attach to that bit of information?' Since she could not deny Dalit's demonstration of motherly devotion towards her daughter, the adoption official tried to discredit her with the supposedly shocking information that she had been 'fraternising with Arabs', as if this in itself were proof that she was unworthy of being a mother.

During Tal's hospitalisation, it transpired that Tal had been born with a constricted intestine, and needed special food. Dalit made sure to feed her according to doctors' orders, and the problem indeed resolved itself within a few weeks, but details of the responsibility she had exhibited towards her daughter continued to be obscured by the reports about her lifestyle. Thus, the fact that she lived in a hostel, occasionally leaving Tal in the care of Mrs N., who lived nearby, was deemed to be 'irresponsible'. She was expected to comply with the condition set by the court, and remain with the baby at Mrs N.'s home twenty-four hours a day, with the exception of Saturday night, when she was allowed to go out. This condition, which has nothing to do with the proper treatment of a child, is not required of any mother in the 'normative' population, especially not an eighteen-year-old single parent, as Dalit was at the time. In marginalised sectors of the population, however, mothers must submit to supervision by social services staff and comply with their every whim and arbitrary rule, even if these undermine their mothering.

Three months after Tal's birth, welfare officials were finally able to point to a slip-up by Dalit that supposedly proved them right to remove Tal from her care. One rainy winter evening, Mrs N. telephoned social services and told them that Dalit had just left her home with Tal in her arms. She would later claim that she did so only because, as Dalit's 'friend' under the terms of the Youth Law, she had undertaken to report any unusual action in Dalit's behaviour. Months later, when she recounted the episode to me in my capacity as expert witness on Dalit's behalf, the story took on an entirely different complexion. The rain, she said, was light, and Dalit had not simply walked out into the street with the baby, but was moving to the home of another member of the organisation, who had even sent a taxi for the purpose. Dalit, too, confirmed that the rain was light, and that she left the house that evening because she could no longer tolerate the lack of privacy and wanted a 'change of scene', as she put it.

In response to Mrs N.'s phone call, welfare officials once again activated the emergency order under the Youth Law, removed Tal from Dalit's care and placed her with an 'intake family' (one that takes in children at a moment's notice). Tal was three months old at the time – an age at which, according to what we know today, a baby is just beginning to discriminate in its smiles to familiar faces.[15] There were no such familiar faces in the intake family – indeed, on that particular day the grandmother in that family had died, so twenty-four hours later, Tal was transferred to yet another family. Even if the welfare officials could not have anticipated this additional transfer, as they later claimed during the legal hearings, they appear to have been oblivious to the effects on the baby of being shunted from one family to another, especially at such a developmentally sensitive stage. As far as they were concerned, protection of the child meant simply removing her from her birth mother's care, and it was this consideration, rather than a wish to improve Tal's situation, that appeared to govern their actions. Ironically, Tal had been taken away from Dalit on the grounds that she was being taken care of by too many figures, which did not allow her to develop the expected differential attachment.

Three days later, a hearing was held at the juvenile court to approve Tal's second removal from Dalit's care. On hearing from the family health centre that the baby's condition was excellent, the judge ordered her to be returned to her mother, and questioned the justification for the emergency order. Tal was returned to her mother, having been away from her for a full week.

On the recommendation of social services, the court did, however, require Dalit to place Tal in daycare, which she did, initially, but when she failed to receive reimbursement for her travel costs, as promised, she stopped. She later explained to me that she was also reluctant to leave Tal in daycare because all the infants there were older than her

– twelve months old or more – while Tal at the time was only three and a half months old, and she was afraid that she would not receive the appropriate care. The authorities' demand to place Tal in daycare is puzzling, as there was no doubt as to the quality of the physical care she was receiving from her mother, and staying in daycare meant that she was exposed to many more figures – the very argument cited for removing her from Dalit in the first place! This demand too, then, appeared to serve no purpose other than to test the extent to which Dalit would comply with the authorities' directives. Dalit responded in kind, refusing to bring Tal to daycare on the grounds that the authorities had not fulfilled their promise, while telling me later that she had done so to protect her daughter.

Dalit's defiance was presented in court as further evidence of her lack of parental capability; her ability was measured not by the nature of her bond with Tal, but by the degree to which she complied with the demands of social services, even when these were not, in her view, in her daughter's best interests. Dalit's opinion, however, was of no consequence to social services. Her role, as they saw it, was simply to disappear from her daughter's life, and she responded by concealing her true thoughts and motivations. Another clash between Dalit and the social services authorities was inevitable.

When Tal turned six months old, a delegation of four welfare officers suddenly turned up on Dalit's doorstep, 'to review the situation'. This was a heavy-handed and ill-judged move. After several weeks of Dalit attempting to avoid any contact with welfare services and hiding her baby from them, clearly a particularly sensitive approach was needed to win her trust and to gain a valid assessment of how well she was caring for her daughter. The surprise visit by a delegation of four officials shows not the merest hint of an attempt to reach some kind of understanding. Indeed, it is unclear what possible purpose such a large delegation could have had, apart from justifying Dalit's sense of being persecuted. If that, indeed, was their intention, they certainly succeeded.

As it happens, Tal was not with Dalit at that moment, nor were there any paraphernalia that suggested that the baby lived there. Dalit was therefore taken in by police for questioning, on the grounds that she had violated the court order by not bringing Tal to daycare. She retorted that the welfare officers were looking for any possible pretext to take away her daughter, and that their visit to her that morning was intended only to see if Tal was with her. In a desperate attempt to do or say anything to prevent Tal from being taken from her, Dalit claimed she did not know where her daughter was and that she had no baby things, although in fact Tal was with a couple from her benefactor organisation, who served as her babysitters from time to time. Social services responded by immediately applying for an injunction to prevent the child from being taken out of the country, but when the welfare officer arrived at the juvenile court to pick up the injunction, he found Tal with her babysitters from the organisation. Having assumed that Tal would be taken away from Dalit anyway and placed for adoption, they had arrived to put in a formal application to adopt her, as this way they could at least ensure that she would be close to her mother. The fact that Dalit had thought that she could stave off the danger of having the baby taken away from her by having a couple from her benefactor organisation pretend to adopt her is indicative of the panic that seized her and robbed her of sound judgement. The court's repeated rulings in favour of Dalit's right to keep her daughter were insufficient in her struggle against a determined social services establishment; her only ally was a group of well-intentioned but hopelessly misguided individuals, a group of recent immigrants from a Western welfare state who interacted mainly among themselves, were utterly cut off from Israeli society and clueless about the Israeli legal system. As one who had been 'cast out into the wilderness', Dalit could only call upon the help of people who were themselves outside the mainstream of society. Thus, she stood defenceless against social services, and worse still, her daughter had been abandoned as well.

The court rejected the couple's request, and Tal was taken from the court by adoption officials, who had taken over her case since it had been decided not only to declare Tal a *ward of court* under the Youth Law,[16] but to petition the court[17] to declare her eligible for adoption, on the grounds of Dalit's alleged parental incapability. Once again, Tal was taken from her mother at a crucial milestone in her development – the age of six months, when the baby 'focuses on one particular figure (or more)'.[18] Although there is no empirical proof that there are critical points in attachment development when damage may be irreversible,[19] there is a tragic irony in the fact that, in the name of concern about too many figures in Tal's life, she was being shunted from one person to another precisely when she was developing her attachment to her mother. The cumulative effect of these upheavals on Tal and her attachment to her mother was apparently not taken into account by the welfare authorities. As far as they were concerned, Dalit no longer existed in Tal's life, so she was eliminated as a potential attachment figure for Tal.

Since Dalit had been marked for exclusion from society, she was not invited to the court hearings that granted the emergency order stripping her of custody of her daughter. Under the terms of the Adoption of Children Law, the emergency order was issued *ex parte*, and Tal was placed with a foster family, which was designated as her adoptive family even before the court had approved her removal from her mother, not because the authorities knew her to be in danger, but because they did not know her true condition. 'Really, why would someone need to hide the truth?' the adoption official later argued in court to justify the emergency order, without knowing the facts of the situation.

To the Eagles' Nest

Approximately four weeks after Tal had been taken away from Dalit, the legal hearing was held on whether to approve the emergency order, as a first stage in the proceedings to declare Tal eligible for adoption. Dalit, whose defiant attitude towards the authorities repeatedly defeated her, rejected the offer of legal representation, not understanding its critical importance. She held the mistaken belief that a court-appointed lawyer would represent the interests of the state, in whose institutions she had no confidence. Dalit, like other parents in her situation, was summoned to legal proceedings where there was a patent inequality between the birth parents and adoption authorities, as described by the court in another case:

> … the values and the conflicting interests in the adoption procedure are unequally represented in court, since most biological parents – the respondents to the adoption application – are from the more disadvantaged sectors of the population, who do not understand why (and by what right) society can interfere with their natural right to raise their child or children, are not familiar with the terms of legal discourse, and lack the skills and resources necessary to ensure that their rights are not compromised.[20]

In Dalit's case, perhaps sensing how she instinctively recoiled from anything smacking of authority, the family court judge decided not to compel her to have representation, but exercised his right under the law to appoint a lawyer for Tal, as a minor. In due course, this lawyer succeeded in persuading Dalit to let him represent her as well. 'I saw him smiling at me with such a nice smile, and I said – OK, let's give it a go', she told me many months later. In so doing, the judge likely prevented further damage to Dalit's struggle for her right to raise her daughter, as the lawyer provided a fiercely committed and excellent representation. The vast majority of parents, if not all, fighting against the forced adoption of their children in court are represented by court-appointed legal aid, as they cannot afford to pay for legal representation themselves. The fees paid to such counsel are paltry, and since virtually all of them work in the private sector, these appointments also come at the expense of far more lucrative work on behalf of their paying clients. Facing them is the full might of the Attorney-General's office, which serves as the SSC's permanent legal counsel, specialises in the issue of adoption and has seemingly limitless resources at its disposal. It is highly unusual, therefore, for a court-appointed legal counsel to conduct such a determined and tenacious court battle as Dalit's lawyer did.

Dalit arrived at court to find that her bond with Tal had been presented by the SSC in a manner calculated to justify Tal's removal from her. To this end, the SSC cited an expert opinion that had been given, two months prior to the emergency order, in preparation for its petition to have Tal declared eligible for adoption. As is usual in such cases, the expert opinion had been based on intelligence and personality tests carried out on Dalit, and on a single observation of her interaction with her daughter. These found, for example, that Dalit did not know who the first Prime Minister of Israel was. While intelligence and general knowledge tests of this sort have little to do with the ability to raise a child, unless the parent is severely mentally challenged, they do serve to elicit feelings of failure in the parent, and to mark him out as a member of the 'wilderness generation'. The psychological tests are designed to justify the parent's exclusion from their child's life, since, in the view of the proponents of such tests, the psychodynamics that the tests are supposed to reveal are thought to be immutable. In Dalit's case, the personality tests carried out on her found, in part, that:

> … the search for immediate gratification, lack of emotional maturity for potential repercussions might lead her to relapse (to the extent that she has indeed stopped) into repeated drug abuse. Apart from the mental and emotional limitations, there is clearly also a difficulty in functioning in complex and uncertain situations, and a difficulty in channelling her behaviour in an appropriate and effective manner. Dalit's level of maturity is low, she is very childish and needs parental figures to take care of her, more than she needs a child herself. According to the findings described below, it appears that Dalit will have difficulties in raising the baby by herself and providing for her emotional, developmental and actual needs.

Since, in this report, the author's impression of Dalit's personality counted for more than the facts, they felt entitled to include the sceptical qualification 'to the extent that she has indeed stopped', even though it was clear and known that Dalit had indeed stopped using drugs. Extrapolating from Dalit's personality as to her parental capability led to the conclusion that she was incapable of caring for her daughter, despite the family health centre's report that Tal's condition was excellent, and the account of the hospitalisation incident, in which Dalit was highly solicitous to Tal's needs.[21]

One sentence in the expert's assessment is worthy of particular notice: 'Dalit ... needs parental figures to take care of her, more than she needs a child herself'. The reference to the maternal instinct – that is, that Dalit was expected to need the baby as much as the baby needed her – was presented by the SSC as evidence that Dalit was deficient and innately incapable of parenting, but the statement 'Dalit needs parental figures' might also have been taken at face value and used as a recommendation to find a family to care for Dalit and support her, given that the SSC clearly had no confidence in the benefactors whom Dalit had found on her own with her meagre abilities. Once again, when the welfare authorities had an opportunity to compensate Dalit for the failure of her adoption and its harsh consequences,[22] they failed to do so. Instead of remembering that the original purpose of personality tests was to find a suitable treatment programme for Dalit, they were using them to evaluate her parental capability, a purpose these tests were not designed for, and to serve as the justification for declaring her child eligible for adoption and for taking the irreversible step of severing the child's contact with her birth mother.

In addition to Dalit's personality assessment, her interaction with Tal was assessed on a spectrum ranging from 'normative' to 'deviant', to see whether, and to what extent, her conduct matched the 'normative' profile of a mother. When Dalit tried to avoid such an examination, this was interpreted by the examiner as an attempt to hide her failure in caring for Tal, rather than as her objection to social services' invasion of her relationship with her daughter. This bias in the examiner's interpretation was evident in the following episode. On arriving at her house, Dalit searched for her house keys, and asked the examiner to hold Tal for a moment while she did so. This, according to the examiner, was a clear deviation from mothering norms: how can a mother entrust a stranger with her daughter? The fact that Dalit changed Tal's diaper in an attempt to calm her crying, but did not wipe the baby's bottom, was also indicative, in the examiner's view, of Dalit's inability to care for the baby, even though the examiner herself admitted that the baby's bottom did not look like it needed cleaning. After Tal had vomited, apparently because of her incessant crying, Dalit changed her clothes, but failed to notice that some of the sick had got onto the baby's hair. Although the examiner did note that

Dalit's omission may have been due to the stressful situation and the knowledge that she was under observation, it did not occur to her that Tal's crying may have also been due, in part, to the tension Dalit was feeling, although it is well known that 'the tension of anxiety when present in the mothering one, induces anxiety in the infant'.[23] Moreover, as we shall see later, the examiner failed to detect a fundamental problem in Dalit's interaction with Tal.

Dalit seemed to have failed the normativity test the examiner had set her, but the test's results were indicative not so much of Dalit's ability to raise Tal, as of the use that the SSC intended to make of it. In this case, as in other cases, the SSC had invited an expert opinion[24] even before the court had called for it, and attached it to the petition to declare Tal eligible for adoption. As the court pointed out in another case, 'The opinions attached to the application are conducted by professionals who have been working with the SSC over a long period, and so it is little surprise that their conclusions are intended to support the application…'[25]

Once an expert opinion had been secured to attest that Dalit was incapable of raising Tal, and the emergency order had been carried out, the SSC was able to continue regulating the contact between the baby and her mother as it saw fit, thus affecting the nature of the bond between them.

The first opportunity Dalit had to see Tal after she had been taken away was a full month later, at the offices of the SSC. Tal, who was then seven months old, arrived with her foster parents after a two-hour drive from their home. She was then handed over to an SSC official – a complete stranger – and from her to Dalit, in an effort to maintain a strict segregation between the foster parents and the birth mother, with no regard for the effect that handling the baby this way might have on her and on her meeting with her mother. As I learned later from the foster father, Tal looked alarmed and frightened when she was handed over to the SSC staff member, and after a month of separation, her mother was a stranger to her too. In her subsequent account of the event to the court, Dalit described the visit as follows:

> The visit at [—] didn't go well: the child was brought to me about half an hour late, or more, and the adoption official took advantage of this [time] to question me thoroughly about my past and future. This bothered me and disturbed me during the visit. Afterwards, when my daughter was brought to me, the adoption official sat and watched how I behaved with the girl, while making notes the whole time. At one point the adoption official left the room, and while she was away, the girl began to cry. She came back in and started asking me if I had done

> anything to the girl. Other staff members also came in to see what had happened. After about an hour, the adoption official ended the visit and took the child away from me.

The description of the meeting, in which Dalit was unable to calm Tal and appeared helpless, was presented as corroborative evidence of her inability to raise her daughter, as if the circumstances of the meeting had no bearing on the child's state or on Dalit's behaviour. It reminded me of the folktale of an eagle that snatched a baby from his mother's arms and placed him in its nest on a clifftop, but, with a superhuman effort, the mother climbed the cliff and managed to retrieve the baby. The mythical ability of that mother illustrates the impossibly high bar that birth parents are required to meet once an emergency order is issued, to prove that they are entitled to raise their children. The SSC puts birth parents through tests that virtually no other parents are expected to face, and very few can hope to pass successfully. For someone like Dalit, whose vulnerability was well known to all, this was not a test but a deliberate hurdle that was meant to defeat her. Her first arranged meeting with her daughter proved to be only the first step in a gruelling and booby-trapped climb to an eagle's nest that would go on for about two years.

That folktale, featuring characters who are not real flesh-and-blood people but illustrative archetypes, very much reflects the case of Dalit and Tal. Dalit was presented as an entity whose entire life had been controlled by the welfare services: from an 'adopted child' she had become a 'juvenile delinquent', or 'girl in distress', then 'a mother of a ward of court'. From there the transition to 'mother lacking parental capability' was virtually self-evident. That final definition doomed her to vanish from her daughter's life from the moment the baby emerged into the world, unless she managed to climb to the proverbial eagle's nest. Tal, too, like her mother, was not perceived as a human being, but as an object. Although ostensibly she was taken away from her mother because of the mother's alleged deficient care and on the pretext of providing her with a permanent caring figure, she was repeatedly passed from one stranger to the next, and at significant points during the formation of her attachment to her mother.

Getting to Know Dalit and Tal

At the start of the hearings on the approval of the emergency order, Dalit's legal counsel was granted permission to appoint me as an expert witness on Dalit's behalf. Before I was introduced to Dalit, I took part in a hearing at which Dalit's legal counsel argued that the emergency order should be revoked and Tal returned to her mother forthwith. However, I cautioned against doing this immediately, given the theoretical and empirical knowledge that babies at that age (eight months) are prone to what is known as 'stranger anxiety',[26] which can be triggered even by familiar figures. To ease Tal's transition back to her mother from the foster family, I suggested putting off her return, and instead holding a series of regular meetings between them for a prescribed period.

A few weeks later, the court ordered the emergency order to be cancelled, as Tal's condition did not justify it. It further ruled that the SSC's statements had been fundamentally flawed, and its contention that many figures were involved when the baby was in Dalit's care was false. As far as it could ascertain, only three caregivers were involved, which is fairly typical of most babies who are placed in daycare while their parents are at work. The judge went on to castigate the welfare services for not offering Dalit the help that she needed, and even seeking to undermine her bond with her daughter by taking her away on three separate occasions within her short life. The court accepted my proposal to defer Tal's return to Dalit for two weeks, during which time she would meet with Dalit five times a week. Further, given Dalit's complaint about the hostile attitude she had encountered from the adoption officials during her meetings with Tal, the court ordered that these meetings be held at a venue unaffiliated with the SSC, and without the presence of the two adoption officials in charge of the case. The mother's legal counsel was to report back to the court after five meetings, and based on that report the court would decide whether Tal should indeed be returned to her mother after fifteen days, or at a later date. The judge made no reference to the state's petition to declare Tal eligible for adoption, which had been submitted at the same time as its request to approve the emergency order, and ordered me to continue my observations and formulate my expert opinion.

My recommendation to the court not to return Tal to her mother before they had a chance to get reacquainted gave the SSC time to appeal to the district court and request deferment of the family court's decision. This request was approved by the district court pending the state's appeal of the family court's ruling. Meanwhile, I met with Dalit and observed her during a meeting with Tal before formulating my opinion.

I first met Dalit in the court corridor. I saw a young woman of solid build, somewhat shabbily dressed, with a weary and lumbering gait and body language of someone with low self-esteem. After exchanging a few words with her, however, I noticed her high cheekbones and almond-shaped eyes. Her face expressed fortitude, and when she was not shutting herself down to shield herself from being hurt, its expression was pleasant and congenial.

In my first conversation with her, I already received a very different impression from that given in the SSC's reports, which had been designed to persuade the courts that she had never formed a significant bond with any other human being. (A history of lack of interpersonal contact is commonly cited as evidence that the mother is incapable of forming an attachment to her children.[27]) She told me about her grief at the death of her grandmother; the good relationship she used to have with her adoptive father; and the fond memories she had of at least one staff member at every institution where she had stayed.

The conversation was flowing and calmly conducted. I felt that Dalit was confiding in me about the internal dialogue she had been holding with herself, and gained the impression of an intelligent and sincere girl who had developed impressive survival mechanisms to make up for her vulnerability. She told me about her relationship with Salim – a West Bank Arab whom she had met while she had been roaming the streets – who she said was Tal's father. With a bashful smile, she told me that she initially took up with him for his money, but over time came to appreciate him as a human being, and fell in love with him. She had just become pregnant by him again, she said, and was toying with the idea of marrying him in a civil ceremony in Cyprus[28] and living together in Israel.

Sometime after that conversation, I observed a meeting between Dalit and Tal. The meeting took place around noon on a very hot day. Dalit was a few minutes late, and Tal, who had been held in the meantime by an adoption official, was crying bitterly. Dalit arrived panting and sweating, took Tal in her arms and the baby fell silent for a moment. Dalit and I entered the room, Dalit looked at Tal, and when Tal gazed back at her, immediately looked away, as if seeing an overly bright light. Tal burst into tears and Dalit placed her on her shoulder in a way that did not allow eye contact, while Tal continued to wail. Dalit then sat her down on her lap with her back towards her. She playfully moved her fingers in front of the baby's eyes to distract her and calm her, but when this did not work either, placed her once again on her shoulder. Eventually Tal buried her head in the crook of her neck and fell asleep – exactly as Dalit had described had happened in previous meetings. While the baby slept, Dalit put her on her lap and sat in a very relaxed manner, gazed at her, stroked her gently and whispered to me, 'Look at her complexion, it's like mocha – amazing...!' She said that Tal already had the feet of a woman, by which she apparently meant that the toes were longer and did not seem to be joined, stroked her hair and remarked how long it was. She told me about the problem Tal had had with the constricted intestine, and how she had helped her overcome that. It was clear to me that in the time before Tal had been taken from her, Dalit had been very well attuned to her needs and completely absorbed in her development.

Tal was breathing deeply. There was a slight hoarseness to her breathing, and I noticed that she clung tightly to a necklace that Dalit was wearing around her neck. Dalit, who could not see this, asked if Tal was holding onto the necklace, as it was something she used to do when she fell asleep in her arms in the past. I wondered if this was a trace of her bond with her mother. Dalit then remarked how Tal had once torn a necklace like that with a *hamsa* that she had been given as an heirloom from her grandmother. Holding Tal in her arms, I thought, perhaps triggered Dalit's longing for her grandmother's love to resurface, which is why she told me again about the special relationship that they used to have.

While Dalit was speaking, Tal tried once again to establish eye contact. She opened her eyes just a crack and gazed at Dalit's face, and Dalit said to me, 'Look – she just smiled'. I changed position so I could see Tal's face, but Dalit said, 'You missed it', referring to Tal's charming smile. Tal continued to gaze at her mother's face while half asleep, as if stealing glances, and even though she was not rewarded with a look back from Dalit, she smiled and went on sleeping. Dalit was enthralled, saying, 'Look at how she looks like me in the shape of her eyes, only her eyelashes are longer'.

The warmth and gentleness that filled the room in those moments starkly contrasted with the attitude and behaviour of the adoption official towards Dalit. At the end of the meeting, Dalit asked if she could wait with Tal in the offices until the taxi that the official had called to take Tal back had arrived, as she did not want to take the baby outside in the searing heat. The adoption official scoffed in reply and dismissed her suggestion, saying that the taxi driver would not be able to tell her when he arrived. So we stood outside, in the oppressive heat, and waited for the taxi. When Dalit suggested that the official check if the taxi had arrived from another direction, this too was dismissed scornfully. Ten minutes later, we discovered that the taxi had indeed arrived from another direction and had already been waiting for several minutes. The official hurried to place the bawling Tal into the taxi. Dalit protested and said that Tal wanted to drink, and offered the baby's bottle to the official, only to have it pushed away brusquely on the grounds that there was no time. Dalit stood there, hurt and fuming. The adoption official made no attempt to hide her dismissal of Dalit's presence in her daughter's life, and I wondered whether the SSC were conducting these meetings merely because they had been ordered to do so by the court.

'Is this all you're doing, then – just talking to me?' Dalit asked as we walked away from that meeting. 'That – and observing what happens between you and Tal', I replied. 'And what did you see?' she asked, curious. I asked her if she found it difficult to look into Tal's eyes, and Dalit immediately admitted she did, adding that this was a problem that had dogged her throughout her life: she was unable to look into people's eyes. When I remarked that I hadn't noticed that in our own meetings, she explained that she only had that problem with people close to her: 'It's because I'm embarrassed', she explained. This is why she had often been accused of lying. I wondered privately if this difficulty was a remnant of a profound pain that she had experienced in the past, which had become seared in her mind and affected her relationship with Tal. Eye contact is crucial to the evolving relationship between a baby and its adult caregiver.[29] The infant uses it to catch the mother's eye, navigate the bond with her and reward her. Lack of eye contact between infant and caregiver affects the nature of the reciprocal interaction between them, but infants can compensate for the absence of one sensual connection by developing another, in their bid to establish contact with the adult.[30] However, to do so requires continuous contact, and this was disrupted when Tal was repeatedly removed from her mother's care. Moreover, the lack of eye contact likely deprived not only Tal but Dalit as well, who was thereby denied the reward of her daughter's gaze, and possibly explained why she limited the amount of time that she spent with her daughter while Tal was still in her care. In a landmark paper published in 1971 about blind infants, Selma Fraiberg showed that problems of deficient attentiveness by parents to their babies – even when this is the result of the parents' profound difficulties – can be resolved when reciprocal interaction between them is established, thanks to the immediate reward that the baby's response gives the parent. However, for that to happen, the parent must be aware of the effect that the lack of eye contact has on their baby's responses to her, and to learn the baby's alternative signals.[31] The importance of this difficulty to the relationship between Dalit and Tal became apparent to Dalit only after I had observed their interaction, but by then, the contact between her and Tal had already effectively been severed. The nature and frequency of their meetings at that time did not allow her to overcome the barrier that had arisen between them due to Dalit's inability to establish eye contact.

The welfare services had no inkling that Dalit had this difficulty when they took Tal away from her, nor was it observed or mentioned by the expert who wrote the expert opinion on their behalf. This is likely because Dalit was assessed not by how she responded to Tal's cues, but by social norms of how a mother should behave, and her willingness to comply with the welfare services' demands. This is also evident in the report submitted to the court by adoption officials about her meetings with Tal:

> In all the meetings to date, Tal has responded by crying, calming down, then falling asleep. The visits, as previously noted, took place at various times of the day, so Tal's falling asleep cannot be attributed in my opinion to tiredness, but as a response to the encounter. The mother, for her part, cooperates, tries to calm her down and sits beside her the whole time she is sleeping.

In stark contrast to this cursory and laconic summary of all the meetings, the report goes into painstaking detail about precisely when and where every meeting was held, the names of the adoption officials present, and Dalit's responses on hearing the prescribed dates and times, for example when she expressed concerns about the timing of the meeting, or surprise when one meeting was set for a Friday.[32] The report appeared to place greater emphasis on the interactions between Dalit and the adoption officials than on her interactions with Tal. Assessing mothering based on the degree to which the mother complies with the demands of the welfare services is not unique to Dalit's case, but is particularly disturbing in this instance. Dalit's life history reveals that the welfare services were never truly interested in her welfare, and she in response established a pattern of defiance to authority that became a pattern of behaviour. One brief episode speaks volumes about this. After one meeting with Tal, I drove her, at her request, in the direction of her home, and when I remarked that she must put on her seat belt, she said, 'Ah, you're one of those'. I smiled and answered that not every rule had to be resisted, and she smiled too in response. The next time we got into the car, she buckled up immediately.

Dalit took advantage of the time provided by the district court's deferment of the family court's decision to return Tal to her, and with the help of her benefactor organisation, rented an apartment near

Mrs N.'s home. The organisation promised to pay the rent and Dalit persuaded the apartment owner to reduce it when she told him she would be moving in with her daughter. With great anticipation and enthusiasm, she began cleaning the apartment and painting what was to be Tal's room. However, when the district court deferred the handover yet again, she lost all interest in the apartment, spent very little time in it, and a few weeks later was asked by the apartment owner to leave, since the reduced rent had been granted on the understanding that she was a single mother, yet no child had been seen. Let down once again, Dalit withdrew into herself, and her face once again took on a blank expression that barely hinted at her feelings. Unwittingly, she was playing the role allotted to her by the authorities, who had no interest in the mental and real harm they were inflicting upon her, as a passive object devoid of all wishes and expectations. To retrieve Tal, she had to fulfil a role of mythic proportions and climb to the proverbial eagle's nest. Myths don't care about their protagonists' mundane difficulties.

As it happens, just at that time Dalit suffered yet another blow, which she spoke little about. During her initial contact with SSC officials, after their attempts to remove Tal from her care, she had formally requested to contact her birth mother. The judge asked for this to be expedited, in the belief that it would be of great significance to Dalit, but the adoption official in charge of Dalit's file told her that her mother did not want to meet her.[33] Dalit knew that her mother had been addicted to drugs in the past, but assumed that she had become rehabilitated as three of her children were now living with her. She now learned that her mother was still addicted to drugs. She expressed surprise that the other three children were still in her mother's custody in that case, but accepted the refusal with resignation, despite her disappointment. Being resigned to her fate, it seems, was her usual way of dealing with disappointment. However, she did revisit the subject later, during the proceedings for regaining custody of Tal.

As part of the evaluation of Dalit's parental capability, I asked to meet with Tal and with the foster parents, as I usually do when giving my expert opinion. As in the case of Elinor in the previous chapter, the adoption officials demanded to be present during the meeting. While the judge rejected their claim that they must be present because I am 'opposed to adoption', he did accept that the foster parents did not know me and might otherwise feel uncomfortable during the meeting, and therefore granted their request. In effect, by demanding to be present during the meeting, the adoption officials were signalling to the foster parents to be wary of me – a message that they received loud and clear. I could not help contrasting the adoption officials' concern to protect the foster parents from the 'unfamiliarity' of meeting me with their uncaring attitude towards Dalit, who was required to meet with more than one expert on her own and to conduct all her meetings with her daughter in a hostile atmosphere with more than one adoption official present (a total of seven different officials, on different occasions).

The latitude given by the court to the SSC in its desire to manage the contact with the foster family was evident in its very choice of the family in question. In the meeting with the foster parents, I discovered that it was a religious Jewish family.[34] During my cross-examination about my expert opinion, I was asked by State Counsel if there was a possibility that Tal's adoption might be open. 'The family that you've chosen obviously rules that out', I answered. The judge gave me a sharp look,[35] and when I explained that I did not know what I was allowed to reveal, told me sternly that I was not allowed to reveal anything. While it subsequently transpired that the reality was more nuanced than that, the fact remained that the court conspicuously avoided tempering the SSC's exclusive control over the information about Tal's designated adoptive family. If this had been an issue of national security, I thought to myself, the judge would have cleared the courtroom and demanded to hear the confidential information.

During my observation of the interaction between Tal, who by now was nine months old, and the foster parents, Tal was more cheerful than I had ever seen her, and very actively cajoling the foster parents to play with her. The foster parents, a warm and cheerful couple, already had a child of their own, a boy of ten. Their confidence in their parental ability was clearly evident in how they played with Tal, who got on with them extremely well. However, it is important to remember that, by law, the question of whether or not they were more capable of raising Tal than Dalit was irrelevant, and could not serve as a basis for denying Dalit's parental rights. The law repeatedly underlines that children must not be removed from their parents simply because other parents may be thought to be more capable.[36] Indeed, it is often the case that adoptive parents are more capable of raising children than the birth parents, are financially better off, and in some cases, as in this one, have already raised children and have some experience. Moreover, the encounter with them is usually held during a 'honeymoon' period in terms of the adjustment difficulties involved, and benefits from the thrill of a new relationship, which designated adoptive parents are certainly motivated to promote.

In my first conversation with the foster parents, they told me about their first encounter with Tal. When she arrived with the adoption officials, they said, she was in a shocking condition: dirty and neglected, her neck muscles so stiff she could not move her right arm, and her smile more like a grimace. During her first night with them, she woke several times in fright. The doctor who examined her on their behalf concluded that the stiffness in her neck and the paralysis of her arm were due to prolonged lying on her side with no stimulation. She recommended massage for the shoulder, and that indeed resolved the problem fairly quickly. This was the first description that raised some doubts in me as to the quality of Dalit's mothering. In court, I recounted the foster parents' description, and added that I found it difficult to reconcile the unusual finding of localised paralysis in the arm and its apparent cause with the fact that there was no general delayed development;[37] I tentatively raised the possibility that it might have to do with the mother's difficulty in establishing eye contact. I was also very surprised that Tal's condition at this point was not included in the adoption officials' reports when justifying their removal of Tal from her mother's care. During my testimony, the adoption officials and State Counsel, who were both present in court, pointedly chose not to refute the impression that Tal's condition had been caused by her mother's deficient care. It served the adoption officials' purpose very well, as it reinforced their projection of Dalit as a negligent and harmful mother.

Children Who Were Abandoned

To understand why Tal was in such a poor condition when she was placed with the foster parents, I asked Dalit's legal counsel to show me the documents that he had received from State Counsel (only after he had expressly petitioned the court to receive them). Among them I found a report by a doctor, appointed by the SSC, who examined Tal the day after she had been taken away from her mother. His findings were summed up in this report:

> I examined a cute baby, [who] establishes eye contact, tracks and smiles, makes noises with communicative intention, extends her hand to a toy. Turns over from stomach to back. Muscle tone within the norm tending to eccentric, most likely due to premature extensive standing up … Occipital flattening of skull, due to prolonged lying on back. Palate and pharynx satisfactory. In summary: a six-month-old baby with no unusual medical finding given today's examination and in the absence of any prior information.

Observing a baby's actions and cues at the age of six months is a reliable indicator of the responses she receives from her surroundings, and what Tal 'reported', in her own way, was that she had just arrived from an environment that was responsive to her cues and that she enjoyed communicating with, as evident also from her great vitality. Further evidence of the appropriate care she had received was the fact that she was normally developed for her age – as indicated, for example, by the fact that she extended her hand to reach a toy, as expected of a six-month-old baby. Any suggestion that the flattening of the back of her head was due to excessive lying on her back – that is, to possible neglect – was belied by her ability to make eye contact and her generally good developmental condition. While a flattening of the back of the skull is empirically associated with a baby's prolonged lying on its back (and with neglect, delayed development and indifference to the environment), it is also characterised by baldness at the back of the head, which was not noted in the doctor's report. In Tal's case, as was apparent to me two months later as well, flatness at the back of the skull may have simply been a congenital feature. Moreover, the doctor's attribution of her stiff leg muscles to premature holding of her in a standing position contradicts the suggestion that she had been left to lie on her back for hours at a time, and suggests instead that she had been physically exercised, and although such exercise is slightly excessive for a baby of that age, it is not unusual with young and inexperienced parents.

Another telling document was a report submitted by the adoption officials to the court. After the doctor's examination, Tal was in the SSC's care for four days before being placed with the foster parents. This tied in with something else the foster parents had told me. They noted that when Tal arrived, she had been fed exclusively on vegetable-based *Materna* baby formula, although children of her age are supposed to receive a more varied diet, such as dairy products, fruits and vegetables. It is unknown who told them that this had been Tal's diet, but the information was not only factually wrong, but potentially harmful. Tal had never been fed *Materna* baby formula, but *Similac* and – on doctor's orders, due to her congenital narrowing of the intestine – a supplement of *Isomil*, against constipation. Clearly, the adoption officials decided to give Tal *Materna*, never thinking of asking Dalit what kind of food she should have, either because they wanted her out of the picture entirely, or because they had no faith in her judgement or ability. Meanwhile, the foster parents accepted the adoption officials' account and assumed that it was the mother who had been feeding the baby the wrong type of formula, despite her evidently good physical development.

Placing Tal with the foster parents in a neglected and dirty condition and hiding the findings of the medical examination indicate that the attempt to erase all traces of the bond between Tal and her mother was more important than actually protecting the baby. Only after the mother's existence had been denied, and all traces of her eradicated, was it possible to deliver Tal to her new family, much as the 'wilderness generation' was decreed to die in the desert before the Children of Israel could enter the Promised Land. This, indeed, is the mindset underpinning adoption procedures in Israel, evident in the words of adoptive parents in another case – 'We thought that, over the years, her memory of her mother would fade' – and in those of the designated adoptive parents of five-year-old Doron (cited in the previous chapter), who objected to an open adoption arrangement because they wanted to 'start with a clean slate', despite his age. Denying the loss involved in separating children from their parents is inextricably accompanied by abandonment, just as Tal was abandoned in the days when she was in the care of the SSC. When the adoption officials were confronted in court with the doctor's report, they addressed two of its findings – the prolonged lying on the back, and the possible premature standing up, based on the leg muscle tone – as indications of neglect, and ignored his remarks about Tal's excellent social development. As for the change in Tal's condition in the short time that she had been in their care, the adoption officials had no explanation. On the witness stand, the adoption official rejected the possibility that Tal was harmed while in their care, and argued that it was not possible for the paralysis in her right arm to develop in such a short period. As for Tal's evident neglect and dirty state, she had no explanation at all. I would like to dwell on this point a little further before continuing with Tal's story.

Even a cursory glimpse behind the wall of secrecy surrounding a child once an emergency order is issued reveals that the SSC cannot deny responsibility for Tal's shocking deterioration while in their care, or for other cases of harm inflicted on children while in their care. Revital (as described in the first chapter) was scalded during her stay with an intake family, and although her case was taken to court, no investigation was ever carried out as mandated by the Prevention of Abuse of Minors and Helpless Law.[38] This would certainly have been investigated if such an 'accident', as the adoption officials described it, had occurred in a family that was not under its remit.

In the case of another child declared eligible for adoption at birth, Noam, the child came to harm while in the SSC's care. Born, after a normal nine-month pregnancy, to a mother who was declared 'mentally challenged', he was tested immediately after birth and found to be normal in all respects, including a genetic test that ruled out mental retardation. However, because of the mother's condition and the concern that he, too, might be mentally challenged, he was placed with a foster family under the auspices of the SSC to evaluate his development prior to being placed for adoption. When he turned one year old, the adoption officials' concerns appeared to have been vindicated. He was indeed significantly delayed in his development, and was brought for an examination at the Children's Medical Centre to determine an appropriate developmental programme for him. However, instead of prescribing a programme for treating the development delay, the doctor found unequivocally that the delay was due to neglect, and called for an investigation of the care that he had received from the foster family. Only then was it discovered that he had been left in bed for hours and days at a time, with no stimulation whatsoever, while the foster parents went about their daily lives, ignoring his need for social contact.[39] In that case, too, no investigation was held into the SSC's liability in the matter.

Nor did the harm end there. Noam was placed with another foster family, and there he enjoyed devoted care, his condition improved greatly and he grew very attached to his new foster parents, confirming the doctor's assessment that his delay had been the result of neglect. Yet he still did not speak. In a second test carried out five months after the first, most of which time he had spent with the new family, it was found that:

> The child is progressing well ... is curious, likes to play, with good concentration ability ... There is a linguistic delay due to the foster family speaking English at home. Motor function satisfactory. The boy is healthy, with normal hearing. It would appear that a large part of the boy's problem was environmental deprivation ... He can thrive in a nurturing family.[40]

These findings show the SSC's continued carelessness. After a long period of little or no communication during his time with the first foster family, who neglected him, Noam was transferred to an English-speaking family, and then, after nearly a year with them, finally placed with his designated adoptive (Hebrew-speaking) family, where he had to learn a new language all over again. It is important to note at this juncture that the adoptive parents had passed all the necessary tests required of people seeking to adopt children with special needs, and were willing to receive him a full two months before Noam was taken away from the first foster family. Noam's placement with the English-speaking foster family, therefore, was entirely unnecessary, and another blow that could have easily been avoided. It also meant that the final adoptive parents received a boy who was indeed developmentally delayed, thereby fully bearing out the adoption officials' prophecy.

The cases of Revital and Noam were both brought to the attention of the court, and yet in both instances the court refrained from ordering an investigation into the responsibility of the adoption officials in question for the harm caused to the children. SSC staff are essentially immune to investigation and punishment. Although these are but two incidents, virtually every child I have known or that I have been told about has been harmed during their emergency accommodation under the auspices of the SSC.

The case of another child, two-year-old Rotem, may explain, at least to some extent, the inherent deficiency in SSC-sponsored care. During the judicial proceedings in her case, Rotem was temporarily placed with her birth parents, who had never cared for her previously, because the intake family with whom she had lived for eight months had gone on holiday, and the court believed that placing the child with her birth parents, with whom she had met on a regular basis, would be an opportunity to see if she could be safely returned to their custody. When I visited Rotem, twenty-four hours after she had been returned to her parents, she did not know how to play. She clutched the hair and dress of her doll as if it were an ordinary object and not a human-shaped doll; when she threw a ball, she did not follow its trajectory with her eyes, as if she did not know that a ball rolls; and she showed no interest whatsoever in the toys strewn about the room. I concluded that there was a substantial delay in her development because she had never attended any educational facility, and that the intake family, who were caring for three other babies at the same time, spent little time interacting with her. To disprove my assessment and to show that Rotem was in fact at a satisfactory developmental state for her age, and that her behaviour was due to her placement with her birth parents, the adoption official provided me with the findings of an expert's observation of the parents' interaction with her when she was five months old. In addition, she provided me with the opinion of a psychologist who examined the girl when she was fourteen months old, who wrote:

> The examination took place in a pleasant and relaxed atmosphere, although the father did express some displeasure towards the SSC official

> who had brought Rotem to the meeting. The two parents were very active during the evaluation, which lasted about an hour and a half, and tried to interest the girl with games and food. (The mother in particular seemed anxious to 'foist' food upon Rotem, even when it was clear that she did not want it.)

Based on these two observations, which were about the parents' behaviour, rather than the child's, and which were carried out many months prior to my evaluation of Rotem's condition, the officials tried to prove that the girl's development was satisfactory when she was two years old. In addition to these documents, they provided a summary of an exam conducted at the paediatric clinic at the hospital a few weeks prior to her placement with her birth parents, which found nothing unusual in her physical examination or any evidence of severe ailment, and that the child was physically adequately developed for her age, alert and sociable. However, there was no assessment of her cognitive development which, unlike the test for alertness and sociability, is not gauged by the child's interaction with the examiner, but by her skills, such as her functional ability to use objects (to roll a ball, for example) and her level of symbolic understanding (e.g. in her attitude towards the doll). In none of the documents presented to me, therefore, was there any indication of Rotem's developmental condition before she was taken from the intake family, and the fact that they were used as such shows ignorance about children's development during infancy and early childhood. Such knowledge is essential to prevent harm to children held in SSC-sponsored emergency care, most of whom are infants or young children.

The wall of secrecy behind which the adoption officials operate is coupled with a lack of any independent oversight of their own operations, which together gives them a position of sovereignty. On the pretext that 'the child must not be sacrificed on the altar of family integrity', they can legally remove a child from his family and then abandon him to his fate, rather like the *homo sacer* practice in ancient Rome.[41] Absolute control over the child is given, therefore, to the very authority with the power to harm him.[42] The emergency order permitting the removal of a child from his parents' care is clearly designed, therefore, not so much to protect the child as to remove the birth parents from his life.

When Tal was placed with the foster family, it was the fourth time within six months that she had been shunted from one place to another. Her whereabouts during the time between her removal from her mother and placement with the foster parents, as well as the identity of her caregivers during that time, when she was in the care of the

SSC, remain unknown. However, whatever happened to her during that time was the reason for her shocking condition and grimace-like smile, and was implicitly used by the adoption officials to make it look as though she had been a victim of neglect by Dalit, and the alleged multiplicity of caregiver figures in her life.

Based on the findings of the medical examination of Tal immediately after she had been taken from her mother, and the foster parents' description of her condition on receiving her, I concluded that Tal had been attached to her mother. Her cheery disposition and communicativeness during the doctor's examination had quickly deteriorated into a grimace within days, due to her severe reaction to the separation. As subsequent events were to prove, the stiffness in her neck was also a reaction to her mother's disappearance. Meanwhile, during my meeting with the foster parents I was also able to corroborate my suspicion that Tal's tight grip of Dalit's necklace was indeed a trace of her bond with her mother; the foster mother said that Tal did not do the same with her own necklace. Although she could not verbalise her attachment to her mother, Tal was able, at the tender age of six months, to communicate it in her own way. In the opinion that I submitted to the court, I recommended that Tal be returned to her mother's custody. There was no question that when Tal was in her care, Dalit treated her responsibly with a full understanding of her developmental needs. Despite Dalit's gaze aversion, which undoubtedly created a difficulty in the communication between them, and despite the repeated disruptions to the bond between them and despite the alienation that had crept into their relationship due to their enforced separation, there were clearly still traces of Tal's discriminating attachment to her mother.

The State v Dalit

In Dalit's story, more than in any other that I recount in this book, the authorities' determination to use all the seemingly unlimited resources at their disposal to achieve their legal aims was starkly apparent. Although they ultimately failed, this came at a very heavy price indeed (in every sense of the word).

Approximately two weeks after the family court had denied the emergency order, State Counsel appealed the ruling at the district court. With the consent of both parties, the district court ordered the hearings to return to the family court, to re-examine the opinion of the SSC-appointed expert, and mine, and decide accordingly whether or not to approve the emergency order. These repeat hearings therefore focused on the two expert opinions. The mother's legal counsel rejected the validity of personality tests as a means of assessing parental capability, and although the court took no principled stand against the use of personality tests, it accepted the mother's counsel's dispute of the validity of the SSC expert's opinion, criticised certain ethical flaws in the opinion of the SSC-appointed expert, and disqualified it, effectively rejecting the normative benchmark that had guided the SSC's actions and assessments of Dalit. The judge also recalled that in his previous ruling he had attributed the difficulties in Dalit's mothering to the conditions under which she was required to care for her daughter (as I had pointed out), and saw no need to change his decision about cancelling the emergency order. Accordingly, he ordered that Tal, who by now was ten months old, be returned to her mother immediately. He further ordered that Dalit be cared for and supervised by a welfare service other than the SSC, and be provided with the support network she needed to ensure that Tal received orderly care. He also noted that Dalit required the services of a communication clinician, to help deal with the difficulty in establishing eye contact with the baby, and ordered the social worker to submit monthly monitoring reports to the court.

With these recommendations, the court effectively prescribed the conditions necessary for raising Tal, and explicitly agreed with the view that Dalit's mothering difficulties had nothing to do with an alleged defect in her personality. The treatment programme prescribed by the judge was also a way to assess Dalit's ability to raise Tal *in vivo*. Accordingly, the court did not set a date for a hearing on the state's petition to declare the child eligible for adoption.

Tal's return to her mother was supposed to take place the day after the ruling in the family court, but when Dalit arrived at the offices of the SSC the next day, only minutes before Tal was supposed to go home with her, she was told that a stay of execution had been ordered. The state, she learned, had just submitted an appeal of the family court's second ruling to the district court. The promise to return Tal to Dalit was broken for the second time, and Dalit's hopes were dashed.

At these appeal hearings, which took place about a month later, the judge accepted the SSC's position unreservedly, and also offered the view that, judging by the family court's decisions, it appeared that that court 'was willing to assume that at present the respondent is indeed not capable of taking care of the minor because of her conduct or condition', but made no mention of the fact that this assessment was attributed to her life circumstances at that time. The district court therefore overturned the family court's ruling, after rejecting the evidence on which it was based. In addition, the judge disagreed with the family court's view that the harm that Tal might incur by being removed from the foster family should not be a factor in the decision as to whether or not to return her to her mother's care, although he did agree that the decision to place Tal with the foster family in the first place had been hasty. However, to minimise any further upheavals, he ruled that Tal should remain with the foster family for now pursuant to the emergency order, pending the family court's decision on the state's petition to declare her eligible for adoption.

By this time, as previously noted, Dalit had become pregnant once again, and the baby's father had been accompanying her throughout the proceedings. The district court accepted the state's argument that returning Tal to her mother at this juncture, when the mother was in her final months of pregnancy, was inappropriate, because if she had problems dealing with one child, she would find it twice as hard to handle two. As we shall see later, this argument had other aspects.

The mother's counsel filed an appeal against the district court's ruling with the Supreme Court, and while this was pending Dalit gave birth to a healthy baby girl of normal weight. She called her 'Yasmin' – a name that is both Hebrew and Arabic – as an expression of her deepening relationship with her boyfriend, the baby's father. The next day, she asked Mrs N. to hurry and pick her up from the hospital, before social services took her new baby away from her too. Her concerns were justified: social services had indeed filed a request to declare the baby a ward of court, but since Dalit's whereabouts were now unknown to them, they could not carry it out.

In a telephone conversation with me, Dalit told me that unlike when Tal was born, she felt nothing towards Yasmin, even when she held her in her arms, because she was afraid that Yasmin would be taken away from her. It was clear to me that she was severely depressed. I asked her if it would help if she and I spoke by telephone on a daily basis about her feelings towards Yasmin, and she replied that it would, very much. Unfortunately, this proved very difficult, because Dalit was now residing in a village in the Palestinian Authority territory, at the home of her partner's parents, where telephone communications were unreliable. When I asked if she was making eye contact with the baby, I sensed her smile on the telephone (as one does over a shared private confidence): 'I'm trying', she said. 'It's hard, though….' I urged her not to give up, and with a more determined voice she replied that she had no intention of doing so. This reassured me somewhat about her mental state.

Contrary to the adoption officials' forecast at the district court, Dalit's difficulty in relating to her second daughter appeared related to Tal's forcible removal. Her limitation lay not in the practical difficulty of taking care of two babies, but in the fact that her motherhood of Tal had been severed. To acknowledge this, one must accept the fact that parenting is affected by the very existence of a child in the parent's life and the importance of the child to them. This effect cannot be predicted before the child is born, as the SSC did when it decided to take Tal away from Dalit even before the child was born, or as the district court did when it agreed with the adoption officials that she would have difficulty caring for two babies.

There was no knowing what might have happened to Dalit's mothering of Yasmin were it not for the considerable support she received from Yasmin's father, Salim, and his family, and the dedicated handling of the case by her lawyer, who insisted on Dalit's right to regain custody of Tal, and made clear to her that her status as Tal's mother was still very much valid. The phenomenon of parents who fail repeatedly in raising children after previous children have been taken away from them is usually interpreted as evidence of a personality defect. However, it could also be explained as an effect of their mourning over the death of their parenthood of the children who have been taken from them, or an outcome of their fear that their other children might be taken from them as well. Perhaps both explanations are correct, or correct in varying degrees from one parent to another. This is a question that has yet to be studied systematically.

Dalit's appeal of the district court ruling concerning her custody of Tal was heard when Yasmin was about two weeks old. Dalit arrived at the Supreme Court with Yasmin in her arms, and sat crying in the courtroom, but no hearing took place. The panel of three judges instantly threw out the district court's ruling, stating that:

> The [district court's] ruling cannot stand, since in the case before us the conditions were not met for taking such an extreme measure as removing a child from her mother, which may also affect the outcome of the main proceedings, namely the petition to declare her daughter [henceforth, the minor] eligible for adoption. ... However, the minor's well-being requires that she continue to remain with the foster family where she currently resides, for an interim period, pending a ruling in the main case, while maintaining contact between the minor and her mother through regular visits....

Legally speaking, the Supreme Court's position was a tremendous achievement in Dalit's struggle, but Dalit protested: 'What good is it if Tal isn't being returned to me?' Like many other birth parents who, in the words of another court cited earlier, 'are not familiar with legal discourse in court', she failed to understand that the court was in fact upholding her rights. Her lawyer tried to explain the significance of the Supreme Court's ruling to her, but all she knew was that Tal was not coming home with her that day, nor was any date set for her to do so. As far as she was concerned, the outcome of this hearing was just another stage in her deprivation and humiliation. To some extent, she was right. The fact that her rights had been upheld did not bring Tal back to her, and their continued separation would only further weaken the bond between them.

The hearings at the family court on the state's petition to declare Tal eligible for adoption went on for ten months, during which time the judge ordered that regular meetings be held between the mother and daughter, initially under the supervision of the welfare services. Dalit's counsel, who joined one of the meetings, later described it to the court:

> It was a fairly difficult experience. The child arrived nearly an hour late, during which time we sat in a room no more than 70 or 80 sq. ft in size. Tal arrived strangely sleepy and fairly apathetic. There wasn't even a carpet on the floor, the conditions were uncomfortable, and on top of that every few minutes someone entered the room, asking questions or making remarks. First it was a secretary, then it was someone else, then an adoption official, whom the court had expressly forbidden to be present at the meetings. Someone told Dalit that she should not have taken Yasmin out of the house that day because it was cold. All this made one uneasy and certainly added to the feelings that Dalit already had from the past, of being viewed with suspicion, and of being in a hostile environment.

Two weeks later the judge ordered the meetings to be held at Dalit's home at least twice a week, and for three hours on each occasion. This ruling was never implemented, however, because Dalit had moved in with her partner in the Palestinian Authority territory, to which there was very limited access. A few meetings were held at the welfare services offices, but the bond between mother and daughter appeared to continue to wane, and Dalit said that there was no point in continuing the meetings because she did not believe that Tal would ever be returned to her.

The meetings became a test of compliance with the court's orders, and as might be expected, Dalit repeatedly failed it. Her lawyer's position was particularly difficult. He had to fight on two fronts: on the one hand, striving to ensure continued cooperation by his client, who was withdrawing into her shell and becoming indifferent to her own interests in an attempt to shield herself from repeated disappointments;

and on the other, battling against the obstacles placed in his path by the authorities. Were it not for the lawyer's tireless efforts, Dalit's feelings of defeat and humiliation would have likely dictated the outcome of the legal proceedings.

The meetings between Dalit and Tal became a stick for the SSC to beat Dalit with. When she failed to arrive at meetings, she supposedly 'proved' that she had no interest in Tal, and when she did turn up for a meeting, their report about its outcome was invariably negative. The adoption officials' contribution to Dalit's anguish during these meetings is evident in her counsel's account of another meeting at which he was present. The adoption official, he said, ordered him to leave the room, and when he refused, threatened to contact the Attorney-General's office. When she saw that the threat did not deter him, she relented. She was clearly not motivated by a desire to protect Dalit's privacy, as she saw no problem with her own presence at the meeting, and her conduct indeed proved as much. During that meeting, Dalit was initially unresponsive, and so too was Tal, but when Dalit held out a sweet to her, the ice between them melted and they smiled at each other. Tal began licking the sweet and coughed, at which point the adoption official, who sat very close to Dalit, explained to her that Tal was coughing because of the sweet: the sugar was stimulating her phlegm. No court order can prevent such an episode, and were it not for the lawyer's presence, this deliberately disruptive interference, just as the intimacy was beginning to form between Dalit and Tal, would not have been recorded anywhere. It was later omitted from the adoption official's account of the meeting. The inherent denial of the loss involved in adoption is evident in the fact that supervision of meetings between child and birth parents is placed in the hands of the very officials whose petition to declare the child eligible for adoption is being heard in court. As a party to the legal proceedings, they are naturally interested in bolstering their contention and proving to the court that it is essential to keep the child apart from her birth parent. Thus, for example, during one of the hearings, Dalit described how Tal, who by now had begun to walk, ran around and played with her at several meetings. These details were not mentioned in the reports filed by the SSC.

To help in its decision on the state's petition to declare Tal eligible for adoption, the court appointed an expert on its behalf, who met with Dalit and Yasmin at the offices of Dalit's legal counsel, and observed their interaction. His findings stated: 'I have no doubt that Dalit, as she is today, has parental capability and is a worthy mother for her young daughter Yasmin'. He particularly noted Dalit's ability to establish eye contact with her daughter, which I saw as confirmation of Dalit's success in overcoming the inhibition that had previously undermined her contact with Tal, and of the benefit of interaction with her second baby. Immediately after Yasmin's birth, Dalit had forced herself to look her in the eye, and after a few days the difficulty that she had previously experienced had passed. To emphasise how significant this is, I should add that Dalit was still unable to look her own partner in the eye.

However, the SSC saw things differently. Previously, the adoption officials had pointed to Dalit's difficulty in establishing eye contact with Tal as a 'personality defect'. Since Dalit had now proven that, unlike personality traits, which are immutable, she was able to overcome the problem and establish eye contact with Yasmin, they were obliged to change tack. Now they cited Dalit's ability to establish eye contact with Yasmin as proof that she had been *unwilling* to make that effort in her relationship with Tal. They, who had been unable to spot Dalit's difficulty in interacting with her daughter and help her overcome it, now used it to accuse her of deliberate neglect. Once again, a parent's difficulty, or failure, was presented as either something immutable, or as a manifestation of deliberate and conscious harm, either of which, according to the SSC, justified removing the parent from their children's lives.

However, despite confirming that Dalit had demonstrated her ability to raise her daughter, the expert recommended to the court to consider carefully

> whether Tal's interests did indeed call for removing her from the home in which she had been living for a year and a half, and transferring her to another home, to parents to whom she is not attached, and to a different sociocultural context.

Although returning the child to her mother's custody, as difficult as it would be, would not cause irreparable harm, the expert continued, he did hope that:

> Dalit would understand that although the doubts about her parental capability may have been offensive and hurtful, Tal's well-being was more important than her need to win the legal battle and to prove that the authorities had been wrong to take Tal away from her.

These words echoed the statements made by the authorities in the 1950s, when Israeli society encouraged new immigrants to send their children to institutions that applied Zionist ideology in their education programmes, as a sign of their willingness to give precedence to their children's educational needs rather than keeping them at home.

However, the twists and turns of Dalit's case, as we shall see, ultimately validated the expert's warning and highlighted the irreparable consequences that ensue when protection of the child is equated with excluding the birth parents.

Despite the expert's recommendation, the family court decided, a full fifteen months after the state's first application in this case, to reject the state's petition to declare Tal eligible for adoption, and ordered her to be returned to her mother. While the protracted legal proceedings had deepened the divide between Dalit and her daughter, it had allowed the judge, as he noted, to assess how Dalit had developed and matured during that time. He then lambasted the welfare services, both for how they had treated Dalit after she had fled from her adoptive family, as cited above, and for their callous and persistent intervention in her care of Tal and disruption of the bond between them. He further added:

> The possibility has not escaped my attention that the [adoption] officials were possibly motivated, perhaps unconsciously, by the long list of families waiting to adopt, in relation to the small number of children who are placed for adoption voluntarily by their parents.

The court's decision to return Tal to Dalit's custody, with no reference to her partner Salim, should be explained. During the hearings, it was learned that Dalit and Salim had tried to hide the fact that he was not, in fact, Tal's father, which is why he had not complied with the court's order to submit to a paternity test. This emerged when adoption officials investigated and found that Dalit had become pregnant with Tal when Salim was in prison for residing illegally in Israel. The true father was another young Arab man, and she met Salim in the early months of her pregnancy with Tal. Although Salim was determined, like her, to assume custody over Tal and to be a full partner in raising her, she was not his daughter, therefore he had no legal status in the court case. The petition was therefore discussed only in relation to Dalit.

Once again, the state asked for a stay of execution of the family court order, to enable it to appeal the decision to the district court, and once again, this was granted. Dalit's counsel then made a special appeal to the Attorney-General himself, as the person in charge of the State Counsels at the court hearings, to ask that the state withdraw its appeal, since there had already been six court rulings ordering Tal to be returned to her mother and stating that her removal had been unwarranted and groundless. In light of those rulings, he argued, filing yet another appeal would be an abuse of the state's prerogative and further exacerbate the already enormous harm that had been inflicted on the mother and her daughter. The Attorney-General, however, rejected this request. The appeal was submitted to the district court, and this time, about two months later, the district court rejected the state's appeal, and ordered Tal be returned to her mother. It further ordered the state to pay the mother's legal costs for the appeal hearings. Once again, the state asked the district court to stay execution of the ruling, to allow it to appeal to the Supreme Court, and once again, the court granted the request. This time, the state did not appeal the court's actual decision to return Tal to her mother's custody, but the manner in which it was to do so. It asked for Tal be returned to her mother gradually, under the supervision of the welfare services who would monitor her adjustment, and that her permanent return to Dalit be approved only after Dalit had proven that she was capable of caring for the child over a period of six months. This was a clear reflection of the SSC's view that the state must control the relationship between parents and children for its own sake, regardless of the consequences, as evident from the state's continuing failure to provide Dalit with the support and protection she needed.

The Supreme Court rejected this appeal, however, reaffirming the family court's ruling, stating that a gradual return of Tal to her mother's custody over a period of a week would suffice. Its dim view of the state's appeal was evident in its charging the state with further litigation costs (a highly exceptional occurrence, since these costs, in effect, are saddled on the taxpayer; in the case of Dalit and Tal, however, it happened twice).

In total, these appeals filed by the state deferred the return of Tal to her mother by another five months. By this time, Tal was two years and three months old, and she had lived with the foster family from the age of six months.

Tal's Return to Dalit

Following the Supreme Court's ruling, the family court accepted the joint request by adoption officials and Dalit's legal counsel for me to oversee Tal's return, and to support her mother. Dalit's lawyer also informed me that, in the interim, Dalit had married her partner, had converted to Islam for the purpose, and was now pregnant for a third time. When I phoned her to congratulate her on her marriage and on the final ruling regarding Tal, she was very excited. In the following days, she phoned me several times, in marked contrast to her behaviour until then. Now that Tal's return was only days away, she could no longer wait: 'I'm on pins and needles', she told me. I was surprised, not only by her initiative in phoning me, but also by the vitality that was evident in her tone of voice and in her direct and personal way of addressing me. Previously, whenever I had phoned her to let her know that, despite the discouraging legal proceedings, someone was rooting for her, her voice had been very flat, and occasionally, when I introduced myself at the start of the conversation, I wondered if she even remembered who I was. Now I realised that her apathy on those occasions, even to the point of not showing up to one of the critical hearings at the family court, was a sign of her deep depression and despair.

One evening she rang me and asked, 'And what about Salim and Yasmin? Tal needs to get used to them, too'. This was a good point, which none of us professionals had thought about. At her request, her legal counsel asked the court to approve her request to have Salim, a resident of the Palestinian Authority, enter Israel and join her for her meetings with Tal. As we shall see later, this issue became a growing concern for Dalit, ultimately assuming a symbolic as well as practical significance. As she saw it, Salim's permit to enter Israel, like the court's decision to return Tal to her, was another symbolic indication of her return 'from the wilderness'.

Tal's return to her mother precipitated a crisis – first and foremost in Tal's life, of course, but also in the life of her mother and of the foster family. Crisis theories point out that to prevent the imbalance that occurs in a crisis situation from becoming a permanent and persistent dysfunctional state requires immediate and intensive intervention, and leveraging the previous equilibrium to create a new, enhanced stable condition.[43] The court's decision to complete Tal's return to Dalit within the space of a week fully bore out these theories.

All the meetings, with the exception of one visit by Tal to the home of Salim's family in the village, took place in the town of the foster family, to spare Tal the discomfort of the long journey involved. To this end, Dalit and I were provided with a taxi service, and the venue provided by the local welfare services was almost always available for the exclusive use of these meetings, allowing Dalit, the foster parents and especially Tal to adjust their physical intimacy as they saw fit. At least two adoption officials were present at every meeting, per standard SSC protocol. Each meeting lasted two hours, and with each passing day there was a noticeable change in Dalit and the foster parents, who were very conscious of the short timeframe involved and the purpose of the meetings. Tal's behaviour indicated that she, too, understood the threat of imminent parting from the foster parents.

Most of the time she clung to them and recoiled from Dalit, but every so often she wavered, and Dalit would seize these moments to create some intimacy between them.

Overall, Tal's return to her mother was a heartrending experience. What follows is a chronological description of events, based on the notes I made during that week.

Wednesday

The meeting took place in the early afternoon. Dalit arrived early to meet with me ahead of time, very excited, and wearing her best clothes and makeup. The previous evening I had asked her if she wanted to bring some toys to the meeting, and she said that she didn't know what to bring; perhaps she might bring a book that she has at home. I brought a stuffed bunny rabbit as a soft toy for her to give to Tal, and a ball for them to play with together. Dalit suggested that she bring Yasmin with her, as she was not sure there would be anyone to take care of her in her absence. I advised against it, as I thought it would be better for her to be attentive only to Tal at their first meeting.

Before we got into the taxi, Dalit bought some sweets for Tal. She was extremely nervous. While we were waiting for the taxi, she said, 'OK, now you can tell me about the foster family'. I told her that they were young, with a son of their own who was older than Tal, and religious Jews. 'Wow, what a great match', she said, sardonically. During the ride, she took great pleasure in going into detail about Yasmin, who was fifteen months old at the time, and about her life with Salim's family. She had had many doubts about converting to Islam, but she had no doubts about Salim himself. He's a good person, she said, and she loved him, but the decision to convert to Islam was not easy. She felt that she was accepted by his family, however, and was particularly appreciative of her mother-in-law who, she said, was very open-minded and avoided criticising her for her 'immodest attire', which is very different from what is conventionally worn by women in the village, and went out of her way to treat her particularly well, lest she be accused of discriminating against 'the Jewish girl'. Dalit then talked about her own family of origin, and how she knew nothing about them. Although she had come to terms with the fact that her birth mother wanted nothing to do with her, she did have brothers and sisters, and she wondered why she was prevented from knowing anything about them.[44] It is no coincidence that this question arose at this time. Dalit was on her way to renewing her relationship with her eldest daughter, and the importance of genealogical ties and one's place in the family tree often resurfaces in one's consciousness whenever thoughts about the next generation become prominent.

The conversation ended on our arrival at the meeting place. Tzippi, the foster mother, was waiting for us at the entrance, a good-looking woman, tastefully dressed, whose head covering only enhanced her appeal. She welcomed Dalit very warmly. Dalit was startled by Tzippi's presence, drew back for a moment and took out a cigarette to calm down. An adoption official also stood at the entrance. Seeing her, Dalit whispered to me, 'What's *she* doing here? The judge said that she couldn't be at the meetings…' Her unexpected encounter with the foster mother had unsettled her somewhat. The joy that had previously shone from her face gave way to fright, and it was easier for her, it seems, to vent her feelings about the adoption official.

We entered the room and waited for the adoptive father, Isaac, to arrive with Tal. Dalit was tense and subdued. A few minutes later Isaac arrived, with Tal in his arms. Tzippi and (another) adoption official joined us in the room. Dalit sat stone-faced, hardly daring to look at Tal, who also looked somewhat frightened. Tal was thin and fragile-looking, with very long hair, and her right eye was half-shut. We all sat in a circle and Isaac encouraged Tal to 'high-five' us all, noting the name of everyone in the room, with particular emphasis of the words 'Mummy Dalit'. Tal played along and did so cheerfully with a smile, if a little tensely, then rushed back to Isaac's arms. Isaac's expression was open and very warm; now and again, his eyes teared up. We learned that Tal still did not speak. She could say 'Mummy' and 'Daddy', somewhat indistinctly, and a few syllables, though she did appear to understand everything said to her.

Isaac tried to break the tension in the room by telling us how he and Tzippi had spent the past few days explaining to Tal that she was about to return to her 'Mummy Dalit'. They had no doubt that she understood what this meant, which is why, they thought, she was tense in her right shoulder and neck, and her right eye was half-shut. Tal's shoulder was raised in an apparent gesture of refusal, her way of reacting to her imminent separation from her foster family, much as she had responded nearly two years earlier when she had first been brought to the foster family after being taken away from Dalit.

Dalit sat with her head down, looking as though she wanted nothing more than to be swallowed up by the earth. Her smart and festive appearance suddenly appeared out of place, at odds with her posture and blank facial expression. Time and again, the foster parents tried to steer Tal towards Dalit, but while they did so, Isaac asked Dalit why she had not shown up at some of the meetings that had been arranged by the court.

I was sitting next to Dalit. She was being confronted with this criticism at the very moment she was being rejected by her own daughter, in the presence of the foster parents, whom Tal clearly preferred to be with, and of an adoption official whom she felt oppressed by, as at previous meetings with Tal. She evidently felt under attack and I could feel how, in her desire to defend herself, she was slowly wrapping herself in the armour that other people interpreted as defiance. I therefore answered on her behalf, and explained that Dalit had been very hurt. First, when in the middle of her labour with Tal, she was told that her baby would be taken from her at birth. Later, throughout the entire legal proceedings, she was faced with repeated disappointments and humiliations. It was no surprise therefore, I continued, that she was not always keen to come to meetings, which were very difficult for her as Tal had become increasingly estranged from her. Isaac fell silent for a moment, but repeated his admonition that Dalit knew that Tal had travelled a long way, and caused her to do so for nothing. 'At least something would have been waiting for her at the end of the road', he said. Isaac was clearly less concerned about Tal herself or the disappointment she felt (as far as he was concerned, the meetings with Dalit were themselves not important) than with the great effort and inconvenience that had been caused to Tal, Tzippi and himself in their efforts to comply with the court orders, when Dalit herself did not bother to attend. 'Weren't you worried about Tal?' he persisted. Once again I answered on Dalit's behalf, explaining that no, she had not been worried about Tal, because it was clear that Tal was being well cared for. As a case in point, I cited how, when I had been present at one of the meetings and Tal was crying, Dalit had said, 'They've probably sent some food along with her'.

Isaac and Tzippi then told Dalit how Tal used to wake up in a fright during her first nights at their home, to which Dalit replied herself: 'That wasn't because of me; it was because of the previous families she had been with'. This was a revelation to Isaac and Tzippi. Apparently they had no idea that Tal had come to them after being placed with two other families, and that just before she was brought to them she had spent a few days in the care of the SSC itself. I added that the paralysis in her arm and her grimacing smile appeared during the few days she had been at the SSC before being delivered to them. This information, too, clearly stunned them. They sat momentarily at a loss as to what to say, as their image of Dalit visibly changed from an abusive mother to one who had herself been victimised. Finally they said, 'Well, at least you should know that Tal got everything from us that we could give her. She's received the best possible care. That should be some comfort to you'. Dalit replied, 'Comfort, no; reassurance, yes'.

The empathy that the foster parents felt on hearing the circumstances of Tal's birth changed again to shock when Dalit told them that she had married and converted to Islam. Tzippi said, 'So Tal will be getting a double whammy: not only is she leaving us, but the religious lifestyle that we observe will change as well'. Dalit said nothing in reply.

At this point, the foster parents turned their attention to the question of Tal's father, and Dalit's partner. 'Why do you keep going out with Arab guys?' they asked. 'Because a Jewish guy wouldn't give me what he gives me', Dalit replied, adding that she too had been adopted. The meaning was clear and painful: as she saw it, she wasn't good enough to belong to the mainstream Jewish society by partnering with a Jewish man. In an effort to keep the atmosphere amicable, the foster parents said something about how it was best not to dwell on the past, but Dalit did not reply. They looked embarrassed, and as they could not find a way to connect with Dalit, they played with Tal. She responded happily, and yet her joyful cries seemed somewhat forced. I wondered if this was a sign of the tension she felt at the prospect of her imminent parting from her foster parents, which, they thought, she understood well. Dalit gave her the stuffed bunny that we had brought with us, then offered her some sweets. Isaac remarked that these were bad for her teeth, but Dalit said nothing in response. Tal was happy to wear the necklace of sweets around her neck, and for a moment there was a twinkle of joy in her eyes as she looked at Dalit. Despite the great pain that was evident in the foster parents' faces, they played with her with great affection, and tried to involve Dalit too. Dalit was so troubled by Tal's avoidance of her, however, that she withdrew into her shell. Isaac and Tzippi suggested that Tal take the stuffed bunny and bring it back the next day. As they left, they asked Tal to wave goodbye to Dalit.

On the taxi ride back, Dalit spoke about how disappointed she was. She regretted not having brought Yasmin with her, as she had suggested the evening before. With hindsight, I also thought that perhaps I had been wrong to talk her out of it. I had not appreciated quite how much she and Tal had become estranged from one another; I remembered how they had interacted during the meetings when I had observed them together, and I wanted her to be free to give Tal her full attention without being distracted by Yasmin. I now thought that Yasmin's presence might possibly have made it easier for Dalit to bridge the gap between her and Tal. From Dalit's remarks after the meeting, she had clearly felt isolated and under attack. She felt the need for her husband's protection, and possibly also thought that Yasmin's presence might have demonstrated her success as a mother. She was very hurt by Tal's reaction to her. When I asked her if she was angry at the foster parents, she said, 'Angry, no. Jealous, yes'. As we drove home, she was very quiet.

Thursday

This time, the meeting took place in the morning. Dalit was dressed more casually, and during our taxi ride there and back expressed the hope that her husband would be allowed to enter Israel so as to take part in future meetings. Once again, she spoke at length about him and Yasmin. He came across as a kind-hearted, protective and intelligent person. Her lack of any contact with her adoptive or birth family clearly bothered her, and perhaps her partner as well. After Yasmin's birth, he had phoned Dalit's adoptive mother to tell her about the birth, and suggested that they all meet for a conciliatory reunion. The adoptive mother responded by extending her congratulations to Dalit, but said that her husband wanted no more to do with her since the episode with the police. Dalit said she couldn't blame him: he had really loved her, but she had let him down badly. The parents' generation – Dalit's birth mother, her adoptive parents, her mother-in-law – were continually present in spirit during our trips to see Tal. The renewed contact with Tal appeared to have triggered a yearning within Dalit for parental support of some kind; in its absence, she sought her husband's presence instead.

Aside from that, however, during these taxi rides Dalit was animated and exuberant, as she had been in all our conversations since the Supreme Court's final decision to return Tal to her. But once we reached the meeting venue, she would fall silent, stricken with anxiety. As we waited for the arrival of Tal and the foster parents, Dalit wondered why we always had to wait for them on each occasion. I replied that it may be because of their past experiences, when she herself had not shown up at previous meetings, which meant that they now preferred not to set out before they knew for sure that we had arrived. This explanation failed to satisfy her. She had no appreciation of how strongly they had felt about her absences from previous meetings, perhaps because she saw herself only as a victim of the repeated cancellations of court rulings. As far as she was concerned, those meetings with Tal had been an arbitrary demand of the courts, in response to which she rebelled as she did against all authority.

When the foster parents arrived with Tal in their arms, it was clear from Tzippi's expression that she was much more distant this time. Isaac left the room for a few minutes. Tzippi began kicking the ball towards Tal, who kicked it back to her, while Dalit sat apart, utterly frozen. Tzippi's face remained expressionless, and she pointedly avoided kicking the ball towards Dalit to involve her in the game. I joined in and kicked the ball towards Dalit, and she began taking part, but with some apprehension. We found that Tzippi and Isaac had forgotten to bring the stuffed bunny rabbit with them, although the toy had been meant, in part, as a means of bridging the gap between the two parties. Dalit perhaps did not think that this mattered very much, but for me, Tzippi and Isaac's omission was indicative of the awkwardness they felt after the previous session, and their reluctance to come to terms with Tal's imminent return to Dalit.

The atmosphere in the room was very tense, and to relieve it a little I suggested that we all go outside to the playground. I went out with Dalit and Tal, and Tzippi joined us. Tal darted between her and Isaac, who remained inside. Dalit sat on one of the swings, clearly unsure as to where she fitted in the picture. Presently, however, Isaac came out as well, and played with Tal near Dalit, while trying constantly to steer Tal towards her. I remarked to Tzippi that she appeared to be more reserved than the day before, and she replied angrily that she couldn't understand why it was that at the previous meeting, when they entered the room with Tal, Dalit looked at her without the merest glimmer of joy or enthusiasm in her eyes. 'Anyone who passes us in the street stops to say, "Oh, what an adorable baby!" So how is it that she reacts like that when she sees her own child?'

The implication was clear: how could she return Tal to someone who was so indifferent, when she herself loved her so much and was so attached to her? I tried to reassure her by saying that people respond in different ways, but she only scoffed when I said this, and when I remarked that she was angry, said there was no point in talking about anger. She went back inside, leaving me with the vegetable platter she had been nibbling on. Isaac took her place, invited me to help myself from the vegetable platter, and continued to try and bring Tal and Dalit together. I was moved by his sincere efforts. His eyes were tearful the whole time, and he was acting against his own wishes, but since he had been ordered to return Tal to Dalit, he thought it better to help Dalit and thereby make things easier for Tal. He suggested to Tal that she offer Dalit something from the platter, and each time she approached Dalit, he asked me if it would be best if he were to move away.

Tal continued to dash between Isaac, who was still outside, and Tzippi, who was now inside the building. Isaac encouraged Dalit to approach Tal, and Dalit did so, but Tal still avoided her. Dalit came back to us, saying, 'She doesn't want to'. Isaac repeatedly encouraged her. 'Don't give up so quickly', he suggested, but Dalit replied, 'Every time I look at her face, I hate them [the adoption officials]'. Isaac suggested that she stop thinking about them, but given Tal's repeated rejections, which Dalit felt like a slap in her face as she tried to make a connection, it was hard to expect her to overcome the feelings of rage. It seemed as if she experienced her bond with her daughter as a stump, which she could not coax back to life to heal the rift between them.

Towards the end of the meeting, Dalit gave up and stopped even trying to get close to Tal. The sun beat down on our heads and we went back inside. Dalit sat gloomily by the entrance while the foster parents and the adoption official played happily with Tal. I thought how galling it must be for her to witness even the adoption official having more success with Tal than she had, as Tal's own mother. She clung to her cellphone and engaged in frequent conversations with Salim, who was closely following events from afar. She then suddenly announced that she could not be there the next day.

We all fell silent in astonishment. Apparently, Salim had just told her that she had to take Yasmin to the clinic the next day, to get her shots. He himself couldn't do so because Yasmin was registered under Dalit's name, and it wasn't possible to put off the appointment to another date. The adoption official responded by immediately phoning the Department of Public Health, who told her that in fact it was possible to postpone the vaccination by a week, but Dalit argued that bureaucracy within the Palestinian Authority made that impossible. Isaac, somewhat hesitatingly, said, 'But we thought the whole point was that we had to have an unbroken series of meetings', to which Dalit replied that she could take Tal home with her for the Sabbath. Once again, everyone fell silent. I remarked that it was too early to do that, and the meeting ended with the agreement that Dalit would let everyone know if she was arriving the next day.

On the ride back, Dalit vented her feelings of despair and rage. She felt wretched and defeated. It was a mistake, she thought, to allow the foster parents to be present at the meetings, because as long as they were there, Tal would refuse to go near her. 'It won't work!' she kept repeating. She felt the whole idea of the meetings was a mistake, from start to finish, and she wanted out.

I suggested that she try to put off Yasmin's inoculation, and bring her along with her the next day, so that she and Tal could get to know each other, and then, at the end of the meeting, we would offer to take Tal with us after the weekend. This suggestion placated her somewhat, but the feeling of failure and hurt did not go away. She pointed out the irony of the adoption officials downplaying the importance of Yasmin's inoculation the next day when, in the past, they had vilified her for not ensuring that Tal got her shots on time. Nonetheless, she would try to postpone Yasmin's appointment. Between her expressions of anger and hurt, she spoke about how Salim, unlike her, had a knack for playing with children: all the village children came to play with him. When I asked her if, when she had been 'on pins and needles' in anticipation of Tal's return, she had thought it would be this hard, she said no.

When we arrived in town, she decided to go to her lawyer to get a letter stating the purpose of her request to grant her husband an entry permit into Israel. As he handed her the letter, he managed to cheer her up somewhat: 'This process will not take forever, you know', he told her. 'This, too, shall pass, at some point', he said. His words of reassurance were important because Dalit's feelings of defeat were beginning to affect me, too. Although I had been asked to chaperone Dalit during this week given that my expert opinion, almost two years earlier, had supported Tal's return to her care, I discovered that the adoption officials thought that I had been in close contact with her throughout that entire period. They must have said as much to the adoptive parents, because when they criticised Dalit for her absences from some of the meetings in the past, Isaac had turned to me and said, 'You're her minder – you should have made sure that she showed up for the meetings'. In fact, not only was I not her 'minder' throughout this period; I thought that the court's demand to hold these meetings, after all its previous rulings had been repeatedly stayed, placed impossible demands on Dalit and did not do anything to foster the bond between her and Tal. I had been made out to be Dalit's spokeswoman, as it were, during the process of returning Tal to her, although I was not close to her and did not really know her well. Dalit had been obliged to endure these interminable proceedings on her own, without the support of anyone close to her.

More than anything, Dalit was afraid of having to compete against the foster parents. When I suggested to her, before the handover, that she ask for the chance to visit the foster family at their home in order to get to know what Tal's image of 'home' looked like, she said that it wasn't easy for her, since '[Tal] calls the foster mother "Mum"'.

Her difficulty stemmed from the fact that she was being measured against the adoption officials' and foster parents' expectations of what a 'mother' should be like, while ignoring her previous trials and tribulations when she still had Tal in her care. As one of the adoption officials told me, 'I see a mother who has fought to get her girl back, but when she does see her, doesn't run towards her'. When I replied that Dalit was afraid that she would be let down once again, as had happened on previous occasions, I discovered that this official knew nothing about the previous course of events prior to the Supreme Court's decision. She had joined the team in charge of Dalit's case only midway through, and *had not read the file*. This was revealing. The fact that she had not read the case file speaks volumes about the SSC's indifference to understanding the context of a painful adoption case, and yet her ignorance did not stop her from criticising Dalit's conduct. Once again, the image of the eagle's nest came to mind. Dalit was expected to climb a precipice and retrieve her infant, and the merest stumble she made on the way served as evidence of her incapability. It was doubly difficult to challenge this image when Dalit was becoming progressively more withdrawn in the face of her failure to re-establish a bond with Tal.

That evening, I spoke with Dalit on the phone, and she sounded more cheerful. She was convinced that this time her husband would receive permission to join her for the meeting on the following Sunday. She decided to come the next day without Yasmin. Her husband categorically refused to put off the inoculation to the following week, and decided, instead, to go with her to the local police station to apply for a one-day postponement. That would mean the inoculation would be on a Saturday, and since that was the Jewish Sabbath, Dalit would not be travelling to meet Tal anyway.

Friday

In the morning, Dalit was particularly alert and active, and more talkative than ever, in marked contrast to her mood the day before. I did not understand why this was, but I chose not to ask her. She spoke scathingly about the SSC, and I replied that it was better that she vent her anger with me in the taxi this way, so that at the meeting she would be better able to pay attention to Tal and focus on her, rather than on her own anger at the adoption officials.

On our arrival, I suggested to Dalit that we go into the toy shop and buy Tal a present. This time, Dalit was happy to do so. As she toured the shop, she was initially stumped: what can one buy for a girl of two? At last she found a doll. When she met with Tal and gave her the doll, Isaac remarked, in a very friendly manner, 'Tal loves dolls very much; she has a lot of them at home. We were all standing at the entrance to the venue where the meetings were held. This time, we learned, the adoption officials and the foster parents had decided to leave Tal alone with Dalit, to put Dalit more at ease. Tal stood next to her foster parents and refused to approach Dalit, who responded in kind, facing her, frozen and immobile. One of the adoption officials stepped forward and suggested to Dalit that she pick up Tal and hold her, but Dalit made no response. I went up to her, touched her lightly on the shoulder and repeated the adoption official's suggestion. Dalit snapped at me, 'Why don't *you* go upset her yourself – why should I do it?'

Dalit's sensitivity to Tal's situation was touching. Her reply summed up her situation, as she saw it: as if it were not bad enough that Tal had been forcibly taken away from her, Tal now saw her as a threat. I kept my touch on her shoulder and explained that if I picked Tal up, it would only make things worse, as she would be coming first to me, and then to Dalit. 'We're doing something that hurts her a great deal', I said. 'And just as you give a child a vaccination shot despite the pain that it gives her, you should pick her up now. Without any pain whatsoever it's not going to happen.'

This time she relented, and said, 'OK, give me a moment'. A minute later, she held Tal in her arms. Tal cried, Dalit entered one of the rooms that were available for our meetings, and the foster parents began to say goodbye. Tal's tears were an expression of protest, but coupled with an apparent resignation to her fate; more of a bleat than a furious or demanding cry. The foster parents stayed around for a few more minutes, until she stopped crying.

After they left, Dalit and Tal went outside together into the playground. Tal rode about on a tricycle, and Dalit chatted with her; they appeared to be absorbed in deep and enjoyable conversation. The adoption officials and I watched them out of earshot, and when the foster parents phoned a short time later, the adoption officials reassured them that Tal appeared to be relaxed and feeling well. The calm and gentleness that I had witnessed in Dalit during my observations nearly two years earlier were once again in evidence. Dalit had been right: she was indeed able to establish a rapport with Tal, but only when she was not forced to compete with the foster parents, or made to feel that she was being tested. Tal was fascinated by a bulldozer that was working nearby, and the conversation between mother and daughter went on for about forty minutes. The adoption officials then suggested that we ask the foster parents to return, as it was a Friday and the Sabbath eve was set to start early.[45] Dalit agreed, and went back inside with Tal, where they began to sing and play together on a xylophone. Tal chirped away happily. At that moment, the foster parents entered the next room and observed the two through a one-way mirror. Isaac's eyes filled with tears, but Tzippi sat in the corner, pale and scowling, seemingly wanting no part, however passive, in what was going on. It felt as though she were watching Tal's life after she was taken from them.

When the two of them entered the room, Tal ran to them happily, without crying in protest. We sat down to plan the remaining meetings in the following week, but Tzippi could not bring herself to take part. She looked as though she were about to faint. We suggested that Dalit bring Yasmin with her on Sunday, and that Tal visit Dalit at her home on Monday. I then hurried to leave with Dalit, as I felt that our presence at that moment had become difficult for Isaac and Tzippi. I felt very sorry for them. They had become very attached to Tal, and although they were aware of her legal status when she was placed with them, the attachment they had formed with her, had been in anticipation of a joint future. Their efforts to create a pleasant atmosphere at the meetings, despite Dalit's initial rebuffs, filled me with admiration, and the endless pain in Isaac's eyes triggered my compassion.

As we left, Dalit got into the taxi with a sense of relief and triumph. I was pleased that she had managed to get through to Tal this time, even without Salim and Yasmin being present, and proved to herself that she was able to do it. During the ride itself, however, she was very quiet. The next day, she rang to say that Yasmin had indeed received her inoculation at the nearby village, but that her husband refused to let Yasmin go with her to the meeting on Sunday, for fear that the adoption officials would take her away and he would not be able to protect her once they were in Israeli territory. His concern was not entirely groundless. Social services had, after all, sought to declare the baby a 'ward of the court at birth', and were prevented from doing so only because Dalit and Yasmin had gone into Palestinian Authority territory, where Israeli civil law did not apply.

Sunday

This time, Dalit was in high spirits throughout the taxi ride. She was convinced that Salim would receive a permit to enter Israel (from the West Bank) the next day, and join her in her meeting with Tal. She spoke about how, on Saturday, she had cleaned the house and cooked (she explained that she had only learned to cook at her husband's house, and that the women in his family made fun of her because, in their culture, girls learned to cook as young as twelve years old). When I asked if she had any further thoughts after the successful meeting on Friday, she replied that she had, and had talked it over with her husband. Yasmin is developing so well, she said, and Tal is delayed in her development. She therefore wondered to what extent that was her fault. The fact that she allowed herself to even ask these questions after the successful meeting the previous Friday was no coincidence. When one is not made to feel like an utter failure, one is able to contemplate one's accountability.

As we approached the meeting place, a tense silence fell in the taxi. I wondered how the foster parents, and especially Tzippi, would relate to us after we had left them in such pain on the previous occasion. A few minutes after our arrival, Tzippi emerged from a taxi, wearing an elegant hat and a warm smile, and looking more beautiful than ever. All traces of the agitation she had felt the previous Friday had completely vanished from her face. While we waited for Isaac and Tal to arrive, Dalit and Tzippi sat in the lobby and fell into conversation. They then left the building together, still chatting freely, while the adoption officials and I watched them from the side. Tzippi called out to us, 'Don't worry, we're getting along fine'. When Isaac arrived with Tal, he joined them in conversation. This lasted throughout the entire meeting, which was, as usual, about two hours. Tal flitted between them as the adults turned their attention alternately from her to each other. At the end of the meeting it was decided that Tzippi would bring Tal to an agreed meeting point the next day, and Dalit would take her home from there; two days later, on Wednesday, Tal would be handed over to Dalit's custody for good. Before we parted, Tzippi said to me, 'We have so many reasons to bless the good Lord'. When I asked her what for, she said only, 'You probably thought that I was dying there on Friday, but I looked within myself over the Sabbath and found things that helped me', without going into any more detail. After Dalit told me about what they had talked about, I wondered if the reason for Tzippi's good humour was that she was thanking God for preventing her from tearing a child away from her mother.

On the ride back, Dalit told me about her conversation with Tzippi and Isaac. It had begun with Tzippi's question whether it was true that Dalit was told that Tal would be taken from her while she was in labour. Tzippi told Dalit that after she had heard that from me, she had gone to her mother and told her how stunned she was. Throughout their conversation with Dalit, both she and Isaac were curious to know about Dalit's life and how she had taken care of Tal, comparing her account with the one they had received from the SSC. For example, they asked Dalit about Tal's condition when she was taken from her. They told her that when they were first contacted by the SSC to collect Tal, they were asked to bring clothes for her, and when they arrived, were shocked at the state she was in, and the seemingly paralysed right arm. They were surprised when they heard Dalit's version of events, but then Isaac said to Tzippi, 'Don't you remember? Every time the courts decided to return Tal to her mother, we said to each other that the adoption officials must not be telling us the whole story?'

They suggested to Dalit that she come live next to them with Tal and Yasmin, to which Dalit replied that she no longer needed that. She had a home and a family, her husband gave her everything she needed, and she felt safe with him. They then asked her if it was OK if they sent Tal along with all her clothes and toys, as well as pictures, and Dalit readily agreed.

From Dalit's description, Isaac and Tzippi appeared to have listened to her story with great interest. This was the first time that her own views and feelings had not been dismissed by someone who saw themselves as representing Tal's interests. Dalit was very pleased afterwards, and said that the foster parents' positive attitude to her may have been partly due to how she related to them.

'You know who told me to behave with them like that?' she asked. 'Salim. He said to me, "Be nice to them".' It was clearly important to her that I credited her husband's contribution to the breakthrough that had taken place in her relationship with the foster parents. Indeed, Salim did seem to be present in spirit at all the meetings, partly because of his frequent phone conversations with Dalit, but also through what she said about him.

Monday

I joined Dalit at the designated meeting place, in anticipation of Tal's arrival. As we waited, a group of schoolchildren walked by, and Dalit said that she envied them: she used to love school outings. This was not the first time that I heard her intimate that her childhood had been cut short. She had been torn away from any environment that might have given her a sense of childhood since the age of twelve, and had had to fight for survival ever since. On another occasion, she told me that she was sorry that she had only one girlfriend who was 'all right': 'Because wherever I've been, all my girlfriends have been, you know, that sort'.

The minutes went by, and still Tal had not arrived. Dalit told me that she would take her down to her mother-in-law's house in the village, where she would find sheep to keep her interested, and lots of children among the family relatives to play with. She seemed worried that Tal wouldn't enjoy staying at her house, as if she didn't trust herself, and had prepared various distractions to keep her amused. Her mother-in-law, she said, was also excited about Tal's arrival. The day before, she had gone into town and bought her some clothes.

Finally, Tzippi and Tal arrived in an SSC vehicle, with one of the adoption officials. At first, Tal refused to go to Dalit, but when Dalit bought them both some ice cream, she relented. Tzippi then made a discreet exit from Tal's sight and left her crying and protesting (in her half-hearted manner) in Dalit's arms. Dalit hurried to get her into the taxi she had ordered, saying, 'Come, let's go to Daddy!'

I protested to her that she wasn't telling Tal the truth. Dalit, clearly a little irked, replied that what she meant was that she was taking Tal to someone who would be her daddy from now on. It struck me that she could not bear Tal's crying, and tried to stop it in any way that was available to her. At all the meetings that week, she appeared as someone who had been hurt in the past, who therefore identified with Tal's desperate neediness and found it difficult to act the part of the protective adult.

The visit with Dalit to the village lasted four hours. Dalit put off the end as much as possible. When we met again at the end of the visit, Tal was very quiet, perhaps tired as well. Dalit told me that she had played and enjoyed herself, that the children liked her very much, but, as Dalit had expected, her presence troubled Yasmin, who understood that she would now have to give up her privileged status of being the only child. Before they returned, Dalit gave Tal a shower and dressed her in the clothes that Tzippi had sent with her, with which Tal happily complied. When Tal saw Tzippi approach in the darkness, she ran to her with great enthusiasm and jumped into her arms. Tzippi asked Tal to say goodbye to Dalit and Tal gave her a warm kiss. It was clear that she had enjoyed herself. Tzippi squeezed Dalit's shoulder and whispered in her ear, 'Dalit, take care of yourself!' Dalit said that her husband wanted to thank them for how they had taken care of Tal, and would join her at the meeting the next day.

Dalit then turned to go and see her lawyer. Once again, he had a letter that was supposed to help Salim get an entry permit into Israel. I invited her to come with me, but she was in a hurry and wanted to get into a taxi that waited nearby. I urged her to come with me all the same, because I had something for her. 'For me?' she asked, in total astonishment. Although I knew that Dalit had always lived with a sense of perpetual abandonment, her astonishment at realising that the gift was for her caused shivers down my spine. We went to my car, and I gave her two bedside table lamps for Tal and Yasmin, a gift from her lawyer and me.

Tuesday

Dalit delayed her departure from home until the last minute, because at that very moment her husband was waiting at the police station to receive his long-awaited entry permit. Their plan was that he would come with her and they would spend the night at his sister's, who lived near the town where the meetings were being held, and he would help her bring Tal home the next day. Finally, she rang to say that she was leaving the house alone because her husband had not received the entry permit into Israel after all. She was in an angry mood, and slept the whole way to the meeting.

Tzippi and Isaac had brought Tal's belongings with them, and showed Dalit the album that Tal's friends had given her at the farewell party held for her at the nursery that morning. The adoption official suggested that they advise Dalit about Tal's preferences, details of her daily routine and so on, which they did, but almost absent-mindedly, as though they and Dalit were now so engrossed in their newfound friendship that they no longer needed our intervention as professionals. However, throughout the visit Dalit avoided any contact with Tal, and when I urged her to forget about the disappointment about her husband and focus on Tal, she snapped, 'You've got no idea what I'm going through right now, so leave me alone!'

For their part, Isaac and Tzippi respected the distance that Dalit kept from Tal, and Tal, for her part, reciprocated by adamantly refusing to approach her. Isaac and Tzippi guessed that she was acting this way because she had been told that she would be going with Dalit the next day and not returning home with them.

After Dalit explained to me why she was behaving the way she was, I understood that she was pulling back just before the critical moment, and so too, perhaps, was Tal. A retreat of this sort is akin to stepping back before leaping across a chasm, and is characteristic of the final moment of an intervention in a crisis. Dalit confessed that she was afraid that, once again, something would happen at the last minute to prevent her from getting Tal back. She had not let on about any of this in the taxi on the way to the meeting. I don't know if I could have reassured her in any way, but this time the situation was fundamentally different. Now that the Supreme Court had spoken, there was no way that the ruling could be stayed. Moreover, the adoption officials themselves were now clearly willing to comply with the court order, and had tried to help Dalit to connect with Tal. But none of these arguments, however sound, put her mind at rest. It was also possible that she was in fact anxious about something else entirely, such as the prospect of the difficulties she might encounter once Tal was back in her care, much as she had encountered in her meetings with her. Such an emotionally intricate and charged situation as Dalit now found herself in naturally has complexities that are not obvious even to the person involved.

Wednesday

Dalit arrived at the meeting venue without me. When I arrived, she was sitting by herself, and remarked that, unlike all previous occasions, no taxi was waiting to take us back. We later learned that this was merely an oversight on someone's part, but Dalit saw it as proof of the SSC's last-minute change of heart about returning Tal to her. The adoption officials, however, quickly ordered another taxi, and meanwhile the foster parents arrived with Tal, their eyes red with weeping. They had spent the day at a family picnic, after a blessing ceremony held for Tal at the synagogue. They had asked their son to help them load Tal's things into the car, but he had refused. He couldn't bring himself to do it.

We had agreed ahead of time to keep this meeting short. Tzippi and Isaac asked to speak with Dalit privately, and gave her some anti-fever medication; they were convinced that Tal would develop a temperature later. They then hugged and kissed Tal and said goodbye to her. Tzippi fell on Dalit's neck, hugged her and wept bitterly. Then they left, closing the door behind them. Dalit took Tal, who was wailing desperately, and tried to draw her attention to the toys in the room. After making sure that the foster parents had gone, she went out with Tal into the playground, sat on a swing next to hers and chatted with her. When the taxi arrived, Tal was very quiet and withdrawn. She allowed Dalit to buckle her seat belt, held on tightly to the drinking bottle she had received from her foster parents, and after a few minutes fell asleep and slept the whole way. I was very tense. Dalit looked at me, very surprised; she herself was very calm, and rested her arm on Tal.

We arrived in town after dark. Tal woke up and went on holding tightly to her drinking bottle, with an expression of utter dejection.

We sat and waited for a taxi that would take Dalit and Tal to their home. I thought to myself that Tal probably felt lost. This was the fifth time she had been handed from one person to another, and she had no way of knowing if this was to be the last time. When the taxi arrived, Tal got in without so much as a glance back at me. I left them with a heavy heart, and hoped that, before long, I would once again see her cheerful and happy.

Tal and Dalit Together Again

In the first days after Tal's return, I spoke with Dalit on the phone every day. She told me that Tal was agreeing to eat only raw food, while their food was almost exclusively fried. Tal slept a great deal, and at night fell asleep with Dalit in her bed, but did not develop a temperature as the foster parents had feared. When she was awake, she played with the other children and appeared to be in a good mood.

A week later, I visited them at their home, which had been built on Israeli territory before Salim had been banned from entering the country, and he stayed in it illegally from time to time.[46] The home certainly did not have much by way of stimulation for children, to put it mildly, but Salim appeared to exhibit much warmth towards the two girls and tried to persuade Yasmin, the younger girl, to accept Tal. Yasmin, a cheerful and energetic child, was very skilled at capturing everyone's attention, and turning every object in her path into a plaything. Tal appeared to feel very much at home. She was quiet and enjoyed the opportunity to cuddle up to Salim, who had been presented as her father. When Salim escorted me on my way out, Tal ran after him and 'scolded' him, as though angry that he was presuming to leave her. This was the first time that I saw her protesting vigorously about anything, which I understood as a sign that she had become attached to Salim and was not afraid to assert her rights. Dalit told me that she related to men more easily, but my impression was that she had formed a good rapport with Dalit as well, and felt secure in Dalit's response to her. The gentleness that I had observed in Dalit's attitude in the past had returned. Although she was not naturally physically expressive like her husband, she did relate to Tal easily and naturally on a physical level, and accompanied her actions with warm and appropriate motherly talk. She now made eye contact with Tal quite naturally, but the verbal interaction between them was still limited because Tal's speech was still undeveloped and her vocabulary very limited. Added to this was the unfamiliarity of the spoken language at home. While Dalit and Salim spoke to Tal in Hebrew, the rest of the family – the grandmother (Dalit's mother-in-law, who had welcomed Tal warmly) and the other children and adults – spoke only Arabic.

My visit to Dalit's home was my final duty in my court-appointed capacity as supervisor of Tal's return to her mother, but having come this far, I decided not to sever all contact with Dalit. I therefore kept in touch with her for several months, as did the foster parents, mainly by telephone, to receive detailed reports of Tal's behaviour and mood, and to give Dalit advice on how to deal with certain situations. Approximately ten days after Tal's return to Dalit, Salim invited the foster parents to visit, which they did, with their son. Dalit told me that the children had played together, and Tzippi had told Dalit how, now that she saw how well developed Yasmin was, she understood why Dalit had been so upset at having Tal taken from her. Towards the end of the visit, when the foster parents were about to leave, Dalit tried to hide Tal. Salim stopped her, explaining that Tal must get used to the fact that the foster parents leave while she stays. In the event, Tal did cry a little, but then calmed down.

Over time, the two families began to meet regularly at a nearby shopping centre, in effect creating for themselves, without state intervention, the very situation that the authorities had sought in their final appeal to the Supreme Court, namely that Tal be returned to her mother gradually over a period of several months, while maintaining contact with the foster parents. Although this may have made things easier for Tal, it did pose some difficulties for Dalit. Two days after Tal's return to her, Dalit complained to me that the foster mother was 'moaning at me on the phone'. When Salim overheard her, he grabbed the receiver and told me not to listen, because 'we are not about to cut the ties with the foster parents', who were 'good people'. Tzippi and Isaac's goodwill, the sincere love that they had for Tal, and Dalit's ability to make amends, all moved me a great deal. I had not imagined that things would change so profoundly.

A month after Tal had returned to her mother, the foster parents asked – almost demanded – that Tal be sent over to spend the *seder* (Passover meal) with them, or that Dalit come with her. Dalit found it hard to refuse, and although she thought that the timing of the visit was premature, eventually she relented and spent a second Passover holiday meal with Isaac and Tzippi's family. She told me that she felt at ease while she was there, 'they're nice people', and when Tal needed something during the visit, she turned to Dalit, not to the foster parents. After that visit, however, Dalit avoided any further contact. Whenever she met with the foster parents, Dalit explained to me,

Tal would stop saying even the few words that she spoke, and took several days to return to her usual speech, which was limited enough as it was.

By that time, I assumed that contact between the foster parents and Dalit and Salim had begun to fade, as usually happens in such cases, and the issue would resolve itself. In one of our conversations, Dalit confessed that 'the jealousy is just killing me', and she wanted no further contact with the foster parents. Salim, too, she said, had become disenchanted with them. They had promised to get him an entry permit into Israel, but failed to do so. Only with hindsight did I realise that Dalit suspected that something was not quite right, but perhaps couldn't put her finger on it.

About a month later, I met with Tal and Dalit to visit an amusement park together. We agreed to meet at the spot from which Tal had been taken to her first visit to Dalit's home. When Tal saw me, she rushed towards me, and when I picked her up in my arms she laid her head on my shoulder, as though she wanted to cry. It was a difficult moment for the three of us – Tal, Dalit and me. I assumed that she had run to me in the hope, perhaps, that it meant that the foster parents would be present, as on past occasions involving me. Dalit was taken aback by her reaction. She, too, guessed that this was a remnant of Tal's loss of the foster parents, but rather than admit as much, tried to dismiss it on the grounds that I resembled a neighbour of hers whom Tal liked very much. She did not, she said, see any indication in Tal's behaviour that she missed the foster parents or was unhappy about living with her. When I asked Tal if she would like to go for a drive, she nodded, climbed down from my arms on her own and happily got into my car. As we drove, I heard happy noises from the back. Dalit, who was sitting next to her, explained that Tal was clapping hands and playing on the cellphone.

On the way, we stopped for Dalit to visit the bank. The moment she disappeared from our sight, Tal's shoulder went up – her tell-tale sign of distress over parting. At the amusement park itself, she accepted every invitation of mine to play, but preferred to play with Dalit. She clearly saw Dalit as her 'safe base' from which to make sorties when something caught her eye, but whenever she was asked by Dalit to stop running and wait for her, she complied. Two months after I had left her with a heavy heart, gazing around her with a lost look on her face, I saw her laughing, playing happily, with a cheerful and warm look in her eyes. She had grown a great deal, in height and in weight. The thin figure that I saw during our meeting before she was finally returned to Dalit, with the raised shoulder and semi-closed eye that broadcast sadness and wretchedness, and the seemingly feigned cheeriness with which she played when she had first met Dalit again, had all disappeared. Instead, I saw before me a sturdy, tanned and relaxed child. Although the traces of the loss of her foster parents were apparent in her dash towards me, she seemed to be sure of her bond with Dalit.

The question of finding her a suitable educational framework, however, was still unresolved. To diagnose the source of her delayed speech, which worried Dalit a great deal, Dalit needed Tal's medical file, but the SSC had not given it to her. Three months after Tal had returned to Dalit, Dalit's lawyer was obliged once again to resort to legal means to ensure that Tal's medical files were given to her mother.

Exclusion and Alienation

Although Dalit's motherhood was now officially recognised and she had found a warm and loving family, she was still living in the wilderness in another sense – she was now a resident of the Palestinian Territories. 'I wouldn't have minded if [Salim] had been an Israeli Arab', she explained to me at one of our meetings, 'but him being a "Territories Arab" makes us so helpless!'

True enough, the Israeli authorities were still refusing to issue her husband an entry permit into Israel. As a result, the good financial situation that she had reported when Tal was returned to her deteriorated within weeks. Salim, who had worked as a builder, became unemployed. None of the people in his area could afford to fix up their houses, or build new ones, and as a resident of the Palestinian Territories, he was prevented from working in Israel. Dalit's conversations with me began to be dominated by complaints about lack of money and her husband's forced idleness. I tried to find someone to pay for Tal's transportation to a bilingual educational institution that Dalit had chosen for her, since Salim could not drive her, it being on Israeli territory, but to no avail. Tal, Dalit told me, was stuck at home with nothing to do all day. From time to time she would tag along with Salim as he went about his errands, which, according to Dalit, she enjoyed very much. The family's life had no regular pattern. Sometimes they would sleep late, sometimes they would leave the house early if they had errands to do, and on other occasions they would take part in family celebrations that went on late into the night. Dalit appeared not to be initiating any purposeful activity with Tal, despite Tzippi and Isaac's advice to provide her with constant stimulation, 'otherwise she wilts', as they put it. I wondered to what extent the lifestyle at home was affected by Salim's despondency over not finding any work, or his despair at being persistently denied entry into Israel. Both he and Dalit believed that this was due to the authorities' concern that he might try to avenge his brother's death at the hands of Israeli security forces (which, the authorities claimed, had been 'accidental').

As if that were not enough, complications had just been found in Dalit's latest pregnancy, and she had to go to hospital for tests. On one occasion, she had to be rushed to hospital in the middle of the night while Tal was asleep, and she didn't have the chance to say goodbye. Salim, as it happens, had just been arrested by the Palestinian authorities until he paid the traditional financial compensation for running over and injuring a youth in the village. Sometime later, Dalit told me that Tal had stopped talking altogether during those days, and sank into what looked like depression, which Dalit attributed to her own disappearance the night of her hospitalisation, coupled with her husband's absence. I suggested that she talk to Tal about what had happened, even if she did not respond verbally. Dalit said nothing in response, and I don't know if she acted on my advice.

Apart from her concern about Tal's condition, Dalit was fully occupied with trying to secure an entry permit for Salim, so he might be by her side when their new child was born. She had learned that her baby was in breech position, and that if it did not turn around in the next two weeks, she would have to return to the hospital. She did not do so, however, and when I urged her two weeks later to check in, she said, 'You sound just like Salim's mum'. She said she was afraid she might be operated on, but my sense was that the real reason was that she didn't want to give birth without Salim beside her. I feared for her and for Tal, but since they were often at Salim's mother's house, in the area under Palestinian Authority jurisdiction, I could not meet with them. Shortly afterwards, Dalit told me on the phone that Tal had starting speaking again, as before, and was once more behaving normally.

A few days later, Dalit told me that she had phoned the foster parents, having not spoken to them for three months. Salim had urged her to do so, saying that it would be wrong for her to lose touch with them completely, even if the foster parents were not making the effort. She told me that Tzippi was very glad to hear from her, and had suggested that they meet in town. Dalit hesitated, but I told her that this might be an opportunity for Tal to see the foster parents again, since Dalit was about to give birth, and after that, no doubt, some time would pass before they could meet again. Salim agreed. Dalit was unsure, but eventually relented.

Two days later, after meeting with Tzippi, Dalit rang me of her own accord (something that she rarely did) to bring me up to date. This time she was flustered. Tzippi had tried to persuade her to leave Tal with them for two or three months after the birth of the new baby, and when Dalit refused, on the grounds that any further upheaval would be harmful to Tal, Tzippi had made an unusual offer. If Dalit and Salim signed a legal agreement to move somewhere near the foster parents, say in the town where Salim's sister lived, and have Tal live with the foster parents and attend local daycare, they would procure Salim an entry permit that would allow him to live and work in Israel. Dalit's immediate reaction was to reject the offer out of hand, as she saw it as an offer to 'sell' Tal in exchange for a work permit for her husband.

'Look how low they're willing to sink', she said, and repeatedly talked about how profoundly offended she was by such an offer. She was particularly alarmed by something else Tzippi had said, namely that if Dalit did not agree, they had 'ways' of getting Tal returned to them. Dalit added that when she met with Tzippi, Tal had shied away from Tzippi and clung to Salim's nephew, who had escorted them; only after Tzippi bought her clothes did she agree to approach her. Moreover, Dalit noted that after the meeting Tal did not react by falling mute again, as she had on previous occasions.

Five days later, on a Friday, Dalit rang me from her lawyer's office. He had given her a letter addressed to the Welfare Coordinator of the (Israeli) Civil Administration of the Palestinian Territories, asking that her husband receive an entry permit when Dalit was about to give birth. As Dalit always reacted when she thought her husband was about to get an entry permit, she was in a cheery mood, and said that Tal felt well too, and that she was going to sort out the entry permit with the Welfare Coordinator on the following Sunday. But Sunday came and went.

On Tuesday morning, I received a call from Dalit's lawyer. The day before, on Monday, Dalit had arrived in court, escorted by the Welfare Coordinator and an adoption official, and announced that she wanted to return Tal to the foster family. Tal, she explained, was in a state of constant depression whenever she was with her, that it was hard for her, Dalit, to see her this way, and that she knew that Tal would be happier with the foster family. The adoption official then testified that Dalit had arrived at the offices of the Welfare Coordinator the day before, and had offered to return Tal to her foster parents. The Welfare Coordinator had then held a telephone conference with the adoption official and with Tzippi, and Tzippi declared that she was willing to take Tal back, but only under the terms of an official adoption. The adoption official agreed: if Tal were returned to Tzippi under any other arrangement, she would end up being mentally disturbed. Dalit told the judge she did not know how she could help Tal, and that I, too, as the supervisor of Tal's return to Dalit, had been unable to help her. The judge granted the two parties twenty-one days to submit a mutually acceptable petition.

This news caught the lawyer, and me, utterly by surprise. I was unable to get hold of Dalit by telephone, as she had changed both hers and Salim's cellphone numbers, and had severed all contact with her lawyer. Since time was of the essence, I wrote to the court, without her permission, with details of our conversation in which she had told me about Tzippi's offer of a permit in exchange for Tal's return. The judge ordered this information to be forwarded to both parties. My letter was received the same day as Dalit's written petition for Tal to be returned to the foster family under an open adoption arrangement. It included an explicit statement that the two parties had agreed for the hearing to be held without legal representation by either side. It goes without saying which of the two sides benefited from this arrangement.

A few weeks later, before the hearing took place, Dalit telephoned her lawyer, and me. I hurried to visit her at her Israeli home. A month had passed since she had given birth to her third child, a boy, whom she named after Salim's deceased brother. The family had insisted on it, and Dalit had reluctantly agreed. Despite the complications towards the end of the pregnancy, the birth itself had been easy, the baby was born at a good weight and Dalit was very happy about him. Salim had been by her side at the birth, having finally received an entry permit thanks to the intervention of someone whom they knew only by his first name; his precise position was unknown to them, but Dalit understood that he had something to do with the Israeli security establishment. After the delivery and while Dalit was still in hospital, Salim brought Tal there, as previously arranged between the two families. She was handed over to the foster parents and taken home with them.

In a way, this episode might be seen as a kind of repeat of the circumstances of Tal's birth, when she was taken from Dalit immediately after birth, only this time Dalit was the one to hand her over. It might be interpreted as an unconscious attempt by Dalit to repeat the traumatic event in which Tal was taken from her. Psychoanalytic theory talks about the inevitability of traumatic events compulsively repeating themselves, as the person turns their participation in the event from passive to active, in a retroactive attempt to overcome it. The meaning of the repetition, however, as an expression of an unconscious need, is not apparent to the person themselves, and when they do understand what they have done, they may regret it.[47]

In fact, Dalit did regret her decision after the event. The chain of events, beginning with the meeting with the Welfare Coordinator, created the conditions that made it possible to take Tal away from Dalit immediately, even when the court tried to put it off. It does not take an unusually suspicious mind to connect the dots in this case: the appearance of the anonymous intermediary; the entry permit granted to Salim to be by Dalit's side when she gave birth; the coordinated arrival of the foster parents and Tal at the hospital, and Tal's handover to the foster parents.

Pending the court's ruling on the request, it was agreed that Dalit and her husband would meet with Tal regularly, and Salim's entry permit into Israel on each occasion would be provided by the Civil Administration's Liaison and Coordination Office (LCO). One can only wonder why, when the courts had repeatedly asked for Salim to be granted permission to escort his wife on her trips into Israel, it had always been turned down, both when Tal had been returned to Dalit and in the weeks before the birth of their son, while now he was granted not just a one-off permit but a repeat pass whenever he visited Tal. The answer lies with the rules (or whims) of the LCO.

When I visited Dalit, she told me that she had decided to give up her daughter to the foster parents because she had felt helpless seeing Tal constantly depressed, refusing to speak and often refusing even to enter the house. When I asked her how long that had been going on, as only a few weeks earlier she had told me that her condition had improved, she said that Tal had acted like that for a whole day. This did not make sense to me. Dalit, after all, knew that there would always be crises; why did she rush to give Tal up instead of dealing with the crisis? Dalit gave me an embarrassed smile, and when I asked if she did this to get an entry permit for Salim, she replied, 'Yes. What can I do? My head's all messed up!'

'Great! Now she's admitting that her head's all messed up. I told her not to do this!' said Salim, who was sitting with us. Dalit protested: 'I thought that I was saving three people this way! He's not working, we have no money. You should have seen how Tal sat on Isaac's lap when he came here to visit. We had to take Tal outside when he left, so she wouldn't see him leave. It's true that at my last meeting with Tzippi, Tal didn't want to go near her, but then she's always more attached to men'. Then she added, 'I thought Tal would be happier with them, and my husband would get a permit to work in Israel, and that way I'd be saving our two children. But now I'm sorry I did it. I understand now that we were conned – my husband won't get a permit to work in Israel, and I miss Tal and don't want her to have problems when she grows up, like I did because I was adopted. We'll be visiting her today. Look at how they're running after us now with an entry permit! Usually the Welfare Coordinator drops off the permit at the village entrance. Today she's on holiday'.

Sure enough, within minutes the intermediary rang to say that the entry permit was waiting for them at the LCO. 'You see how they're running after us now, and how they're so anxious for us to take the permit?' Salim asked me.

Although they couldn't afford to travel to the LCO office to pick up the permit, Dalit was determined to visit Tal. 'Even if I have to crawl there on my hands and knees, I'll get there', she said, with the intensity of someone who has been wronged and is determined to stand up for her rights. I gave them some money to have the permit delivered to them by taxi from the LCO, and they borrowed a car from a friend to visit Tal.

On the way back they got a flat tyre and had to stop by the wayside. Since they had no spare tyre, and of course no roadside assistance insurance, they waited for hours for their friend to come and rescue them. It was very cold outside, and the baby was with them in the cold. The permit's validity had expired, but they were still in Israeli jurisdiction. It was three a.m. by the time they got home. Such is the fate of people relegated to live 'in the wilderness'. About the visit itself, Dalit said only that it was 'OK'. This time, Tal had approached her, possibly because she had brought the baby with her.

Dalit then described to me the chain of events leading to Tal's return to the foster family. When she arrived at the office of the Welfare Coordinator (at the LCO), the Coordinator arranged a meeting with SSC officials, and took her to another office. From Dalit's description, I recognised it as the SSC's head office, where they met a woman who identified herself as an adoption official, but told Dalit that she was seeing her on this occasion not in that capacity but as a friend who wanted to help her. Dalit could not understand how the official was able to talk about Tal's distress, and only with hindsight connected it with Tzippi's dark hint at their previous meeting that they had 'ways of getting Tal returned to them'. At the moment of the meeting, she didn't think about it. She couldn't account for why her 'head just went upside down', as she put it, to explain her feeling of things getting out of control. Tal's regression; their worsening financial situation since Salim had been denied entry into Israel and couldn't find work; the impending birth; and her desperate need for Salim to be by her side during delivery were all affecting her. The adoption official's offer of 'friendship' must have seemed like a godsend, and she was willing to hand Tal over to the foster family on a temporary basis. In court, she objected to a closed adoption, but agreed to an open adoption with the foster parents. She said that she was told such an adoption was a 'temporary solution'.

It is entirely possible that Dalit genuinely believed that an open adoption would be a temporary arrangement due to her misunderstanding, rather than because she had been told so by the adoption official. Nonetheless, adoption officials, like all professional social workers, are entrusted with protecting the interests of people seeking their help, who are usually people in need of representation. Is it not their job to ensure that those who approach them understand what their rights are? In this case, the officials were perfectly aware that Dalit and the foster parents had agreed to conduct the hearings without lawyers on either side, and did nothing to stop this, as if this would have promoted equality under the law, as required.

From a professional standpoint, too, the official's conduct raises serious questions. Did she not know that re-establishing the mother–daughter bond after a long separation takes time? An adoptive family is given at least six months before an adoption order is issued, to enable it and the child to adjust to the new situation, while Dalit's meeting with the adoption official took place only five months after Tal had been returned to her. Is it not obvious that in a process such as this, doubts emerge and there are moments of despair? Moreover, Dalit was in the final stages of pregnancy at the time, a time when a woman's mental equilibrium may be temporarily disturbed. Yet despite all this, instead of trying to postpone the decision and provide Dalit with the support that she needed, particularly given how sensitive she was to Tal's distress, the official chose to focus only on the arguments for returning Tal to the foster parents. Dalit's vulnerability appears to have been exploited to remove her, once again, from Tal's life.

One cannot always say for certain that adoption officials deliberately ignore the rules of good governance and professional ethics, but on this occasion it was undeniable. Several weeks later, when the court rejected the agreement that had been reached between Dalit and the foster parents and appointed her legal counsel to continue to represent her at the hearings about whether Tal should be returned to the foster parents, the lawyer arranged for Dalit to be interviewed in the media. In response to her revelations, a spokesman for the Ministry of Welfare stated:

> All her claims, as if someone from the service had tried to persuade her to hand over her daughter to the designated adoptive family, are figments of her imagination. The truth is the precise opposite: she arrived at the service with a request to allow her to place her daughter in adoption, and the SSC denied her many pleadings and did not allow her to sign the adoption agreement.

This, indeed, is what the adoption official should have done, but did not. The timeline alone shows this account to be false. On Sunday, Dalit met with the adoption official, and on Monday morning the two of them were already in court, where the adoption official demanded that Tal be adopted by the foster parents. The spokesman's statement was not only false, but an attempt to denigrate Dalit, whose claims were dismissed as 'figments of her imagination'.

Dalit admitted that she regretted her decision; she missed Tal very much. She knew that she could not hope to match the kind of upbringing that the foster parents could provide, but believed that children are better off growing up with their birth parents, as she herself knew all too well from first-hand experience. Her husband was angry at her for giving Tal up, as were his mother and family members. They loved Tal very much because she was so delicate. She had avoided her lawyer after meeting the adoption official because she felt that she had 'betrayed him' after he had fought so hard for her to get Tal back. She seemed to find herself perennially in a bind: when she did not receive support, she was offended; when she was helped, she was afraid of disappointing her helpers, just as she had disappointed her adoptive father. She had chosen not to inform me, either, of her intentions, because she assumed that I would accuse her of 'selling' Tal for an entry permit for her husband. This was a clear example of projection. When Tzippi first offered to take Tal in return for an entry permit for Salim, Dalit had been appalled, saying that it was 'like selling Tal', and now she was attributing that same response to me, feeling guilty about what she had done. It was as though Dalit had been determined at that moment to surrender Tal, despite the ambivalence that she felt, and any consultation with me would have raised doubts in her, which she wanted to avoid. She took comfort in the thought that even if she were wrong, Tal at least would be happy with her foster parents.

According to Dalit, the court issued an interim order appointing her and the foster parents as Tal's joint guardians. In addition, it ordered Tal to undergo psychiatric and neurological tests to establish the reason for her developmental delay. At the hearing, Dalit insisted that Tal's name not be removed from her own ID card as her daughter. 'It would be as if she were dead!' she said, undoubtedly echoing her sense of being as good as dead to her own birth mother.

In our conversations, Dalit gave a glimpse into the conflict that now raged within her. On the one hand, she was tormented by the knowledge that Tal was not living with her, and every piece of her clothing was a reminder of her; on the other hand ('when I'm honest about it', as she put it), she felt it was better for Tal to grow up with the foster parents. When Tal had been returned to her, she found it difficult to bond with her, as she had not raised her, nor could she admire every little achievement of hers as she did of her second daughter, Yasmin. She didn't find it easy to hug and kiss Tal, while she hugged and kissed Yasmin all the time. She talked about how worried she was about Tal's developmental delay, and feared that she would not be able to afford to give Tal the care that she needed. When Tal was living with them, she said, there was a permanent atmosphere of mourning (although I couldn't tell if she meant this was due to Tal's mere presence, or because she thought that Tal was mourning over her separation from the foster parents). When I reminded her how cheerful Tal had been on our drive to the amusement park, Dalit said that that day was different, special.

A mourning period usually lasts several months,[48] and Tal was still in the final stages of that period, when the difficulties actually peak. Had she been in an educational setting of some kind, with stimuli other than Dalit and Salim (especially given Dalit's limitations in this regard), Tal's mourning response might have receded in the face of the distractions of daily life. Dalit's identification with Tal's feelings of loss appeared to paralyse her, and her ability to identify with her daughter's despair was not countered by a sense that she, as an adult, could protect Tal. None of these details had come to light when I had spoken with Dalit while Tal was in her care, and with hindsight I wonder if I had truly made it possible for her to speak frankly to me about her feelings during that time.

To back up her contention that Tal would be better off growing up with the foster parents, Dalit then pointed out that the last time she had been to see her she saw a 'different' child (which she said with warmth and love), a child who kicked mischievously at items, who was finally potty-trained, and whose vocabulary had grown. Tal responded to her presence at the most recent meetings, apparently because Dalit had brought the baby boy with her, and Tal 'loved him to bits'. At the same time, she noted that Salim wanted Tal to be back with them. I remarked that whenever I raised the possibility of having Tal returned to her, she presented reasons against it, but when I said that perhaps it would really be better for Tal to remain with the foster family, she objected to that too. Dalit agreed: 'My mother-in-law says that I have a good demon and a bad demon inside me', she said (an accurate description of ambivalence, I thought to myself), 'and the bad demon is the one who gave up Tal'. But, she added, she felt that she would be doing Tal a disservice if she took her back, and she couldn't ignore the fact that whenever they visited Tal, Tal was afraid that she would do just that. During one of Tal's medical tests, for example, when Salim entered the neurologist's room with her and Tzippi remained outside in the corridor, Tal took fright and shouted, 'No! No!' 'That was so embarrassing', Dalit said. When I asked if it had been a mistake to return Tal to her in the first place, she said yes, she now thinks that perhaps it was. On another occasion, she said that the mistake lay in the fact that Tal went on seeing the foster parents from time to time. If it weren't for that, she thought, Tal would have adjusted. When I asked her what it was that she thought Tal was saying to her in her behaviour while she was with her, she responded, 'I felt as though she were saying, "Who are you, anyway?"'

Those four words likely summed up the feeling that had dogged Dalit throughout her life. The estrangement between herself and her daughter that took root once Tal was taken away only exacerbated the feeling. Ultimately, she had failed in her struggle to overcome the feeling of defeat that had always plagued her and that grew even stronger when her husband was persistently denied entry into Israel. Once again, as she had done two years before when she handed Tal over to the benefactor couple who had petitioned the court to adopt her, by returning Tal to the foster parents Dalit had taken a step that was more desperate than premeditated.

At the back of her mind, Dalit was haunted by the thought that perhaps she had caused Tal's delayed development in the first months of her life. She had, after all, not cared for her with the same devotion with which she now cared for Yasmin and her baby son. She had not had the wherewithal to do so at the time; she was very young and wanted to spend time with her friends, and felt lonely and persecuted by social services. Added to that, I thought to myself, the lack of eye contact was possibly another barrier. Had she been given help with that at the time, she could have overcome it, just as she had with Yasmin. She had clearly forgotten about the warm rapport that she had formed with Tal during my first observations of their interaction. I asked if she had claimed that she was unable to form an attachment as a pretext for the exchange of Tal for the promise of an entry permit, or whether she had returned Tal because of an actual lack of a bond between them (and the exchange for the permit was meant to disguise this). She replied that both explanations were true. I believed her. Few women are asked to face the tests that she had to endure, and perhaps for that reason popular folklore has no stories that describe what she had to go through; these might have given an insight into such complex predicaments, as folktales often do. She had to extract an understanding of the situation from within herself, and in every conversation between us she offered a different explanation, reflecting her state at that moment.

At times, it seems to me that she preferred things to continue as they were – Tal growing up with the foster parents, while staying in touch with her – but Dalit was forever speculating about the future. How would Tal feel when she grew up and understood the difference between the observant Jewish lifestyle of her adoptive family and her mother's Muslim family? How would her siblings, who wouldn't know her, feel? Dalit was constantly troubled by her own adoption story and feelings of abandonment, and did not want that to happen to Tal. In effect, Dalit's doubts were a sign of her dilemma between wanting to compensate Tal for the harm Tal had incurred while living with Dalit in unsuitable conditions, and therefore relinquishing her to a family 'who can give her more than I can', and the fear that the denial of Tal's genealogical ties would come to hurt her and leave her with a sense of loss, as Dalit herself had experienced.[49]

The arrangement by which Tal grew up with the foster parents and maintained contact with Dalit was something I could accept as positive, in part because I believe that a child does not 'belong' to anyone. However, in this case, the sharp differences in social-religious background between the two families precluded any possibility of continuity in Tal's existence. In addition, Dalit felt that the foster parents were not entirely sincere in their intentions. There had already been an erosion in their cooperation with her, she said. They did not always keep their promise of maintaining regular meetings, occasionally denying Dalit's requests for such on various pretexts, even though she now made sure to show up for every meeting. Moreover, various difficulties suddenly began to emerge in the provision of an entry permit for Salim, which he still needed in order to accompany her on the visits. For one meeting, Tzippi and Isaac showed up with the intermediary who had arranged the entry permits, and another man, both armed with handguns.[50] They placed these conspicuously on the table while Dalit sat there alone, helpless, facing them and the foster parents. As the court hearings over the permanent arrangement for Tal proceeded, the tensions between the two parties increased.

Dalit's description of Tal's difficulties during the time she had spent with her, her hurried decision to return Tal to the foster parents, her inner struggle about whether to have Tal returned to her, all raise questions as to whether the court's decision to return Tal to her had been the right one. As previously noted, the court ruled that Tal should be returned to her mother based on Dalit's right to raise her, but this came about only after a protracted legal battle, during which time all traces of Tal's attachment to her mother had been obliterated in favour of a strong bond with the foster family. It must have been obvious to everyone, therefore, that returning Tal to her mother would be a long and painful process, one that would be fraught with risks. Should the court have avoided such a ruling, for that reason? If the authorities had acted in the spirit of the law – for example by considering the child's religious affiliation a legal requirement and choosing an adoptive family whose religious affiliation was the same as the child's – it would have been possible for the court to choose an alternative by arranging an open adoption that would have given Dalit the option of staying in touch with Tal. Although Tal's religious affiliations were complex,[51] was it really necessary to choose a foster family that was the diametric opposite of the birth family? The adoption officials argued that they had no choice. That particular family was chosen because few designated adoptive families are willing to accept a child who has not yet been declared eligible for adoption, as was the case with Tal. This is, indeed, a dilemma. The adoption officials were forced to choose between this family and a foster family that was not designated to adopt Tal and from which she would have had to be subsequently transferred to the final adoptive family once (or if) the court declared her eligible for adoption. The problem was particularly acute since Tal had already been transferred several times after being taken from her mother, due to the actions of the welfare officials, and therefore her situation precluded any further transfers. Because of this, it seems, the differences in ethnic or religious affiliation were less important in the eyes of the adoption officials, and the court, as previously noted, refrained from enquiring about the chosen family. Since the Adoption of Children Law itself has no interest in preserving the traces of the birth parents in the life of the adopted child, the choice of adoptive family is not regulated by the courts and is left to the discretion of the adoption officials.

But perhaps this was not the case. Perhaps the marked contrast in family background was a deliberate ploy to ensure that Tal would be adopted, and all ties with Dalit ultimately severed, given the impracticality of reconciling the differences between the two families. If that is the case, the entire course of events, from start to finish, was of the adoption officials' making, ultimately leading to a stark choice between severing ties with the foster family or with the birth mother. I shared Dalit's concern. How would the conflict that Tal might experience when she grows up and understands affect her?

Nonetheless, this failure was not necessarily preordained. There is no denying that the situation resulted from Dalit's hastiness to return Tal to the foster parents at a time of acute crisis in her life. Given the support that she received from her husband and his family for keeping Tal, had she not been so hasty, or had she been prevented from returning Tal, the outcome might have been different. Although I myself did not experience Dalit's pain, I too had been conflicted about returning Tal to her care previously, as much as I was now about her being returned to the foster parents. Ultimately, however, the answer to these musings may have been found in Tal's plaintive cries of 'No! No!' when she was momentarily separated from the foster mother, and perhaps it was best that she remain with the foster parents after all.

Dalit's End

A few weeks after Dalit's intimidating meeting with the foster parents, I was able to persuade her to join me for a trip to the beach. The previous summer, when she was pregnant, she had expressed her wish to do so, since her husband's status as a resident of the Palestinian Authority meant that she had been denied that pleasure.[52] Yasmin was spending the day at her grandmother's house in the village, so we travelled with her son, who was about a year old at the time – beautifully developed, happy, cheerful and unfailingly successful in captivating everyone with his communicative smiles (as had been said about Tal when she was first taken from Dalit, and as I had seen with Yasmin at that age). Unfortunately, there was a temporary ban on swimming in the sea that day, but despite the disappointment, Dalit managed to enjoy herself and played with her son. She spoke constantly about her attachment to Tal and how she missed her, but also about her joy in raising her son. When we parted, at the entrance to the village, she said to me, 'Thanks, Mili. I enjoyed myself, all the same!'

That was the last time I saw her.

Over the following weeks, we spoke occasionally on the phone, and Dalit was determined once more to get Tal back. To my surprise, her previous doubts and deliberations had vanished without trace.

Then one evening, her lawyer telephoned me with the news that Dalit had been found dead at her home in Israel, while her baby played beside her. She had been knifed to death. She was twenty-two when she died. Her body had been taken to the Forensic Institute. I was unable to get hold of Salim, because he had been arrested that evening as a suspect. I found it hard to believe that he was responsible. I tried to find out when her funeral was, but was told two days later that her body had already been taken from the Forensic Institute and buried in a ceremony at a Jewish cemetery, where a temporary sign above her grave presented her as the daughter of her adoptive father. I do not know if her adoptive parents had been present at the ceremony, but when I visited her grave a year later, I saw that they had erected a headstone on which they had inscribed, among other things, the words 'Our dear daughter'. Dalit did not see herself that way.

Salim was released from detention after lengthy questioning. He was taken off the list of suspects and asked by police to help in the search for the killer, but he had no idea who it could have been. To the best of my knowledge, the culprit is still unknown, as are the motives for her killing. The children are growing up in the village with their grandmother, and Salim is still hoping to receive permission to live in Israel and raise his children there. Will the children ever know who their mother was? Will they ever visit her grave, or will they grow up, like her, not knowing who she was?

Tal is in the care of the foster family, as their adoptive daughter. All contact between them and Salim has been severed. In the past, the foster parents would talk to him occasionally on the phone, but since Dalit's murder he hasn't heard from them at all. They have avoided all contact, and he was very hurt by the fact that they did not even telephone to offer their condolences.

Dalit's murder completed the process of rendering her redundant, and removed from the world a young woman who had always experienced herself as a burden. I thought it particularly important to document her life, and asked the court for permission to include it in this book, despite a publication ban imposed on her case. In the following chapter, I will describe the legal proceedings leading up to my being granted permission to publicise the story, and discuss the question of secrecy and its implications for adoption policy.

This book is dedicated to Dalit. I thought it would be appropriate to give her full name and possibly her Muslim one, as well, but since

I could not receive her permission, I did not appeal to the court to ask for permission to do so, as would be required under the Adoption of Children Law, which imposes secrecy on all the individuals involved. As a result, even the dedication at the start of this book is complicit in obliterating her identity, the same obliteration that she had fought against when seeking to prevent her removal from her daughter's life and the blurring of the traces of her loss. She wanted, with every fibre of her soul, for her daughter Tal not to live with a similarly obliterated identity.

Notes

1. Ophir, *The Order of Evils*, 108.
2. Numbers 32:13, 'And the Lord's anger was kindled against Israel, and he made them wander in the wilderness forty years, until all the generation, that had done evil in the sight of the Lord, was consumed'; Mishnah Tractate Sanhedrin 10:3, 'The generation of the wilderness has no portion in the world to come and they will not stand in judgement, as it is written there, "In the wilderness they will be consumed and there they will die"'.
3. Bracha Habas, *The Youth Aliyah Book* (Jerusalem: Youth Aliyah Bureau, 1941), 281, 293, 471 [Hebrew]. This mindset was also reflected in the preference for communal (residential) schooling on the kibbutz, which was designed to protect children from what the kibbutz movement at the time regarded as the 'pathology' of family relationships. Ya'ara Bar-On, 'The Family in the Kibbutz', in Aviad Kleinberg (ed.), *The Love of Mothers and the Fear of Fathers: Rethinking the Israeli Family* (Jerusalem: Keter, 2004), 20 [Hebrew].
4. Eli Amir, *Scapegoat* (Tel Aviv: Am Oved, 1983) [Hebrew]; *Ruah Kadim*, film (Israel: David Ben-Chetrit, 2002) [Hebrew].
5. Seventy-six per cent of the population in Israel are Jews. Therefore, unless noted otherwise, all parents and children referred to in this book are Jewish. This point is of particular significance in the present story.
6. Shifman, *Family Law in Israel*, 54.
7. Knowing one's own adoption story carries great importance for the adoptee. Elsbeth Neil, 'The Reasons Why Young Children Are Placed for Adoption: Findings from a Recently Placed Sample and a Discussion of Implications for Subsequent Identity Development', *Child and Family Social Work* 5 (2000), 303–16.
8. Modell, *Kinship with Strangers*, 2–3.
9. On the question of predictions in the area of adoption, see Chapter 4: Interlude.
10. Hence the power imparted by the absence of words in the play *Passing Shadow* written and directed by Michael Gurevitch (Khan Theatre, 1999 [Hebrew]), which depicts a family in which the taboo of incest is broken.

11. Michel Foucault, *Discipline and Punish: The Birth of the Prison*, trans. Alan Sheridan (New York: Pantheon Books, 1977).
12. Resolution Committee (Planning Committee, Treatment and Evaluation), http//www.Kolzchut.org.il.
13. Unlike emergency orders issued under the ACL 12(c), which states that application must be made to the court within fourteen days, the Youth Law stipulates that application to the courts to remove a minor from his or her parents must be made within seven days (Youth Law 11a).
14. Since the emergency order had been issued under the ACL, as described below, the management of the case had been handed over from local social services to adoption officials.
15. Bowlby, *Attachment*, 301.
16. For more on the term 'ward of court', see Chapter 1.
17. Unlike previous hearings in this case, which were held at the juvenile court, this application, like all adoption cases, was heard at the family court.
18. Bowlby, *Attachment*, 302.
19. Ross A. Thompson, 'Sensitive Periods in Attachment?' in Donald B. Bailey et al. (eds), *Critical Thinking about Critical Periods* (Baltimore, MD: Paul H. Brookes, 2001), 83–106.
20. AF (Jerusalem) 16/01, *A-G v Anon*, LP 2001 (3) 131, para 9 (2001).
21. On this matter, see the ruling of the Deputy Chief Justice Elon, CA 418/88, *Anon v A-G*, 8:

    For the court to determine that, in its estimation, the parent is not capable of taking care of his children properly, it must be presented with factual proof that in practice the parent did indeed fail to take care of his child. It is not enough, therefore, that the court should have presented to it a psychological opinion or some other kind of assessment, that the parent is mentally, intellectually, or emotionally deficient, that he is incapable of taking care of his children or any other assessment. Proof must be presented as to the actual effect of this incapability on the child, and that the child has suffered from it and been harmed by it.
22. In the United States as well, preference is given to adoption over investing resources to support families. Modell, *Sealed and Secret Kinship*, 197.
23. Harry Stuck Sullivan, *The Interpersonal Theory of Psychiatry* (New York: Norton, 1953), 41.
24. On the selection of experts on the SSC's behalf, see Chapter 4: Interlude.
25. AF (Jerusalem) 16/01, *A-G v Anon*, para 13.
26. René A. Spitz, *The First Year of Life* (New York: International Universities Press, 1965), 150; Bowlby, *Attachment*, 327.
27. John Bowlby, *Child Care and the Growth of Love* (Harmondsworth: Penguin Books, 1965). For reservations about this view, see Ann M. Clarke and Alan Douglas Benson Clarke, *Early Experience: Myth and Evidence* (New York: The Free Press, 1979); Michael Rutter, *Maternal Deprivation Reassessed* (Harmondsworth: Penguin Books, 1972).
28. Since the law in Israel does not allow Jews to marry non-Jews in Israel, 'mixed' couples marry outside Israel; Cyprus is the nearest country with

which Israel has friendly relations. These marriages are subsequently recognised by the state.

29. Brazelton, Koslowski and Main, 'The Origins of Reciprocity'; Daniel N. Stern, 'Missteps in the Dance', in *The First Relationship* (Cambridge, MA: Harvard University Press, 1977), 109–28.
30. Fraiberg, 'Intervention in Infancy'.
31. Fraiberg (ed.), *Clinical Studies in Infant Mental Health: The First Year of Life* (New York: Basic Books, 1980).
32. In Israel, Friday, as the day before the Jewish Sabbath, is the first day of the weekend, akin to Saturday in Europe or North America.
33. An adoptee's access to their adoption file upon reaching the age of eighteen is at the discretion of adoption officials (ACL 30, 3(b)), who point out that it may be done only with the consent of the birth parents.
34. In Israel, there are gradations of religiosity. This family was not ultra-Orthodox, where the men wear distinctive long black coats and hats and side curls, but 'National Religious', where the only visible difference from secular Israelis is a small knitted skullcap for the men, and a stylish headscarf for the women. This and their way of life suggested that they (like many of the 'National Religious') also held nationalist views that had a bearing upon their attitude to Dalit's choice of partners.
35. Details of the adoptive family are normally revealed to the court only during the adoption order hearings, i.e. at least six months after the child has already been with the designated adoptive family (ACL 6). See also Chapter 4: Interlude.
36. CA 680/77, *Anon v Tel Aviv Municipality*, Ruling 32 399 (3) (1978).
37. For more on this, see the description of Revital in Chapter 1.
38. Amendment 26 to the Penal Code, 1999.
39. This story was told to me by Noam's adoptive mother, who had adopted him when he was approximately two years old.
40. From the report by the Children's Medical Centre in Jerusalem given to me by Noam's adoptive mother.
41. In the ancient Roman republic (as early as the fifth century BC), the authorities could declare anyone to be a *homo sacer* (lit., 'sacred man' or 'accursed man'), which meant that he was banned from society and stripped of all rights and all functions in civil religion, and that he could be killed by anyone, with impunity. Giorgio Agamben, *Homo Sacer: Sovereign Power and Bare Life*, trans. Daniel Heller-Roazen (Stanford, CA: Stanford University Press, 1998), 71.
42. Mass and Ophir, 'Care, Supervision and Abandonment'.
43. Eliezer Witztum, 'Between Intervention in Crisis and Short-Term Psychotherapy', in Haim Dasberg, Joseph A. Itzigsohn and Gaby I. Shefler (eds), *Brief Psychotherapy* (Jerusalem: Magnes Press, 1985), 53–66 [Hebrew]; Howard J. Parad and Gerald Caplan, 'A Framework for Studying Families in Crisis', *Journal of Social Work* 5 (1960), 3–15.
44. On the significance of the discovery and meeting the adoptee's brother, see Jackie Kay, *Red Dust Road: An Autobiographical Journey* (London: Picador, 2010), 245–87.

45. In Judaism, the Sabbath starts at sunset on Friday.
46. The precise details of the patchwork of jurisdictions in the West Bank are beyond the scope of this book, and only tangentially relevant. The Byzantine complexity of territorial boundaries during this messy transition phase before a permanent settlement means that a Palestinian Arab can wake up one day to find that the house he built in his village is now on the 'wrong' side of a new border, while his parents' house is on the other.
47. Otto Fenichel, *The Psychoanalytic Theory of Neurosis* (New York: Norton, 1945), 543.
48. Rutter, *Maternal Deprivation Reassessed*, 29.
49. Ophir, *The Order of Evils*, 130.
50. It is not unusual for members of the security forces in Israel to carry handguns.
51. The law states that a child must be adopted by a member of the same faith (ACL, 5). See also the UN Convention on the Rights of the Child, article 20 (3). However, the children of a Muslim father and a Jewish mother present a problem, since according to the Jewish faith they are Jewish, but under Islamic law they are Muslim. When this occurs, it is worth raising this issue before the court *before* the child is placed with a foster or adoptive family and forms an attachment to it, but the law states that information about the adoptive or foster family can be revealed to the court only at the stage that the adoption order is deliberated in court, i.e. at least six months after the child has already lived with the family in question.
52. The Palestinian Territory has no access to the sea.

4

INTERLUDE

Between Secrecy and Privacy: On the Publication of Dalit and Tal's Story

Background

This interlude was written after legal proceedings over whether I should be permitted to publish the story of Dalit and Tal described in the previous chapter. These proceedings, which centred on whether the publication ban that had been imposed in this case should also apply to academic publication, shed light on the role played by secrecy in adoption processes in Israel. While I have already touched upon the implications of secrecy for the adoption proceedings and for the contact between the children and their parents in the previous chapters, mostly with regard to how it contributes to denying the loss of the children's genealogical ties, the proceedings over permitting publication of Dalit and Tal's story engender an examination of secrecy as a social construct, and of how it is similar to, and different from, the protection of privacy. Accordingly, after a brief description of the legal debate over the publication of Dalit and Tal's particular story, I shall discuss the issue of secrecy in relation to adoption policy in general, and its ramifications for the legal debate in question.

Given the very strict nature of the secrecy set out in the Israeli Adoption of Children Law,[1] I had already looked into the question of permission to publish the book during its first draft. To this end, I consulted a judge with considerable experience in adoption matters, who read the book's draft and explicitly assured me that as long as the identity of the members of the adoption triangle was not revealed, the law would not preclude publication of the story as it was written. I then received an identical second opinion from a lawyer specialising in the field. With these two assurances in hand, I continued my work on the book, but a subsequent development in Tal and Dalit's adoption case was published in the media, and since that did contain certain identifying details, a publication ban on that particular story was issued. As a result, I thought I ought to verify that the ban did not extend to publishing the story as part of the book. Although I suspected that approaching the court on this matter would delay the book's publication, I realised it was unavoidable when another lawyer, who specialises in publication-related matters, made clear to me the seriousness of publication bans in general, particularly in relation to the Adoption of Children Law.

Since I was applying to the court about publication of Dalit and Tal's story, I thought I might as well ask for explicit permission to publish the book's other three chapters, rather than rely on the implicit permission arising from the interpretation of the law by the first two legal experts I had consulted. In my petition, I based my claim on the grounds of academic freedom and freedom of speech, attached a synopsis of all four chapters, and added that the full manuscript would be made available to the court, if required.

Within days, the judge who presided over the proceedings concerning the three cases of the children of the Ziv family, Elinor and Daniel (whose story follows this chapter) permitted the publication of their stories (on condition, of course, that the identity of those involved remains confidential), since the rulings of those cases were already in the public domain. With regard to Dalit and Tal's story, however, I applied to another judge, who was considering an additional petition at the same time about the same case on behalf of a different publication, and decided to combine the proceedings in the two cases.[2] The judge named State Counsel as respondent to my petition,[3] and, after reading the chapter synopsis, State Counsel immediately objected to its publication, but asked to read the full manuscript before giving their final position. The actual hearing in court about my petition and the state's response took place only after repeated deferrals by State Counsel and the other petitioners.[4] At the hearing, the SSC, through State Counsel, its legal representative, opposed publication of the chapter on the grounds of secrecy, as prescribed by the Adoption of Children Law.

However, the Guardian *ad Litem* whom the judge had appointed for the minor[5] stated that he saw no reason to deny academic publication of the adoption case of Dalit and Tal. In response, State Counsel withdrew its objection, and the court permitted the chapter to be published, with the sole caveat that any statements by any participant in the proceedings that might be injurious to any third party be presented strictly as their quoted views, rather than as fact. These proceedings took sixteen months,[6] confirming my suspicion that applying to the court would delay publication of the book.

This chapter is different from others in the book, in that the theoretical discussion about secrecy in adoption proceedings represents the substance of the chapter, with episodes from various cases serving only to illustrate these issues. This is in contrast to the other chapters, where the focus is the story, with the related theoretical and empirical debate and analysis interwoven. The chapter's conclusion includes description and discussion of the legal proceedings about the publication permission, and my chosen method of presenting all cases in the book, in light of the distinction between secrecy and privacy.

Secrecy, Privacy and Publicity

The sociologist Georg Simmel saw the secret as man's greatest achievement. The ability to hide information, or any other aspect of human activity, by positive or negative means, is indicative, in his view, of restraint of the natural childish tendency to express any thought and allow access to any information. Secrecy extends reality by offering an additional world that exists beside, and substantially influences, the visible one. The very existence of a secret, and its nature, determine the relationship between the partners to the secret: even if one of the parties is unaware of the secret, they are still subject to its impact, and the fact that they are unaware of its existence simply means that they are unable to circumscribe it or counter that impact.[7]

The secret establishes a clear distinction between the one 'in the know' and those who are not.[8] This confers upon the secret the aura of a highly valuable asset. Its obscurity gives it an aura of mystery, and its holders assume a special status. The importance of a secret lies in the person's ability to keep it, but the barriers imposed by the secret give the challenge of breaking it a magical quality as significant as that of the aura surrounding the secret itself.[9] The secret per se is a neutral social construct. It may serve a sublime purpose, or hide a malicious intent and the existence of something sinister. Although secrets are not inherently or directly linked to evil, evil is directly and essentially bound up in secrecy. A secret may therefore be morally wrong, but, Simmel says, this possibility should not obscure its importance.[10]

Discovering a secret may be destructive, as in the legend of Pandora's Box, which tells how, in retribution for Prometheus's theft and divulgence of the secret of fire to human mortals, Zeus gives a box to the beautiful and reckless Pandora, warning her never to open it. Curiosity gets the better of her, and when she does open it, all the world's evils and sufferings burst out and blight the human race forever. However, secrets can also be destructive when kept hidden, and the evil within them defeated only by breaking through the shroud of secrecy, as in the story of the Sphinx upon the walls of Thebes who killed anyone who could not correctly answer her riddle, until Oedipus managed to do so.[11]

As a social construct, secrecy serves the sovereign, who has the power to determine what information is made known and what is not. The question is, when is secrecy functional, and when is it symbolic? That is, when is it limited by its purpose, and when does it extend beyond its original purpose to become an end in itself? The answer to this question reveals how important secrets are to understanding human interaction, and is encapsulated in the basic values underpinning the structure of society. Every democratic society views openness as a desirable condition, since it ensures that information about the events and circumstances impacting everyone's life is available to all members of society, who can thereby influence crucial decisions that govern them. However, to maintain such openness requires an autonomous mechanism of some kind, and ensuring the autonomy of such a mechanism in itself requires secrecy. The question then becomes, what is the logic of valuing openness so highly? At the same time, the evolution of openness reveals the cultural schema that distinguishes between things that are public and whose openness should be preserved and promoted, and those that are intrinsically autonomous and concern the affairs of individuals, and as such should remain confidential.[12]

The historical evolution of a society might be described in terms of the changes in what it considers secret, as that varies from one period to another with the nature of the regime. Thus, for example, prior to the seventeenth and eighteenth centuries, no details were published about taxation, government debt or the size of the army. However, espionage and treason have always revealed the inconsistency in attitudes towards the protection of secrets. As societies became more democratic, one of the notable political trends, in Edward Shils' view, was public pressure on governments to stop withholding information.[13] In the nineteenth century, openness began to extend to national issues, and governments began to regularly publish material that had previously been considered impossible for publication.[14] The principle of proportional taxation brought about a further reduction of areas in which the government protected its own privacy. In parallel with the push for ever-greater public disclosure and freedom of the press as befitting a constitutional and democratic regime, there were increasing calls to enshrine and protect individual privacy as another hallmark of liberty. The perpetual tension between openness and privacy gives secrets a magical quality, due not necessarily to the practical need to protect the state's interests, but to the fateful aura surrounding them, as if secrecy were a cosmic attribute that confers upon government officials a mysterious authority.

Immanuel Kant viewed secrecy as indicative of immoral activity, as did Jeremy Bentham, who argued that secrecy is a tool in the service of conspiracy, and therefore has no place in a well-governed regime, while openness is a guarantee for the establishment of good and protection from the continued existence of evil.[15] However, Bentham did state three types of instances where openness can be detrimental: when it is of benefit to the enemy; when it harms the innocent; and when it results in unduly harsh punishment of the guilty.[16] Woodrow Wilson, however, declared that in matters of government there is no legitimate privacy. If the government is fair in its guiding principles, and blameless in its actions, there is no reason why it should not exercise openness in all related proceedings.[17]

The delicate balance between openness and privacy is undermined by the fear of conspiracy.[18] As early as the first decade of the twentieth century, there was a growing concern in Europe and the United States about revolutions and terrorist acts. Every so often, conspiracy theories sprang up, spurring calls to uphold secrecy as a value in its own right. This mindset runs contrary to the nature of a civil society of diverse occupations, where the citizen's life does not revolve around his or her relationship with central government. Life in such a society cannot be conducted under the perpetual threat of conspiracy, and requires an appreciation of the fundamental difference between targeted secrecy in response to a specific and undeniable threat, and a constant obsession with secrecy and invasion of privacy to prevent conspiracies. Shils sees secrecy as the enemy of privacy, since, to preserve secrecy, one must invade the privacy of those charged with its protection, to ensure that they are suitably qualified for the role and to ensure that their views are consistent with the nature of the secrets they are supposed to protect.[19] Therefore, in democratic politics, secrecy involves a fundamental paradox that cannot be reconciled through deliberation, however sensitive and differentiated.[20] Privacy cannot be dismissed by any society: there will always be areas that are kept hidden from certain groups. However, privacy and secrecy are not the same thing. Privacy is the individual's ownership of an area that he wishes to isolate, such as his identity, activities or history, all of which were declared part of the private domain with the emergence of individuation. Secrecy, however, extends the private domain beyond the individuality of those affected by it; it is not subject to the latter's will or desire; the penalty for its violation is more severe than that of violating privacy; and the number of people affected by the secret, and excluded by it, is far greater.[21] Shils defines privacy as 'zero relations' between people, between groups, or between a group and an individual, in terms of communication and interaction.[22]

Privacy has always been a privilege of the middle classes and the elites, and has been denied to the lower classes, who lived in highly crowded conditions. Over time, trends such as wider education, growing literacy and greater involvement of citizens in politics led to the first fractures of privacy, as people became more aware of the individuals in society and of each other, and individuals' exclusive ownership of their personal information was loosened. After World War II, governments became ever more intrusive into the privacy of their citizens, on the pretext of preserving national security, aided and abetted by social scientists who were increasingly able to collect information about citizens without personal interaction. This helped authorities to gather information and to break through the privacy barrier. What was once thought of as voyeurism was now recast as 'scientific curiosity', and what was once considered exhibitionism was now 'serving the cause of scientific research'. Shils describes the pluralist society as one in which the integration of openness and privacy parallels the integration of knowledge and sensitivity, or the integration of autonomy and cooperation based on fraternity. In such a society, there is indeed room for functional secrecy born of necessity and established through sober deliberation. There is, however, a big difference between that sort of secrecy and the sort demanded by a 'paranoid ideology', as Shils puts it, which is essentially symbolic rather than functional.[23]

For our purposes, the question is when is secrecy in adoption functional, serving the purpose of protecting the child, and when is it essentially symbolic, serving other interested parties?

Secrecy in Adoption: A Brief History

As previously noted, a 'closed' or 'full' adoption, in which secrecy plays a key and essential part and the birth parents are cut off from both their child and the adoptive parents, is the default option in Israel, where it is often presented as the 'original' form of adoption.[24] It is worthwhile, however, to examine the historical facts.

Adoption dates as far back as the Hammurabi Code in the early second millennium BC, which stated that a person who raised a child that he did not conceive was entitled to regard him as his own child. Yet as late as the early 1600s CE, adoption was not a commonly prescribed solution for children whose parents could not raise them. In the ancient world, adoption was a common means of ensuring continuity in religious orders and temples: children were routinely removed from their parents' care at a young age to be groomed for religious functions. In Rome, adoption served political aims, such as securing an heir to the throne or cementing an alliance between families to secure power. Strengthening ties between families through adoption still exists today in parts of Asia and Africa: when a family is unable to provide adequately for their child, they might hand him or her over to another family, thereby forging a bond between the two families as though they were one extended family.[25]

The history of adoption in the Western world[26] may be traced through the changes in the manner and extent to which birth parents have been excluded from their children's lives or, as Simmel put it, by the changes in the social premises governing which details of the adoption must be hidden and which may be revealed from one period to the next. The United States was the first country in the Western world to use adoption as a conventional solution for children whose parents could not raise them. For a long time, it was customary to place such children with foster families. From the eighteenth century onwards, however, children were placed for adoption on an individual basis, without oversight or official arrangements, in families with whom the child was already acquainted, such as the godparents. In the nineteenth century, with the increasing congestion in towns and cities and the huge growth in destitute populations, shelter homes were established for children to provide them with a better upbringing than they would have received at home. In the mid 1800s, Reverend Charles Loring Brace, a Calvinist minister, established the Orphan Train initiative, which took homeless orphaned or runaway children in New York City and placed them with farm families in upstate New York, the Midwest, New England and other parts of the country, in the belief that life in the countryside would be more congenial for the children and that they would be accepted by their host families not as servants but as family members. In the wake of the great success of this initiative, four more states joined in, to the point where many parents saw the dispatching of their children out west or up north as a way of ensuring them a better life. Since the hosting farmers wanted to secure their legal status through official adoption, and since Brace thought the birth parents were morally depraved and of malicious intent, all contact between the children and their birth parents was cut off and prevented. Brace's unregulated activity, however, ultimately led, from the second half of the nineteenth century onwards, to the development of a professional and bureaucratic establishment to manage the removal of children from their families.

The first modern adoption law is thought to have been enacted in Massachusetts in 1851, to ensure the welfare and well-being of adopted children. It established, for the first time, that adoption revokes the birth parents' right to raise their child, and that due diligence must be taken in choosing the designated adoptive parents, but it did not stipulate that birth parents must be entirely cut off from their child, or that secrecy be imposed on all aspects of the adoption proceedings. Although Brace's approach of excluding birth parents from their children's lives was very much in evidence in adoption practices, the official guiding ethos, judging by the legislation enacted in Minnesota in 1917, for example, actually advocated openness within the adoption triangle, while protecting privacy. In practice, adoptive parents received information about the background of the children placed with them, and birth parents were told nothing about the identity of the adoptive parents, but were informed about their child's development. The importance attributed by adoption agencies at the time to the bond between the child and his birth parents is evident, in part, in their determined efforts to inform birth parents if their child had died. However, this custom was gradually phased out, to the point where birth parents received no information at all about their child's condition. In the early 1940s, general access to legal files of an adoption case was banned altogether, unless there was 'good cause'. However, adoptees were allowed to access their file with the adoption agency, including information about their birth family, upon reaching adulthood. This policy remained in place until the end of World War II.

In the late 1940s, the policy of privacy protection was gradually superseded by one of blanket secrecy, that is, banning any contact or any transfer of information within the adoption triangle. This came about following the merger of two factors: the desire to upgrade the status of social workers, and the change in the typical profile of birth mothers. Classifying adoption as secret gave social workers a status similar to that of doctors and lawyers, who are sworn to client confidentiality. It was also designed to give a competitive advantage to government adoption agencies, which promised to shield adoptive parents from possible future intrusions into their lives by the child's birth parents, over private adoption agencies, which did not guarantee such confidentiality. Uncritical use of psychoanalytic theory, which was presented as the scientific basis for the social workers' work, also contributed to the cult of secrecy, for example by citing the hypothesis that the adoptee must be protected from an Oedipus complex that he might develop towards his birth parents, or from idealising them.[27]The secrecy also developed another aspect: hiding from the adoptee the very fact that he had been adopted. Today, as noted earlier, it is customary to reveal to the adoptee that he was adopted;[28] social workers have rejected the psychoanalytic approach that the adoptee must never discover this.

In the meantime, the profile of birth mothers had changed. During World War II and in its aftermath, many women, some still in their teens, gave birth out of wedlock, and placed their babies for adoption for fear that the child's existence would prevent them from settling down with their husbands or boyfriends who had gone to war, or with new partners. The notion of a 'clean slate', which is now a key argument cited in preserving secrecy in adoption, therefore owes its beginnings to the protection of the welfare of these women, rather than that of their children, as is usually presented today.[29] Adoptees began to demand information about their origins and identity as early as the 1950s, but it was not until the 1970s that this demand had grown into an organised movement throughout the United States, which the birth parents joined.[30] By the 1990s, there were growing demands for adoptions to be open, that is, for contact to be maintained in one form or another between adoptees and their birth parents, throughout childhood and beyond.

The history of adoption in England and Wales reveals different premises from those underpinning adoption policy in the United States, as evident in a different dialectic between concealment and disclosure.[31] Here, even before the Adoption Act had come into effect, registering a child as a member of the adoptive family required the intervention of the courts. Prior to the mid nineteenth century, birth parents who gave up their children for adoption were entitled to be consulted about the designated adoptive parents and to be informed about the whereabouts of their children after they had been adopted.

Even parents whose children had been taken for adoption without their consent, for failing the demands of the English Poor Laws, had this right and were able to maintain contact with their children. From 1873 onwards, however, the principle of the best interests of the child gained the upper hand, but it was not until half a century later, in 1925, that the first commission was appointed to look into the issue. The commission's findings explicitly stated that birth parents must be advised as to the identity of the adoptive parents and allowed access to their children. Adoptive parents objected to this stipulation, for fear that the birth parents might intervene in their lives, but this was rejected by another commission appointed to look into the issue, which found that out of 1,200 cases of adoption in the Birmingham area, only three mothers had troubled the adoptive parents. The recommendations of the commission on the issue of openness in adoption were translated into the first Adoption Act of 1926, but the act's directives with regard to preserving contact between birth parents and children after adoption and access to information (by birth and adoptive parents alike) were not implemented in practice. Gradually, the custom of getting the mother to sign a form that provided no identifying details of the adoptive parents became established practice. In 1932, when this practice was brought to its attention, the House of Lords (in its capacity as the supreme court of the land at the time) ordered the open adoption directives to be implemented, but adoption agencies, in league with the lower law courts, continued to ignore this demand, as well as the legal obligation to have the birth mother appear in court to confirm her decision to place her child for adoption.

In 1949, the principle of secrecy was made an official part of the adoption procedure and applied across the board, applying to contact between the birth parents and the adopted child, the identity of the adoptive parents, and the adoptee's access to their adoption file. One reason for this change was that the pendulum of the 'nature versus nurture' debate had now swung from the notion of genetic dominance (which necessitated contact between birth parents and their children to understand the origins of the child's development) to the belief that the child's environment is the determinant factor, as the Western world, still recovering from World War II, hoped for a better future and sought to distance itself from notions of genetic dominance that were associated with Nazi ideology. According to the new perspective, secrecy also ensured that the adopted child was provided with a new environment that kept him apart from the mother who had given birth to him out of wedlock and was therefore of questionable character. In England and Wales, as in the United States, birth mothers who had placed their children for adoption during World War II and its aftermath did so to conceal the birth of their children from the men who returned from the warfront.

In 1972, a government commission in England and Wales ordered adoption files to be opened to adoptees on reaching the age of eighteen, in a bid for greater openness in adoption. In its wake, the Adoption Act of 1976 stipulated that an adoptee who has reached the age of eighteen must be helped in every way possible to procure their original birth certificate. It was not until the Children Act of 1989, however, which stipulated that the well-being of the child is a paramount principle that contact between adoptees and their birth parents was permitted by the court. The Children Acts of 2002, 2004 and 2006 promoted openness, inasmuch as a section in each act requires consideration of the possibility of involving the birth parents in every action concerning the child, including maintaining contact between them, be it through correspondence, meetings or an outright open adoption arrangement.[32]

In Israel, the trend in adoption policy has run counter to those of both the United States and England and Wales. The first Adoption of Children Law was enacted in 1960, in which the secular Israeli statute rejected the traditional Jewish religious dictum that a person who raises 'an orphan' is not permitted to view him as his own child.[33] Closed adoption (also known in Israel as 'full adoption') was defined as the default option. Some degree of influence from Jewish tradition is apparent, nonetheless, in that open adoption, or 'restricting the results of adoption', as it is referred to in the statute, is stated as an exceptional option, whereby the courts may consider allowing continued contact between the adoptee and his birth parents, in some form or another.[34] In addition, perhaps inspired by the traditional Jewish dictum, Israel pioneered legislation that permitted adoptees to gain access to their adoption file on reaching the age of eighteen.[35] That said, ACL (the Adoption of Children Law of 1981) made the opening of the adoption file, at the adoptee's request, subject to the discretion of the chief social worker under the Law of Adoption.[36] The chief social worker replaces the adoptee in the list of those permitted by law to have access to the adoption file.[37] The issue of the adoptee's birth certificate is not stipulated in the law, but as a rule, the adoptee is issued with a new birth certificate, to make it look as though he or she had been born to the adoptive family. The original certificate is kept in the state archives, and the adoptee has no access to it, even as an adult.[38]

From this historical review, then, it is apparent that in the West secrecy was an integral part of adoption laws only for a period of thirty years or so, and today closed adoption is no longer the norm.[39] In Israel, on the other hand, the so-called 'restricted-result adoption' is still the exception to the rule.[40] This has been justified on the grounds that there is a dearth of 'sufficient research basis on which to base the nature of open adoption',[41] and yet no such research is cited as justification for preferring closed adoption. The reference to scientific justification is, therefore, questionable, particularly since the claim that there is no research basis for open adoption has been repeated in rulings for several years now,[42] implying that there have been no developments in scientific knowledge in this regard. This repeated reference to the need for scientific explanations appears, therefore, to be designed to promote the notion that open adoption is exceptional and that closed adoption should therefore continue to be the default choice.[43]

In the spirit of Simmel's warning against ignoring the importance of secrecy, I should point out that I am not arguing that the blanket implementation of closed adoption and avoidance of an informed debate about open adoption are grounds for abolishing closed adoption completely. Secrecy is undoubtedly called for in cases where the very contact between the child and his birth parents endangers the child. In such cases, all contact between the child and his birth parents should be severed, and the child's whereabouts kept hidden. However, there is a big difference between using secrecy for this purpose and using it as protection against the alleged perpetual looming menace of openness over the adoption, which is essentially no different from the 'paranoid' ideology to which Shils refers. The notion that secrecy and adoption are inextricably bound together has no basis either in the history of adoption or in scientific evidence. I argue, therefore, that other explanations are at play.

Secrecy in Adoption: Possible Explanations

In this section I address the possible underlying reasons for the conventional view in Israel that secrecy is an integral part of adoption, based on my experience and understanding. These include the mystery of the bond between parent and child and of secrecy itself; the power invested in government-based interventions; the bureaucracy underpinning the authority of the SSC, and its alleged expertise, which plays a key part in legal proceedings over adoption without parental consent; the uncertainty of decisions over the child's future and the future of his relationship with his birth parents; and the anxiety involved in interventions in situations that seem to endanger the child, particularly when decisions about adoption are perceived as a threat by the participants in the adoption proceedings.

Mystery

In various mythologies, adoption is associated with the universal figure of a hero born to high-ranking parents who, for one reason or another, is taken away from them, with or without their consent, and adopted by a low-ranking family.[44] The stories of Moses and Oedipus, which were presented in the Introduction of this book as archetypal adoption stories, are exceptions to this rule since both figures were adopted by royalty, but even in those instances, adoption is presented as the first step in the process of their evolution into heroes. Adoption features repeatedly in literature, not always in its modern-day meaning as an official and legal procedure, but always with an emphasis on the secrecy surrounding the origins of a child who ends up in the care of adults who are not his birth parents. The story usually reaches a climax with the revelation of the child's origins. When this revelation results in contact being re-established between the child and his birth parents, the story is one of redemption,[45] even if the child prefers to remain with his adoptive family; when the child fails to discover his origins, the story is a tragedy.[46] These stories are generally rooted in cultures where the boundaries of the family were rigidly defined, and any intimate relationship outside socially prescribed boundaries was strictly prohibited. In these stories, the separation between the child and his birth parents and the distress that he experiences as a result are not necessarily due to the birth parents' indifference or cruelty,[47] but rather are the result of social arrangements or society's attitude towards the child as an artefact or interchangeable object that can be exchanged or handed over to anyone's ownership.[48] Even today, when society no longer recognises adults' 'ownership' of children, the number of stories about adoption in popular culture far exceeds the actual instances of adoption in the population at large, and stories about adoptees seeking their birth identity and discovering their roots continue to hold immense appeal in the media.[49]

The perennial fascination with adoption may be due, perhaps, to its ability to highlight the duality inherent in parenthood – the simultaneous similarity and differences between parents and their children,[50] and their simultaneous relationship of belonging and separateness.[51] It does so by clearly delineating the duality: the separateness and difference are manifest in the severing of contact between the child and his birth parents and providing the child with a different identity, while similarity and belonging are realised in the revelation of the child's origins.[52] Stories of this kind speak to the profound dread of the differences and separateness entailed in parenthood, and provide great consolation when belonging and similarity prevail.[53] In this way, they serve the myth's purpose:[54] to reconcile the belief that parenthood, as a phenomenon, is naturally ordained, with a fixed trajectory that begins with the physiological process of birth and establishes the child's belonging and identity, with the actual complex and unpredictable reality that contains difference and separateness.

Emmanuel Levinas proposes that parenthood 'verges on the mysterious' and defines it as:

> The fact of seeing the possibilities of the other as your own possibilities, of being able to escape the closure of your identity and what is bestowed on you, toward something which is not bestowed on you and which nevertheless is yours – this is paternity.[55]

Parenthood is gradually revealed to parents as their relationship with their child evolves, and has elements of mystery, of the magic that surrounds anything unknown, but also of anxiety induced by the unexpected. Mystery is a secret, but this is because we do not know what is hidden,[56] not because the very knowledge of it is forbidden.

However, mystery has no place in policymaking, and today, when society recognises that the privacy of the family unit can also be used to cover up child abuse, parenthood is subject to state supervision, which constantly seeks to uncover the unknown and render the unexpected into something expected.[57] The duality inherent in the parent's search for similarities to him in his child, while recognising the child's different qualities and otherness, has now been replaced by the notion of 'parental capability',[58] a term that assumes that a 'normal' parent is endowed with an inborn parenting capacity that can be detected in objective tests.[59] By using secrecy, the state separates external reality from internal reality, the objective from the subjective.[60] The secret embodied in the unknown becomes a secret whose very revelation is expressly forbidden. The child is cut off from his parents, and the internal reality – his bond with his parents – is hidden and denied. Enshrining adoption in law is presented as a promise that the child's future sense of belonging and identity will grow out of his relationship with his adoptive parents, implying that merely mandating the adoption can determine the nature of this relationship. The trials and tribulations the adoptive family must undergo as it grapples with the inevitable differences and separateness of their adopted child are shrouded in secrecy,[61] while the mystery of natural parenthood is appropriated by the state by obscuring the child's origins and whereabouts and concealing the difficulties that the adoptive parents experience. As the one in charge of the secret, the state holds the power (or illusion of power) of control over the relationship between parents and child, as though it were, to paraphrase Albert Einstein, an unseen piper whose mysterious tune determines everything.[62] This serves the construction of adoption as the transfer of parenthood to the adoption establishment.[63] Thus, the parent–child bond is replaced by a relationship between state and child; the mystery of the bond is replaced by secrecy; the magic of mystery by authority; and the unknown by a lack of transparency.

Power

Presenting closed adoption as the default option gives secrecy a key role in establishing the SSC and enhancing its authority.[64] The SSC is the only authoritative body pertaining to adoption in Israel, and the exclusive contact, both for birth parents and adoptive parents alike, in all adoption-related matters. This exclusivity, which prevents the leaking of information, is an outcome of the Adoption of Children Law, which charges Israel's Justice Minister with implementing the law, including setting regulations to ensure secrecy.[65] The monopoly and exclusivity granted to the SSC indicates that secrecy is accorded more weight than the principle of fairness, which cautions against operations involving a conflict of interests. Indeed, the assumption behind the imposition of secrecy upon the adoption triangle is that there is an inherent conflict of interests between the birth parents and the adoptive parents that is potentially hazardous,[66] and yet both sets of parents are dealt with exclusively by the SSC. It is worth noting, in this regard, that in its ruling on Tal, the court recommended separating the authority responsible for removing children from their parents from the one that hands these children over to adoptive parents, to prevent situations in which the adoption officials are influenced, consciously or otherwise, by the amount of time that the prospective adoptive parents have to wait until they receive a child.

The difficulty created by the merger of these two functions has clearly not escaped the notice of the adoption authorities themselves. As if to underline that adoption officials act only in the best interests of the child and do not favour either set of parents, the authority was named the 'Service for the Sake of the Child' when it was created following the ACL in 1981. However, actions taken amidst a conflict of interests, under cover of secrecy, create a closed system that obscures the transparency that guarantees the protection of the rights of those served by it. As a result, all three parties – birth parents, prospective adoptive parents and adopted children – are liable to be harmed.

Excluding the birth parents from their children's lives is deemed necessary to 'free the child for adoption', as the procedure is commonly referred to when the child is declared eligible for adoption. The manner in which the birth parents are treated is designed to ensure that they are completely cut off from their children, rather than to promote understanding of their place in their children's lives, and secrecy serves the adoption officials well in achieving this end.[67] In the case of Elinor, for example, the foster parents were given selective information about the birth mother, with the deliberate aim of casting her in a bad light and presenting the girl's adoption as an act of saving the child from a wanton woman. In the case of Tal, the adoption officials achieved the same purpose by concealing critical information. The SSC does not serve as an unbiased authority for birth parents. As far as it is concerned, the birth parents exist only insofar as they must be excluded from their children's lives, and as such they are not worthy even of the little succour that the state might offer them once they have lost their children to adoption.[68] The distress experienced by the birth parents, for whom the SSC is the only authority they can appeal to, is of no interest to that body.[69] From the moment their child is declared eligible for adoption, the SSC ceases to have any interest in the birth parents; they are left to their own devices. It offers them no help, unlike the help it offers to foster parents, who are supported by adoption officials during their 'grieving period' whenever a child under their care is taken away from them. Although it is debatable whether the adoption officials' callous attitude towards birth parents when removing a child from their care makes them the right people to offer support, the fact remains that they are the only ones with the mandate to do so.

Adoptive parents, too, are not immune to the harm that may come from having so much power concentrated in the hands of adoption officials, who are the sole keepers of the secret. In their passionate determination to promote adoptions at all costs, the officials seek to present the courts with *faits accomplis*. This has led them on more than one occasion to conceal the real facts from the designated adoptive parents too,[70] as in the cases of Elinor and Tal, and in the case of Daniel, as will be recounted in the next chapter. In this respect, the designated adoptive parents fare no better than the birth parents: they, too, are not party to the 'secret', and may be adversely affected.

The need to maintain strict segregation between the birth parents and the designated adoptive parents during the adoption officials' respective dealings with them dictates the SSC's work procedures. One adoption official takes the child from the birth parents' care; another escorts him to a secret venue or to the prospective adoptive parents.[71] The ramifications of these procedures for the child highlight the paradox in the presumption that an authority operating with a conflict of interests can be neutral and impartial, since passing the child from one adoption official to another negates the one possible advantage that might arise from having the same body deal with both sets of parents, namely to provide the child with continual interaction with a single figure who can provide him with a sense of continuity during the upheaval of the transition from one set of parents to the other. Thus, even the children, whose protection is ostensibly the main purpose of the Service for the Sake of the Child, are adversely affected, as various adoption officials flit in and out of their lives on behalf of the authority controlling their fate.

Despite repeated censure by the courts for the actions and liberties taken by adoption officials in abuse of their exclusive authority,[72] the SSC's unassailable status shields their work from the scrutiny of any oversight that might prevent repeated harm to children and parents.[73]

The SSC's hegemony might have been an advantage from a research standpoint, for example in resolving the problem of uniformity when selecting a sample, but in reality its method of operation precludes its involvement in any reliable scientific study, as it uses secrecy to control the outcome of studies, for example by having a say in the selection of research samples.[74] Furthermore, as in any organisation, secrecy serves the competition between facilities that offer various solutions for children who are removed from their home,[75] but unlike those facilities, whose operational details are available to the public, enabling failures to be uncovered, the secrecy surrounding the fate of adopted children makes it possible to cover up failures and present adoption as the best option. The failure of Dalit's own adoption, for example, was only discovered by the court when the question of her daughter being declared eligible for adoption came up. Instances of adoption that fail to live up to the promise of a successful bond between adoptive parents and the child are neither documented nor made known to the courts.[76] The change in adoptees' legal identity means that they effectively 'disappear', precluding any follow-up of their situations by independent bodies after they have been adopted. As the court said on one occasion, when it ruled in favour of adoption, 'There is no one to monitor the minor in question, to ensure that the decision to declare him eligible for adoption was indeed to his benefit'.[77] In this way, adoption authorities can present adoption as the preferred solution for children of failed parents, not because it is known to be so, but because neither the courts nor the public know its outcomes. Michel Foucault has already pointed out, 'For it [power], secrecy is not in the nature of an abuse – it is indispensable to its operation'.[78]

Bureaucracy and Expertise

A bureaucratic system whose operation is based on a monopolistic authority granted by statute can entrench its dominance over other systems, by controlling the disclosure of information that would reveal its intentions.[79] As noted earlier, the history of adoption in the United States was one of ever-expanding circles of exclusion from the secret, until the adoptees themselves began to reverse this trend. In Israel, on the other hand, secrecy is still considered fundamental to the institution of adoption, and the SSC is in charge of its scope. Indeed, such is the control that the SSC has over its privileged circle of confidants, that it is not only able to decide who to exclude from it, but it is also able to include individuals who are actually forbidden by law to be party to the secret, for example by leaking copies of expert opinions which have been commissioned as part of court proceedings to foster parents or to designated adoptive parents.[80] In its ruling in the case of Elinor, for example, the court declared this practice illegal, in addition to its many other criticisms of the SSC. However, this did not result in any legal sanctions of the SSC by any supervisory body, confirming the claim that authorities apply strict administrative secrecy and expand it to the maximum possible extent, especially when officials are driven by a fervent sense of mission and a conviction that they, as the representative authority, are above ordinary moral considerations.[81] It is highly doubtful that this was the legislators' intention when the Adoption of Children Law was enacted, but like any bureaucratic apparatus, the SSC uses its maximum authority under the law to implement and interpret it as it sees fit.[82]

The bureaucratic nature of the SSC is also evident in how the actions of the adoption officials are determined by their rank in the service's administrative hierarchy, rather than by the required responses to the needs of the individuals involved. Unlike a professional organisation, where the worker's role is determined by their function,[83] here administrative hierarchy dictates the actions taken.[84] In one such example, as I recounted in the previous chapter, no fewer than four welfare officials turned up on Dalit's doorstep to call on her after she had consistently eluded them over several months. When asked in court why four people were needed for this purpose, the adoption official gave a classic bureaucratic reply: one was the regional adoption official, the second was the regional inspector, the third was the director of Dalit's local welfare office, and the fourth a Youth Law welfare official. The sensitivity that was needed when seeking to re-establish contact with Dalit was replaced by bureaucratic rationale.

The lack of any consideration for the individual, a consistent theme in the flagrant invasion of the privacy of the parties to the adoption, serves to shield the privacy of the adoption officials, who operate like members of a secret society, which the SSC is clearly not, since its existence and purpose are known to all. While adoption officials do not actually cover their faces with masks like members of secret societies to prevent their identification and erase any trace of individual differences between them, they do present themselves as interchangeable.[85] For example, one official may observe the meetings between a child and his mother, while another signs off on the observation report that is submitted to the court, and yet another appears in court and testifies on the SSC's behalf (none of which is mentioned in the report itself). In this way, the adoption officials absolve themselves of any personal responsibility for their actions,[86] and present themselves as the representatives of a secret apparatus, whose existence, like that of any such system, is predicated on an 'all or nothing' choice:[87] either to leave the child with his parents, or to cut him off from them entirely and change his identity.[88] Thus, when the SSC petitions the court to declare a child eligible for adoption, no other alternative is offered, and adoption is presented as the only solution that serves the best interests of the child.[89] Whenever a child is returned to his parents after being taken away from them pursuant to an emergency order, it is defined as a 'trial run'. Adoption, on the other hand, is never defined as such,[90] despite the dramatic change that it introduces in the child's life, including a changed identity, sometimes at a crucial stage in his development, when the issue of identity plays a key role.

'Power is tolerable only on condition that it mask a substantial part of itself', argued Foucault.[91] One of the mechanisms of power is the central role ascribed to expertise in declaring a child eligible for adoption on grounds of his parents' inability to raise him. As previously mentioned, one of the reasons for maintaining secrecy in adoption is to elevate the professional status of social workers. Secrecy bestows upon adoption officials a mantle of unique expertise. As one adoption official wrote in a report submitted to the court during the proceedings in the case of Elinor, 'This is not the place to give a lesson in adoption procedures. This subject must be studied before we are subjected to any criticism, since we are the only experts in the field'.

It is highly doubtful that anyone can lay claim to exclusive expertise in the area of adoption, as it does not involve only knowledge based on empirical findings, and because implementing that knowledge in any given case is subject to interpretation based on moral grounds. To reach an informed decision about a given adoption, the court must be presented with as many perspectives as possible on a child's situation, but the aura of secrecy surrounding adoption officials gives them a special status and disproportionate say in determining the nature and scope of the information and viewpoints presented in court. Despite the crucial role played by expert opinions in assessing 'parental capability', the law offers no hard and fast definition of what constitutes an 'expert' in this context. An expert is appointed by the court under section 20 of the Evidence Ordinance:

> The court may, unless it apprehends a miscarriage of justice, admit as evidence, in writing, an opinion by an expert as to a matter of science, research, art or professional knowledge (hereinafter referred to as 'opinion') and a certificate by a physician as to the state of health of a person (hereinafter referred to as a 'medical certificate').[92]

Generally, those appointed to such a position are professionals from the mental health field: psychologists, psychiatrists and social workers.[93]

The practice of appointing an expert witness who is acceptable to all parties concerned gives adoption officials great power.[94] Given that they are regularly called upon to testify in family courts, experts are inclined to avoid disagreeing with the SSC's position, to ensure that their services are called on again in future. As one family court judge pointed out:

> If we add to all this the court's common practice of not appointing an expert who is not acceptable to both parties (which is exploited by State Counsel to reject experts that are not to its liking), and the interest of experts to 'please' the petitioner so that they may [be called upon to] testify again in future, and the fact that in most cases the parents involved do not exhibit manifestly good parental skills, one may easily imagine that the expert appointed on the court's behalf will find it very difficult to deviate from the general position outlined in the documents and in the opinions provided to him – [particularly given the] risk that if, heaven forfend, his recommendation that the minor be returned to his parents proves to be wrong, the blame would be placed squarely

> on him (while no such risk exists for someone who goes along with the generally accepted view)…[95]

In many cases, two opinions are presented in court: one appended to the state's petition to declare the child eligible for adoption, the other submitted by the court-appointed expert whose appointment State Counsel has also agreed to. The opinions of experts appointed exclusively on the parents' behalf are given in only very few cases.[96]

In addition to the SSC's influence over court-appointed experts and the scope of information presented during court proceedings, the court views the testimonies of the adoption officials themselves as impartial expert opinions,[97] even when it is clear that the situation that they themselves have created, as those in charge of controlling and monitoring contact between the child and his parents prior to their petition to the court, advances their position in court proceedings in which they are an interested party. Under the guise of secrecy, the adoption officials can exercise control and blur the distinction 'between providing a professional assessment, and contributing to the circumstances on which the petition is based'.[98]

At the court hearings, the testimony of the SSC is pitted against the testimony of the parents, as though they were two sides of equal weight. In reality, given their influence over court-appointed experts and over the information presented in court, and their status as 'experts' themselves, as well as a party to the proceedings, the weight of the SSC's position is effectively trebled, and the principle of equality before the law is compromised.

Since adoption officials are seen as experts, they have exclusive authority in the selection of designated adoptive families. As noted earlier, details of the chosen family are revealed to the court only once the adoption order has been issued, at least six months after the child has been placed with the family. By that time, however, the child has likely become attached to that family and the court finds it difficult to reject the adoption order petition, even if the family has failed to meet the minimum statutory conditions for that purpose, such as being of the same religion as the adoptee.[99] In the case of Tal, for example, the adoption officials ignored the child's complex religious background and focused exclusively on her mother's religious affiliation, and when State Counsel raised the possibility of an open adoption, the court studiously avoided the religious issue, even though that information is crucial to an informed definition about the appropriate type of adoption. According to a Supreme Court ruling, the decision about the type of adoption – 'full' or 'open' – must be made *prior* to the child's placement with the adoptive family,[100] and clearly the religion of the child must be taken into account in the arrangements. Even within the Jewish community, this clause is open to abuse, as the question of religious affiliation is determined purely by nominal affiliation,[101] resulting in children from secular Jewish families, or from families of uncertain religious affiliation, being placed with Orthodox Jewish families, with predictable difficulties arising whenever the option of open adoption is raised, due to the contrasting lifestyles and values between the two families.[102] As described in the previous chapter, adoption officials fiercely protect their exclusive prerogative of choosing the adoptive family and the secrecy in which it is done by every means possible, and thus retain their control in deciding the type of adoption.

Certainty and Anxiety

The petition to declare a child eligible for adoption is made when, in the authorities' view, the child is in danger and adoption is expected to ensure his welfare. In situations of this sort, a forecast is required, which raises questions of certainty and anxiety. The veil of secrecy surrounding the adoptee hides the progress of the child's adjustment to the adoptive family, who, despite having wished and waited for the child for many years, often find themselves facing many unforeseen situations. In particular, it is worth examining the phenomenon of adoptive parents seized with anxiety and depression shortly after the adoption has got under way, which in recent years has been designated a 'syndrome' and likened to postpartum depression.[103] The 'discovery' of this 'syndrome' speaks volumes about the authorities' expectation of adoption as an unqualified success. Otherwise why would it be surprising that people who have endured years of selection procedures and long waits and have finally been found worthy of raising a child of their own react with anxiety when the child finally arrives at their home? It is only natural that people in such a situation should suddenly be plagued by apprehensions about the difficulties that might arise in raising their adopted child, for fear that they might fail in the adoption and not live up to the trust that has been placed in them. Why would such an understandable reaction of anxiety and depression in such a situation be defined as a pathology, if not to foster the myth that adoption compensates fully for the loss of the natural bond between a child and his birth parents, and that there are no uncertainties in the actual adoption process?[104] As one Supreme Court judge pointed out:

> There is much that is unknown and uncertain in the ramifications of the decision that is required of us. It is difficult to predict the future of the minor's natural family, nor can there be any certainty in knowing how the life circumstances of the adoptive family may develop over time. The decision that is called for is based not on a clear forecast of the future, but on a range of considerations based on primary life experience and fundamental values underpinning the autonomy of the natural family and the institution of adoption.[105]

Recognising the uncertainty that is inherent to any attempt to forecast a child's future when making a decision regarding his adoption raises anxiety, and in a bid to dispel that anxiety, one common strategy is to deny that the disappearance of the child's birth parents and his genealogical ties constitutes an irreplaceable loss. Only the child can attest to this loss, but his testimony is not always available during the proceedings on whether to declare him eligible for adoption, in part because the loss is not necessarily experienced until some time later. The legal proceedings are therefore often conducted without the child's testimony,[106] and the court must base its rulings on value judgements that do not remove the uncertainty. However, as noted in previous chapters, even when the child's testimony is presented in court, the adoption officials dismiss it and draw the court's attention to the damage that the birth parents have caused, or are likely to cause, to the child. In this way, they foster the common notion in Israel that adoption is compensation for the damage done to the child, be it the harm inflicted by his birth parents or the simple fact that he, unlike any other child, is denied the right of growing up with his birth parents. Presenting the birth parents' disappearance as 'damage' is telling, as it suggests that it can be quantified and compensated for, thereby rendering the child's testimony unnecessary.[107] Since the legal hearings focus on calculating this damage and those responsible for it, attention is drawn away from the uncertainty involved in the adoption proposal itself, so that it may continue to be presented as a failsafe solution that guarantees the child's welfare.[108]

Certainty is critical to relieving the anxiety that no doubt constantly weighs upon the adoption officials in their work, due to the weight of responsibility involved in protecting children in jeopardy, and because of the somewhat threatening nature of their relationship with the birth parents. (This is a threat that works both ways: the adoption officials are a threat to the birth parents, and feel threatened by them as well.) The anxiety that overshadows their contact with the birth parents may explain the belligerency with which they enforce emergency orders[109] that grant them the right to remove a child from his family prior to court approval. When details emerged in court of how the children of the Ziv family were taken away from their mother, State Counsel (representing the adoption officials) clashed with the court over whether it was justified to exercise the emergency order before an assessment had been made of the mother's ability to raise the children on her own once the abusive father was removed. In the hearings concerning the removal of Tal from her mother's care, it transpired that the SSC had exercised the emergency order before finding out the true facts of the situation. While executing emergency orders when conditions (as prescribed by law) do not quite warrant them may relieve the adoption officials' concern for the children who may be abused or neglected by their parents, it does not eliminate anxiety, but merely transmits it to the parents. The threat of having their children taken away was enough to drive the mothers in question to desperate acts. In the case of the Ziv family, the mother declared that her youngest child was in fact the son of another man, in the hope that she might be allowed to keep him for that reason. In the case of Dalit, she offered her daughter to a solicitous couple who wanted to help her. Anxiety is a poor guide: it spurs adoption officials and parents alike to commit actions that are aimed at relieving the anxiety, rather than resolving problems at their source.

It is highly doubtful that the adoption officials succeed in relieving their anxiety by such actions, even when they shield themselves behind a wall of secrecy. Unlike contagious diseases, anxiety cannot be blocked by isolating its subjects. On the contrary, isolation only confirms and heightens the threat that induced the anxiety in the first place. Perhaps it is because of this anxiety that adoption officials insist on arranging meetings of birth parents and children in the presence of two or more adoption officials, arguing that it helps them to gain an accurate assessment of the situation and support for the heavy responsibility placed on their shoulders. From a professional standpoint, there is no justification for the presence of more than one adoption official during meetings with birth parents or with a child. While it is undoubtedly true that dealing with anxiety-provoking situations that demand careful observation and scrutiny does require support, the social work profession has a plethora of support measures that it has pioneered[110] to help social workers cope with such situations, usually involving experienced and senior professionals who assess the social worker's approach, identify blind spots or areas requiring further input, and help draw up a suitable treatment programme. However, such support is provided not *during* their encounters with their clients, but after, or, if possible, before, to help in preparation.

Conducting a professional observation of a meeting is intended not only to capture external events, but to gain an understanding of the significance and meaning that each person at the meeting attributes to the situation. This sort of understanding can only be achieved by establishing a personal and perhaps even intimate rapport.[111] Perhaps, in its attempt to deflect this anxiety, the SSC sought to support its workers in a manner that enabled it to retain control, since the very presence of two adoption officials puts birth parents at a disadvantage. As a result, instead of the meeting allowing the officials to gauge the relationship between the parents and child with all its nuances and complexities, the expanded presence of the adoption officials makes them look like 'minders' on the authorities' behalf. Anxiety is therefore replaced by fortification, which in turn, like a self-fulfilling prophecy, magnifies the alleged threat posed by the birth parents and justifies the fortification. In the case of the Ziv family, for example, in its effort to create the impression that the mother was a threat to her children, the adoption officials even insisted that she should not be present at the court hearings to determine the future of her motherhood. In the case of Dalit and Tal, the officials thought it more important to 'save' the child from the mother's care than to consider the impact of such an action on her development at that particular age and at that particular juncture in her bond with her mother. In the SSC's eyes, every failed parent is akin to Oedipus's father, who sought to have Oedipus killed.[112]

In their attempt to extricate themselves from this vicious circle, oscillating endlessly between secrecy and anxiety, the adoption officials constantly expand their circle of control,[113] at times in violation of professional protocol. As one judge put it in her ruling:

> I find a further failing in the conduct of social services in the manner in which the minors were removed from their parents' care. According to the welfare officer's report, a police escort was requested for this purpose, a reasonable request in light of the concerns raised by the father's threats against the social workers in the past. However, the welfare officer then agreed to the police officers' suggestion that she remain in the patrol car while they went to the petitioners' home, removed the minors themselves and brought them back to the car. Such conduct, as the welfare officer has agreed with me in the hearing, is clearly unacceptable and contrary to the minors' interests. Welfare officials must receive clear action guidance in cases such as these, and policemen, too, should be briefed as to the proper manner to execute a removal of this sort, so that this instance does not recur.[114]

Protection from anxiety gives secrecy a symbolic significance and violates the privacy and autonomy of the parents and their children, as well as the principle of open government, which is supposed to protect citizens from arbitrary government action. Imposing secrecy on adoption procedures creates a paradox, as it undermines the very circumscription of parental privacy that is built into adoption without parental consent. Legislation that enables the state to invade the intimacy of a family relationship is aimed at protecting children whose home has turned from a haven into a trap, when the parents abuse the privacy and autonomy granted to them to harm their children. However, the wall of secrecy that surrounds these children from the moment they are taken away from their parents only recreates the danger they were exposed to within their birth family. In the case of the Ziv family, the mother responded to the perceived threat posed by the adoption officials by trying to hide her children. When police discovered their whereabouts, they were forcibly removed to a secret location and the mother was denied access to them for several months. In the case of Elinor, she was seized from her nursery school without so much as the chance to say goodbye to her mother and grandmother; meetings with her mother were abruptly terminated after Elinor threw a tantrum on one occasion; and a telephone call between her and the mother was hastily terminated when she mentioned the name of her foster brother. These examples demonstrate the harm caused to children by the belief that children must be hidden from their parents. The children of the Ziv family lost all trust in adults (according to the staff of the children's home where they were kept), and Elinor ceased to pine for her mother and instead saw her as a threat (according to the adoption officials' testimony in court). Hiding children behind a wall of secrecy presents the parents as menacing and dangerous figures who might impair the development of their children even after they are placed for adoption.

I was able to experience myself just how secrecy feeds the anxiety surrounding adoption when the question of the legality of this book's publication first arose. As is customary in such matters, I was asked to submit the manuscript to a reader working on behalf of the publishing house, and she, a lawyer by training, advised me to seek further legal opinions regarding the publication of Dalit and Tal's story, given that a publication ban had been imposed on it. After the judge whom I had consulted privately saw no difficulty in publication of the first draft, I consulted with another judge, who took a more conservative view. It was not just the publication ban that prevented publication, he said, but also the fact that I was exposing the mother's life story, which I had pieced together in the course of the court hearings. His opinion was particularly significant for me, since he had no issues with the criticisms I had made about the adoption service in my manuscript, although he did question the need for quite such a detailed description, and wondered if this was the right way to present it. Among the arguments that he raised, one comment in particular stood out in my mind.

'You can't possibly write this: do you have any idea what it's like to rule that a child should be taken away from its parents?' he asked me. I had no reason to believe that the alarm in his voice was due to his own personal views, as I had seen him in the past taking bold decisions while presiding over adoption proceedings; rather, he was referring to the anxiety surrounding adoption per se. By now, that anxiety began to affect me, too, and I began a series of consultations, in an attempt to avoid any delay that would ensue if I had to apply to the courts for permission to publish the story. However, apart from two lawyers, one who insisted that disguising the identity of the parties to the adoption triangle would suffice and that I could publish this case (particularly given that court rulings in the case were in the public domain), and the other, a specialist in issues of publication and media, who warned me that any unauthorised revelation (particularly one involving a publication ban) would be dealt with very severely under the Adoption of Children Law, all the other experts I spoke to avoided taking any clear position.

'No one is giving you a clear-cut answer because everyone wants to be certain', I was told by one of them, who feared that any accusations levelled against me for violation of secrecy would only strengthen the hand of those objecting to my criticism of the adoption service, thus revealing yet another aspect of the anxiety generated by the grip of secrecy over adoption.

The dread that took hold of me during these consultations was different from the concerns I usually have when making court submissions of expert assessments of the ability of parents to raise their children. It seemed to confirm the supernatural power of secrecy, as though I was holding Pandora's Box in my very hands. In the end, when I did finally appeal to the court on this matter, I felt relieved: it was a way of reining in secrecy to within its functional boundaries. At the same time, the experience gave me insight into the trepidation that secrecy generates and feeds, which is what drove me to devote this chapter to an examination of its significance and how it is distinct from privacy.

On Publication of the Chapter and the Book

The Canonical Status of Secrecy

The public nature of adoption proceedings as a legally sanctioned governmental act is manifest in the stipulation that all adoption-related court rulings are in the public domain, while the identity of those involved is concealed, to protect their privacy. Based on that position, I received permission to publish three of the book's chapters without any legal proceedings on the strict understanding, of course, that I could not reveal the identities of the parties to the adoption triangle. The legal proceedings over the publication of Dalit and Tal's story, however, were conducted under the regulations of secrecy. The court appointed State Counsel as the SSC's legal representative, as respondents to my petition. Thus, the SSC was effectively given the option of declaring its own autonomy as the one with the authority to decide the boundary between permitted and forbidden and to prevent any disclosure of its working methods.[115] In effect, the court granted the SSC ownership of the secret.

The issue of secrecy in adoption has acquired a canonical status in Israel, which deters any attempt to scrutinise adoption procedures. This is evident, in part, in the reply to my request by State Counsel after they had read the synopsis that I had submitted to the court:

> Judging by the aforementioned examples, it is clear that the facts on which the petitioner, Dr Mass, is seeking to base her research are untrue and tendentious, and might harm the adoption system in Israel and adoptees, on the pretext of 'scientific research'. For this reason, and as long as we have not received a full description of the case involved in the material provided by Dr Mass, State Counsel objects to the publication in its current form for the aforesaid reasons.

The derisive reference to my work as 'scientific research' in quotation marks was repeated once the hearings got under way, when State Counsel argued that the full version of the chapter (which they had received by then) was highly tendentious and based on preconceived ideas, and therefore unworthy of being defined as research. This objection, however, was dismissed out of hand by the judge because it was irrelevant to the matter at hand, and because State Counsel was not a scientific authority. Moreover, by arguing that the research must not be published because of the alleged invalidity of its facts, State Counsel was purporting to appoint itself as the representative of the Ministry of Truth,[116] with the power to decide what is and what is not permitted for publication. Such an argument indicates a basic lack of understanding of the freedom of expression as enshrined by Israel's Court of Appeal in a ruling that stated that it is an inalienable right that enables all other rights, and is not contingent upon the truthfulness of the facts being presented.[117]

Setting aside its unsubstantiated claim that the facts in my book were untrue, State Counsel's declaration that publication of Dalit and Tal's story must be forbidden in order to protect the adoption system is worthy of closer examination. Although the court did not respond to this argument, it may be understood as an attempt to forestall any public debate about the adoption system. It suggests that State Counsel did not believe that the government's actions in a democracy should be subject to public scrutiny; indeed, in court the State Counsel went even further, arguing that since the hearings pertained to the Adoption of Children Law, the issue of publication required a stricter level of protection than applicable to publication in other domains. In support of her reasoning, she cited the publication ban that had been imposed in this particular case, but ignored the fact that at the end of the original hearings of this adoption case in the family court, State Counsel's request to ban publication of the ruling had been denied. The publication ban was ultimately issued not because of the inherent risks of publishing a case involving adoption, but because at a later stage in the case, after the family court and district court rulings had been published, several news items appeared in the media with details that could be used to reveal the identity of the birth mother and the designated adoptive family in question. At that time, the judge had also been advised that there was a photographer in court during the proceedings, who was continuing to cover the story for publication in the media. By ignoring these facts, and citing the Adoption of Children Law, State Counsel was justifying the ever-present concerns about conspiracy, that is, arguing for secrecy of the symbolic, non-functional type.

Furthermore, by citing harm to 'adoptees' in the list of possible harms that publication of Dalit and Tal's story might inflict upon the adoption system, State Counsel was trying to portray a cultural structure that defines adopted children as a uniform group about which personal and autonomous details must be kept secret in order to protect the group.[118] However, equating the protection of this group with protecting the secrecy of the adoption system appropriates the rights of adoptees and undermines their right to autonomy. By casting itself as the representative of 'adoptees', State Counsel was implying that when birth parents' rights over their children are revoked, these rights revert not to the children but to the state,[119] as though guardianship over the children, which the state assumes on removing the children from their birth parents, remains with the state even after they have been adopted. This is in express contravention of the law, which clearly states that once the adoption order is issued, the adoptive parents are the child's guardians.[120] State Counsel's presumption to speak on behalf of the adoptees thus illustrates how the autonomy of the adoptive parents and adoptees alike is compromised when excessive use of secrecy allows their rights to be appropriated by the state.

'We're talking about the people's lives', declared State Counsel, arguing that merely banning publication of the identities of those involved in the case was not enough to protect the minor's privacy, since the case had such unique characteristics that would make it easy to identify those involved even without exposing identifying details (although, as previously noted, these characteristics had already been included in previous publications of the court's rulings). 'When the minor's friends study social work', she explained, 'they will read this research and recognise her'. (The minor in question was aged five at the time.) She further argued that the story is delivered in minute detail, to an 'invasive' degree, implying that I was treating the people involved as mere playthings. She insisted that they would undoubtedly have something to say about this, and that it would be wrong to reach a decision without hearing their own opinion.

The argument about the invasiveness of the manuscript, which had also been raised by one of the judges whom I consulted, is a serious one, which I will return to later in this chapter. However, the manner in which I had allegedly manipulated the individuals in the case was already well known to these individuals, as the material was the same that I had presented in the expert opinions that I submitted to the court. In general, expert opinions are not supposed to be shown to the designated adoptive parents, who often frankly confide their thoughts and feelings to experts, and while the way in which they were presented might be construed as being critical, my criticism was not aimed at them but against the social mindset behind current adoption practices.

In my response to State Counsel's statement, I told the court that I agreed that the publication was about people's lives. Precisely for that reason, I added, the state cannot operate under cover of secrecy and stifle all discussion of the topic. Since State Counsel was unable to point to any details in the manuscript that might identify those involved, I said, academic freedom must be protected. The court then asked me if I had received permission from Dalit's adoptive parents (who had not been a party to the legal proceedings described in my text) to publish details about them, to which I replied that what is written about them in the book is cited merely as the subjective views of those being quoted, rather than as facts. Furthermore, in the book their identity is concealed and details of their relationship with Dalit are, in any event, in the public domain, since they appear in the family court rulings and in the summaries submitted at the case hearings.

On conclusion of this debate, the judge decided to appoint an attorney as Guardian *ad Litem* (GAL) for the minor, to examine whether the publication of my research might be injurious to her interests. The GAL focused on the question of whether it was possible to protect the minor from inappropriate reactions by those surrounding her to her life story. When he found that the rulings in this case had been published before the publication ban, and that the entire story had been featured in the printed press as well as in interviews on television and radio (nine in all, according to his list), he stated that he doubted there was any justification to impose the ban only with regard to my book, and that to do so would also be tantamount to limiting academic freedom. He also drew a distinction between privacy and secrecy of the sort that the state was seeking to impose with regard to the publication of Dalit and Tal's story. With respect to State Counsel's claim that 'the facts on which the petitioner, Dr Mass, is seeking to base her research are untrue and tendentious', he wrote:

> The concern raised by State Counsel is not about harm to the welfare of the minor in question, but about harm to the adoption system and to adoptees. And while Dr Mass's research is sharply critical of the social services and the part they played in removing the minor from the deceased, to my mind this criticism is not harmful to the minor's welfare – indeed, perhaps quite the opposite. This criticism puts forward a comprehensive explanation for the rupture created between the minor and the deceased, which makes it clear that the deceased had not abandoned the minor, nor had she lost interest in her, or ceased to love her, etc., even when the minor was handed back to the foster family by the deceased after regaining custody of her.

The appointment of the GAL put an end to the state's claim of ownership over secrecy, and since the report placed the protection of the minor's privacy at the heart of its opinion, it became apparent that arguments in favour of protecting the adoption system had no place in this discussion.

Protection of Privacy

Shils' insight that social sciences have broken through the privacy barrier, and his somewhat wry observation that 'what was once voyeurism has now become scientific curiosity and what was once exhibitionism now serves as scientific research',[121] might apply also to a book such as this, which goes into great detail when describing the intimate bond between children and their parents. Such, in any event, was State Counsel's contention when she claimed that my manuscript was 'invasive and intrusive', adding: 'It's like a game [to her], flagrantly and callously turning the subjects of this case into game pieces'. However, my decision to provide a detailed description of my observations of the children and their parents and the various actions taken during the legal proceedings, while appearing to verge on invasion of privacy, was driven by the objective I had set for my book, namely to expose the systematic denial of loss that is inherent in current adoption procedures. Acknowledging this loss requires the child's testimony, which is not always heard; when criticism is made in the media about the actions of the adoption services, it focuses on the birth parents' complaints rather than on the children's testimonies, because the children have disappeared behind the wall of secrecy. However, hearing the children's testimony is hampered not only by its active concealment, but also by the fact that children often do not testify openly and directly – or even verbally – and therefore their testimony can only be inferred from careful observation of their interaction with their parents.[122] In the case of the children of the Ziv family, for example, determining the significance of the bond between the children and their mother required close observation, while also taking into account the effects of the conditions under which the meetings were held, the irregularity of the meetings, and the evident changes in their relationship when the meetings began to be held on a regular basis, as scheduled. In the case of Elinor, the meetings between her and her mother were renewed only after I had asked for this to happen so that I might be able to complete my expert opinion. Elinor's questions during the meetings – whether her mother knew when she was born, and whether she had breastfed her – attested to the importance that she attributed to her belonging to the mother, after having been told that she would not see her mother again before the age of eighteen. In the case of Tal, traces of the bond between her and her mother could be detected only through close observation of the interaction between them, which allowed me to understand the effect that their forced separation had had, as was also evident from the marked contrast between the report of the doctor who examined her immediately after being taken from her mother and the foster parents' description of her condition when they received her. Only by describing the respective contexts in which these non-verbal testimonies were given – that is, by detailing the process of the children's removal from their mothers and the conditions under which the meetings were held – can they be understood, despite their fragmented, hesitant and elusive nature. Only on the basis of these observations can one form an expert opinion for submission in court, as described in previous chapters, and therefore, although it involved a measure of invasion of privacy of the relationship between children and their parents, it would be wrong to suggest that the observations themselves were gratuitous or constituted a form of voyeurism.

For many years I did avoid publishing my observations, lest they be considered 'exhibitionism in the guise of scientific research', as Shils might put it. Instead, I restricted myself to providing a coherent and succinct position in court, thinking that in this way I was contributing to improving current practices. But I have come to realise that even when the SSC changes its work practices, as in the wake of the court's scathing criticism of its misrepresentation of the facts surrounding Elinor's placement with her foster parents, its officials persist, on the pretext of secrecy, in trying to present the court with *faits accomplis*. Time and again I have seen the enormous power of secrecy, and how it has thwarted any informed debate in adoption proceedings. By continuing to avoid publication of my testimony, therefore, I would be partly complicit in the ever-expanding circle of secrecy and obstruction of children's testimonies.

I cannot deny that at first I did harbour many concerns about providing a detailed description of the chain of events in each of the cases described in the book, since my participation in the proceedings as an expert witness made me party to the secret and imposed upon me an obligation that was somewhat driven by the fear projected by secrecy, the same fear that blurs the distinction between symbolic secrecy and functional secrecy. The manner in which I present my testimony in this book is also not conventional. Usually, the accounts provided by research subjects are divided into quotations and presented in accordance with the researcher's proposed analysis of the themes arising during the interviews with the subjects, or according to the situations that the researchers were exposed to during the research, to protect the research subjects' privacy even from other participants in the events in question.[123] This is not the case in detailed descriptions of adoption cases, but because of the changes in the identifying details, only someone with an intimate knowledge of the stories could identify those involved, and in this case, as the GAL pointed out, 'the book does not make any new or additional revelations about the story to someone who is familiar with it'. I opted for the approach of presenting full stories to counter the repeated denial of the children's loss. This denial is presented as justified by the anger and sense of alienation from birth parents invoked in us when hearing about their failed parenting, and by the sympathy we feel for adoptive parents who so desperately want a child. When parental failures are presented, in particular when compared with designated adoptive parents' alleged devotion and competence, the unique significance of the child's bond with his birth parents is replaced with the assumption that the child, like us, is angry and feels alienated from his parents due to their failure. To make the children's testimony present in the court's proceedings, I had to expose the fallacy of the equation implicit in the state's position, between the parents' failure and the denial of the loss experienced by the children. I attempted to do so by highlighting the hopeless entanglements that arise between the parents' difficulties and the state's attempts to control the parent–child bond while undermining the parents' ability to care for their children and by drawing attention to the suppression of the children's testimonies.

I have already used excerpts from my experience in other contexts to illustrate the strategies used by the adoption service.[124] However, as Foucault pointed out, 'no strategy could achieve comprehensive effects if it did not gain support from precise and tenuous relations, serving not as its point of application or final outcome, but as its prop and anchor point'.[125] To document these 'precise and tenuous relations', I had to describe the events preceding the court's rulings, and their effects on those involved, in minute detail. My decision to include my thoughts and commentary about the actions of the adoption services in the description of the events themselves in each case was designed to highlight what Foucault calls 'the double conditioning of a strategy by the specificity of possible tactics, and of tactics by the envelope that makes them work'.[126]

The GAL's opinion also pointed out why it is important to provide a detailed presentation from the standpoint of the best interests of the child:

> The research explains and demonstrates the circumstances that led to the deceased taking this step, the objective hardships she endured due to her background, which made it difficult for her to forge a bond with the minor, and the supreme efforts she made to ward off the demons that plagued her, for her daughter's sake. I believe that if this research

> [ever] reaches the minor, a scientific explanation of this sort might in fact put to rest some of the questions that will undoubtedly arise in her heart in future, and demonstrate to her the intensity of her mother's devotion and love towards her, and that this knowledge will significantly contribute to her development, happiness and mental well-being. I should note that my position in this matter is not based on training in psychology or in the therapeutic realm, but on my many years of experience of dealing with questions that preoccupy children caught up in family crises in general, and in cases of adoption in particular.

The GAL's position is a recognition of the profound significance of the image of a parent in their child's mind, even when the parent has disappeared as a result of adoption, and a rejection of the adoption service's interpretation of the best interests of the child, which removes the birth parents from their children's lives while besmirching their image. The GAL's words may also be read as a warning of the damage inflicted on the child by the secrecy surrounding the parents' disappearance from his life.

State Counsel's claim that in my writing I had invaded 'the innermost corners of the minor's soul' was also disputed by the GAL:

> To my mind, this claim is factually untrue ... These descriptions are certainly no different in essence, nor do they raise any more grave concerns about the harm to the minor's best interests, than any description in the welfare reports periodically submitted to the family court in any ordinary custody case – reports that are available for the inspection of the children about whom they are written upon reaching adulthood.

He concluded that 'the risk that publishing Dr Mass's research would be inimical to the best interests of the minor is extremely low – and even that risk may be eliminated almost entirely, if need be, by changing additional identifying details'.

In response to the GAL's statement, State Counsel withdrew its objection:

> With regard to Dr Mass's petition to publish the research, *we have no objection to its publication*.[127] However, we do request that Dr Mass emphasise that certain passages that may be harmful to third parties, such as the mother's adoptive parents, are presented as the subjective accounts of the people being quoted, rather than as facts.

I accepted this qualification, which, as previously noted, was fully consistent with what I had said during the legal proceedings. Accordingly, the court ruled:

> In light of the petition, the respondent's consent (subject to the qualification to which the petitioner has agreed) and the GAL's own position, I

> grant the petition and hereby permit publication of the research, subject to the qualification that Dr Mass emphasise in her published research, in relation to statements that may be injurious to third parties, that they are presented as subjective accounts of the people being quoted rather than as facts.

In the end, the considerations behind the principle of privacy overcame the symbolic meaning of secrecy, which had given the state hegemonic control over the secret and enabled it to censor any interpretation that differed from its own.[128] But the turning point in these legal proceedings, and the court's ruling, cannot compensate for the serious harm caused to the continuity of work on the book and the considerable delay in its publication, due to the protracted legal wrangling over an issue that, regarding the publication of that particular chapter at least, was quite uncomplicated and straightforward.[129] The court's conduct highlights the vulnerability of the requirement that governmental procedures concerning adoption be made public, and validates the claim that, 'when the fetish status of the secret is achieved, it is the skin of the secret that vibrates with sacred light, intimation of the *public* secret within'.[130] Indeed, 'the sacred and the secret have been linked from earliest times. Both elicit feelings of what Rudolf Otto has dubbed *the numinous consciousness* – which combines the daunting and the fascinating, dread and allure'.[131]

The secret bestows upon adoption an almost sacred status, which in turn serves the work of the SSC. This topic is further explored in the next chapter.

Notes

1. ACL 34.
2. In describing the legal proceedings on my petition, I have chosen to make no references to the other petition, except for aspects that directly related to the debate in my petition. See notes 3 and 4 below.
3. The judge did so because State Counsel had been named as respondent by the petitioner in the other petition; in the case of the other three chapters in the book, however, since I had applied to the court merely for clarification of one point, I did not think that a respondent would be necessary.
4. Two of these were at State Counsel's request, which I learned about only after they had been approved by the court; the other two were at the request of the other petitioners, which I objected to, but they too were approved by the court.
5. A Guardian *ad Litem* (henceforth GAL) is appointed by the court to represent the interests of a minor in cases where the court determines that

the parents, or the minor's guardian, as the case may be, unable to do so. 'The basic premise guiding the Sub-Committee is that children must be provided legal representation only if it can be assumed that their parents are unable to represent them ... due to conflict of interest or some other reason, or because their child has grown up and has formulated an independent will....' *Report of Sub-Committee: Separate Representation of Children in Civil Actions*, ed. Att. Sharon Primor-Eldar, under direction by Sub-Committee Chair, Att. Tamar Morag, the Committee on Fundamental Child- and Justice-Related Principles and their Implementation in Legislation (Jerusalem: Hamol, 2003), 65 [Hebrew].

6. By comparison, the debate over disclosure of national security-related documents lasted two years, and was roundly criticised *for taking so long. See* Yossi Melman, 'A History Reserved for Close Associates Only', *Haaretz*, 16 April 2009 [Hebrew].
7. Georg Simmel, 'Secrecy', in *The Sociology of Georg Simmel*, trans. and ed. Kurt Wolff (Glencoe, IL: The Free Press, 1950), 330–44.
8. Fran Lloyd and Catherine O'Brien, *Secret Spaces, Forbidden Places* (New York: Berghahn Books, 2000), xviii.
9. Simmel, 'Secrecy', 333.
10. Ibid., 331; Sissela Bok, *Secrets: On the Ethics of Concealment and Revelation* (Oxford: Oxford University Press, 1984), 6.
11. Ibid., 3–4.
12. Simmel, 'Secrecy', 337.
13. Edward A. Shils, *The Torment of Secrecy* (Glencoe, IL: The Free Press, 1956), 21–35.
14. Ibid.
15. Quoted in ibid., 175.
16. Quoted in Bok, *Secrets*, 171, 174.
17. Carl J. Friedrich, *The Pathology of Politics* (New York: Harper and Row, 1972), 181. Notably, however, Wilson himself did not uphold his own standards in this regard once he had been elected President of the United States. See Bok, *Secrets*, 171.
18. Shils, *Torment of Secrecy*, 21–35.
19. Ibid., 201.
20. Ibid., 40.
21. 'Today, in the nuclear age, the ratio between the few in the know and the large populations who are affected by the secret but are excluded from it has grown to unprecedented proportions.' Elias Canetti, *Crowds and Power* (Harmondsworth: Penguin Books, 1981), 345.
22. Edward Shils, 'Privacy: Its Constitution and Vicissitudes', *Law and Contemporary Problems* 31 (1966), 281–306.
23. Shils, *Torment of Secrecy*, 235.
24. See CA 653/95, *Anon v A-G*, ruling 49 (2) 383, 392 (1995); CA 2169/98, *Anon v A-G*, 264; FAP 3640/06, *Anon v A-G* (unpub.), Takdin Rulings Database, http://www.takdin.co.il (last modified 21 June 2006).
25. O'Halloran, *Politics of Adoption*, 1.

26. The following review of the history of adoption is taken from E. Wayne Carp, 'The Ephemeral Age of Secrecy', in *Family Matters*, 102–37; Elizabeth E. Cole and Kathryn Donley, 'History Values and Placement Policy Issues in Adoption', in Brodzinsky and Shechter, *The Psychology of Adoption*, 273–79.
27. Sigmund Freud, 'Family Romances', in James Starchy (ed.), *The Standard Edition of the Complete Psychological Works of Sigmund Freud*, vol. 9 (London: Hogarth Press, 1959), 235–342.
28. Carp, *Family Matters*, 136.
29. Ruth Zafran puts forward a different thesis, whereby the strict separation between birth and adoptive parents came about due to the weakness of the birth mothers, many of whom had given birth out of wedlock and suffered from social disgrace. Excluding them was meant, therefore, as a form of punishment. Ruth Zafran, 'The Closed Records Policy as a Reflection of the Statuses of the Parties and as Indication of Prevailing Social Conception', in *The Right of Offspring to Seek Out Their Biological Parents* (Ph.D. diss., Faculty of Law, Hebrew University of Jerusalem, 2004), 255–68 [Hebrew].
30. Katarina Wegar, *Adoption, Identity and Kinship: The Debate over Sealed Records* (New Haven, CT: Yale University Press, 1997), 19; Modell, *Sealed and Secret Kinship*, 69.
31. Murray Ryburn, 'Secrecy and Openness in Adoption: A Historical Perspective', *Social Policy and Administration* 29 (1995), 150–68.
32. O'Halloran, *Politics of Adoption*, 203.
33. Shifman, *Family Law in Israel*, 54.
34. Adoption of Children Law, 1960, 13, whereby the adoption creates the same set of duties and rights between adoptive parent and adoptee as between birth parents and their children; it grants the adoptive parent the rights given to parents with regard to their children; the duties and rights between the adoptee and his birth parents and other relatives are terminated (with the exception of the adoptee's right of inheritance) and their rights in relation to him, although the court may restrict the said results of the adoption order. The same directive appears also in ACL 16(1).
35. See Adoption of Children Law, 1960, 27: 'The adoption register will not be viewable to anyone apart from: (1) the Attorney General or his legal representative; (2) a marriage registrar or any other person so authorised, in their official capacity; (3) the adoptee on reaching the age of eighteen'. See also Shifman, *Family Law in Israel*, 61.
36. ACL 30(b). On the existing provisions, and the proposed provision of allowing the adoptee to receive information about his birth family while protecting its privacy, see Zafran, *Right of Offspring*, 255–68.
37. ACL 30(a).
38. In Ronit Krown Kertsner's film *The Aforementioned Minor* [Hebrew], a grown-up adoptee is shown being denied access to her original birth certificate. The director of the SSC at that time justified this refusal on the grounds that 'a legal act was done that cancels this thing – the blood tie', and an adoption official explains to the adoptee, 'A person can't have two

birth certificates'. The adoptee protests: 'But I do have two birth certificates!' On the link between the birth certificate and the adoptee's sense of identity, see Kander, *A Flower Named Sigal*; on the profound significance that the birth certificate has for the adoptee, see Alon Alexander Krasucky, *The Last Krasucky*, film (Israel, 2009) [Hebrew, English, Polish].

39. Susan M. Wolfgram, 'Openness in Adoption: What We Know So Far – A Critical Review of the Literature', *Social Work* 53 (2008), 133–42.
40. CA 653/95, *Anon v A-G*, 392: 'The preferred rule is usually the full adoption … The open adoption is considered anomalous'; CA 2169/98, *Anon v A-G*, 264: 'The cumulative weight of the various considerations has led the Israeli ruling to the conclusion that the rule is the "full" or "closed" adoption. The "open" adoption is the exception and anomalous. This is also implicit from the structure of the law, which regards the "full" adoption a natural outcome of the adoption order … The "open" adoption is possible only in exceptional cases'; FAP 3640/06, *Anon v A-G*; FAP 10791/05, *Anon v A-G* (unpub.), Takdin Rulings Database, http://www.takdin.co.il (last modified 9 February 2006).
41. CA 2169/98, 265: 'In the absence of sufficient research basis, this court should maintain its basic approach'.
42. FAP 3646/06, *Anon v A-G*; FAP 778/09, *A-G v 1. Anon. 2. Att. Yaron Hod (Minor's Guardian ad Litem)*; FAP 778/09, *1. Anon 2. Anon v 1. Anon 2. A-G 3. Att. Yaron Hod (Minor's Guardian ad Litem)*. However, as I shall detail in Chapter 5, since 1998 many further studies have appeared on the subject of open adoption.
43. It should be noted that the Supreme Court in Israel has repeatedly called on the legislature to enshrine the legal status of 'open' adoption in law. CA 4616/94, *A-G v Anon*, RT, 308, 289 (4); CA 653/95, *Anon v A-G*, 396; CA 2169/98, *Anon v A-G*, 278. This call has yet to be acknowledged.
44. Otto Rank, *The Myth of the Birth of the Hero* (New York: Vintage Books, 1964).
45. For example, Charles Dickens, *Oliver Twist* (London: Richard Bentley, 1837–1838); Dickens, *Great Expectations* (London: Chapman and Hall, 1860–1861); George Elliot, *Silas Marner* (Edinburgh: William Blackwood and Sons, 1861); Elliot, *Daniel Deronda* (Edinburgh: William Blackwood and Sons, 1876); Thomas Hardy, *The Mayor of Casterbridge* (London: Smith, Elder, 1886). For a discussion of the questions of adoption in two of George Elliot's books, see Marianne Novy, 'Adoption in Silas Marner and Daniel Deronda', in *Imagining Adoption: Essays on Literature and Culture* (Ann Arbor, MI: University of Michigan Press, 1994), 35–36.
46. Eugène Scribe (libretto), Jacques Fromental Halévy (music), *The Jewess*, opera (1835); Khaled Hosseini, *The Kite Runner* (New York: Riverhead Books, 2003).
47. Indeed, the birth parents in these stories are usually depicted as victims of their own life circumstances. In Israel, on the other hand, the archetypal birth parent is likened more to Oedipus's father, who sought to kill him. See the Introduction to this volume.

48. Martha C. Nussbaum, 'Objectification', in *Sex and Social Justice* (Oxford: Oxford University Press, 1999), 213–39, the child in a closed adoption is presented as fulfilling the needs of the adoptive parents, rather than as a person with his own identity and needs. See Garry Leonard, 'Immaculate Deception – Adoption in Albee's Plays', in Novy, *Imagining Adoption*, 111–32. The opposite – and unusual – view of adoption, whereby the adoptive father sees his child as a charge held in trust for a predetermined period, which he must then return to the birth parents, is offered in Dror Burstein, *Kinship* (Jerusalem: Keter, 2005) [Hebrew].
49. Wegar, *Adoption, Identity and Kinship*, 97; Barbara Melosh, 'Adoption Challenged', in *Strangers and Kin: The American Way of Adoption* (Cambridge, MA: Harvard University Press, 2002), 239–86.
50. The title of the documentary film, *Green Eyes*, by Ronen Israelski (UK-Israel, 1995–1996) [Hebrew], alludes to the striking resemblance between the adoptee's green eyes and his birth mother's, but the film ends with the adoptee's declaration that he feels that he belongs to his adoptive family. See Nancy K. Gish, 'Adoption, Identity and Voice – Jackie's Kay Inventions of Self', in Novy, *Imagining Adoption*, 171–91; Paris De Soto, 'Genealogy Revised in Secrets and Lies', in Novy, *Imagining Adoption*, 193–206.
51. Julie Berebitzky, 'Redefining "Real" Motherhood: Representation of Adoptive Mothers 1900–1950', in Novy, *Imagining Adoption*, 83–95; Margot Gayle Backus, 'I Am Your Mother; She Was a Carrying Case: Adoption, Class and Sexual Orientation in Jeanette Winterson's "Oranges Are Not the Only Fruit"', in Novy, *Imagining Adoption*, 133–40.
52. Jan Van Stavern, 'A Junction of Amends: Sandra McPherson's Poetics of Adoption', in Novy, *Imagining Adoption*, 151–70.
53. Of particular note in this regard is the book by Sami Michael, *Pigeons at Trafalgar Square* (Tel Aviv: Am Oved, 2006) [Hebrew], in which belonging and similarity overcome nationalist animosity, which emphasises difference and separateness.
54. On the use of myth to bridge the gap between belief and reality, see Murray Edelman, *Politics and Symbolic Action* (Chicago, IL: Markham, 1964), 54.
55. Emmanuel Levinas, *Ethics and Infinity: Conversations with Phillip Nemo*, trans. Richard Cohen (Pittsburgh, PA: Duquesne University, 1965), 70.
56. On the difficulty in creating a coherent explanation for parenting, see Lisa Baraitser, '"Oi, Mother! Keep Ye' Hair On!" Impossible Transformation of Maternal Subjectivity', *Studies in Gender and Sexuality* 7 (2008), 217–38.
57. The state's oversight is also maintained by means of doctors and correctional institutions. See Michel Foucault, 'The Eye of Power', in *Power/Knowledge*, ed. Colin Gordon, trans. Colin Gordon et al. (New York: Pantheon Books, 1980), 147–65.
58. On the role of language in hiding the world that lies beyond the reach of power, see Lloyd and O'Brien, *Secret Spaces, Forbidden Places*, 122; and George Orwell, *1984* (London: Secker and Warburg, 1949).
59. Modell claims that adoption policy in the United States since 1997 has brought about a simplification of parenthood. See Modell, *Sealed and Secret Kinship*, 127.

60. On the practice of secrecy as the generator of contrast between what is defined by the secret as 'inner reality' and 'external reality', and between the 'subjective' and the 'objective', see D.A. Miller, *The Novel and the Police* (Berkeley, CA: University of California Press, 1988), 207.
61. On the question of separateness in adoption, see David H. Kirk, 'A Dilemma of Adoptive Parenthood: Incongruous Role Obligations', in *Exploring Adoptive Family Life* (Port Angeles, WA: Ben Simon Publications, 1988), 27–37. See also Kander, *A Flower Named Sigal*.
62. Quoted in Normand Berlin, *The Secret Cause* (Amherst, MA: University of Massachusetts Press, 1981), 2.
63. Today, as noted earlier, the very adoption of a child is not a secret, and there is no attempt, at least not explicitly, to cover up the fact that the child is not biologically related to the adoptive family. According to adoption officials, the SSC holds workshops for adopted children to discuss the question of their belonging. The adoption is carried out in the hope that the feeling of belonging and similarity will naturally emerge from the relationship forged within the adoptive family, but the strict adherence to the closed adoption model, which necessitates secrecy, still follows the 'as if begotten model' (Modell, *Kinship with Strangers,* 2), which attempts to cover up the differences and separateness.
64. Canetti, *Crowds and Power*, 338.
65. ACL 36(a).
66. See FAP 6509/04, *Biological Parents v Anon and Anon, Minor's Designated Adoptive Parents*, 59 (1), 596, 619 (2006): 'Direct contact between the parents and the adoptive parents or personal contact between them naturally creates tremendous emotional difficulties. The two parties may be drawn against their better judgement into a protracted, painful legal battle. Revealing the adoptive parents and birth parents to each other is undesirable, and is liable to hurt the child and cause irreparable harm to him and to the entire delicate fabric of the adoption'.
67. Robert K. Merton, *Social Theory and Social Structure* (Glencoe, IL: The Free Press, 1955), 197.
68. The law in England and Wales requires that birth parents be provided support and counselling both during and after the adoption proceedings. O'Halloran, *Politics of Adoption,* 205; Elsbeth Neil, 'The Mental Stress of Birth Relatives of Adopted Children: "Disease" or "Unease"? Findings from a UK Study', *Health and Social Care* 21 (2013), 191–99.
69. On the need to address the birth parents' feelings and expectations and the absence of such a response, see Shifman, *Family Law in Israel*, 226.
70. For example, Judge Procaccia's decision, FAP 377/05, *Anon and Anon, Minor's Designated Adoptive Parents v Biological Parents*, 211: 'However, the SSC was impatient. Although the welfare officials have spoken about the horrendous contradiction between the mother's declared desire to hand over her child to adoption the next day, and her physical devotion to her baby that led her to stay by his side and not leave him for the entire time that he was in hospital, they had no compunction about procuring her

consent to adoption only a week after his birth. Adoption procedures were begun immediately after that'.

71. In England and Wales, the law states: 'Every child is to have a named social worker who will be responsible for the child and will be required to explain to him or her the matters arising at every stage of the process'. O'Halloran, *Politics of Adoption*, 189.
72. CA 488/77, *Anons v A-G*; CA 166/81, *Anon v A-G*; CA 320/84, *Anon v A-G*; CA 138/85, *Anon v A-G*; CA 3236/90, *Anons v A-G*; CA 6953/94, *Anon v A-G*; AF (Rishon Lezion) 67/02, *Minor v A-G*; Miscellaneous Civil Appeals (MCA) 370/09, *A-G v 1. Anon 2. Anon v 1. Anon. 2. A-G 3. Att. Yaron Hod (Minor's Guardian ad Litem)*.
73. In one highly controversial case, the Supreme Court explicitly defended adoption officials. In a majority ruling, it avoided any criticism of their actions, although the fact that the chain of events had developed into a full-blown 'incident' was, in no small part, due to their actions. See FAP 377/05, *Anon and Anon, Minor's Designated Adoptive Parents v Biological Parents*, and Mass, 'Baby at a Crossroads'.
74. On the difficulty involved in research sampling involving adoptees, see Tovah Lichtenstein, *Genealogical Embarrassment and Search Patterns: Adult Adoptees Searching for Their Biological Parents* (Ph.D. diss., Bar-Ilan University, 1992), 67 [Hebrew]. In follow-up studies carried out in Israel, the SSC, which has an explicit interest in showing adoption to be the preferred option for children who cannot be raised by their parents, took part in selecting the sample under the guise of secrecy. In one study, the adopted children who were among the research subjects were interviewed only by SSC staff, while the children from the control groups were interviewed by the researchers. See Anita Weiner and Eugene Weiner, *Expanding the Options in Child Placement* (London: University Press of America, 1990). A follow-on study was conducted twenty-five years later with the same research population: Anita Weiner and Haggai Kupermintz, 'Facing Adulthood Alone: Long-Term Impact of Family Break-Up and Infant Institutions, a Longitudinal Study', *British Journal of Social Work* 31 (2001), 213–34. Involvement of SSC staff in this study is noted, but not detailed. Another study, in which the sample was chosen in collaboration with the SSC, involved the children's adoptive parents: Rivkin and Baumgold, *Follow-up of Older Children Who Have Been Adopted*. Two studies were conducted, apparently with the same sample selected in collaboration with the Ministry of Welfare's Center for Treatment of Adoptees and their Parents: Beatriz Priel, Bella Kantor and Avi Besser, 'Two Maternal Representations: A Study of Israeli Adopted Children', *Psychoanalytic Psychology* 17 (2000), 128–45; Priel et al., 'Adjustment among Adopted Children: The Role of Maternal Self-Reflectiveness', *Family Relations* 49 (2000), 389–96. In another study conducted by an SSC official, the subjects responded to an appeal by SSC staff: Ilana Gleitman, *The Functioning and Emotional State of Adolescents Adopted before and after the Age of Two as Babies, and Adolescents Adopted after the Age of Two* (Ph.D. diss., Tel Aviv University, 2008) [Hebrew]. The exception to all these is a study that

recruited adoptees directly, through a school: Alina Brickman Schellekes, *Cognitive, Emotional and Social Adjustment of Adopted Children as Compared to Non-adopted Children and Children Raised in Institutions*' (MA thesis, Tel-Aviv University, 1985) [Hebrew]. This study found that adopted children had problems in adjustment, compared with children in control groups.

75. Max Weber, *From Max Weber: Essays in Sociology*, trans. Hans H. Gerth, introduction by Wright Mills, (New York: Oxford University Press, 1958), 232.
76. As noted in Chapter 2, there is still no systematic research and documentation of cases where adopted children are sent by their adoptive families to institutions; in addition, cases of failed adoptions are not publicised. In one such case, the daughter of a female drug addict was removed from her custody at the age of six, but was finally adopted only at the age of nine, after three years in a children's home. Her adoptive mother eventually sent her to an institution because of difficulties in their relationship. At the age of sixteen, she discovered that her half-brother on her father's side was at the same institution, and through him she made contact with her birth mother. She refused to return to her adoptive mother and remained with her birth mother, who had rehabilitated herself and had started a family, having had another son in the interim. Although the SSC and social services knew that the daughter had gone back to her mother, no official petition was made to the court to cancel the adoption, which meant that the daughter remained registered on her adoptive mother's identity card. This resulted in endless bureaucratic difficulties in all her dealings with authorities, from child allowance payments through to military conscription papers. Among other things, it meant that she could not be conscripted, much to her disappointment, because her adoptive mother refused to provide access to her medical records, which might have changed the decision of the military authorities.
77. AF 16/01, *A-G v Anon*, para 15. At a meeting held on 25 January 2007, at the Hebrew University's School of Social Work and Social Welfare in Jerusalem, staff researchers complained that the SSC was obstructing studies on adoption in Israel. In response, adoption officials at the meeting said that this was unavoidable, for reasons of secrecy.
78. Michel Foucault, Introduction, in *History of Sexuality*, vol. 1, trans. Robert Hurley (New York: Penguin Books, 1978), 86.
79. See Weber, *From Max Weber*, 233.
80. According to some officials in the justice system, the SSC sometimes also 'boycotts' judges who have been sharply critical of its practices by simply not referring adoption cases to them, on the pretext of the regional jurisdiction of the birth parents or the adoptive ones, to suit.
81. Bok, *Secrets*, 177.
82. Weber, *From Max Weber*, 232.
83. Amitai Etzioni, 'Administrative and Professional Authority', in *Modern Organizations* (Englewood Cliffs, NJ: Prentice-Hall, 1964), 75–93.
84. Ibid., 224; Merton, *Social Theory*, 195.
85. Georg Simmel, 'The Secret Society', in *The Sociology of Georg Simmel*, trans. and ed. Kurt Wolff, 345–376, here 345 and 374.

86. See AF (Rishon Lezion) 67/02, *Minor v A-G*, para 19 (h): 'The court must decide which of the two civil servants ... is speaking the truth'.
87. Simmel, 'The Secret Society', 346.
88. Thus, for example, in the case of a nine-year-old boy whose mother neglected him whenever she had difficulties finding suitable living accommodation, and although she was likely using this as a means to pressure the authorities into acceding to her demand for an apartment in the town where her family lived, the only solution considered was adoption. The court heard the child's expressed wish to return to his mother, who was now in a stable relationship with a man she had been living with for some years, and whose housing problem had been resolved. Despite the added prospect of help from her adult daughters, who had fought with her against their brother's adoption, the court decided to declare him eligible for adoption nonetheless. However, in recognition of the child's strong connection with his family, it stated that the adoption was contingent upon his remaining in touch with them, in a manner prescribed by the court (note, however, that even in an open adoption such as this, the child's identity must be changed). See FA 2080/07, *Anon v. the State of Israel* (unpub.), Takdin Rulings Database, http://www.takdin.co.il (last modified 12 March 2008).
89. Modell states that this is the case in American adoption policy (*Sealed and Secret Kinship*, 95).
90. Barkai and Mass, *The Meanings of 'Parental Capability'*, 81–85; FAP 3329/08, *Anon v A-G* (unpub.), Takdin Rulings Database, http://www.takdin.co.il, Judge Danziger's Decision, para 8 (18 June 2006). Justice Danziger dissented from the majority decision, which saw the child's return to his mother as a 'trial run', but not so his adoption.
91. Foucault, *History of Sexuality*, 86.
92. Evidence Ordinance (New Version) 5731-1971, State of Israel's Laws, ch. 2: *Written Evidence*, Article 3 *Testimony of Experts and Public Servants*.
93. For a review of the issue of expertise in the issue of adoption, see Vered Ben-David, *Social Exclusion and Forced Adoption: An Analysis of the Personal and Family Characteristics of Children Adopted without Their Parents' Consent* (MA diss., Faculty of Social Welfare and Health Studies, School of Social Work, Haifa University, 2006), 7 [Hebrew]; Mass, '"Parental Capability"'.
94. The district court's ruling in what became known as the 'Disputed Baby Affair' is a clear illustration of the SSC's method of choosing experts. FA (District, Tel Aviv-Jaffa) 4/04, *Anon and Anon, Minor's Designated Adoptive Parents v Anon and Anon, Biological Parents*, Takdin-District 6517, (4) 2004, decision of Judge Rotlevy, ruling 41: 'The court was not informed until the day of the hearing on Nov. 7, 2004, that Dr Weil had agreed with the SSC that he would provide expert opinions to the SSC on demand. If we had known this, we would have chosen another expert. It is regrettable that Dr Weil chose not to direct our attention to this prior to his appointment, nor did he note it when detailing his professional experience, nor did State Counsel or the SSC. Judge Rotlevy accepted the expert's opinion

and relied on it in her decision because 'there was only an appearance of conflict of interest, not a significant conflict'.

95. AF 16/01, *A-G v Anon*, para 15. Since the court prefers to appoint experts with the consent of both parties, the SSC effectively has power of veto in this matter, and some judges accept its position unquestioningly. In the interests of full disclosure, I should point out that I myself belong to the group of experts blacklisted by the SSC. In 1987, the SSC had recommended me as a court expert in three cases. In one of them I did not recommend adoption, and since then I have been marked out as someone who 'opposes adoption'. One adoption official even said this when the court wanted to charge me with the task of returning Elinor to her mother's care (Chapter 2). Moreover, the adoption officials demand to be present during my observations of children living with foster or adoptive families, as part of my evaluation procedures. When judges accede to this demand, they are effectively allowing the adoption officials to interfere with the expert's work.
96. Ben-David, *Social Exclusion and Forced Adoption*.
97. AF (Jerusalem) 16/01, *A-G v Anon*, para 9.
98. AF (Beer-Sheba) 32/05, *A-G v Anon*, para 7(c).
99. ACL 5; *UN Convention of the Rights of the Child*, Article 20(3).
100. CA 2169/98, *Anon v A-G*.
101. Lili Galili, 'Not According to Section 5', *Ha'aretz*, 27 May 2005 [Hebrew]; David Regev, 'Suing the Ministry of Welfare for Millions Because of a "Bad Adoption"', *Yediot Aharonot*, 27 October 2006 [Hebrew].
102. FAP 778/09, *A-G v 1. Anon 2. Att. Yaron Hod (Minor's Guardian ad Litem)*; MCA 370/09, *A-G v 1. Anon 2. Anon v 1. Anon 2. A-G 3. Att. Yaron Hod (Minor's Guardian ad Litem)*.
103. Limor Gal, 'As Tears Go By', *Ha'aretz* (weekend supplement), 23 May 2008 [Hebrew].
104. On the uncertainty inherent in any forecast, see Berlin, *The Secret Cause*, 9. On the creation of a mediating myth, see Edelman, *Politics and Symbolic Action*, 54.
105. FAP 377/05, *Anon and Anon, Minor's Designated Adoptive Parents v Biological Parents*, 227.
106. The child's testimony in court is required by law only at the stage of granting the adoption order (i.e. six months after he has been placed with the designated adoptive family) and only from the age of nine. ACL 7.
107. Indeed, the Sub-Committee on Separate Representation of the Child concluded that in cases of involuntary adoption, the child's testimony is not needed, since court hearings in these cases take place after there has been intervention by social services in the parent–child relationship; therefore the testimony of social services would suffice. *Report of Sub-Committee: Separate Representation of Children in Civil Actions*, s 5.5.3.
108. Mass, 'Baby at a Crossroads', 222–25.
109. On the perception of adoption workers as using excessive force, see Derek Kirton, 'Kinship by Design in England: Refiguring Adoption from Blair to Coalition', *Child and Family Social Work* 18 (2013), 97–106.

110. Rudolf Ekstein and Robert A. Wallerstein, *The Teaching and Learning of Psychotherapy* (New York: International Universities Press, 1958), 246.
111. Max van Manen, 'Phenomenology of Practice', *Phenomenology and Practice* 1 (2007): 11–30.
112. Mass, 'Adoption in the Bondage of the Oedipal Myth'.
113. For a dramatic description of the anxiety-driven expansion of control, see J.M. Coetzee, *Waiting for the Barbarians* (London: Secker and Warburg, 1980).
114. FAP 7360/08, *Anon. and Anon. v A-G, Anon. and Anon.* (unpub.), Takdin Rulings Database, http://www.takdin.co.il (last modified 31 August 2008).
115. Lloyd and O'Brien, *Secret Spaces, Forbidden Places*, xviii.
116. A reference borrowed, of course, from George Orwell's book, *1984*. Arguments of this sort have been cited in the United States in response to criticism of the censorship imposed by the adoption agencies on the information given to adoptees about their origins, with the implicit message that it contains an awful truth. See Carp, *Family Matters*, 154.
117. See Court of Appeal (CoA) 399/85, *Kahane v Israel Broadcasting Authority*, MA 255(3).
118. Simmel, 'Secrecy'.
119. Mandell, *Where Are the Children?*
120. ACL 16.
121. Shils, 'Privacy', 299.
122. One can learn more about the difficulty adoptees have in speaking about their loss from Shai Golden's book, *The Good Son*. The book, written by an adoptee on reaching adulthood, reveals the confusion and vagueness surrounding his identity, and the struggle for himself and his brother to achieve a sense of belonging.
123. For example, Carolyn Thomas et al., *Adopted Children Speaking* (London: British Agencies for Adoption and Fostering, 1999); Ha'elyon, *Adopted*.
124. Mili Mass, 'On State Intervention in Parent–Child Relationship: The Case of Involuntary Adoption Due to "Parental Incapability"', *Law Review, Netanya Academic College Law School* 4 (published in honour of Prof. Avner H. Shaki) (2005), 589–616 [Hebrew]; Mass and Ophir, 'Care, Supervision and Abandonment'; Mass, 'Baby at a Crossroads'.
125. Foucault, *History of Sexuality*, 99.
126. Ibid., 100.
127. Emphasis in the original.
128. For more on censorship, in particular that imposed by the Catholic Church in the sixteenth century on the Talmud for offering commentary on the Holy Scriptures that the Church did not endorse, see Amnon Raz-Karkotzkin, *The Censor, the Editor and the Text* (Jerusalem: Magnes, 2005) [Hebrew].
129. As noted previously, the legal proceedings went on for over sixteen months, although the court held only one hearing on the matter. As noted, permission to publish the remaining three chapters was given within days.

130. Michael Taussig, *Defacement* (Stanford, CA: Stanford University Press, 1999), 58. Emphasis in the original.
131. Canetti, *Crowds and Power*, 344. Emphasis in the original.

5

'Sacred Calling'

Daniel's Story

On Faith

The decision to define Daniel's adoption as open – that is, with continued contact between him and his birth mother – was taken out of concern that his adoption would be accompanied by an acute sense of loss if this contact were severed.[1] The adoption officials also agreed that the state should not inflict on Daniel repeated disappearances by his mother, who had already left him on numerous occasions for long periods of time before the petition to declare him eligible for adoption. They, too, recognised the importance of preserving some contact between him and his mother after the adoption. Daniel himself, in his way, testified to the loss that he had experienced with his mother's disappearances and to the importance that he attributed to continuity in his life before and after the adoption. Nonetheless, his need to understand the particular arrangement of his open adoption was not taken into account. No one answered him when he asked 'But why?' in astonishment when, at the end of the meeting with his mother and grandmother, he was forbidden by the adoption officials to escort his grandmother, who was in a wheelchair, outside the offices of the SSC, where his adoptive mother was waiting for him. No one had told him, and he did not understand, that his mother and grandmother were barred from having any contact with his adoptive mother.

The way in which Daniel's 'open adoption' was implemented reveals how entrenched the authorities' view is that any contact between birth parents and adoptive parents is strictly taboo, almost incestuous. While this kind of compartmentalisation is conventional in cases of closed adoption, its sweeping application across the board, including in cases of open adoption, indicates the doctrinal nature of the supreme importance attributed to it. The very notion of segregation runs counter to the thinking behind open adoption, which is designed to ensure continuity in the adoptee's existence.

In an open adoption, as its name indicates, contact between the adoptee and his birth parents is maintained, and a connection of some sort is formed between the latter and the adoptive parents. The permitted contact between both sets of 'significant others' in the adoptee's life is in acknowledgement of his past attachments and experiences,[2] and when circumstances preclude such contact in person – between the birth parents and the child – it may be maintained by other means, for example through written correspondence or telephone conversations between any two or all three parties of the adoption.

Daniel's story is one in which the SSC attempted to muzzle the challenge inherent in the open adoption approach – a challenge to the belief that there must not be any contact whatsoever between birth parents and adoptive parents. As with any belief system, its practice is regarded as a 'sacred calling', as indeed the work of the adoption officials is publicly referred to whenever any reservations are expressed about their actions.[3] Such an expression is designed to fend off any criticism, likening it to blasphemy. And it is no mere figure of speech: there are considerable parallels between the ceremonial nature of missionary work and the SSC's standard protocols. By creating emotional dependency on bureaucratic symbols and status, and encouraging the staff to become personally invested in areas that require expertise and authority, the organisation gains recognition of its special prerogative to imbue protocols, conceived for the sake of administrative efficiency, with moral significance in their own right.[4] Maintaining these ritualistic procedures blocks any attempt to examine the degree to which the beliefs underpinning the SSC's work are warranted, while at the same time silencing the child's voice. Thus, the portrayal of open adoption as something anomalous is preserved. It is worth dwelling briefly on this point, before introducing Daniel's story.

The Status of Open Adoption

A number of factors have brought about dramatic changes in the institution of adoption in recent decades, including the decline in the number of babies placed for adoption in the United States in the 1960s and 1970s; the growing demand by women for the right to motherhood irrespective of their marital status; their desire and willingness to raise children even if born out of wedlock; and changes in social values and norms. Over time, the campaign for the right of adoptees to access their adoption files has broadened its demands to include the right to have continued contact with their birth parents after adoption. A group of birth mothers who regretted the loss of the children they had placed for adoption also began a campaign to remove the ban on all contact between them and their children. In the face of such growing demands for open adoption, an intense ideological struggle developed between its proponents and the advocates of closed adoptions. Citing the small number of instances where open adoption was already successfully implemented, and the abandonment of the public perception of pregnancy out of wedlock as a pathological or moral defect, proponents of open adoption argued that there no longer seemed to be a need to protect the adoptee from all contact with his birth mother. Psychoanalytic theory, which by its nature lends itself to various interpretations, was enlisted by both sides of the argument in support of their respective claims. Thus, in response to the claims of birth mothers whose regret over giving up their children for adoption had spurred them to campaign for continued access to their children, opponents argued that it was precisely such continued contact that prevented birth mothers from recovering and getting on with their lives.[5] However, what ultimately clinched the broader application of open adoption was not the ideological argument, but the low number of babies placed for adoption, a fact that helped the cause of birth mothers who were demanding access to the children who had been adopted.[6] The arguments in favour of open adoption were based on the inherent advantages not only for the birth mothers, but also for the adoptees themselves. It meant that they were saved from 'genealogical bewilderment',[7] the anxiety and confusion caused by the taboo on the disclosure of any information about their origins. Open adoption reduced adoptive parents' anxieties about the birth mothers, and made it easier for them to get closer to their adopted children. Together, these factors contributed to the trend of removing the element of secrecy from adoption. Studies and observations of the damage caused to adoptees by the secrecy surrounding their adoption gave the impetus for new policies, particularly in England and Wales, that granted adoptees access to information about their adoptions, and reports about the suffering of birth parents led to growing support for open adoption.[8] Nonetheless, and despite the growing practice of open adoption, the two approaches, closed and open adoption, remained at loggerheads, with prominent cases being cited in support of one position or the other.[9]

In Israel, judicial rulings continue to portray open adoption as the exception to the rule,[10] while closed adoption is presented as the default option. Closed adoption sets out to create a 'normal' family: a parental couple whose relationship with their children is exclusive. Here too, as in the issue of parental capability discussed in Chapter 1 in the case of the Ziv family children, normality is replaced by normativity, and the 'normal' family model is cast as one that the adoptive family must also be adjusted to suit. This view is backed up by the concept of the 'psychological parent', which reflects the notion that the most important component is a child's bond with his principal adult caregiver, whoever that may be (i.e. not necessarily the birth parent). Joseph Goldstein, Anna Freud and Albert Solnit (who coined the term) suggest that safe and constant care – that is, creating a reality in which the child's place in a family, and the place of parental figures in his life, are assured and unequivocal – is what allows the child's bond with his birth parents to be superseded by a bond with substitute parents.[11] The insistence on defining the adoptive family as 'normal' fosters the need for secrecy and for the severing of all ties between the child and his birth parents, to secure the exclusivity of the child's bond with his adoptive parents. Yet, despite this, the argument does not extend to considering unmarried parents as candidates for becoming adoptive parents. In fact, unmarried applicants are not included in the definition of an 'adopter' under the Adoption of Children Law, although they too are capable of forming an exclusive bond with an adoptee.[12] The real intention, therefore, behind the argument about the need for an exclusive bond is to ensure that children are transferred from marginal families to mainstream 'standard' families that society is interested in cultivating.[13] Try as it may, however, the 'normal' appearance of an adoptive family does not diminish the looming presence of the adoption in its life, nor does it exorcise the ghosts of the birth parents, which return to haunt it from time to time. In the documentary film *Green Eyes*, in which the adoptee describes meeting his birth mother as an adult, there is a dramatic scene captured in a video recorded during his *bar mitzvah* celebrations. When it was the turn of the adoptive father to light the last candle, which had been reserved for him as a mark of respect, a friend of the family suddenly pushed him aside and lit the candle in his stead. Years later, the friend explained the reason for this odd behaviour: since there was no knowing who would see the video recording of the event, he feared that the birth parents might identify the adoptive father, thereby learning the whereabouts of the boy, and abduct him.[14]

The life of the adoptee is forever shadowed by a secret.[15] A recurring theme in the testimonies of adoptees is that, in reality, they live with two sets of parents: the adoptive parents with whom they reside, and those in their imagination, the birth parents.[16] Proponents of open adoption point out that allowing the child to maintain open and direct contact with the birth parents would actually be less threatening to the child and to the adoptive parents than the ghosts of the birth parents that might haunt their relationship. However, the customary practice in Israel of maintaining strict segregation between birth parents and adoptive parents, even in cases where the adoption has been defined as open, preserves the menacing nature of the secret.

The belief in the paramount importance of maintaining strict segregation between birth parents and adoptive parents is based on the notion that adoption is compensation for the damage caused to the child for not growing up with his birth parents.[17] Continued contact between the child and his birth parents might therefore be tolerated as part of the compensation, but not out of recognition of the importance of continuity in the adoptee's life, nor as a means of preventing the loss involved in adoption. The transfer of children from the margins of society to mainstream families bolsters this perception, and the prevention of all contact between the adoptive parents and birth parents is perhaps also designed to shield the adoptive parents from the birth parents, who are perceived to be non-normative.

Paradoxically, a common argument for making adoption contingent upon complete severance of ties between a child and his birth parents is that if adoptive parents are not offered an exclusive bond with their adopted child, no one will be willing to adopt. It is difficult to avoid thinking that this attitude is nothing more than simple possessiveness.[18] This contradiction is all the more striking in Israel, given the Judaic religious dictum that adoptive parents must not regard their adopted child as their own.[19]

Furthermore, the belief that it is vital for adoptive parents to have an exclusive bond with the adoptee ignores studies that indicate that adoptive parents who are partners to an open adoption and meet the birth parents report a greater sense of autonomy in their relationship with their children.[20] Such parents are freed of fears that perhaps some unpalatable information about the adopted child had been kept from them, and their empathy towards the child is enhanced by virtue of their familiarity with his birth parents. The premise that secrecy is essential to protecting the bond between adoptive parents and their adopted children is no longer generally accepted in Western countries,[21] but in Israel, as described in Chapter 4: Interlude, the SSC has enshrined strict segregation and secrecy as an essential component of adoption.[22]

In Israel, open adoption is perceived as being mainly in the interests of the birth parents. While in recent years there has indeed been a growing number of birth parents asking for their children's adoption to be open, many of these requests have been denied in court, while the principle underlying open adoption – that is, sparing the adoptee the loss entailed in the disappearance of his birth parents from his life – is not always taken into account.[23] Moreover, although the cooperation of the designated adoptive parents is essential to the success of an open adoption, this form of adoption is often presented to the adoptive parents as an unavoidable condition – the outcome of a court ruling that prescribes regular meetings between the adoptee and his birth parents, rather than as a response to the child's need for continuity in his life. Implementing open adoptions in this way dooms them to failure.

The strict prevention of any contact between birth parents and the adoptee and adoptive parents in closed adoption preserves the SSC's sovereignty, by virtue of the secrecy surrounding its operations and its power to rewrite the adoptee's history, in practice or by default.[24] In this way, the adoption officials can present reality as they see fit, and present the outcome as the only one possible. This is one of the hallmarks of a body that casts itself as a supreme authority entitled to set its own rules and regulations. The result is a closed circle in which it is impossible to test the premise that strict segregation is indeed essential to the success of adoption. Rather, this premise must be accepted unquestioningly, on faith. Indeed, the adoption apparatus operates somewhat like a religious order, which, in service of the faith, establishes certain protocols whose significance is implicit in their strict enforcement, irrespective of the special circumstances that might apply in each individual case. Faith cannot be served half-heartedly. One must submit to it totally and it, in turn, prescribes the order's operations and validates them. Thus, for example, when a child's adoption has been designated as open, the child's meetings with his birth parents are immediately suspended for two months, to enable him to form a bond with his adoptive parents. This standard procedure is referred to by the SSC as a 'cooling off' period, an expression that unwittingly confirms the significance of the child's bond with his birth parents that gave rise to the open adoption in the first place.[25] One might well wonder why the child's bonding with his adoptive parents requires the suspension of his contact with his birth parents. Does that not undermine the very open nature of the adoption? Does it not signal to the child that his bond with his birth parents is a hindrance in his relationship with his adoptive parents? However, faith does not require reasoning. Its justification lies in the very adherence to its tenets, and its realisation is contingent upon the execution of protocols that are justified by virtue of their uniformity.

The way in which open adoption – or 'adoption with contact',[26] as it is referred to by the SSC – is implemented in Israel tightens the SSC's control over the lives of the child and his adoptive parents and ensures that all contact between them and his birth parents is strictly controlled. While the adoptee may be entitled to meet with his birth parents from time to time, these encounters are conducted exclusively at the offices of the SSC, on dates and at times in accordance with the SSC's schedule, without the presence of the adoptive parents and under the watchful eye of adoption officials. In these circumstances, when contact between the child and his birth parents takes place in such an artificial setting, the intimacy of the relationship is lost, and it loses its unique meaning. The significance of the bond between parent and child, as in any intimate bond, arises from spontaneous contact and shared activities. But in these meetings, policed as they are by the SSC, the parents' physical presence is no substitute for a genuine bond. Moreover, meetings held in this way neither counter nor alleviate antagonism between birth parents and adoptive parents, but actually perpetuate it. The meetings become an inconvenient burden for the adoptive parents, who are required to abide by a regime of meetings between the child in their care and individuals whom they have never met, and who have presumably failed in their duty as parents considering that the child was removed from their custody. Rendering this antagonism redundant would very likely undermine the adoption officials' sovereign status, which they struggle to prevent by establishing procedures that serve to reinforce it.

The story of Daniel's adoption, which was defined as an open one, reveals the lengths to which the SSC will go to protect its dogmatic belief in the imperative of preserving the exclusive bond between the adoptive parents and the child, and thereby also the governing interest inherent in maintaining strict segregation between birth parents and adoptive parents.

The Mother's Wanderings

The ruling in Daniel's case recounts his history and that of his mother prior to the state's petition to declare him eligible for adoption. The mother had immigrated to Israel with her own mother and stepfather when she was sixteen. In her country of origin, her life had been one of continual transitions, a pattern that continued after their arrival in Israel. After falling out with her parents, she constantly moved from one place to another as a result of chance encounters with people she had known only a short time. Two years after her arrival in Israel, she returned to her place of birth where she took up again with a childhood boyfriend and became pregnant. The relationship did not last. At the age of nineteen, six months into her pregnancy, she returned to Israel, where she gave birth to Daniel. She refused to provide any further details about Daniel's father.

In the first months of Daniel's life, the mother lived with her stepfather – who in the interim had divorced her mother – and cared for her son with the help of the next-door neighbours. When relations with her stepfather soured, she moved in with a nearby family who offered her a room. During this time, she did not work, and lived exclusively off social assistance payments. Several months later, she moved to another town, leaving Daniel in the care of her host family, but visiting him frequently. She later claimed that she had no choice, as she had to find work to support herself and her son. Nothing is known of the nature of her contact with Daniel during these visits, or how he responded to her at that time after being left with various families during her repeated absences.

When Daniel reached the age of two, or thereabouts, the host family refused to continue to host them any longer, apparently because the mother had fallen behind in the agreed upon payments. The mother then rented an apartment in another town where she lived with Daniel. She began a relationship with a married man who supported her financially, and with the addition of social assistance was able to support herself and her son for a while. Approximately five months later, she left that town and returned to her previous place of work. Once again, she placed Daniel with the family she had previously stayed with, and once again, after a few months, they asked her to take him back. From time to time she would ask her mother or other people to mind Daniel and disappear without saying when she would return. When Daniel was three years old, she took up with another man by whom she became pregnant. Given her lack of any permanent abode or stable framework of any kind, she voluntarily placed the baby for adoption. She then became pregnant again, but this time chose to undergo an abortion.

It is difficult to precisely trace the mother's doings over the months that followed, as she herself appears to have difficulties reconstructing what happened to her during that time. She would generally rent an apartment, but being unable to pay the rent would soon be required to leave and move somewhere else. However, she later denied the authorities' claim that she neglected her son during this time. She visited Daniel often, she said, cared for him devotedly, and did not leave him with strangers before verifying that they cared for him properly, even if she had known them only for a short time.

When Daniel was approximately four years old, she left him with her mother. Sometime later, however, the grandmother was hospitalised at a rehabilitation centre, and after a fruitless search for the mother, contacted social services, who placed Daniel with a foster family. For a full year after that, the mother had virtually no contact with Daniel, although she knew that her mother's condition had deteriorated and that Daniel had been placed with a foster family. The mother later denied this account, however, claiming that she had often visited her son while he was with his grandmother, and meant to take him back, but was waiting for an apartment that she had rented to be vacated of its present tenants and renovated, whereupon she would take him to live with her. This took longer than she had expected (she could not recall quite how long), and meanwhile the grandmother's condition had worsened. The court rejected the mother's explanation for her absence from Daniel's life and believed that she was self-absorbed and that her son's welfare had been pushed aside as he had become a nuisance in her life.

When the grandmother asked social services to appoint Daniel's foster parents as his guardians, the authorities became aware of the boy's condition. He was five years old by that time. Before they could reach a decision in the matter, the foster family itself demanded that Daniel be taken away from them, as he had been stealing items of silver and jewellery from their home. In an expedited procedure, Daniel was transferred to a children's home run by the SSC, where he stayed pending resolution of a legal hearing concerning the identity of his guardian. His entire life up to that point had been an endless catalogue of transitions and wanderings, either with his mother or in the care of strangers. Throughout that time, the mother had focused on her own needs, in her attempt to survive in a new country and to find herself a place to live, a job, and perhaps a social environment in which she could feel that she belonged. Meanwhile, Daniel's needs were virtually ignored.

The staff at the children's home described Daniel as a sad child, emotionally and cognitively delayed for his age, who did not talk openly about his feelings. He appeared to have set up a barrier between himself and the world. He was thin and pale, very fragile, with delicate features, unintelligible speech and a babyish manner. When he walked, he did so on tiptoe, like a bird. The psychologist treating him at the children's home noted that, 'this is a child who is emotionally very impaired, and who, without intensive treatment and a stable family framework was under significant risk'. The court attributed the boy's grave condition to the history of his relationship with his mother:

> From the moment of his birth until his arrival at the children's home he has experienced numerous and frequent transitions, including long periods in which he was left by his mother in the care of people of various sorts. Little wonder, therefore, that these experiences of abandonment and transience left their mark on the minor!. The foster parents told the social worker that during his time with them the minor had been temperamental, prone to crying at night and even hitting himself without being able to explain why. He addressed his caretaker as 'Mum' within a day after arriving at the children's home. His nursery teacher told the social services official that he showed signs of severe distress.

For seven months the SSC tried to locate the mother, and when they finally managed to do so, with the help of a neighbour of the foster family where Daniel had stayed in the past, they petitioned the courts to declare him eligible for adoption, with the recommendation that the adoption outcome be restricted in relation to the grandmother (i.e. that she might continue to have contact with the boy after his adoption). The adoption officials had no difficulty with this: as far as they were concerned, an adoption that is open in relation to the grandmother does not challenge the exclusivity of the bond between the child and his adoptive parents, as it does not threaten the image of the adoptive family as normal. This assumes, of course, that such contact would take place strictly in accordance with how open adoption is perceived in Israel, namely through arranged meetings at predetermined times, at the offices of the SSC, and under the supervision of adoption officials. All contact between the mother and Daniel, however, would be banned.[27]

Assessing the Relationship between Mother and Daniel

Once the legal proceedings got under way, the mother made sure to attend all meetings with Daniel and to take part in the court hearings. This indicated a sincere desire to regain custody of Daniel, which the court noted and responded to by doubling the frequency of their meetings:

> It would appear that since contact with Daniel has been renewed there has been a change in the mother's behavioural pattern. This is evident not only in her consistent declarations that Daniel is the most precious thing to her, that she is not willing to give him up and that she will never run out on him again or repeat the mistakes that she had made in the past as she began looking for work and for shared accommodation with a long-time female friend. It is also evident in her active participation in the legal hearings, maintaining close contact with her legal counsel, showing up for all hearings and displaying sincere efforts to persuade the court to return her son to her care. In addition, the mother has shown a serious and responsible attitude to her renewed contact with the son, and after requesting and being granted more frequent and longer visits, has proven that she is capable of living up to the commitment of these more frequent visits.

The SSC officials recognised the positive effect that the renewed contact between Daniel and his mother had had, and noted how it helped to calm the boy and to stimulate progress in his speech, which had become clearer, albeit still markedly babyish in its manner. That said, it would be wrong to attribute the improvements in Daniel's condition exclusively to the renewal of his contact with his mother, as he was living at that time in a facility that addresses such difficulties and was receiving intensive psychological treatment.

Despite the noticeable change in the mother's behaviour, the SSC still insisted that she was not capable of raising Daniel, and that he must be declared eligible for adoption without any concessions towards the mother or any continued contact between her and her son. The petition to 'restrict the result' of the adoption towards the grandmother, however, remained as it was.

The mother's legal counsel asked the court to appoint me as an expert witness to assess her ability to raise Daniel, but State Counsel objected to this on the grounds that 'it was generally known' that I objected to adoption. This was not, as I have previously noted, the first time that my participation in legal proceedings had been opposed on the grounds that I was 'opposed to adoption'.[28] However, on this occasion, as it turned out, and unlike other cases described in this book, there was no disagreement between me and the adoption officials as to the mother's capability. I, too, believed that Fanny, the mother, was not capable of raising Daniel, not only because of her track record as a mother, but also because of her inability to relate to his needs, even after she had begun attending regular meetings with him. I had learned that much from my meetings with her, in which I saw a young woman in her mid twenties, who looked older than her age, with an attractive and interesting facial expression that changed from one meeting to the next – at times dignified and impressive, on other occasions vulgar and coarse. Her tone of speech was measured and created the impression that she considered her words carefully, but this was deceptive. In my conversations with her, it struck me that she appeared to lack an 'internal dialogue', and rather than look into the reasons for the choices she made, she saw the world as the chain of arbitrary events that dictated her life. Although her lifestyle and outlook on the world were possibly affected in part by her sense of rootlessness following her immigration to Israel, I saw no hint of possible change in the future. Her claim that she was fighting to retain custody of her son because she could no longer have children after her abortion was indicative more of her need to have some sort of ownership over a child than of a distinct attachment to Daniel. She appeared to be completely oblivious to the impact that her repeated disappearances had had on him. She claimed that she was merely trying to establish appropriate living conditions for them, which, she said, was sufficient justification for leaving her son with strangers. Her perception of her role as a mother noticeably lacked an understanding of the protection she was supposed to have provided for Daniel – in the past as well as at present and in the future. Thus, for example, she was considering continuing to live with her female friend, and had no compunction about telling me about a certain man who had been stalking her friend and pestering her at home. 'And you want to bring Daniel to such a home?' I asked. 'That's not a problem', she replied. 'We've already notified the police.'

This perception of her role as a mother was accompanied by an absence of any understanding of Daniel's innate dependency. When I asked about the good memories she had of Daniel, she laughed and recounted certain embarrassing moments in which he was either hurt or about to get hurt, for example when he dunked his head into the bath water and was afraid that he had drowned. I thought this indicated a remarkable lack of awareness of the child's vulnerability and need for adult protection and guidance. This lack of awareness might be explained by her response when I asked her to give me an example of an unpleasant memory about Daniel. She thought that Daniel acted in a sexually suggestive manner towards women, which indicated that she viewed him more as a grown man than as a small child who was dependent on her.

Fanny's limitations as a mother were strikingly evident during the two meetings with Daniel that I observed. She repeatedly ignored his cues of yearning for close contact with her, such as his attempts to create physical contact, his interest in her life and his efforts to please her. She kept trying to educate him, for example by remarking that his fingernails needed trimming, or pulling his thumb out of his mouth and forbidding him to suck it. When they played together, she reacted gleefully when he did not understand that he had the advantage, much as she had done when she had told me about the time he had panicked in the bathtub. Daniel, not understanding why she was laughing, was embarrassed, and she exploited this too, as though he were her equal in the game. At one point during the meeting, her friend entered the room and gave Daniel a pair of new shoes on his mother's behalf. Apparently, at their previous meeting Fanny had promised to buy him new shoes, but Daniel, who had never seen Fanny's friend before, was taken aback, and Fanny, who was seeing the shoes for the first time herself, marvelled at how smart they looked. It was evident that she thought that the shoes were what was important to him, rather than the fact that she had remembered to keep her promise to him.

At neither meeting was there any sign of intimacy between the two, despite Daniel's repeated attempts to approach her and touch her. On both occasions, however, just before the end of the session, they did begin, with great enjoyment, to play a game of clapping that involved close coordination, followed by rubbing their noses together. I could not explain the meaning of this sudden intimacy – whether it was because the meeting was about to end and the mother no longer felt the need to guard against it, or because they both recalled a game that they used to share. Either way, there was no mistaking the pleasure they both felt from this primal sensual intimacy.

In the wake of these two observation sessions, I argued that Daniel should not be returned to Fanny's custody, despite the responsible manner in which she had shown up for all the scheduled meetings. I concluded that she was unable to conduct a lifestyle that suited Daniel's need for protection, and based on her pattern of interaction with him, I saw no reason to believe that she would be able to develop an attentive attitude towards him if he were returned to her care. Indeed, if he were to be returned to her, I feared that they would enter a destructive cyclical relationship, in which she would keep him at arm's length, exposing him to further harm, leading him to respond negatively towards her, which in turn would confirm her assumption that he did not need her, leading her to become yet more distant, and so on, in an ever-worsening spiral. Nonetheless, I recommended that the adoption be left open in relation to the mother, as well as to the grandmother, based not on Fanny's ability to change, but because Daniel clearly attached great importance to staying in touch with her, despite her deficient mothering, and because of the positive effect this would have on him. On the latter point, his carers at the children's home were in agreement: Daniel always arrived at the meetings with his mother with a very keen, clear and expectant expression – in stark contrast to his dark and inscrutable face whenever I saw him at the children's home. The grandmother's testimony confirmed as much. Before he began his regular meetings with his mother, she told me, he would start every telephone conversation with her with the question, 'Where is Mum?', and refuse to continue the conversation until he received an answer. I concluded that Daniel keenly felt his mother's disappearance as a loss. Although he received proper attention and stimulation at the children's home, it was clearly no substitute for a bond with his mother.

In court, I argued that the state must not inflict a repeated loss on Daniel by 'closing' the adoption and severing his ties with his mother completely, and therefore I recommended that, whichever solution was ultimately proposed, priority be given to his continued contact with his mother. The best solution, I said, would be an open adoption, but if no family could be found who would agree to this, a foster family should be appointed to act as Daniel's legal guardians. They could then take decisions independently, while contact with his mother would be maintained. In the recommendation I submitted to the court, I argued that Daniel should be recognised as a person with his own rights, whose attachment to his mother must be inferred not from her actions or omissions, but from his own needs.

Just as I was submitting my opinion to the court, the adoption officials announced that a couple had been found who were interested in adopting Daniel, and were amenable to maintaining an open adoption in relation to the grandmother. They had doubts, however, as to whether the same concession should extend to the mother as well, although they did not rule it out. The judge asked to meet with the couple in the presence of the adoption officials and myself. This appeared to threaten the adoption officials' exclusive monopoly over the process of selection of adoptive parents,[29] and, in collaboration with State Counsel, they sought to derail this suggestion. Several days later, they asked to postpone the meeting with the couple, and since the mother's legal counsel had no objection, this was granted.

Preserving the Adversarial Nature of Legal Proceedings

Since I disagreed with the mother with regard to the advisability of returning Daniel to her, her counsel argued that I should no longer be on record as an expert witness on her behalf, but rather on behalf of the court itself. State Counsel objected to this suggestion without stating why, even though, contrary to their earlier prognostication, I had not actually opposed the adoption option. Apparently, the very fact that I acknowledge the possibility that a child who is forcibly cut off from his birth parents experiences it as a loss was enough to brand me as someone who questioned the very legitimacy of the adoption institution.

Granting the request of the mother's legal counsel, the court ruled that I should be noted for the record as an expert on its behalf, but given State Counsel's objection also decided to appoint another expert on its behalf. Several days later, State Counsel issued an announcement stating the name of the second expert witness, and noting me as a witness appointed on the mother's behalf, which the judge immediately rejected, stating that a court decision cannot be cancelled by an 'announcement on behalf of State Counsel'. Meanwhile, I went beyond the call of duty and formally asked the court if I could attend the hearings, although they are generally held *in camera*. From the transcripts of the hearings, I had learned that the SSC's interpretation of my recommendation for an open adoption would distort its true spirit, and I wanted to present an alternative interpretation, one that posits that continuity in the child's life is overwhelmingly important. State Counsel objected to my request, on the grounds that my role was only to provide an opinion and that that role had ended once I had submitted it. The court overruled this objection, too, on the grounds that

> the test for determining parental capability is not a simple one to implement, given the vagueness of the conditions involved that can neither be measured nor quantified, and because of the element of forecasting that plays a considerable role. Furthermore, an expert opinion is based on impressions and an assessment that is susceptible to norms and beliefs … Unlike the opinion of experts in other fields, an expert opinion in the context of adoption proceedings, although it relates to a given situation, cannot be seen as pertaining to a fixed condition, given that the process itself is of a dynamic nature. In addition, by the nature of things, during

> the evidence hearings stage, additional facts and information may arise, and changes may occur that may affect the final ruling. In any event, the notion that the expert witness is merely someone whose role it is to submit their opinion and then submit to cross-examination about it, as claimed by State Counsel, is not applicable to adoption proceedings.

With these words, the judge established not only that the participation and presence of the expert witness in court hearings is an integral part of his or her role, but also that the justice system in Israel, which is fundamentally adversarial by nature, is unsuited to judicial deliberations over adoptions.[30] As she further noted in her decision:

> The purpose [of the adversarial method used] in presenting the (factual or judicial) circumstances of an event or series of events is to determine which of them is the most trustworthy, logical and plausible. It charges all parties to the debate with responsibility for presenting the evidence, with each party doing its utmost to prove its version of events and disprove the account of the other party, with the final judicial decision based, in part, on an examination of the trustworthiness, degree of proof, acceptability etc. of each account. Unfortunately, however, adoption proceedings are not about the presentation of two accounts, that of the state versus that of the birth parents, or at least, it is not supposed to be that way. Rather, adoption proceedings are supposed to focus initially on assessing the respondents' parental capability, and then on finding a solution that best serves the interests and needs of the minor, given his parents' shortcomings.

The fact that the debate over whether an issue such as adoption can be resolved in the Israeli judicial system, given its adversarial nature, arose specifically in relation to a case that centred on whether or not to accept the open adoption model is likely no coincidence. This form of adoption was conceived to prevent conflict between the birth parents and adoptive parents, as its name suggests, and, like the open debate that the judge was seeking to promote in these proceedings, it is supposed to be open. As I described in Chapter 2, depicting Elinor's story, the judge in another case in which the possibility of an open adoption was discussed also departed from standard protocol by taking part in the evaluation of the bond between the child and his mother, and tried to persuade the foster parents to consent to the child's continued contact with his mother.

In her explanation of the reasoning behind her decision to permit my presence at the judicial hearings, the judge was effectively expressing her opinion that it is not the ritualistic rules that are supposed to dictate the nature of the legal debate, but the nature of the issue at hand. The confrontation between the court's position, which sought to 'open up' the adoption procedure and liberate it from the shackles of adversarial litigation, and that of the adoption officials, who barricaded themselves behind the customary rules, continued throughout Daniel's adoption hearings. The judge's decision indicated that she wished to defuse the inherent conflict in the legal proceedings, and I too tried to act in that spirit. Since I believed that it was possible to reconcile my recommendation (that Daniel's adoption be left open towards the mother as well as the grandmother) with the SSC's position that it be open only towards the grandmother, I suggested to the mother's legal counsel that we meet with the adoption officials to see if it was possible to hammer out a settlement that was agreeable to all sides. The mother's legal counsel agreed, although she still represented the mother's position, which was to regain custody of Daniel. The mother's position had been gravely undermined by my assessment that she would be unable to raise her son, but she seized upon my recommendation that continued contact between her and Daniel be an essential component of any future arrangement. In the event, however, we did not reach an agreement at that meeting. My position, that priority should be given to continued contact between Daniel and his mother under any proposal – if need be through a foster family, if no family was found who would agree to an open adoption in relation to the mother – was unacceptable to the adoption officials, for whom fostering offered neither stability nor continuity. This was the conventional view, although it had not been supported by empirical evidence.[31]

The dispute returned, therefore, to the court, pending receipt of the second expert opinion. Meanwhile, an additional dispute emerged between the adoption officials and me, this time about what open adoption actually meant. During the hearings, I expressed reservations about the total ban on any contact between the birth parents and adoptive parents,[32] in part because it is actually more onerous to the adoptive parents as it means that they have little say in deciding the meeting dates, and no first-hand knowledge about the birth parents with whom the child is meeting. Under those terms, I argued, it is no surprise that it is difficult to find adoptive parents who would agree to an open adoption. To this, the adoption officials countered that, 'in some circumstances open adoption can be perceived by people as something threatening', ignoring the fact that the SSC, which has held a monopoly over all adoptions for about twenty years, is responsible for making such arrangements appear threatening by the manner in which it presents and implements open adoptions. According to the adoption officials, with whom the courts tend to agree,[33] the confrontation between birth parents and adoptive parents might be exacerbated in cases where the birth parents object to the adoption and refuse to accept that they are incapable of raising the child, as in the case of Daniel's mother. However, this argument ignores the dynamics that come into play once the court declares a child eligible for adoption,[34] at which point the birth parents come to understand that, if they are to have any continued contact with the child, they need to cooperate. In Daniel's case, in the view of the adoption officials, any continued contact with the mother would be contingent upon the nature of the bond he formed with his adoptive parents. Such an arrangement helps to support the premise that adoption offers 'a clean slate', a premise undermined by the open adoption model. In Daniel's case, the premise of 'a clean slate' also meant overlooking the mother's repeated disappearances, which had clearly left their mark on Daniel. I replied that the profound significance that his mother's presence had in Daniel's life was an unavoidable factor that he brought with him to the adoption, as intrinsic as the colour of his hair.

A full six months passed before the second expert appointed on behalf of the court submitted her opinion. In it, she described Daniel's grave condition: that he was in despair and depressed, and despite a general improvement in his condition since his arrival at the children's home, was still significantly delayed in his cognitive abilities. She underlined the urgent need to have him adopted, but she, too, recommended that this be of an open nature. She did not think that the mother would harm Daniel if they remained in touch. She characterised Daniel's relation to his mother as being 'more like to a sister than a mother', which corroborated my assessment that the mother was incapable of protecting Daniel or responding to his neediness. As the expert noted, the fact that the grandmother was the one who had given Daniel motherly care might explain why he saw his mother as belonging to his own generation, rather than to the parents' generation.

The expert recommended that in the run-up to Daniel's handover to the adoptive family, the frequency of the mother's visits be reduced, and that the first meeting with her should take place two or three months after his adoption. This recommendation was consistent with the SSC's policy that an 'adoption with contact' required a 'cooling off period' of two months, during which time the child is kept apart from his birth parents so that he may form a bond with his adoptive parents. The court noted the similarity between the other expert's recommendation and mine, and asked to meet with the prospective adoptive parents who had submitted their candidacy several months earlier. However, it was told that they were no longer candidates because the adoption officials had thought it unfair for them to have to wait so long. This was a telling argument, as it suggested that the SSC thought it more important to protect the designated adoptive parents than to protect the child. It was clear that it would be difficult to find alternative adoptive parents for Daniel, not only because of the intent to make it an open adoption, but also because his condition meant that he had special educational needs, which prospective adoptive parents are generally reluctant to take on. It also appeared to be at odds with the standard procedure in other cases, where the child was placed with their designated adoptive family long before he or she was declared eligible for adoption. However, understanding the SSC's special role in the placement of children in adoption may help to explain this contradiction. The selection of candidates for adoptive families and placing of children with them are its exclusive preserve: the Holy of Holies that only it has access to. The judge's suggestion to meet with Daniel's prospective adoptive parents was a potential invasion of this sacred precinct, which the adoption officials responded to first by deferring the proposed meeting, and then by rendering it inapplicable by withdrawing the prospective couple's candidacy altogether.

As the court began preparing its ruling, the mother's legal counsel argued that the two expert opinions had been submitted during the time when the mother was meeting with Daniel every fortnight, but given the increased frequency of the meetings over the previous several months at the court's instigation, the mother's conduct ought to be reassessed. The judge asked if I agreed with this argument, and I replied that it had some merit. State Counsel objected, however, on the grounds that it would lead to a further delay in the court's decision and Daniel could not wait any longer. Objecting to the very limited delay that would be incurred by conducting one further observation of a meeting between the mother and her son, on the pretext that a solution for Daniel's condition was urgently needed, was highly disingenuous given that the legal proceedings had been considerably delayed by the SSC's earlier insistence on soliciting a second expert opinion. That opinion had taken a full six months to deliver, and the SSC had accepted the expert's advance notice that this delay would occur without demur. In addition, the SSC had cancelled the candidacy of the original couple who had offered to adopt Daniel, which meant that a new, and very protracted, search for different candidates had to be made. However, as with all self-appointed supreme authorities, the passage of time is measured not by the calendar, but by its own definitions. The judge asked me how quickly I could deliver a new assessment observation, and I replied that I could do so within a few hours after the observation, at a date to suit the SSC staff. The court therefore granted the mother's legal counsel's request and decided that I should hold an additional observation of a meeting between Daniel and his mother. This took place a few days later.

During this observation, I saw a considerable change in Daniel. His gait had become fairly assured, and his appeals to his mother more assertive and less anxious. Fanny's interventions in her son's actions were no longer quite as intrusive and abrupt as in the past, and this time she watched what he was doing before trying to educate him. Thus, instead of simply pulling his thumb out of his mouth, as she had done at the previous meeting I had witnessed, she explained to him that it was better for him not to suck his thumb. The meeting was more relaxed than the ones I had previously observed, and it was evident that the regularity of the meetings and their frequency had helped to improve the bond between them. Nonetheless, Fanny was still mostly concerned with making remarks and attempting to educate Daniel. I saw no improvement in her ability to respond to his appeals for attention, although she expected Daniel to respond to her own appeals. As on the previous occasions, Fanny responded to Daniel's attempts at physical intimacy only as the meeting was drawing to a close. I therefore reported to the court that the mother was still not capable of responding to Daniel's cues of his need for dependency, and the only lesson she appeared to have learned from the previous occasions was to comply with the regime of regular visits. Therefore, despite the significant improvement in the interaction between them, I saw no need to revise my previous assessment, and argued that the mother was not in a position to resume custody of Daniel. I stated that the mother's presence in Daniel's life was essential, and that her disappearance would consume all his mental energy. I therefore reiterated my previous recommendation of an open adoption, in recognition of the importance of continuity in a child's life.[35]

Daniel was declared eligible for adoption, but in her ruling the judge emphasised that a family must be found who would agree to his continued contact with his mother. In response, State Counsel agreed to opening the adoption towards the mother (as well as the grandmother), but asked the court to limit the number of meetings with Daniel to three times a year. This might be seen as yet further evidence of the ritualistic nature that the SSC sought to ascribe to adoption. This adoption would involve a relationship between the three sides of the adoption triangle, and one of the sides – that of the adoptive parents – was still unknown. The perception of open adoption as nothing more than an arrangement of meetings of a predetermined number and duration, by a supreme authority, is indicative of an approach that ignores the fact that the relationship between the three parties of the adoption triangle cannot be governed by decree from 'above'. Indeed, such a perception is a travesty of the spirit and purpose of the open adoption model, which seeks to allow continuity in the child's life, and which by its very nature is dynamic and will undoubtedly be affected, in part, by the nature of his relationship with his adoptive parents. The court agreed with me on this point, and rejected State Counsel's request to limit the number of meetings or their duration. It further stipulated that if suitable prospective adoptive parents were not found within three months, the case would return to court.

A Failed Attempt at Dialogue

The court appointed me to monitor Daniel's adoption until he was settled with an adoptive family. This involved a dialogue between me, with my position that all parties of the adoption should be involved in the adoption process, and the SSC, whose position, as conveyed to me by two or more adoption officials at every meeting we held, was that the adoption must be carried out strictly in accordance with its standard protocols.

The dialogue between us was opened by one adoption official with the following words: 'I agree with what you said in court, that the state must not repeat what the mother has done and bring about further severance of contact between her and Daniel'. I was pleased to hear that we were in agreement on this initial premise, but in time I learned that there was a considerable difference between what I understood by severance of contact and how the adoption officials understood it. I saw it as a loss of something irreplaceable, the effects of which would be erased only once Daniel's contact with his mother was restored, while the adoption officials thought of the severance as damage that is 'expressible in terms of an exchange system' to determine the appropriate compensation.[36] Therefore, as they saw it, the frequency of the meetings between Daniel and his mother could be established even before the adoptive parents had been found, and before Daniel had formed any attachment to them or experienced the effect that it would have on his attachment to his mother. In the SSC's estimate, three meetings a year would be adequate compensation for the damage caused by Daniel's separation from his mother. The perception of adoption as compensation for damage explains how the SSC implemented the decision to find Daniel an open adoption arrangement.

Since open adoption involves a triangle of three inseparable sides – the child, the birth parents and the adoptive parents – I suggested that when suitable candidates were found, they would meet not only with the child, as was customary, but also with his mother. The adoption officials accepted this suggestion with understanding, as they did not regard the mother as a threat to the prospective adoptive parents, but they preferred to decide on the matter only after considering it in the light of the SSC's standard procedures. In addition, I asked to be part of the process of choosing the prospective adoptive parents. This, too, was met with the reply that it required further consideration by the SSC's management. Besides these suggestions, there was an unspoken understanding between us that my monitoring of Daniel's adoption would not involve meetings with Daniel. I thought it would be inappropriate for me to intervene in a treatment process that was already under way. I also decided to let the SSC decide on how our collaboration should proceed, and I was kept up to date at every important juncture in the process.

Daniel's adoption was delayed because no suitable adoptive parents were found among the applicants that the SSC had on file at the time. Accordingly, a public appeal was put out in the media, in which the proposed open adoption was presented as it should be: as a response to the child's need for continued contact with his mother. When the three-month deadline set by the court for finding suitable candidates had come and gone, and only a few enquiries had been received, an extension was granted, but Daniel was becoming impatient and more temperamental after the public appeal, in which he himself had taken part. By this time, he had spent two years at the children's home and had seen many children come and go. While it is common to hear birth parents accuse children's homes of neglecting the children in their care, the woman who did eventually adopt Daniel was shocked at how carelessly he had been dressed, in clothes that were both tasteless and unsuited for the weather. Daniel's impatience may therefore have been due not only to the delay in finding him an adoptive family, but also to the indifference exhibited by the staff at the children's home, even towards a child who had been staying with them for months or indeed years.

The urgency in Daniel's condition required a quick resolution, but the lives of families on the margins of society are often beset by sharp and unexpected turns. While we were planning Daniel's adoption, his mother became pregnant again, quite unexpectedly this time, since she said she had been told that she could not have any more children. As in the past, she was not in a stable relationship with the man by whom she was pregnant. The staff of the children's home advised her to tell Daniel about her pregnancy in their presence, and Daniel reacted furiously on learning that his mother would be taking care of a baby while he was being abandoned and given up for adoption by strangers. In the event, the pregnancy ended in a miscarriage, but Daniel reacted badly to that news too. The adoption officials reported that he drew a picture of the three children whom his mother had abandoned: himself, the child who had been given up for adoption, and the baby that had been lost in the miscarriage.

Around this time, a woman by the name of Ruth applied to the SSC to adopt a child. She told them she was unmarried, but believed that she was capable of raising a child with special needs. What stood in her favour was that she enjoyed a very close relationship with her family and friends, and had a stable and thriving professional career. The adoption official in charge – Daniel's case coordinator – advised me that her colleague had met with Ruth and found her very suitable for adopting Daniel. I asked if I could speak with her colleague, or with Ruth herself, but was denied, which I saw as yet another attempt to prevent any incursion by anyone outside the appointed 'priesthood' to be involved in selecting candidates for adoptive parents. The adoption officials argued that the usual 'cooling off period' of two months after Daniel's placement must be observed, in which Daniel was not to meet with his birth mother, because 'he cannot form an attachment with two figures at once'. This was further evidence of the ritualistic nature of the SSC's procedures, given that Daniel was already attached to his mother. Indeed, the opposite is true: the attachment that Daniel would be forming with his designated adoptive parent would be made at the expense of his enforced cut-off from his mother. The uniform application of the 'cooling off period' in all cases once again reveals the extent of the belief that the contact between the adopted child and adoptive parent must be exclusive, even in the case of an open adoption. The implementation of the open adoption that was decided in Daniel's case was not based on a recognition of the importance of continuity in his life, but was a token concession to the *Zeitgeist* that acknowledges the open adoption model as an option to be considered.[37]

I was invited to a meeting with the children's home staff and director and the psychologist treating Daniel, to discuss how Daniel would be handed over to Ruth's care. Since they all agreed that Daniel needed continuity in his life, it was suggested that the psychologist continue to see him on a regular basis, even after his placement with Ruth. This clearly illustrated the meaning that the adoption officials attributed to the damage caused to Daniel by his separation from his mother. Since they did not regard his mother's disappearance from his life as irreplaceable, they thought that it was possible to maintain continuity in Daniel's life by merely continuing his contact with the children's home psychologist.

During this discussion, the SSC staff argued that my opposition to the idea of a 'cooling off period' was biased. There was some truth to this, since Daniel had not yet been handed over to Ruth's care, and my opinion was not based on his testimony, which could indicate how significant his attachment to his mother was in his formation of a new bond with Ruth. I therefore suggested that instead of us debating over the SSC's bias, or mine, that we not predetermine whether or how Daniel should meet with his mother, but let the psychologist, who was meeting with him on a regular basis, make an assessment of Daniel's wishes in this regard. In response, the psychologist expressed her concern that this would mean that we were effectively charging Daniel with the serious responsibility of whether or not he should meet with his mother, but I countered that a distinction should be made between expressing a desire and making a decision. Daniel would be given the option of telling the psychologist what he wanted, but the decision would ultimately be taken by the adoption officials. This suggestion was met with silence, but at the next meeting it was fiercely criticised for the alleged nonchalance with which I supposedly drew a distinction between desire and responsibility, as if it were a trivial matter. The SSC's opposition to my proposal reveals how important it was for them to deny the child's subjective view in order to preserve the ritual nature of the adoption process.

The demand to observe a 'cooling off period', which the adoption officials had raised immediately after the open adoption solution had been proposed, was being raised again, but this time it was attributed to Ruth herself. This ongoing dispute revealed the opposition of the children's home staff to the very decision about open adoption in Daniel's case. I discovered that throughout the period during which I was meeting with the adoption officials, opposition to the open adoption plan had been brewing among the staff of the children's home who had been in direct contact with Daniel and who were supposed to be preparing him for the adoption. This opposition grew when they learned of the mother's latest pregnancy. As they saw it, the mother had proven herself to be utterly irresponsible and had hurt Daniel once again. The fact that I agreed that the mother was irresponsible and had recommended that she be denied the right to raise him was not counted in my favour. The very fact that I recognised the uniqueness and importance of Daniel's bond with his mother marked me out as someone opposed to adoption. Faith, as noted earlier, can only be served totally, and not by halves.

In my conversations with the adoption officials, it gradually became apparent to me that, although they had said that they were interested in working with me as the court-appointed monitor of the case, this collaboration would consist of nothing more than informational updates from them. My requests to meet with the prospective adoptive parent and to introduce her to the birth mother before her introduction to Daniel were repeatedly deferred, and ultimately denied. This is not to say that the SSC had been insincere. For an organisation accustomed to working in secret, the mere provision of information is a marked sign of willingness to cooperate, but as I came to realise, the information I was being given was designed to protect the secrecy of their operations, rather than mitigate it. Such information as was provided was not always reliable and was certainly incomplete.

In court, the adoption official announced that Ruth, the prospective adoptive parent, had agreed to adopt Daniel on condition that his meetings with his mother be limited to four times a year. This detail had not been conveyed to me by the SSC when they had first told me about her. The official claimed that this was an unintentional omission on their part, even though the question of 'rationing' the meetings had arisen immediately after the judge's ruling that the adoption should be open, and was always at the centre of my discussions with the adoption officials. But even more significant than this omission was the fact that the open adoption was being defined as a highly regulated regime of meetings between the boy and his birth mother, even before he had begun to form a bond with his adoptive mother. In court, State Counsel underlined the urgency of transferring Daniel to his designated adoptive mother's care, because the delay in finding him a family had brought about a deterioration in his condition. The fact that the urgency had been caused, in part, by the authorities' actions was not mentioned, and rightly so, since under the circumstances, time was of the essence. Yet, when talking about the SSC's operations, it is impossible not to point out that it is the licence given to it to operate as a secretive monopoly that gives rise to the very reality that bolsters its position, and it then presents that reality disingenuously in court, while hiding the part played by its officials.[38] However, due to the urgency of Daniel's condition and Ruth's strong desire to adopt, and the very good impression that she had made on the adoption officials, the court was persuaded to grant the state's petition and hand Daniel over to Ruth as a designated adoptive mother. In addition, the court ordered a two-month suspension of meetings between Daniel and his mother. It did, however, reject the state's request to set a pre-set limit to the number of meetings with his mother after the two-month suspension. This, it said, would be determined after an assessment had been made about the quality of Daniel's bond with his adoptive mother.

Daniel was placed in Ruth's care, but the next meeting between him and his birth mother did not take place after the two months of the requisite 'cooling off period'. The mother had to travel abroad to find a cure for her ill mother, and when she notified her legal counsel to that effect, it was too late to arrange a meeting before they set off. Quite how urgent the trip actually was is unclear, especially since it proved to be pointless, because the grandmother did not have the necessary medical insurance. Due to the mother's lack of judgement, and possibly the grandmother's too, the cut-off between Daniel and his mother was longer than the court had prescribed – in this instance, four months. At this point, a court hearing was held at which an adoption official reported that Daniel was acclimatising well to life with his designated adoptive mother. He was progressing nicely at an ordinary school, his childish speech and gait had improved, and he was gradually adjusting to the routine in his new home, with occasional regressions, as to be expected in the first period of his life with a new family. The official noted that Daniel had never mentioned the possibility of meeting his mother; indeed, she said, he had mentioned her only once, when a staff member of the children's home came to visit him. It is easy to interpret such omissions as meaning that the birth parents are no longer important to the child, as though all trace of them had been erased in the new family setting. This phenomenon has been noted with other adoptees as well.[39] However, the taboo imposed on any contact between the child and his birth parents in a closed adoption means that it is impossible to examine what it means when a child makes no mention of birth parents. In Daniel's case, however, it was different, as shall presently be apparent.

The SSC staff believed that my role as monitor of Daniel's adoption was undermined by our differences over the meaning of open adoption, and therefore that it was pointless for it to continue. I, too, was torn as to whether or not I should continue. On one hand, I doubted whether there was any benefit to my continued involvement in Daniel's adoption process, given the manner in which I had been made a party to it; on the other hand, I wanted to try and preserve the limited degree of openness that remained in this case. I therefore expressed regret that the SSC continued to insist on a total ban on any contact between Daniel's birth mother and designated adoptive mother, and questioned the adoption officials' claim that such a meeting would pose a threat to the adoptive mother.

In her decision, the judge once again rejected the state's petition to limit Daniel's contact with his birth mother to four meetings a year, and ordered that three such meetings be held within the next five months, with the first one to take place immediately. She further ordered that the SSC report to her at the end of the five-month period, and that I submit a report after I had met with Fanny, with Daniel and with Ruth.

In the Shadow of Compartmentalisation

The first meeting between Daniel and his mother, after four months of not seeing each other, resulted in two dramatic reports – one by the adoption official about Daniel's reaction, and the other by me about the mother's response. The adoption official reported that Daniel wept bitterly after the meeting, asked to grow up with his mother, said that he did not want to stay with Ruth any longer and that he had difficulty calming down and falling asleep that night. This disruption, said the adoption official, was a direct consequence of meeting with his mother, an explanation which, in my view, was yet another example of the adoption officials' denial of the child's testimony of the importance of the continuity of such contact, and of their attempts to erase all traces of his loss. To my mind, Daniel's response was a sign that his previous avoidance of asking to see his mother after being placed with Ruth did not mean that he was renouncing his attachment to his mother, but that he was trying to adjust to his new situation. His silence seemed to have been a forced acquiescence to a situation in which he was prevented from expressing his loss. These silences create the impression that the traces of the loss have been erased, and when they reappear again, the loss is not always identified as such. I surmised that Daniel's reaction was a reflection of the difficulty created by the 'cooling off period', that the enforced interruption of his contact with his mother reignited his sense of loss and was accompanied by an anxiety that the renewed meeting with his mother would not ensure continued contact between them.

By contrast, Fanny's reaction to the meeting with Daniel was truly exuberant. In her conversation with me, she told me excitedly how

Daniel had made such a marked improvement in the short time that he had been living with Ruth. She said 'Good on her!' several times, adding, 'If the judge were to give me Daniel today, I wouldn't know what to do with him'.

Her enthusiasm cheered me, too. This was the first time that I had seen her able to enjoy Daniel and treat him as a person in his own right, rather than someone who 'belonged' to her. There could be no more emphatic refutation of the adoption officials' claim at the start of the proceedings, that Fanny's objection to Daniel's adoption was sufficient cause not to 'open' Daniel's adoption towards her. Clearly, her opposition during the legal proceedings had not been at all indicative of her position now that the adoption had gone ahead. Despite her problematic conduct during her interactions with Daniel, the child's best interests were now more important to her than protecting her right to raise him. She may even have come to recognise her own limitations when she saw quite how positive life with Ruth had been for Daniel, especially in terms of his progress at school, which was important to her. While one could not be sure from this reaction that she would continue to maintain that attitude, since emotional attachments by their very nature can vary over time, her reaction indicated an ability to appreciate what Ruth and Daniel had forged together.

In light of Daniel's emotional reaction to the meeting with his mother, I believed that more frequent meetings between them would have a calming effect on him (as indeed proved to be the case), and that I could raise that possibility in my conversation with Ruth. But the adoption official argued that, in view of Daniel's behaviour after the meeting with his mother, which gave Ruth much concern, Ruth would view a meeting with me as a threat, and therefore it should be put off. I later learned that Ruth had been obliged to meet with more than one adoption official prior to her selection as Daniel's adoptive mother, in keeping with the SSC's standard protocol, and her anger about that was directed at the idea of meeting with me as well.

The debate over the issue of my meeting with Ruth once again brought up the adoption officials' request to limit the annual meetings between Daniel and his mother to four, on the grounds that any other arrangement would leave Ruth in a state of uncertainty and anxiety. This repeated portrayal of Ruth as someone who was easily intimidated and given to anxiety was strikingly at odds with the image that I had been given previously, of a self-made woman who held a very responsible position at work and had shown considerable courage in accepting Daniel into her care, given how poorly he was at that time, and the fact that she had brought about a marked improvement in his condition, which undoubtedly required a high degree of determination and persistence. All of this suggested that she was a resolute person who was not easily intimidated, and yet the adoption officials chose to portray her as someone fragile, presumably to ensure their continued exclusive access to her. Subsequently, in my discussions with Ruth, I learned that the adoption officials had assured her that the meetings between Daniel and his mother would be limited to four times a year, in flagrant contradiction of the court's ruling. Furthermore, they did not report this to the court, even when the judge ordered three meetings to be held between Daniel and his mother over the next five months, pending further hearings.

Following the judge's decision, I met with Ruth twice. The first meeting took place after Daniel had met with his mother three times over five months, as prescribed by the court. During my meetings with Ruth, she expressed anger that the assurances she had been given by the SSC that Daniel would meet with his mother only four times a year had been violated. 'They must abide by the price that had been agreed upon', she told me, repeatedly. As she saw it, Daniel's meetings with his mother were a kind of tax that she had to pay for the privilege of adopting him, rather than a response to his need for continuity. She pointed out that these meetings disrupted the routine that she was trying to create, at great effort, and that Daniel's bond with his birth mother was not that important to him. She attributed Daniel's anxiety about the meetings to his fear that *she* herself might abandon him. She said she was not interested in adopting Daniel in an open adoption arrangement, and that his contacts with his mother were imposed on her. The arrangement had been presented to her as a commitment to four meetings a year, and considering herself a fair-minded person, she had agreed. That said, now that she had become attached to Daniel, she declared that she was willing to go along with as many as twenty-four meetings a year.

Since the open adoption had been presented to Ruth as a series of pre-set meetings between Daniel and his mother, it is little surprise that she did not acknowledge the significance of continued contact between Daniel and his mother. This might also explain why Daniel did not mention his mother after moving into his new home, or ask to meet with her. He would be unlikely to express how important that contact was, given that Ruth was dismissive of it, even if she did not say so in as many words in his presence. Ruth's use of terms such as 'agreement' and 'price' indicated that she perceived the adoption as compensation for the damage incurred to Daniel by his mother,[40] a view no doubt reinforced by her success in improving Daniel's condition, in contrast to the harm caused by his mother. Ruth perceived Daniel's bond with herself as a substitute for the one that he had had with his birth mother, and since the relationship with her was proven to be more beneficial, the compensation for the limited contact with his mother might even amount to no more than one meeting a year, as indeed she suggested in the heat of anger over the violation of the assurances given to her and her indignation over the open nature of the adoption.[41]

Ruth was willing to accept the challenges involved in raising Daniel and was happy that her efforts appeared to be paying off. It was clear from her description that she was totally devoted to raising Daniel and helping him to develop, and that she had great respect for him. She attributed his progress to his excellent natural abilities. She later told me how much pleasure she gained from raising Daniel, about the joy they had playing together, and the warm relationship that was developing between Daniel and her family. When I remarked that all this was clearly evident in her descriptions, she beamed. She said that she was happy with Daniel, and with undisguised pride spoke about how she had won an award for her work despite the great amount of time and effort she had invested in raising Daniel. At school he had caught up with his classmates and had even been advanced a year, so that he was now with his own age group. It was quite impressive that despite his troubled past, his innate talent for writing and drawing appeared to have survived intact.

Since I had been present at the second meeting between Daniel and his mother, I could see the great progress that he had made. He now walked fully erect and no longer tiptoed in that strange bird-like manner that he had previously. His voice was still somewhat childish, but he spoke in a louder and more confident voice, and addressed his mother directly and articulately. When Fanny expressed admiration of the shoes he was wearing and asked where they were from, he hesitated for a moment, looked her in the eye and said, somewhat hesitantly, 'Ruth bought them for me', but Fanny completely missed his implicit appeal for her approval of his life with Ruth. When, in reply to a question put to him by Fanny, he told his mother that he was still using the school backpack that she had bought him – 'the one with the Dalmatian' – she expressed surprise that it was still in usable condition, completely oblivious to the possibility that Daniel was hinting to her that he was using that particular backpack because he had received it from her. Later Daniel suggested to his mother that she take a drink from the bottle that he had brought with him, explaining clearly and without hesitation, 'Taste it, it's good – Mum made it', by which he meant Ruth had made it. Fanny took a sip and said, 'It's nice, but a bit sour', once again unaware of this implicit attempt to receive her approval of his bond with Ruth. There was no change in her ability to understand Daniel's vulnerability. She was still incapable of identifying his attempts to express how important his bond with her was for him, and as in the previous meetings between them that I had observed, Daniel received her reactions with a mixture of disappointment and resignation. At the end of the visit, he feared that Ruth would not be waiting for him at the place where he had ordered her to 'Wait for me, and don't move!' Happily, he did find her in precisely that spot.

In the room in which we were sitting, one of the two adoption officials who had arrived for the meeting was also present, but she did not take advantage of her presence to convey Daniel's appeals to his mother and help the communication between them. Although providing such help would probably not have changed the mother's behaviour, Daniel might have felt that his attempts to convey his feelings to her were not falling on deaf ears. The adoption official could have softened Daniel's disappointment in his mother's insensibility instead of limiting her role to that of mere supervision,[42] but in fact her conduct was a perfect illustration of the ritualistic character of the SSC's work. The purpose of the adoption officials' presence at these meetings is simply to be there.

The authorities' invasion of the relationship between parent and child can, of course, be used to advantage. One opportunity for this arose when Fanny told the adoption official and me before the meeting that she was intending to buy Daniel an expensive electric toy car. We were taken aback by its high price, and the adoption official reminded Fanny how happy Daniel was at their previous meeting when Fanny had brought him a ball, as he had asked for on the previous occasion. It was not the price of the gift that was important, the adoption official explained, but the fact that she remembered to fulfil his request. In my conversation with the adoption official after the meeting, I remarked that it was important to consult with Ruth before the mother bought Daniel such an expensive item. I thought this would serve two purposes: to protect the lifestyle that Ruth had created with Daniel from practices that she might not have approved of; and to help start some form of mediation between Ruth and the mother. Daniel's desire to bridge between the two women was evident when he said to his mother, 'Next time, come with me to the car', in other words, come and meet Ruth.[43] The adoption official agreed that this was what he wanted, but Ruth, she said, was still not ready for it. She did not point out that Ruth had been opposed to the very idea of an open adoption; that I learned only later, when I spoke with Ruth myself.

In the conversation that I held with Fanny after the meeting, I received further confirmation of my earlier assessments that she was utterly lacking in judgement on how she conducted her life. She told me excitedly that she was hoping to become pregnant again, this time by a boyfriend who had moved in with her two weeks previously. I learned that she knew very little about him, and what she did know sounded suspicious to me, though obviously not to her. He was a convicted felon, she admitted, but now he had become religious. 'All the convicts become religious', she said, waving her hand dismissively. Clearly, the bad experiences she had had in the past had not equipped her to see warning signs. Two months later, I learned that she had left him after he had beaten her and after she had learned that he had been physically abusive towards other women in his life. I still did not get the impression, however, that this experience had raised any doubts in her mind about the hastiness with which she entered into such relationships.

The next meeting between Daniel and his mother might, to a large extent, serve as a perfect illustration of what an open adoption should look like. This time, the adoption officials asked Fanny what she was thinking of bringing for Daniel, and when they told Ruth that the birth mother was thinking of bringing clothes, Ruth remarked that she had just bought him a great many clothes for the winter, but that Daniel was expecting the car that Fanny had promised. Two days before the meeting, Ruth also told the adoption official that Daniel had been talking a great deal about the *kucharikas*[44] that his grandmother used to make, and since his grandmother was supposed to attend the meeting, he asked if she could bring some with her. When the adoption officials passed this on to the grandmother, she said that she had already prepared some *kucharikas*, as she knew that Daniel loved them. This kind of exchange neatly encapsulates the spirit of the open adoption model, and creates continuity between the child's past and ties with his birth family and his present existence with his adoptive family.

The meeting – which took place, as usual, at the offices of the SSC – felt like a festive occasion, perhaps because of the grandmother's excitement. She was dressed in her best clothes and told me with a bright face that that day was her birthday and that seeing Daniel was her gift. The table in the room was covered with a handsome tablecloth, on which were placed the gifts that had been brought for Daniel, in the manner of a birthday party. Beside the gifts was a box containing the *kucharikas*. Daniel arrived, beaming with pleasure, and showed his grandmother that he was wearing the jacket that she had bought him a few years earlier. His entire bearing spoke of confidence, and his bright eyes gazed happily at his grandmother and mother. His grandmother showed him the *kucharikas* that she had prepared, but Daniel said that he didn't want to eat just yet. Fanny tried to get the toy car that she had bought to work while Daniel looked on with curiosity, but he lost interest after she failed to get it to work immediately. After fifteen minutes or so, Daniel declared that he was now ready to eat, asked that he be served only a limited amount, and ate with obvious enjoyment. The mother helped herself to some of the *kucharikas*, and Daniel protested, for fear that she might finish them all. The mother, true to form, explained to him that she had not yet eaten lunch and that she was going to work immediately after the meeting, as though she were trying to educate him to consider her needs as well. The special significance that the *kucharikas* held for Daniel completely eluded her. Daniel asked for a second helping, and ate it quickly. His grandmother asked him to eat more slowly, but when I quipped that he had to eat quickly before his mother polished them all off, he laughed out loud. When he finished eating, he told his mother proudly that he had received a score of 100 on his geometry test, but she was so preoccupied with getting the car to work that she did not appear to notice. I repeated what he had said, noting that it was important to him that his mother knows about his achievements. Neither the mother nor the grandmother knew what the word 'geometry' meant (in their country of origin they called it something else), and when Daniel explained it to her, clearly and coherently, the mother, anxious to save face, expressed her appreciation by telling Daniel that he was like his grandfather – her father and her mother's first husband – who was an engineer. There was evident satisfaction in her voice, since she was very attached to her father, who had remained in their country of origin. On two more occasions, I was obliged to direct her attention to his appeals, and she accepted my comments and responded to them. Her reactions on hearing of Daniel's achievements – such as his joining the Art Club thanks to his talents in drawing – pleased him a great deal. While the mother continued to struggle to make the car work, the grandmother took an interest in Daniel's life, asking him how many pupils were in his class, and whether he could send her some of his drawings. At this point, the adoption official who had been sitting in the room interjected that this could be done through her, and Daniel willingly agreed to write his pet name for his grandmother on the drawing that he would draw for her. This, I thought to myself, is what a child in an open adoption looks like: living in a secure environment, yet staying in touch with the significant people from his past.

At the end of the meeting, Daniel began pushing his grandmother's wheelchair towards the door, but the adoption official stopped him, to prevent a chance meeting between the mother and grandmother and Ruth, who was waiting just outside. Daniel backed away, and with evident astonishment, and the expression of a lost child, asked 'But why?' several times. He received no answer from anyone.

The bewilderment in Daniel's voice was a jarring contrast to the convivial atmosphere that had prevailed throughout the meeting and the preparations that had been made so painstakingly and lovingly by the adoption officials, Ruth, the grandmother and the mother (who had made sure to fulfil her promise). Daniel's reaction indicated the estrangement that had entered his life with the prohibition of any contact between Ruth and his mother and grandmother. No one, it seems, had told him about that segregation, or explained what it meant. Even the fact that his adoption was supposed to be an open one did not entitle him to recognition of his status as an independent person, as one who wanted his mother and grandmother to be part of his life, or to an explanation as to why his contacts with them were so circumscribed. The efforts involved in ensuring that he grew up with Ruth while maintaining contact with his mother and grandmother were made for his sake, but he was not party to those efforts.

In a telephone conversation that I had with Ruth after the meeting, I raised the question of Daniel's attachment to his mother, but she tended to dismiss its significance. 'Only the presents interest him', she said, ignoring my remark about how he missed his grandmother's *kucharikas*.[45] She remarked how he often asked for certain toys or things to eat, and once he received them, lost all interest. She appeared to take heed when I told her that children who have been deprived are more interested in proof that their requests are being granted than in the actual items they are asking for. Nonetheless, to understand Daniel's craving for his grandmother's *kucharikas* required a more nuanced explanation. It was as though, in his requests, Daniel was searching for something that had disappeared from his life, but was unable to say what it was, and therefore fulfilling his requests could not return that something to him.[46] The *kucharikas* were therefore symbolic of regaining something lost. They had the taste of belonging.[47]

Fanny's ability to provide a *kucharikas-like* connection with Daniel was clearly very poor. To make the most of the meetings that they had in such an artificial setting requires an ability to play with the child and engage him in conversation, an ability that she certainly did not have. From the way in which she interacted with Daniel, it was clear that she herself needed help if the spirit of the court's decision to make Daniel's adoption an open one, and not just its letter, were to be upheld. Thus, for example, during her meetings with Daniel she repeatedly asked if she and Daniel could go out for a walk together, as they used to do when she visited at the children's home. This was not an idle request: having limited imagination of her own, she needed stimulations, such as a shopping centre, for the meeting to be enjoyable for them both. But the strict regimentation of the meetings precluded this, and perhaps as a result, during the most recent meetings that I witnessed between them, even the intimacy and the cuddles that Daniel used to initiate before parting with his mother were gone.

After meeting with Ruth, with Daniel and with his mother, I recommended to the court that Daniel and his mother meet every two months – not because I thought that was the appropriate frequency, but because that was the pattern that they had become accustomed to, and I saw no need to change it. I do not know whether or not the court accepted this recommendation, as I was not asked to continue to monitor Daniel's adoption. This, then, marked the end of my involvement in Daniel's adoption process.

The Vindication of Faith

Sometime later, the adoption officials informed the court that Daniel was angry with his mother and did not want to meet with her any more. Perhaps he now felt more secure in his relationship with Ruth and was able to express his anger towards his mother for not raising him – or perhaps for her disappearances in the past. Relationships, by their nature, are dynamic and variable, but the highly artificial manner in which Daniel was permitted to see his mother, the fact that the open adoption was not to Ruth's liking from the outset, Fanny's inability to make the most of the meetings with Daniel, which took place at a venue of the SSC's choosing – all of these factors may have eventually led to Daniel's expressions of anger becoming a permanent feature, and may have precipitated the reality in which the mother no longer played a part. These factors may have conveyed to the child the message that one can resolve a problem by removing the object of one's anger. This is precisely the opposite of the message that we usually try to convey to children. Ideally, we encourage children to continue to engage when they become angry, so that they may allow themselves to experience and express the widest possible range of emotions without repercussions.

The alienation and estrangement between Daniel and his mother began to seep into the first meetings that were held after he had been placed in Ruth's care, at which I was still present. The meetings did not provide Daniel with the contact that he needed to gain a sense of continuity in his existence. It is unclear what Daniel understood from these regimented meetings, especially when he was forbidden from achieving his wish of forging a connection between his birth mother and adoptive mother. One might say, metaphorically speaking, that Daniel's contacts with his mother were given to him much like his mother had given him the shoes – the shoes, rather than the significance of a kept promise, were presented as the main thing. An open adoption conducted in this manner did not prevent the loss; instead of a true bond with the mother, it only offered her physical presence. It is doubtful that it justified the growing bitterness that it induced in the adoptive mother, and it may serve as evidence against open adoption as a viable option in general.

The success of an open adoption depends, as its name suggests, on the degree of openness that exists between the parties involved, rather than in the structural framework of the relationship between them.[48] In the story of Daniel's adoption, however, the openness was reduced to haggling over the frequency of meetings between him and his mother.[49] This interpretation is one that the adoption officials have managed to institutionalise. The court had tried to intervene in what the SSC workers conceive of as their exclusive 'territory', as it were, namely in the selection of prospective adoptive parents and deciding on the nature of the adoption, but had failed. The adoption officials' zealousness preserved the strict segregation within the adoption triangle, in stark contrast to the spirit of open adoption. The very negotiation over the frequency of meetings, instead of understanding Daniel's need for a sense of continuity in his life, and the total preclusion of any contact between the birth mother and adoptive mother, eradicate the meaning of this type of adoption and turned the openness into a burden on the relationship between Daniel and his adoptive mother, while preserving the ritualistic nature of the SSC's work. The validity of a dogma is proven by examining it in a closed circle in which premises and conclusions are indistinguishable: premises are conclusions, and vice versa. Thus, in debates about open adoption, adoption officials repeatedly present examples of its failure, while ignoring the fact that perhaps they are the ones who laid the groundwork for failure, for example by placing Daniel with an adoptive mother who did not want him to have any further contact with his mother; or by presenting the concept of open adoption to the potential adoptive mother as nothing more than a handful of meetings a year between the boy and his mother, a kind of 'price' that she must pay, as she put it; or by failing to inform the court that the adoptive mother objected to this form of adoption. Understanding that an open adoption is meant to preserve a sense of continuity in the adoptee's life is essential if the designated adoptive parents are to give informed consent; if no suitable candidates are found for this sort of adoption, the SSC must alert the court to that effect, so that it may reconsider its decision. The consent of the designated adoptive parents to the spirit of open adoption is necessary not only for its success, but also out of fairness to them.

The conditions under which Daniel's open adoption was implemented revealed once more the denial of the loss inherent in adoption, even if it assumed a different form from the one embodied in the proceedings concerning a closed adoption. Since the disappearance of the birth parents from the child's life is thought of in terms of damage that can be compensated for, rather than as a loss, it is possible to believe that the bond between the adoptee and his adoptive parents must be an exclusive one, even when the court declares the adoption to be an open one. This form of adoption, as we noted earlier, is referred to by the SSC as 'adoption with contact' – a term that preserves the adoption officials' exclusive prerogative of strictly controlling the contact between the adopted child and his birth parents. In this way, the SSC secures its status as a kind of priestly sect serving in the 'Holy of Holies', beyond the reach of civilian authorities – that is to say, beyond the jurisdiction of the law courts.

To preserve the ritualistic nature of the adoption officials' work, the child's position as subject is denied, as listening to his voice might lead to a deviation from the ritualistic rules. The SSC staff refused to listen to Daniel when they demanded a 'cooling off period' in his contacts with his birth mother after his adoption, and when they refused to allow any contact between his birth mother and his adoptive mother, or to pay any heed to his desires in that regard, and explain it to him.[50]

I never saw Daniel again, but his bewilderment and feelings of hurt when he was prevented from escorting his wheelchair-bound grandmother outside stayed with me for a long time.

Notes

1. As previously noted, the Adoption of Children Law in Israel permits the court to 'restrict the results' of adoption, i.e. to permit, in exceptional cases, continued contact between the adoptee and his birth parents. ACL 16(1).
2. According to June Thoburn, 'Studies of children who cannot grow up with their natural parents all clearly indicate that there are two essential conditions for ensuring their welfare: the feeling of continuity of belonging to a family with which the child has formed a bond (generally referred to as *permanence*) and the sense of identity that is best achieved by maintaining contact with a significant period from his past'. Quoted in Ryburn, *Open Adoption*, 78.
3. See, for example, Protocol #11 of the Knesset Labor, Welfare and Health Committee, 8 April 2003, http://www.knesset.gov.il/protocols/data/html/avoda/2003-05-20.html; AC (Rishon Lezion) 67/02, *Minor v A-G*, Tak-Fam 2003 (2) 27; Ruth B. Caplan and Gerald Caplan, *Helping the Helpers Not to Harm: Iatrogenic Damage and Community Mental Health* (New York: Brunner-Routledge, 2001), 92; FAP 778/09, *A-G v 1. Anon 2. Att. Yaron Hod (Guardian Ad Litem)*; MCA 370/09, *1. Anon. 2. Anon v 1. Anon 2. A-G 3. Att. Yaron Hod (Guardian Ad Litem)*, decision of Judge Rubinstein, para 14.
4. Merton, *Social Theory and Social Structure*, 202.
5. Karen Manch, 'Birth Mother Grief and the Challenge of Adoption Reunion Contact', *American Journal of Orthopsychiatry* 84 (2014), 409–19.
6. Richard P. Barth, 'Adolescent Mothers' Beliefs about Open Adoption', *Social Casework* 68 (1987), 323–31.
7. Tim O'Shaughnessy, *Adoption, Social Work and Social Theory: Making the Connections* (Brookfield, VT: Ashgate Publishing, 1994), 119.
8. Ryburn, *Open Adoption*, 87–92; Roy Parker, *Adoption Now: Messages from Research* (Chichester: Department of Health, Wiley, 1999), 45–58; Jerica M. Berge et al., 'Adolescents' Feelings about Openness in Adoption', *Child Welfare* 85(6) (2006), 1011–39; Marianne Berry et al., 'The Role of Open Adoption in the Adjustment of Adopted Children and Their Families', *Children and Youth Service Review* 20(1–2) (1998), 151–70; Lynn van Korff, Harold D. Grotevant and Ruth C. McRoy, 'Openness Arrangement and Psychosocial Adjustment in Adolescent Adoptees', *Journal of Family Psychology* 20(3) (2006), 531–34; Jerica Berge et al., 'Adolescents' Satisfaction with Contact in Adoption', *Child and Adolescent Social Work Journal* 21 (2004), 175–90; Richard Sullivan and Ellie Lathrop, 'Openness in Adoption: Retrospective Lessons and Prospective Choices', *Children and Youth Services Review* 26 (2004), 393–411; Lois Wright, Cynthia Flynn and Wendy Welch, 'Adolescent Adoption and the Birth Family', *Journal of Public Child Welfare* 1 (2007), 35–63.
9. In support of open adoption, see E. Wayne Carp, 'From Open Records to Open Adoption Epilogue: The Prospects for Adoption', in *Family Matters*, 196–234; Judith S. Modell, 'Conclusions', in *Kinship with Strangers*, 225–38. For opposing views, see Dean Byrd, 'The Case for Confidential Adoption', *Public Welfare* 4 (1988), 20–23; Beverly Hughes, 'Openness and Contact

in Adoption: A Child Centered Perspective', *British Journal of Social Work* 25 (1995), 729–74; Indira Vyas, 'Openness in Adoption: Some Concerns', in Margaret Adcock, Jeanne Kaniuk and Richard White (eds), *Exploring Openness in Adoption* (Croydon, Surrey: Significant Publications, 1993), 57-67; Thomas et al., *Adopted Children Speaking*; Janette Logan and Carol Smith, *'Face to Face Contact Post Adoption: Views from the Triangle'*, *British Journal of Social Work* 35 (2005), 3–25.

10. CA 95/653, *Anons. V A-G*, 392; CA 98/2169, *Anon v A-G*, 264; CA 05/10791, *Anon v A-G and Anon.*
11. Joseph Goldstein, Anna Freud and Albert J. Solnit, *Beyond the Best Interests of the Child* (New York: The Free Press, 1979), 17. For criticism of the lack of empirical basis for the authors' position, see Caplan and Caplan, *Helping the Helpers Not to Harm*, 96–97; Marsha Garrison, 'Why Terminate Parental Rights?', *Stanford Law Review* 35(3) (1983), 423–59; Daniel Katkin, Bruce Bullingham and Murray Levine, 'Above and Beyond the Best Interests of the Child: An Inquiry into the Relationship between Social Science and Social Action', *Law and Society Review* 8 (1974), 669–87; Case Comments, 'Adoption: Psychological Parenthood as the Controlling Factor in Determining the Best Interests of the Child', *Rutgers Law Review* 26 (1973), 693–713; Nigel Lowe et al., *Supporting Adoption: Reframing the Approach* (London: BAAF, 1999), 39.
12. The Adoption of Children Law states that adoption can only be by 'a man and his wife, together' (ACL 3). Single mothers and same-sex couples can, subject to availability, adopt children who are perceived as less desirable, such as children who are past infancy or have special needs. See SSC, *Adopting Another Way: Information for Prospective Adopters* (Jerusalem: Ministry of Labor and Welfare, 2001), 7; Yossi Tamir and Zohar Neuman, *Issues in Implementing International Adoption in Israel* (Jerusalem: Paul Baerwald School of Social Work, 2005), 23 [Hebrew]; Zvi Triger, 'The Child's Worst Interests: Social-Legal Taboos on Same-Sex Parenting and Their Impact on the Child's Well-Being', *Israel Studies Review* 28(2) (2013), 264–81 [Hebrew].
13. Mass and Ophir, 'Care, Supervision and Abandonment'.
14. Ronen Israelski, *Green Eyes*, documentary film (UK-Israel, 1995–1996) [Hebrew].
15. See Chapter 2.
16. Brinich, 'Some Potential Effects of Adoption', 107–13; Nickman, 'Losses in Adoption', 365–91; Ryburn, *Open Adoption*, 21–32; Polly Toynbee, *Lost Children: The Story of Adopted Children Searching for Their Mothers* (London: Hutchinson, 1985); Golden, *The Good Son*. See also, from a court ruling: 'In a series of decisions, the courts ruled that the previous world view, which attributed little weight to "blood ties", was wrong' (Family Court (FC) Tel Aviv 87471, *Anon (Minor) v Anon*, DCR Family Matters Rulings, vol. 2001, 801, 858).
17. On damage that can be compensated for, see Ophir, *The Order of Evils*, 127.
18. Shifman, *Family Law in Israel*, 218.
19. Ibid., 54.

20. Harold G. Grotevant et al., 'Adoptive Family System Dynamics: Variations by Level of Openness in the Adoption', *Family Process* 33(2) (1994), 125–44; Barbara Yngvessen, 'Negotiating Motherhood: Identity and Differences in "Open" Adoptions', *Law and Society Review* 31 (1997), 31–80; Deborah H. Siegel, 'Open Adoption of Infants: Adoptive Parents' Perceptions of Advantages and Disadvantages', *Social Work* 38 (1993), 15–23. A further study by Deborah H. Siegel found that adoptive parents were often committed to maintaining contact with the birth parents, despite the difficulties and obstacles that that entailed: 'Open Adoption and Adolescence', *Families in Society* 89 (2008), 366–74.
21. See Wolfgram, 'Openness in Adoption'.
22. Mili Mass, 'On State Intervention in Parent–Child Relationship'; Mass and Ophir, 'Care, Supervision and Abandonment'.
23. For example, FAP 10791/05, *Anon v A-G*; FAP 3534/06, *Anon v A-G* and *Anon* (unpub.), takdin.co.il (21 May 2006); FAP 3646/06, *Anon v A-G*; FAP 6593/06, *Anon v A-G* (unpub.), takdin.co.il (22 March 2007); FAP 1845/07, *Anon v A-G*.
24. Mass and Ophir, 'Care, Supervision and Abandonment'.
25. In the past, when the child was placed in a residential facility, the common practice was to prevent any meetings between him and his birth parents, at least initially, on the grounds that this would help him adjust to his new surroundings. This practice was discontinued when experience showed that the parents' visits actually reduced the child's anxiety about the unfamiliarity of the new setting, and protected him from the feeling of abandonment, similar to the change in the authorities' attitude towards parents' visits to hospitals, as described in Chapter 2.
26. Eva Arbel, 'Case Presentation: Adoption with Contact: Fantasy versus Reality', Seminar lecture at TLM Israel, 30 November 2004 [Hebrew].
27. In an article about a unique open adoption initiative by the SSC, in which grandparents were permitted to visit their grandchildren but not allowed to tell the children's parents – their own children – about it, one participant was quoted as saying, 'I agreed to these conditions because I had no choice – I wanted to continue to see him. He's my favourite grandson, and I didn't want to give up on him … At first he would ask me about his mum, and I would tell him that she wasn't around. On one occasion I told him that she was ill, but usually I would avoid the question'. David Regev, 'Grandma's Secret', *Yediot Aharonot*, 11 March 2010, 6 [Hebrew].
28. See Chapter 4: Interlude.
29. AC (Rishon Lezion) 67/02, *Minor v A-G*, para 22: 'The adoption officials believe that they, and they alone, understand what "the best interests of the child" means, and that the end justifies the means…'.
30. Ruth Zafran, 'The Discourse of Relationship as a Foundation for Resolving Family-Related Issues: Some Notes on Concern and Justice', in Orna Ben Naftali and Hannah Naveh (eds), *Proceedings of Love* (Tel Aviv: Ramot, Tel Aviv University, 2005), 605–55 [Hebrew].

31. Daphna Oizerman, Rami Benvenisti and Dalia Ben-Rabi, 'Children in Foster Care: Family Background and Situation at the Time of Placement', *Society and Welfare* 11 (1991), 227–47 [Hebrew].
32. Elsbeth Neil, *Supporting Direct Contact after Adoption* (London: BAAF, 2011).
33. CA 10791/05, *Anon v A-G*, and CA 6593/06, *Anon v A-G*.
34. Murray Ryburn, 'A Study of Post Adoption Contact in Compulsory Adoption', *British Journal of Social Work* 26 (1996), 627–46.
35. James L. Gritter, *The Spirit of Open Adoption* (Washington: Child Welfare League of America, 1997).
36. Ophir, *The Order of Evils*, 129.
37. Asaf Peled, 'Forget about Mum', *Yediot Aharonot* (weekly supplement), 12 May 2006 [Hebrew].
38. See Chapter 2.
39. Golden, *The Good Son*.
40. Ophir, *The Order of Evils*, 132.
41. Elsbeth Neil, 'Post Adoption Contact and Openness in Adoptive Parents' Minds: Consequences for Child Development', *British Journal of Social Work* 39 (2009), 5–23.
42. Elsbeth Neil, 'Contact after Adoption: The Role of Agencies in Making and Supporting Plans', *Adoption and Fostering Journal* 26 (2002), 25–38.
43. Elsbeth Neil, 'The Contact after Adoption Study: Face to Face Contact', in Elsbeth Neil and David Howe (eds), *Contact in Adoption and Permanent Foster Care: Research, Theory and Practice* (London: BAAF, 2004), 65–84.
44. A traditional Sephardi Jewish dish made of aubergines and/or squash cut in the shape of shoes and filled with cheese and eggs and baked in the oven.
45. Elsbeth Neil, 'Understanding Other People's Perspectives: Tasks for Adopters in Open Adoption', *Adoption Quarterly* 6 (2003), 3–20.
46. Ophir, *The Order of Evils*, 93.
47. David Howe and Julia Feast, *Adoption, Search and Reunion: The Long-Term Experiences of Adopted Adults* (London: BAAF, 2003); Yair Ronen, 'The Child's Right to Identity as a Right of Belonging', *Tel Aviv University Law Review 26 (2003)*, 935–84 [Hebrew].
48. David M. Brodzinsky, 'Family Structural Openness and Communication Openness as Predictors in the Adjustment of Adopted Children', *Adoption Quarterly* 9 (2006), 1–18.
49. Ophir, *The Order of Evils*, 145.
50. Joan Fratter, Rena Phillips and Emma McWilliam, *Adoption with Contact: Implications for Policy and Practice* (London: BAAF, 1996).

Epilogue

Not Blame, But Loss

By documenting the cases cited in this book, I sought to highlight the need to change the moral conception behind the declaration of a child as eligible for adoption due to 'parental incapability'. Instead of a moral position that equates responsibility with culpability, thereby incriminating the parent and presenting 'protection of the child' to mean severing the contact between them, I propose one that seeks to enable parental responsibility through intervention aimed at preventing unnecessary loss to the child.[1] To put it in terms of the two mythological stories of adoption featured at the start of this book, I am proposing that adoption in Israel be modelled on the story of Moses, who maintained contact with his mother during his infancy, rather than that of Oedipus, who was hidden from his father, who had sought to have him killed. The reasons why Jochebed, Moses' mother, was forced to give him up were clearly very different from the reasons for the adoption of the children in this book, in that the parents in these cases played a (possibly significant) part in creating a situation that endangered their children, but that difference is not at the heart of the moral perspective I am seeking to promote. A comparison between parents based on their measure of responsibility is necessarily cast in terms of moral judgement, whereby responsibility is equated with culpability. What I am proposing, however, is a view aimed at preventing unnecessary suffering to the child, which highlights the contrast between Oedipus's tragic detachment from his past, and Moses' preserved ties with his family and his people.

The cases I have presented illustrate the state's incriminatory attitude towards failing parents and the call to punish them. The prevailing view – that parents who fail in their parenting do so out of malicious intent[2] – is evident in public discourse, which continually cites instances of allegedly intentional harm inflicted by parents on their children in various guises, in an attempt to draw public attention to such cases and alert the public to the danger that such parents represent. For example, in a well-known midday radio programme,[3] the presenter announced that she was about to let listeners participate in a drama that was taking place at that very moment. A woman who was about to give birth had arrived with her husband at the hospital, and when they saw officials from social services and the police waiting for them, they had fled and were now hiding 'at a sensitive place', as they put it, so that their baby would not be taken from them, as their other children had been in the past. It should be noted that no court order had been issued at that time to remove the baby from their care at birth; indeed, it is doubtful that such an order could have been issued, despite past court rulings about the couple's previous children. Those court rulings explicitly stated that the statutory definition of parental capability 'does not refer to the parents' ability to properly raise any child, but their capability of raising a particular child, namely, the one at the centre of the court hearings'.[4] For such an order to be issued, therefore, there must be a child in question, and in this instance the child had not yet been born. Nonetheless, social services officials were apparently already waiting at the hospital with the intention of executing the emergency order to remove the child from his parents' care, before the court had sanctioned it. As a result, the real danger to the baby's well-being was due to the possibility of being delivered in a place of hiding rather than at the hospital. Because of this, perhaps, the director-general of the Israeli Ministry of Welfare and Social Services was prompted to be interviewed during the broadcast, and declared that he personally guaranteed that the baby would not be taken from the parents, provided the woman delivered it at the hospital. He added:

> In Israel, children are not taken away forcibly. There are children who are in situations of grave and dreadful risk. Children are taken away only when there is no other choice in the matter. We believe that a child should be with his family. The moment that there is danger, we transfer him to an emergency facility where the children remain in contact with their parents. There is no alternative but to save the children … Just in the past week, I read about parents who were arrested on suspicion that they had starved and neglected their two-year-old son, and the judge had written that they were 'unworthy of being parents and must be separated from the child as soon as possible'. Last week, a mother

> stabbed her five-year-old daughter, nearly killing her, because the child had 'annoyed' her (she loves her two-year-old daughter more); a father who raped his daughter; a child complained that her father had attacked her; a mother tried to murder her daughter; [another mother] suspected of murdering her daughter because she was a prostitute – all this just in the last week. One must remember that the welfare and health of the children are what is important. We do not remove children without court approval. In one family, a mother cut her child with a paring knife. No one takes children away, and no one abducts children in the State of Israel.

The official's promise that the child would not be taken from the couple – a promise blurred by the litany of extreme cases of parental abuse – in fact confirmed the couple's claim that he had set out to deny. In the event, the mother did arrive at the hospital and gave birth to a baby, and the baby was not taken from her at that time.

Citing of media reports of horrific instances of child abuse is typical of the response provided by representatives of the authorities whenever protests are made about children being forcibly removed from their parents, even when the parents pose no threat to them. Extreme examples of abuse or neglect are presented in these instances to invoke public outrage against the parents, and criticism is responded to by citing universally accepted norms rather than addressing the actual circumstances of these parents, thereby entrenching a moral judgement that equates responsibility with culpability. Elements of this approach are clearly evident in the cases described in this book, where the children were being raised by single mothers living in poverty. While the fact that the mothers were single parents was not the reason why the children were removed from their care, it undoubtedly contributed to their poverty and to the harsh living conditions that made it difficult for them to raise their children. In none of the state's petitions to declare these children eligible for adoption was there any reference to the mothers' hardships; instead, their failure as parents was presented as proof of their insensitivity towards their children and of their presumably harmful behaviour.

With regard to the risk inherent in blaming the parents for being incapable of raising their children, the Supreme Court stated in one of its rulings:

> We never suggested that 'bad' parents are unworthy of raising their children, or that the state is entitled to deny them that right and place their children 'for their own benefit' with other parents who are better than them … We all know where such thinking may ultimately lead us.[5]

However, the ruling stops short of offering an alternative moral point of view, leaving the prevailing notion that a parent's ability to raise their child is an innate mechanism that is triggered automatically at the child's birth, in response to the human newborn's need for protection and care over a prolonged period. Although this is ostensibly a scientific statement devoid of any moral bias, in reality it gives rise to the kind of adoption policies that the above ruling warns about. The supposedly objective scientific portrayal of parenthood conceals realities that society seeks to downplay, such as 'class blindness', which makes it possible to ignore the birth mothers' living circumstances and present the pretext of 'lack of parental capability' as though there were no difference between the living conditions that the children's birth parents must contend with, and those of the adoptive parents. In this way, adoption makes it possible to transfer children from families at the margins of society to well-to-do families, and from 'non-normative' families to 'normative' ones, since the Adoption of Children Law defines the adoptive parents as 'a man and woman jointly'.[6]

The pervasiveness of the hidden social attitude in the allegedly scientific construction of parenthood is apparent, for example, in the conclusions of the National Commission of Inquiry into the disappearance of 1,053 children of Jewish Yemenite immigrants in the early 1950s.[7] The medical treatment of the babies born to these immigrants, who were housed in tent camps set up to accommodate them during that period, was entirely in the hands of immigration authorities. While it is very likely that had the mothers been left to treat their children by themselves, in accordance with their traditional methods and customs, the incidences of illness and mortality of their infants would have been much higher, not least because the treatment provided by the authorities was adapted for life conditions in Israel, the commission concluded that the immigrants' failings in terms of sanitation and medical knowledge were due to grave defects in their *parenting*. The commission unquestioningly accepted the immigration authorities' assertion that they did not bother to search for the babies' parents once the babies had recovered during their hospitalisation – or even notify parents whose children had died in hospital – because they assumed that the parents had abandoned them. The parents' deviation from conventional Israeli standards of hygienic care at the time were interpreted as an inherent personality defect,[8] as it were, which is perhaps why the commission members saw nothing implausible about the notion that 'mothers who had carried their babies in their womb for nine months, then in their arms on an exhausting trek all the way from Yemen to Israel on foot, would abandon them once they arrived in the country'.[9] The commission's conclusions reveal the attitude that deviation from conventional norms justifies the removal of mothers from their children's lives.

The denial of the parents' position as subject embodied in the notion that parental capability is a manifestation of a natural mechanism also leads to a disregard of the child's position as a subject in his own right. Because the child is viewed as nothing more than the object of the parental mechanism, he may be shunted around like an inanimate object.[10] In the conclusions of its report, the commission referred to the Yemenite children who had disappeared as having 'disappeared to their parents' [*sic*],[11] as if the fact that they were now living under false identities, or had died as unnamed persons stripped of any identity or belonging, did not constitute an actual disappearance. The sixty-nine children whose remains were not found when graves were opened, according to the commission's report, are thought to have been placed for adoption instead of being returned to their parents. They were presented not as distinct and identifiable individuals, but as objects that had 'disappeared' from their parents' sight through 'fortuitous adoption placement', in the words of the commission, as there is no surviving documentation about them.[12] Although there was no adoption law on the statute books in Israel at that time, the adoption of a child did still require some legal registration that should have left some kind of record. The disappearance of these children was therefore not only 'to' their parents. Even if they were physically 'present' for their adoptive parents, with whom they may have been placed in the manner of abandoned items in Lost and Found, they had disappeared as individuals with certain identities given to them at birth by their parents. The commission's approval of the way the children were allegedly adopted denied their parents' role in establishing their identity, and thereby disregarded the children's meaningless existence devoid of their identity.

The commission's conclusions were submitted in 2001 – approximately fifty years after the children in question had disappeared – and stated that there was no substance to the claim that state authorities had conspired to abduct them (the key contention at the centre of the inquiry). To my mind, the focus on the claim of conspiracy was a distraction that negated any benefit that might have been derived from the inquiry in the first place, since evidence of conspiracy is always difficult to find. Instead, the commission might have focused on the normative framework that made the disappearance of these children possible. A normative framework, unlike a conspiracy, is not limited to any single affair or period, as evident from the fact that the wording of the commission's conclusions does not merely reiterate and confirm the norms that guided the state authorities' conduct in that affair, but also reflects the mindset governing adoption procedures to this day.

By passing moral judgement on the birth parents, current adoption procedures focus on their conduct and deny the child their personhood. The proceedings are designed to determine whether the parent is guilty or innocent, and the bond between parent and child is inferred from the parent's actions or failures.[13] This is illustrated in the case of a baby whom the state had sought to declare eligible for adoption when the mother, who had voluntarily consented to this, refused to disclose the father's identity.[14] Both the family court and the district court had rejected this petition until the state authorities had located the father and informed him that his son might be given up for adoption. On appeal, however, the Israeli Supreme Court overturned these rulings in a majority decision of a special expanded panel of judges, and ordered the baby to be declared eligible for adoption even without the father's knowledge. It reasoned that the mother's right to privacy must be respected, noting that she had agreed to disclose the father's identity after being promised that this information would be revealed to the minor only upon his reaching the age of eighteen, as prescribed by law. It further reasoned that their decision was based on the father's behaviour. According to the mother, he had left her when she told him that she might be pregnant. Such a reaction, according to the majority opinion, indicated that he would not be a good father.[15] However, the dissenting justice disagreed. Locating the father, she said, was essential to protecting the child's interests, and the mother's privacy must not be given precedence over the need to locate the father. As for the censuring of the father, the human psyche is complex, said the dissenting judge, and the father's reaction on learning that his girlfriend was pregnant does not necessarily indicate that he would respond the same way to the news of his son's birth.[16]

The disagreement between the judges in this ruling might be thought of as a dispute between two views of morality, one based on universal moral norms, the other rooted in the reality of human existence, where the moral issue concerns a person in distress and is aimed at preventing the production and dissemination of unnecessary harm.[17] One way to follow the latter moral view is to try and determine whether the damage in question can be quantified and compensated for, or whether it is irreplaceable and can be resolved only by restoring to them what has been lost.[18] The majority decision in this ruling focused on the parents' responsibility for their disappearance from their son's life as a result of his adoption. However, in this case the court chose to absolve the mother of responsibility and protect her, placing the blame for the situation squarely on the father, while deeming him incapable of raising the child. As a result, adoption is presented in this case as compensation to the child for the damage inflicted on him by the disappearance of his genealogical ties. Conversely, the dissenting opinion sought to prevent the child from incurring an irreplaceable loss, an objective that, according to this opinion, trumps the mother's right to privacy and questions the assumption that the father would not be capable of raising his child, taking into account the possible effect of the change of circumstances on his behaviour.

The link between the weight given to the parents' conduct and the meaning given to their disappearance from their child's life, which is inherent in the adoption, is clearly evident in the debate reflected in a Supreme Court ruling in another case that was widely publicised in the media and referred to as the '*Disputed Baby Affair*'. Here, too, the majority opinion in the ruling overturned the decisions of the two lower courts, and stated that the baby must be kept in the custody of his designated adoptive parents, who had received him after he had been declared eligible for adoption without the father's knowledge, because the mother, who decided to give him up for adoption, refused to disclose his identity. The father learned of his son's birth only after the mother had changed her mind about placing the baby for adoption,[19] whereupon he petitioned the court for custody of the child. In this case, more weight was given to the opinion of experts who argued that the baby would be caused irreparable damage by being taken away from his designated adoptive parents – with whom he had lived for a year and a half, from the age of ten days old – over that of another expert who stated that although the baby's removal from designated adoptive parents would cause him pain, it would not necessarily cause him irreparable damage,[20] whereas leaving him with the adoptive parents might result in a lifelong loss. The majority opinion had focused on rejecting the parents' claim to the baby on the grounds that he was of their own 'flesh and blood', stating that, 'judging by universal norms',[21] the parents were responsible for the situation that had come about and were therefore incapable of raising the child, omitting the fact that the adoption would be denying the child's right to his own 'blood relations'.

Once again, the minority opinion by the dissenting judge in the ruling argued that the child should be returned to his birth parents, that the mother's severe distress when she parted from the baby meant that her decision to give up her son for adoption was not made with a sound mind. Based on observations of the father's behaviour, the dissenting judge also disputed the court's assessment that he was unable to raise his son, and underlined the unique bonds that a child has with his birth parents, well beyond the purely biological meaning of the term 'blood relations':

> The term 'the best interests of the child' is a complex and multifaceted one, involving many factors – material, cultural and social – but the dominant factor is that of the natural bond of the biological family. This is the chief artery through which the blood flows to the child's life capillaries; it is what gives him his sense of belonging and existential confidence.[22]

The dissenting judge's opinion about 'blood relations' highlights the limitations of the supposedly 'scientific' perception of the bond between parents and their children, which presents the child as merely the object of a biological process, and denies him his independent position as a party to the proceedings.[23] It is, perhaps, no coincidence that the court-appointed *Guardians ad Litem* appointed in the two legal proceedings cited above (which established the children's positions as parties to the legal disputes) stated the need to protect the child's genealogical ties, both in the first case, by demanding that the authorities try and track down the absentee father, and in the second case, by returning the baby to his birth parents.[24]

Acknowledging the fact that a child experiences the disappearance of his birth parents from his life as a loss,[25] an aching void that cannot be compensated for, means that the position as subject of both the birth parents and the child are validated. The place of the parents in the child's life is defined through the genealogical ties, whose unique significance to the child is recognised when it is at the heart of the legal debate. In the cases described in this book, I presented the arguments put forward by the birth parents' legal counsels to address the circumstances under which the parents had acted as they had and had failed in their parenting. The court was willing to consider viewing the parents' disappearance in terms of the meaning that the children attributed to their bond with their parents, rather than simply incriminating the parents. However, as it pointed out, '[the court] did not have the tools to turn back the wheels of time',[26] and the decision to restore the parents' presence to their children's lives, once the bond between them has been distorted by the authorities' regimented intervention, does not always ensure that the unique bond can be restored.[27] The damage inflicted on children who are forcibly separated from their parents and handed over to strangers – often more than once – and the intrusive effect of social services on the bond between parents and children, is not compensated for, and often cannot be.

For those who refuse to recognise the existence of the loss incurred by adopted children, the testimony of adoptees who re-encounter their birth parents in adulthood but are left unmoved by the experience is cited as proof that 'blood relations' are insignificant; it is as if the special bond can be triggered like a conditioned reflex. However, while the encounter in adulthood may provide the child with knowledge of their identity and restore the physical presence of their parents in their life, it may not reignite the uniqueness of the bond between them.[28] In the documentary film *Into the Arms of Strangers: Stories of the Kindertransport*,[29] about Jewish children sent by their parents from Czechoslovakia, Austria and Germany to England shortly before World War II, one of the interviewees tells how, on arrival in England he had been placed with a foster family who raised him lovingly and to whom he became very attached. After the war, he learned that his parents had survived, and he met with them on a street in Paris, approximately nine years after they had parted. As he approached the appointed rendezvous, both excited and apprehensive about seeing them again, he opted to look at them first through a shop window, before meeting them face to face. When his father tried to put his arm around him, he instinctively pushed it away, and there was a sense of alienation between him and his mother. From his words – 'I suppose I was lucky, I had people who loved me and my parents had returned to my life' – it appears that, while his parents had indeed returned to his life, the close and loving bond that they used to have did not immediately return. Does this story invalidate the claim that a child experiences the disappearance of his birth parents as a loss?

In other cases, the emotional forfeiture of what has been lost is accompanied by a loss of self,[30] as illustrated in the testimony of a woman of forty who had been adopted immediately at birth after being found in a rubbish bin. In an interview with her, she said that her 'biological mother' (as she pointedly referred to her, rather than 'mother', by which she referred to her adoptive mother) 'does not interest me, nor will I be looking for her'. However, later in the conversation she revealed that she had, in fact, been trying to find clues as to her birth mother's identity, for example by trying to guess if her mother had been the daughter of an ultra-Orthodox family, since the bin in which she had been found stood at the edge of an ultra-Orthodox neighbourhood. She described her life as 'not particularly amazing', as though the expunging of the loss that she had experienced had also obliterated life's very meaning for her, and she said that she was unable to form relationships with men. In her case, the loss of the bond was not with her mother, since that bond had not consciously existed, but, as she put it, in the loss of a sense of belonging:

> Every adopted child senses that something is missing. It's no accident that people are so preoccupied with their origins, where they came from. It's something deeply embedded in the human psyche: everyone wants to feel a sense of belonging – which is also physical – to someone. Every time I see a child who looks like his parents, or brothers who look like one another, it always moves me and surprises me.[31]

As Ophir points out in his book, *Order of Evils*, 'The constant presence of the loss, the unstopping pain, becomes a new pole of identity for the subject who wishes to permanently be what she is now'.[32] As another woman who was adopted in her infancy pointed out, 'I came into the world as a refugee, with no visa or address. The great love that I received was, and still is, very significant, but it cannot heal the pain of abandonment'.[33] 'The loss is annulled, erased', Ophir points out, 'what is not erased is the disappearance itself, as an occurrence, and the experience of loss'.[34]

In my work as an expert witness in adoption cases, I have yet to encounter a case that did not genuinely raise concerns about a child's welfare due to his parents' hardships or inability to raise him. Yet in all of these cases I also witnessed the children's sense of loss over the disappearance of their parents. I am not claiming that adoption erases individual differences, and there are certainly adoptees whose lives are not forever overshadowed by a sense of loss, but it is important to remember that the testimonies of adoptees are almost always heard amidst a public discourse of denunciation of their birth parents, and a ban on their contact with the birth parents dictates how the adoptees participate in this discourse.[35] Perhaps for that reason, many of them have felt obliged, consciously or otherwise, to suppress the sense of loss in their childhood.[36] In the very act of adoption, the state intervenes in the autonomy of the family unit; by denying the loss that the child incurs, it invades the child's private domain, which is supposed to be protected by the right to privacy; and by systematically stifling the children's testimonies, it violates its duty to protect their right to their own opinions and feelings.[37] Presumably, the state does this because it believes that, with time, when the children grow up and present their testimonies, all vestiges of the loss will be erased and become impossible to retrace.[38]

The moral judgement implicit in the decision to declare a child eligible for adoption and equating the parental failure with culpability precludes the distinction between 'unworthy' parents and 'bad' parents, a distinction that is essential if adoption is not to cause unnecessary loss. There are parents who are indeed 'unworthy', because they intentionally harm their children, through abuse or neglect. In those cases, adoption might well compensate the children for the damage caused to them by their parents, denying them their birth right to be raised by their birth parents. They have no choice but to come to terms with the traces of that loss and to recognise it. But in many cases, some of which have been presented in this book, parents fail through no fault of their own, but for lack of competence and ability to overcome their difficulties, and their disappearance from their children's lives is an unnecessary loss that can and should be prevented. The Supreme Court, as a rule, deliberately avoids making any references to any parent's motives, but its assessment of a parent as being incapable of raising a child, and its repercussions on the future of the child's ties with his parents, makes it necessary to distinguish between lack of ability and helplessness, and malicious intent.

To avoid unnecessary loss, it is essential to change the prevailing view of the relationship between parent and child as merely a kinship in the narrow biological sense, a reduction of the parent's position as subject to a 'natural biological' mechanism that is triggered with the child's birth, while denying the child his personhood. Perhaps a different conceptualisation of the relationship between parents and child will bring about an acknowledgement of the child as a person who can testify to his loss when the parent has disappeared. This would look at parenting as an existential experience rather than just a biological association. As previously noted, Levinas saw the bond between parents and child as 'a mystery', not because of the magical aura surrounding it, but because of the elusive and reciprocal nature of parenthood, in which the parent and the child affect each other. The nature of parenting, which evolves through the relationship with the child, is not always fully apparent at any given moment, and may constantly vary. The coexistence of similarity and differences, and of belonging and separateness,[39] makes a parent's relationship with their child unique, and binds the child to the parent through a sense of belonging, rather than of ownership.[40] The child is part of the parents' self; as a person in his own right, he is neither owned by them nor are his prospects and opportunities identical to theirs. Their affiliation is not a function of the parents' actions or failures, but of the meaning that the child attributes to the fact that he is part of the parent, of his genealogy. It does not ordain an exclusive bond, but by the same token, there is no need to sever it when other adults take over the role of parenting the child, provided that mere contact with the parents does not involve any danger to the child. According to the alternative view that I propose, adoption proceedings should be guided by recognition of the child as an independent person with his own genealogical affiliations, even if these do not play a part in his actual upbringing and the parenting role is ceded to other adults.[41]

Notes

1. Ophir, *The Order of Evils*, 12.
2. Carmit Guy, 'In the Name of the "Best Interests of the Child"', *The Seventh Eye* 51 (2004), 10 [Hebrew].
3. *Yael Dan's Doing Lunch*, Galei Tzahal, 2 September 2003, radio programme [Hebrew].
4. See CA 2075/96, *Anon v A-G*, ruling 49, 476, 476 (5) (1996).
5. CA 680/77, *Anon v Tel Aviv Municipality*.
6. ACL 3. See Leroy H. Pelton, 'Child Abuse and Neglect: The Myth of Classlessness', *American Journal of Orthopsychiatry* 48 (1978), 608. In Israel, according to the SSC guidelines, prospective adoptive parents must, at the very least, have a high school education and prove that they have at least an average income and can provide each child with his own room. SSC, *Adopting Another Way*, 7 [Hebrew]. An example of how this plays out in reality is reflected in the words of a woman adopted as a child: 'Suddenly I got up and told him [her adoptive father]: "Do you understand what I'm saying? I used to throw up and was malnourished with you as well as with my biological parents – but interestingly enough, nobody thought of taking me away from you, and nobody thought of applying the law because of it. And you know why? Because *you* are a respected doctor, of the right background, you're educated and not 'primitive', and so everyone assumed that you were not neglecting your children. But that poor woman – my mother, who was barely able to run around between doctors and rabbis, struggled with me without any financial means, in order to save me – nobody made that assumption. Everybody assumed, if she's from such and such a country of origin and doesn't have any money, then obviously she's neglecting her daughter – or maybe even abusing her"'. Walder, *'Please Do Not Uproot What is Planted'*, 89 (emphasis in the original).
7. *Report: Commission of Inquiry into the Disappearance of Yemenite Immigrant Children in the Years 1948–1954* (Jerusalem, 2001) [Hebrew]. It should be noted that the 'Yemenite Children Affair', as this episode is known in Israel's modern history, is an open wound not only to the Yemenite community. The commission referred to here was the third one to inquire into the matter. All three committees were accused of placating public opinion rather than attempting to get at the facts.

8. The vulnerability of immigrant families whose children were taken from them without their consent was raised for debate on several occasions in Israeli parliamentary committees. See Transcript #15 of the Labor, Welfare and Health Committee, 20 May 2003, the 16th Knesset, Session 1 [Hebrew]; and Transcript #285 of a joint meeting of the Immigration, Absorption and Diaspora Committee, and the Children's Rights Committee, 30 November 2005, the 16th Knesset, Session 4 [Hebrew]. This phenomenon is not unique to Israel; see Wegar, *Adoption, Identity and Kinship*, 35.
9. Boaz Sangero, 'Report of the Commission of Inquiry into the Disappearance of Yemenite Immigrant Children', *Theory and Criticism* 21 (2002), 47 [Hebrew].
10. Nussbaum, 'Objectification', 2.
11. *Report: Commission of Inquiry*, 151.
12. Ibid., 73.
13. Mili Mass and Carol van Nijnatten, 'Child Protection and the Conception of Parental Responsibility', *American Journal of Orthopsychiatry* 75 (2005), 220–29.
14. ACL 8(c).
15. FAP 5082/05, *A-G v Anon et al.*, s (3) 201 (2005), Chief Justice Barak decision.
16. Ibid., decision of Justice Procaccia; Ruth Zafran and Noam Peleg, 'The Name of the Father Following FAP 5082/05 *A-G v Anon*', *He'arat Din* 3 (2007), 196 [Hebrew].
17. Ophir, *The Order of Evils*, 127.
18. Ibid., 89.
19. A parent was allowed to renounce his decision to place his child for adoption within six months. ACL 10(a). This was true at the time that this affair took place. In 2010, this section of the ACL, among others, was amended and a parent may now renounce this decision to place his child for adoption within sixty days. ACL, 1981 amendment 8, 10(a).
20. Thompson, 'Sensitive Periods in Attachment?'.
21. Mass, 'Baby at a Crossroads'. For a clear example of the application of universal norms, see FAP 377/05, *Anon and Anon, Minor's Designated Adoptive Parents v Biological Parents*, decision of Deputy Chief Justice Cheshin, 179: 'The father did not run towards his son, to pick him up, hug him tightly, kiss him, or hold him up in the air'. It should be noted that the father did not have access to his son who, at that time, was living with his designated adoptive parents, whose identity and location were confidential.
22. Ibid., decision of Justice Procaccia, 188.
23. FAP 209/54, *Peretz Steiner v A-G*, ruling 9/1, 241, 251 (1955): 'and the child is not an object to be kept and held for the pleasure or the interests of one of the parents, but is a "subject" in his own right'.
24. Much the same occurred in a third case: the court declared the child eligible for adoption in the absence of the father, whom the authorities had been lax in locating, ordering all contact between him and his son be severed, contrary to the recommendation of the *Guardian ad Litem* appointed for the minor. FAP 778/09, *A-G v 1. Anon 2. Att. Yaron Hod (Guardian ad*

Litem); MCA 370/09, *1. Anon 2. Anon v 1. Anon 2. A-G, 3. Att. Yaron Hod (Guardian ad Litem)*. Thus, in all three cases the courts rejected the GAL's argument.

25. Judith Modell, 'Natural Bonds, Legal Boundaries: Modes of Persuasion in Adoption Rhetoric', in Novy, *Imagining Adoption*, 207.
26. AF (J'lm) 22.98, *A-G v Anon*. (unpub.), Nevo Archive, para 8 (handed down 24 July 2000).
27. The ruling warns against excessive intervention by the state. For example, Civil Appeal Authority (CAA) 3009/02, *Anon. v Anon*, ruling 56 (4) (2002), decision of Justice Procaccia. See also Chapter 1.
28. Ophir, *The Order of Evils*, 89; Melosh, *Strangers and Kin*, 247.
29. Mark Jonathan Harris, *Into the Arms of Strangers: Stories of the Kindertransport*, film (UK/USA, 2000).
30. Ophir, *The Order of Evils*, 108.
31. Interview on Yael Dan's *Doing Lunch*, Galei Tzahal, 15 November 2005, radio programme [Hebrew].
32. Ophir, *The Order of Evils*, 97.
33. Rivkaleh Mondlak, *My Child* (Tel Aviv: Miskal, Yediot Aharonot and Chemed Books, 2003), 40 [Hebrew].
34. Ophir, *The Order of Evils*, 89.
35. Ibid. In a study of grown-up former female adoptees, a repeated theme in their accounts was that of abandonment; they emphasised the birth mother's act, rather than their experience of her disappearance. Ha'elyon, *Adopted*, 35 [Hebrew].
36. Zvi Yanai's books talk about a childhood overshadowed by the loss of a brother that was put into words only in adulthood. See Zvi Yanai, *Yours, Sandro* (Jerusalem: Ketter, 2006) [Hebrew]; Yanai, *Too Late* (Jerusalem: Ketter, 2009) [Hebrew].
37. Ophir, *The Order of Evils*, 107.
38. Remnants of the loss might appear as a 'patched identity'. Ha'elyon, *Adopted*, 49.
39. Mili Mass, 'The Need for a Paradigm Shift in Social Work: The Study of Parenting', *Social Work and Social Science Review* 5 (1994), 130–45; Mass, 'The Narrative of Parents', *Journal for the Theory of Social Behaviour* 26 (1996), 423–42.
40. Ronen, 'The Child's Right to Identity as a Right of Belonging'.
41. See Christine Jones, 'Openness in Adoption: Challenging the Narrative of Progress', *Child and Family Social Work* 21 (2016), 85–93; Mili Mass, 'Acknowledging the Child as an Independent Personality: A Proposal for Changing the Adoption of Children Law', *The Family in Law* 3–4 (2009–2010), 139–98 [Hebrew].

Bibliography

'Adoption Narratives', *The Adoption History Project*. Retrieved 11 July 2007 from www.uoregon.edu/~adoption/.

Agamben, Giorgio. *Homo Sacer: Sovereign Power and Bare Life*. Translated by Daniel Heller-Roazen. Stanford, CA: Stanford University Press, 1998.

Ainsworth, Mary D. Slater. *Infancy in Uganda: Infant Care and the Growth of Love*. Baltimore, MD: The Johns Hopkins University Press, 1967.

Almagor, Moshe. 'The Place of the Clinical Psychologist in Assessing Parental Capability'. *Psychology* 8(1) (1999), 39–49 [Hebrew].

Amir, Eli. *Scapegoat*. Tel Aviv: Am Oved, 1983 [Hebrew].

Bable, Anne L. *Ethics in American Adoption*. London: Bergin and Garvey, 1999.

Backus, Margot Gayle. 'I Am Your Mother; She Was a Carrying Case: Adoption, Class and Sexual Orientation in Jeanette Winterson's "Oranges Are Not the Only Fruit"', in Marianne Novy (ed.), *Imagining Adoption: Essays on Literature and Culture* (Ann Arbor, MI: University of Michigan Press, 1994), 133–40.

Baraitser, Lisa. '"Oi, Mother! Keep Ye' Hair On!": Impossible Transformation of Maternal Subjectivity'. *Studies in Gender and Sexuality* 7 (2008), 217–38.

Barkai, Mira, and Mili Mass. *The Meanings of 'Parental Capability' and 'The Best Interests of the Child' in Supreme Court Decisions Regarding the Adoption of Minors*. Jerusalem: Sacher Institute for Legislative Research and Comparative Law, Faculty of Law, The Hebrew University, 1998 [Hebrew].

Bar-On, Ya'ara. 'The Family in the Kibbutz', in Aviad Kleinberg (ed.), *The Love of Mothers and the Fear of Fathers: Rethinking the Israeli Family* (Jerusalem: Keter, 2004), 20 [Hebrew].

Barth, Richard P. 'Adolescent Mothers' Beliefs about Open Adoption'. *Social Casework* 68 (1987), 323–31.

Ben-David, Vered. 'Judicial Bias in Adjudicating the Adoption of Minors in Israel'. *Children and Youth Services* 33(1) (2011), 196–203.

Ben-David, Vered. *Social Exclusion and Forced Adoption: An Analysis of the Personal and Family Characteristics of Children Adopted without Their Parents' Consent*. MA diss., Faculty of Social Welfare and Health Studies, School of Social Work, Haifa University, 2006 [Hebrew].

Benedek, Theresa. 'Motherhood and Nurturing', in James E. Anthony and Theresa Benedek (eds), *Parenthood: Its Psychology and Psychopathology* (Boston, MA: Little Brown, 1970), 153–66.

Benedek, Theresa. 'Parenthood as a Developmental Phase'. *Journal of the American Psychoanalytic Association* 7 (1959), 389–417.

Benedek, Theresa. 'Psychobiological Aspects of Mothering'. *American Journal of Orthopsychiatry* 26 (1956), 272–78.

Benjamin, Jessica. *Bonds of Love*. New York: Pantheon Books, 1988.

Berebitzky, Julie. 'Redefining "Real" Motherhood: Representation of Adoptive Mothers, 1900–1950', in Marianne Novy (ed.), *Imagining Adoption: Essays on Literature and Culture* (Ann Arbor, MI: University of Michigan Press, 1994), 83–95.

Berge, Jerica M., et al. 'Adolescents' Feelings about Openness in Adoption'. *Child Welfare* 85(6) (2006), 1011–39.

Berge, Jerica, et al. 'Adolescents' Satisfaction with Contact in Adoption'. *Child and Adolescent Social Work Journal* 21 (2004), 175–90.

Berger, Maria, et al. 'Some Thoughts on the Question of When to Tell the Child that He Is Adopted'. *Journal of Child Psychotherapy* 8 (1982), 67–88.

Berlin, Normand. *The Secret Cause*. Amherst, MA: University of Massachusetts Press, 1981.

Berry, Marianne, et al. 'The Role of Open Adoption in the Adjustment of Adopted Children and Their Families'. *Children and Youth Service Review* 20(1–2) (1998), 151–70.

Blecher-Prigat, Ayelet. 'On Rights, Boundaries, and Family'. *Tel Aviv University Law Review* 27(2) (2004), 539–86 [Hebrew].

Bok, Sissela. *Secrets: On the Ethics of Concealment and Revelation*. Oxford: Oxford University Press, 1984.

Bowlby, John. *Attachment, vol. 1*. London: Pimlico, 1997.

Bowlby, John. *Child Care and the Growth of Love*. Harmondsworth: Penguin Books, 1965.

Brazelton, T. Berry. 'Evidence of Communication during Neonatal Behavioral Assessment', in Margaret Bullowa (ed.), *Before Speech* (New York: Cambridge University Press, 1979), 79–88.

Brazelton, T. Berry, Barbara Koslowsky and Mary Main. 'The Origins of Reciprocity: The Early Mother–Infant Interaction', in Michael Lewis and Leonard A. Rosenblum (eds), *The Effects of the Infant on Its Caregiver* (New York: Wiley, 1974), 49–76.

Brinich, Paul M. 'Some Potential Effects of Adoption on Self and Object Representation'. *The Psychoanalytic Study of the Child* 35 (1980), 107–34.

Brodzinsky, David M. 'Family Structural Openness and Communication Openness as Predictors in the Adjustment of Adopted Children'. *Adoption Quarterly* 9 (2006), 1–18.

Brodzinsky, David M. 'Stress and the Coping Model of Adoption Adjustment', in David M. Brodzinsky and Marshall D. Shechter (eds), *The Psychology of Adoption* (New York: Oxford University Press, 1990), 3–24.

Burstein, Dror. *Kinship*. Jerusalem: Keter, 2005 [Hebrew].

Byrd, Dean. 'The Case for Confidential Adoption'. *Public Welfare* 4 (1988), 20–23.

Canetti, Elias. *Crowds and Power*. Harmondsworth: Penguin Books, 1981.

Caplan, Ruth B., and Gerald Caplan. *Helping the Helpers Not to Harm: Iatrogenic Damage and Community Mental Health.* New York: Brunner-Routledge, 2001.

Carp, E. Wayne. *Family Matters: Secrecy and Disclosure in the History of Adoption.* Cambridge, MA: Harvard University Press, 1998.

Case Comments. 'Adoption: Psychological Parenthood as the Controlling Factor in Determining the Best Interests of the Child'. *Rutgers Law Review* 26 (1973), 693–713.

Clarke, Ann M., and Alan Douglas Benson Clarke. *Early Experience: Myth and Evidence.* New York: The Free Press, 1979.

Coetzee, J.M. *Waiting for the Barbarians.* London: Secker and Warburg, 1980.

Cole, Elizabeth E., and Kathryn Donley. 'History Values and Placement Policy Issues in Adoption', in David M. Brodzinsky and Marshall D. Shechter (eds), *The Psychology of Adoption* (New York: Oxford University Press, 1990), 273–78.

De Soto, Paris. 'Genealogy Revised in Secrets and Lies', in Marianne Novy (ed.), *Imagining Adoption: Essays on Literature and Culture* (Ann Arbor, MI: University of Michigan Press, 1994), 193–206.

Deutsch, Helena. 'Motherhood and Sexuality'. *Psychoanalytic Quarterly* 2 (1933), 476–88.

Deutsch, Helena. *Neurosis and Character Types.* New York: International Universities Press, 1965.

Dickens, Charles. *Great Expectations* London: Richard Bentley, 1837–1838.

Dickens, Charles. *Oliver Twist* London: Chapman and Hall, 1860–1861.

Downs, Martin. 'When adoption without parental consent breaches human rights', UK Human Rights Blog, 1 October 2013. http://ukhumanrightsblog.com/2013/10/01/when-adoption-without-consent-breaches-human-rights.

DSM-IV-TR. *Diagnostic and Statistical Manual of Mental Disorders*, 4th rev. ed. Washington, DC: American Psychiatric Association, 2000.

Edelman, Murray. *Politics and Symbolic Action.* Chicago, IL: Markham, 1964.

Ekstein, Rudolf, and Robert A. Wallerstein. *The Teaching and Learning of Psychotherapy.* New York: International Universities Press, 1958.

Elliot, George. *Daniel Deronda.* Edinburgh: William Blackwood and Sons, 1876.

Elliot, George. *Silas Marner* Edinburgh: William Blackwood and Sons, 1861.

Etzioni, Amitai. *Modern Organizations.* Englewood Cliffs, NJ: Prentice-Hall, 1964.

Fenichel, Otto. *The Psychoanalytic Theory of Neurosis.* New York: Norton, 1945.

Foucault, Michel. *Discipline and Punish: The Birth of the Prison.* Translated by Alan Sheridan. New York: Pantheon Books, 1977.

Foucault, Michel. *History of Sexuality*, vol. 1. Translated by Robert Hurley. New York: Penguin Books, 1978.

Foucault, Michel. *Power/Knowledge.* Edited by Colin Gordon. Translated by Colin Gordon et al. New York: Pantheon Books, 1980.

Fraiberg, Selma (ed.). *Clinical Studies in Infant Mental Health: The First Year of Life.* New York: Basic Books, 1980.

Fraiberg, Selma. 'Intervention in Infancy: A Program for Blind Infants'. *Journal of the American Academy of Child Psychiatry* 10 (1971), 381–405.

Fratter, Joan, Rena Phillips and Emma McWilliam. *Adoption with Contact: Implications for Policy and Practice*. London: BAAF, 1996.

Freud, S. 'Family Romances', in James Starchy (ed.), *The Standard Edition of the Complete Psychological Works of Sigmund Freud*, vol. 9 (London: Hogarth Press, 1959), 235–342.

Friedrich, Carl J. *The Pathology of Politics*. New York: Harper and Row, 1972.

Gal, Limor. 'As Tears Go By', *Ha'aretz.* weekend supplement, 23 May 2008 [Hebrew].

Galili, Lili. 'Not According to Section 5', *Ha'aretz*, 27 May 2005 [Hebrew].

Garrison, Marsha. 'Why Terminate Parental Rights?' *Stanford Law Review* 35(3) (1983), 423–59.

Gish, Nancy K. 'Adoption, Identity and Voice: Jackie Kay's Inventions of Self', in Marianne Novy (ed.), *Imagining Adoption: Essays on Literature and Culture* (Ann Arbor, MI: University of Michigan Press, 1994) 171–91.

Gleitman, Ilana. *The Functioning and Emotional State of Adolescents Adopted before and after the Age of Two as Babies, and Adolescents Adopted after the Age of Two*. Ph.D. diss., Tel Aviv University, 2008 [Hebrew].

Glick, Yaffa, 'Double Agent', *Tsomet Hasharon*, 24 June 2004 [Hebrew].

Golden, Shai. *The Good Son*. Or-Yehudah: Zmora Bitan Dvir, 2008 [Hebrew].

Goldstein, Joseph, Anna Freud and Albert J. Solnit. *Beyond the Best Interests of the Child*. New York: The Free Press, 1979.

Greene, Ross W. *The Explosive Child*. New York: Harper Collins Publishers, 1998.

Gritter, James L. *The Spirit of Open Adoption*. Washington, DC: Child Welfare League of America, 1997.

Gronrot-Kaplan, Lee. 'Forgive Me for Not Raising You', *Ynet* (column), 7 November 2008, http://ynet.co.il [Hebrew].

Grotevant, Harold D. 'Coming to Terms with Adoption: The Construction of Identity from Adolescence to Adulthood'. *Adoption Quarterly* 1 (1997), 3–27.

Grotevant, Harold D., et al. 'Adoptive Family System Dynamics: Variations by Level of Openness in the Adoption'. *Family Process* 33(2) (1994), 125–44.

Guy, Carmit. 'In the Name of the "Best Interests of the Child"'. *The Seventh Eye* 51 (2004), 10 [Hebrew].

Habas, Bracha. *The Youth Aliyah Book*. Jerusalem: Youth Aliyah Bureau, 1941 [Hebrew].

Ha'elyon, Hila. *Adopted: The Adoption Experience from the Standpoint of Adopted Women in Israel*. Haifa: Pardes, 2010 [Hebrew].

Hardy, Thomas. *The Mayor of Casterbridge*. London: Smith, Elder, 1886.

Harré, Rom, and Paul Secord. *The Explanation of Social Behavior*. Oxford: Blackwell, 1972.

Hilgard, Josephine R. 'Anniversary Reaction in Parent Precipitated by Children'. *Psychiatry* 16 (1953), 73–86.

Hosseini, Khaled. *The Kite Runner*. New York: Riverhead Books, 2003.

Howe, David, and Julia Feast. *Adoption, Search and Reunion: The Long-Term Experiences of Adopted Adults*. London: BAAF, 2003.

Howell, Signe. *The Kinning of Foreigners: Transnational Adoption in a Global Perspective*. New York: Berghahn Books, 2006.

Hrdy, Sarah Blaffer. 'Fitness Tradeoffs in the History and Evolution of Delegated Mothering with Special Reference to Wet-Nursing, Abandonment and Infanticide', in Stefano Parmigiani and Frederick S. vom Saal (eds), *Infanticide and Parental Care* (Chur, Switzerland: Harwood Academic Publishers, 1994), 30–42.

Hughes, Beverly. 'Openness and Contact in Adoption: A Child Centered Perspective'. *British Journal of Social Work* 25 (1995), 729–74.

Jones, Christine. 'Openness in Adoption: Challenging the Narrative of Progress'. *Child and Family Social Work 21* (2016), 85–93.

Kander, Lihi. *A Flower Named Sigal*. Tel Aviv: Tcherikover Publishers, 2000.

Katkin, Daniel, Bruce Bullingham and Murray Levine. 'Above and Beyond the Best Interests of the Child: An Inquiry into the Relationship between Social Science and Social Action'. *Law and Society Review* 8 (1974), 669–87.

Kay, Jackie. *Red Dust Road: An Autobiographical Journey*. London: Picador, 2010.

Kirk, David H. 'A Dilemma of Adoptive Parenthood: Incongruous Role Obligations', in *Exploring Adoptive Family Life* (Port Angeles, WA: Ben Simon Publications, 1988), 27–37.

Kirton, Derek. 'Kinship by Design in England: Refiguring Adoption from Blair to Coalition'. *Child and Family Social Work* 18 (2013), 97–106.

Leonard, Garry. 'Immaculate Deception: Adoption in Albee's Plays', in Marianne Novy (ed.), *Imagining Adoption: Essays on Literature and Culture* (Ann Arbor, MI: University of Michigan Press, 1994), 111–32.

Levinas, Emmanuel. *Ethics and Infinity: Conversations with Phillip Nemo*. Translated by Richard Cohen. Pittsburgh, PA: Duquesne University, 1965.

Lichtenstein, Tovah. *Genealogical Embarrassment and Search Patterns: Adult Adoptees Searching for Their Biological Parents*. Ph.D. diss., Bar-Ilan University, 1992 [Hebrew].

Lilienfeld, Scott O., James M. Wood and Howard N. Garb. 'The Scientific Status of Projective Techniques'. *Psychological Science in the Public Interest* 1 (2000), 27–66.

Livneh, Neri. 'An Abandoned Baby from Africa', *Dad, Mum, and Me* (special supplement) Haaretz: 16 April 2003 [Hebrew].

Lloyd, Fran, and Catherine O'Brien. *Secret Spaces, Forbidden Places*. New York: Berghahn Books, 2000.

Logan, Janettte, and Carol Smith. 'Face to Face Contact Post Adoption: Views from the Triangle'. *British Journal of Social Work* 35 (2005), 3–25.

Lowe, Nigel, Mervyn Murch and Margaret Borkovski. *Supporting Adoption: Reframing the Approach*. London: BAAF, 1999.

Maimon, Nili. *Child Adoption Legislation*. Tel Aviv: Israel Bar Association, 1984 [Hebrew].

Main, Mary. 'Avoidance in the Service of Attachment: A Working Paper', in Klaus Immelman et al. (eds), *Behavioral Development: The Bielfield Interdisciplinary Project* (Cambridge: Cambridge University Press, 1982), 651–93.

Manch, Karen. 'Birth Mother Grief and the Challenge of Adoption Reunion Contact'. *American Journal of Orthopsychiatry* 84 (2014), 409–19.

Mandell, Betty Reid. *Where Are the Children? A Class Analysis of Foster Care and Adoption.* Lexington, MA: Lexington Books, 1977.

Marsh, Peter, and June Thoburn. 'Adoption and Permanence Debate in England and Wales'. *Child and Family Social Work* 7 (2002), 131–32.

Mass, Mili. 'Acknowledging the Child as an Independent Personality: A Proposal for Changing the Adoption of Children Law'. *The Family in Law* 3–4 (2009–2010), 139–98 [Hebrew].

Mass, Mili. 'Adoption in the Bondage of the Oedipal Myth'. *Journal of Psychiatry and Law* 22 (1994), 263–67.

Mass, Mili. 'Baby at a Crossroads: The Dispute over the Meaning of Adoption'. *Tel Aviv University Law Review* 31 (2008), 219–40 [Hebrew].

Mass, Mili. 'The Determinants of Parenthood: Power and Responsibility'. *Human Relations* 50 (1997), 241–60.

Mass, Mili. 'The Narrative of Parents'. *Journal for the Theory of Social Behaviour* 26 (1996), 423–42.

Mass, Mili. 'The Need for a Paradigm Shift in Social Work: The Study of Parenting'. *Social Work and Social Science Review* 5 (1994), 130–45.

Mass, Mili. 'Legal Parenthood and the Continued Parent–Child Relationship: The Moral and Experiential Aspects of Parenting'. *Adoption Quarterly* 2 (1999), 39–69.

Mass, Mili. '"Parental Capability": "Parental Instinct" or "Survival Instinct": On Expert Opinion', in David Yagil et al. (eds), *Psychology, Law and Ethics in Israel: Psychological Evaluations, Psychotherapy and Judicial Decisions* (Tel Aviv: Probook, 2008), 217–35 [Hebrew].

Mass, Mili. 'Risk, Danger and Vulnerability in the Parent–Infant Relationship: A Method for Assessment and Intervention'. *Society and Welfare* 12 (1992), 391–405 [Hebrew].

Mass, Mili. 'On State Intervention in Parent–Child Relationship: The Case of Involuntary Adoption Due to "Parental Incapability"'. *Law Review, Netanya Academic College Law School* 4 (2005), 589–616 [Hebrew].

Mass, Mili. 'When Family Relationship Stumble into the Finality of Legal Proceedings'. *IDC Law Review* 18 (2014) [Hebrew]: 328–362.

Mass, Mili, and Adi Ophir. 'Care, Supervision, and Abandonment: On Non-Consensual and Confidential Adoption'. *Tel Aviv University Law Review* 29 (2006), 257–310 [Hebrew].

Mass, Mili, and Carol van Nijnatten. 'Child Protection and the Conception of Parental Responsibility'. *American Journal of Orthopsychiatry* 75 (2005), 220–29.

Melman, Yossi. 'A History Reserved for Close Associates Only', *Haaretz*, 16 April 2009 [Hebrew].

Melosh, Barbara. *Strangers and Kin: The American Way of Adoption*. Cambridge, MA: Harvard University Press, 2002.

Merton, Robert K. *Social Theory and Social Structure*. Glencoe, IL: The Free Press, 1955.

Michael, Sami. *Pigeons at Trafalgar Square.* Tel Aviv: Am Oved, 2006 [Hebrew].

Miller, D.A. *The Novel and the Police*. Berkeley, CA: University of California Press, 1988.

Modell, J. *Kinship with Strangers: Adoption and Interpretation of Kinship in American Culture*. Berkeley, CA: University of California Press, 1994.

Modell, Judith. 'Natural Bonds, Legal Boundaries: Modes of Persuasion in Adoption Rhetoric', in Marianne Novy (ed.), *Imagining Adoption: Essays on Literature and Culture* (Ann Arbor, MI: University of Michigan Press, 1994), 207–29.

Modell, Judith. *A Sealed and Secret Kinship*. New York: Berghahn Books, 2001.

Mondlak, Rivkaleh. *My Child*. Tel Aviv: Miskal, Yediot Aharonot and Chemed Books, 2003 [Hebrew].

Neil, Elsbeth. 'Contact after Adoption: The Role of Agencies in Making and Supporting Plans'. *Adoption and Fostering Journal* 26 (2002), 25–38.

Neil, Elsbeth. 'The Contact after Adoption Study: Face to Face Contact', in Elsbeth Neil and David Howe (eds), *Contact in Adoption and Permanent Foster Care: Research, Theory and Practice* (London: BAAF, 2004), 65–84.

Neil, Elsbeth. 'The Mental Stress of Birth Relatives of Adopted Children: "Disease" or "Unease"? Findings from a UK Study'. *Health and Social Care* 21 (2013), 191–99.

Neil, Elsbeth. 'Post Adoption Contact and Openness in Adoptive Parents' Minds: Consequences for Child Development'. *British Journal of Social Work* 39 (2009), 5–23.

Neil, Elsbeth. 'The Reasons Why Young Children are Placed for Adoption: Findings from a Recently Placed Sample and a Discussion of Implications for Subsequent Identity Development'. *Child and Family Social Work* 5 (2000), 303–16.

Neil, Elsbeth. *Supporting Direct Contact after Adoption*. London: BAAF, 2011.

Neil, Elsbeth. 'Understanding Other People's Perspectives: Tasks for Adopters in Open Adoption'. *Adoption Quarterly* 6 (2003), 3–20.

Newman, Stephen A. 'Assessing the Quality of Expert Testimony in Cases Involving Children'. *The Journal of Psychiatry and Law* 22 (1994), 181–235.

Nickman, Steven L. 'Losses in Adoption: The Need for Dialogue'. *The Psychoanalytic Study of the Child* 40 (1985), 365–98.

Novy, Marianne. 'Adoption in Silas Marner and Daniel Deronda', in *Imagining Adoption: Essays on Literature and Culture* (Ann Arbor, MI: University of Michigan Press, 1994), 35–56.

Nussbaum, Martha C. 'Objectification', in *Sex and Social Justice* (Oxford: Oxford University Press, 1999), 213–39.

O'Halloran, Kerry. *The Politics of Adoption: International Perspectives on Law, Policy and Practice*. New York: Springer, 2009.

Oizerman, Daphna, Rami Benvenisti and Dalia Ben-Rabi. 'Children in Foster Care: Family Background and Situation at the Time of Placement'. *Society and Welfare* 11 (1991), 227-47 [Hebrew].

Olden, Christine. 'On Adult Empathy with Children'. *The Psychoanalytic Study of the Child* 8 (1953), 111–26.

Oliviero, Ann Ferraris. 'Infanticide in Western Culture: A Historical Overview', in Stefano Parmigiani and Frederick vom Saal (eds), *Infanticide and Parental Care* (Chur, Switzerland: Harwood Academic Publishers, 1994), 105–20.

Ophir, Adi. *The Order of Evils: Toward an Ontology of Morals.* Translated by Rela Mazali and Havi Carel. New York: Zone Books, 2005.

Orwell, George. *1984*. London: Secker and Warburg, 1949.

O'Shaughnessy, Tim. *Adoption, Social Work and Social Theory: Making the Connections.* Brookfield, VT: Ashgate Publishing, 1994.

Parad, Howard J., and Gerald Caplan. 'A Framework for Studying Families in Crisis'. *Journal of Social Work* 5 (1960), 3–15.

Parker, Roy. *Adoption Now: Messages from Research.* Chichester: Department of Health, Wiley, 1999.

Parton, Nigel. 'The Natural History of Child Abuse: A Study of Social Problem Definition'. *British Journal of Social Work* 9 (1979), 431–51.

Peled, Asaf. 'Forget about Mum', *Yediot Aharonot* (weekly supplement) 12 May 2006 [Hebrew].

Pelton, Leroy H. 'Child Abuse and Neglect: The Myth of Classlessness'. *American Journal of Orthopsychiatry* 48 (1978), 608–17.

Plato. *The Complete Works.* Edited by John. M. Cooper. Cambridge: Hackett, 1997.

Priel, Beatriz, Bella Kantor and Avi Besser. 'Two Maternal Representations: A Study of Israeli Adopted Children'. *Psychoanalytic Psychology* 17 (2000), 128–45.

Priel, Beatriz, et al. 'Adjustment among Adopted Children: The Role of Maternal Self-Reflectiveness'. *Family Relations* 49 (2000), 389–96.

Provence, Sally, and Rose C. Lipton. *Infants in Institutions.* New York: International Universities Press, 1962.

Rank, Otto. *The Myth of the Birth of the Hero.* New York: Vintage Books, 1964.

Raz-Karkotzkin, Amnon. *The Censor, the Editor and the Text.* Jerusalem: Magnes, 2005 [Hebrew].

Regev, David. 'Suing the Ministry of Welfare for Millions Because of a "Bad Adoption"', *Yediot Aharonot*, 27 October 2006 [Hebrew].

Regev, David. 'Grandma's Secret', *Yediot Aharonot*, 11 March 2010 [Hebrew].

Report of the Public Committee into the Condition of Children and Youth at Risk and in Distress, chairperson Hillel Schmid. Jerusalem: Prime Minister's Office and Ministry of Welfare, March 2006, 33 [Hebrew].

Report: Commission of Inquiry into the Disappearance of Yemenite Immigrant Children in the Years 1948–1954. Jerusalem, 2001 [Hebrew].

Rivkin, Dori, and Shoshana Baumgold. *Follow-Up of Older Children Who Have Been Adopted.* Jerusalem: Myers-JDC-Brookdale Institute, 2001 [Hebrew].

Robertson, Joyce, and James Robertson. 'Young Children in Brief Separation: A Fresh Look'. *Psychoanalytic Study of the Child* 26 (1971), 264–315.

Ronen, Yair. 'The Child's Right to Identity as a Right to Belonging'. *Tel Aviv University Law Review* 26 (2003), 935–84 [Hebrew].

Rutter, Michael. 'Continuities and Discontinuities in Socioemotional Development: Empirical and Conceptual Perspectives', in Robert N. Emde and Robert J. Harmon (eds), *Continuities and Discontinuities in Development* (New York: Plenum Press, 1978), 41–65.

Rutter, Michael. *Maternal Deprivation Reassessed.* Harmondsworth: Penguin Books, 1972.

Ryburn, Murray. In *Open Adoption: Research, Theory and Practice.* Aldershot: Avebury, 1994.

Ryburn, Murray. 'Secrecy and Openness in Adoption: A Historical Perspective'. *Social Policy and Administration* 29 (1995), 150–68.

Ryburn, Murray. 'A Study of Post-Adoption Contact in Compulsory Adoption'. *British Journal of Social Work* 26 (1996), 627–46.

Sameroff, Arnold J., and Michael J. Chandler. 'Reproductive Risk and the Continuum of Caretaking Casualty', in Frances D. Horowitz (ed.), *Review of Child Development Research*, vol. 4 (Chicago, IL: University of Chicago Press, 1975), 187–244.

Sangero, Boaz. 'Report of the Commission of Inquiry into the Disappearance of Yemenite Immigrant Children'. *Theory and Criticism* 21 (2002), 47–76 [Hebrew].

Schellekes, Alina Brickman. *Cognitive, Emotional and Social Adjustment of Adopted Children as Compared to Non-Adopted Children and Children Raised in Institutions.* MA diss., Tel Aviv University, 1985 [Hebrew].

Shechter, Marshall D., and Doris Bertocci. 'The Meaning of the Search', in David M. Brodzinsky and Marshall D. Shechter (eds), *The Psychology of Adoption* (New York: Oxford University Press, 1990), 62–71.

Shifman, Pinhas. *Family Law in Israel*, Vol. 2. Jerusalem: The Sacher Institute for Legislative Research and Comparative Law, Hebrew University Faculty of Law, 1989 [Hebrew].

Shils, Edward. 'Privacy: Its Constitution and Vicissitudes'. *Law and Contemporary Problems* 31 (1966), 281–306.

Shils, Edward A. *The Torment of Secrecy*. Glencoe, IL: The Free Press, 1956.

Siegel, Deborah H. 'Open Adoption and Adolescence'. *Families in Society* 89 (2008), 366–74.

Siegel, Deborah H. 'Open Adoption of Infants: Adoptive Parents' Perceptions of Advantages and Disadvantages'. *Social Work* 38 (1993), 15–23.

Simmel, Georg. *The Sociology of George Simmel.* Translated and edited by Kurt Wolff. Glencoe, IL: The Free Press, 1950.

Sinai, Ruth and Moshe Reinfeld. 'The Judge Did Not Understand Why the Children Had Been Separated from Their Mother', *Ha'aretz*, 21 September 2000 [Hebrew].

Spitz, René A. *The First Year of Life*. New York: International Universities Press, 1965.

SSC. *Adopting Another Way: Information for Prospective Adopters*. Jerusalem: Ministry of Labor and Welfare, 2001.

Stavern, Jan Van. 'A Junction of Amends: Sandra McPherson's Poetics of Adoption', in Marianne Novy (ed.), *Imagining Adoption: Essays on Literature and Culture* (Ann Arbor, MI: University of Michigan Press, 1994), 151–70.

Stern, Daniel N. *The First Relationship.* Cambridge, MA: Harvard University Press, 1977.

Sullivan, Harry Stuck. *The Interpersonal Theory of Psychiatry*. New York: Norton, 1953.

Sullivan, Richard, and Ellie Lathrop. 'Openness in Adoption: Retrospective Lessons and Prospective Choices'. *Children and Youth Services Review* 26 (2004), 393–411.

Tamir, Yossi, and Zohar Neuman. *Issues in Implementing International Adoption in Israel*. Jerusalem: Paul Baerwald School of Social Work, 2005 [Hebrew].

Taussig, Michael. *Defacement*. Stanford, CA: Stanford University Press, 1999.

Terr, Lenore. *Too Scared to Cry*. New York: Harper and Row, 1990.

Thomas, Carolyn, et al. *Adopted Children Speaking*. London: BAAF, 1999.

Thompson, Ross A. 'Sensitive Periods in Attachment?' in Donald B. Bailey et al. (eds), *Critical Thinking about Critical Periods* (Baltimore, MD: Paul H. Brookes, 2001), 83–106.

Toynbee, Polly. *Lost Children: The Story of Adopted Children Searching for Their Mothers*. London: Hutchinson, 1985.

Triger, Zvi. 'The Child's Worst Interests: Social-Legal Taboos on Same-Sex Parenting and Their Impact on the Child's Well-Being'. *Israel Studies Review* 28(2) (2013), 264–81 [Hebrew].

Tristeliotis, John. *In Search of Origins: The Experience of Adopted Children*. London: Routledge and Kegan Paul, 1973.

Van Korff, Lynn, Harold D. Grotevant and Ruth C. McRoy. 'Openness Arrangement and Psychosocial Adjustment in Adolescent Adoptees'. *Journal of Family Psychology* 20(3) (2006), 531–34.

Van Manen, Max. 'Phenomenology of Practice'. *Phenomenology and Practice* 1(2007), 11–30.

Vyas, Indira. 'Openness in Adoption: Some Concerns', in Margaret Adcock, Jeanne Kaniuk and Richard White (eds), *Exploring Openness in Adoption* (Croydon, Surrey: Significant Publications, 1993), 57–67.

Walder, Haim. 'Please Do Not Uproot What is Planted: The Story of an Adopted Child Who Has Grown Up', in *People Speaking About Themselves: Life Stories* (Bnei Brak: Sifriati Publishing, 2002), 82–91 [Hebrew].

Weber, Max. *From Max Weber: Essays in Sociology*. Translated by Hans H. Gerth. Introduction by Wright Mills. New York: Oxford University Press, 1958.

Wegar, Katarina. *Adoption, Identity and Kinship: The Debate over Sealed Records*. New Haven, CT: Yale University Press, 1997.

Weiner, Anita, and Haggai Kupermintz. 'Facing Adulthood Alone: Long-Term Impact of Family Break-Up and Infant Institutions, a Longitudinal Study'. *British Journal of Social Work* 31 (2001), 213–34.

Weiner, Anita, and Eugene Weiner. *Expanding the Options in Child Placement*. London: University Press of America, 1990.

Wilson, Margo, and Martin Daly. 'The Psychology of Parenting in Evolutionary Perspective and the Case of Human Filicide', in Stefano Parmigiani and Frederick S. vom Saal (eds), *Infanticide and Parental Care* (Chur, Switzerland: Harwood Academic Publishers, 1994), 73–104.

Witztum, Eliezer. 'Between Intervention in Crisis and Short-Term Psychotherapy', in Haim Dasberg, Joseph A. Itzigsohn and Gaby I. Shefler (eds), *Brief Psychotherapy* (Jerusalem: Magnes Press, 1985), 53–66 [Hebrew].

Wolfgram, Susan M. 'Openness in Adoption: What We Know So Far – A Critical Review of the Literature'. *Social Work* 53 (2008), 133–42.

Wright, Lois, Cynthia Flynn and Wendy Welch. 'Adolescent Adoption and the Birth Family'. *Journal of Public Child Welfare* 1 (2007), 35–63.

Yagil, David. 'Considerations and Uncertainties in Diagnosing Parental Capability', in David Yagil et al. (eds), *Psychology, Law and Ethics in Israel: Psychological Evaluations, Psychotherapy and Judicial Decisions* (Tel Aviv: Probook, 2008), 183–205 [Hebrew].

Yanai, Zvi. *Too Late*. Jerusalem: Ketter, 2009 [Hebrew].

Yanai, Zvi. *Yours, Sandro*. Jerusalem: Ketter, 2006 [Hebrew].

Yngvessen, Barbara. 'Negotiating Motherhood: Identity and Differences in "Open" Adoptions'. *Law and Society Review* 31 (1997), 31–80.

Zafran, Ruth. 'The Discourse of Relationship as a Foundation for Resolving Family-Related Issues: Some Notes on Concern and Justice', in *Orna* Ben Naftali and Hannah Naveh (eds), *Proceedings of Love* (Tel Aviv: Ramot, Tel Aviv University, 2005), *605–55* [Hebrew].

Zafran, Ruth. 'The Right of the Adoptee to Track Down the Identity of His Biological Parents: A Critical Observation from a Comparative Viewpoint'. *Family in Law* 1 (2007), 225–55 [Hebrew].

Zafran, Ruth, and Noam Peleg. 'The Name of the Father Following FAP 5082/05 *A-G v Anon*'. *He'arat Din* 3 (2007), 196 [Hebrew].

Index